THE
TROUBLE
WITH
PROSPERITY

THE
TROUBLE
WITH
PROSPERITY

THE LOSS OF FEAR, THE RISE OF
SPECULATION, AND THE RISK
TO AMERICAN SAVINGS

JAMES GRANT

TIMES BOOKS

RANDOM HOUSE

*Grateful acknowledgment is made to the following for permission to reprint
previously published material:*

Dow Jones & Company, Inc.: Excerpt from "Trader Column" by Harry
Nelson from the April 13, 1942 issue of *Barron's*. Copyright © 1942 by
Dow Jones & Company, Inc. All rights reserved worldwide.
Reprinted by permission of *Barron's*.

Fortune: Excerpt from "40 Wall: X-Ray of a Skyscraper" from the July 1939
issue of *Fortune*. Copyright © 1939 by Time, Inc. All rights reserved.
Reprinted by permission of *Fortune*.

Grant's Interest Rate Observer: Excerpt from "Bull Market in Heresy" from the
February 15, 1991 issue of *Grant's Interest Rate Observer* (Vol. 9, No. 3).
Copyright © 1991 by Grant's Interest Rate Observer. Reprinted
by permission of *Grant's Interest Rate Observer*.

The Saturday Evening Post Society: Excerpts from "Guilt-Edged Insecurity"
by Robert Lovett from the April 13, 1937 issue of *The Saturday Evening Post*.
Copyright © 1937 by *The Saturday Evening Post*. Reprinted by
permission of The Saturday Evening Post Society.

Mr. Allan Wilson-Smith: Excerpts from *Crises and Cycles* by Wilhelm Röpke,
translated and adapted by Vera C. Smith (London: William Hodge & Co,
Limited, 1936). Reprinted by permission of Mr. Allan Wilson-Smith.

Library of Congress Cataloging-in-Publication Data
Grant, James
The trouble with prosperity: the loss of fear, the rise of speculation, and
the risk to American savings / James Grant. — 1st ed.
p.   cm.
Includes bibliographical references and index.
ISBN 0-8129-2439-8 (alk. paper)
1. Business cycles—United States—History—20th century.
2. United States—Economic conditions.   I. Title.
HB3743.G73   1996
338.5'42'0973—dc20   96-20991

Random House website address: http://www.randomhouse.com/
Printed in the United States of America on acid-free paper
98765432
First Edition

To Paul J. Isaac,
who somehow knows everything

Acknowledgments

Thanks first to Julieann Kelly and John Crawford, expert and tireless researchers, as well as to the staff of *Grant's Interest Rate Observer*, especially Ruth Hlavacek, nonpareil editor; Jay Diamond and Sue Egan, nonpareil overall; and Jeff Uscher, our resident expert on Japan (who should not be blamed for any misapprehensions of my own about his area of expertise).

Special thanks to the friends who read the chapters of this book, Paul J. Isaac and Gert von der Linde. Steve Wasserman of Times Books read every word.

In addition to sources named in the text or notes, I am indebted to the people who so kindly shared their point of view on recent financial events. Thus, on banking and the miracle cure of American credit: Mark Alpert, Peter Bakstansky, David Berry, Richard P. Eide Jr., Peter Ryerson Fisher, David Gale, John Keefe, Orin Kramer, Donald L. Kohn, James B. Lee Jr., John F. Lee, Eugene Ludwig, James J. McDermott Jr., John G. Medlin, Clarence F. Michalis, John M. Morris, John Neff, Ernest T. Patrikis, Charles Peabody, Jerome H. Powell, Thomas F. Robards, William Seidman, Valerie Simson, Barton Sotnick, Jim Tisch, Tom Tisch, Josh Welch, Richard C. Yancey. Rachel Strauber contributed her professional banking research talents.

Concerning real estate, including downtown Manhattan real estate: Tom Ferris, Joseph Harkins, Dale Hemmerdinger, Jan

Hyde, John Loeb, Robert McCormack, Patricia Rich, Howard Rubin, Andrew Sachs, Douglas Shorenstein, David Singleton, James G. Stein, Edmund Yu.

On the general topic of cycles, financial and economic: Peter Bernstein, James S. Chanos, Alexander Crutchfield, Raymond F. DeVoe Jr., Roger Garrison, Erich Heinemann, Allan Kaplan, Fred D. Kalkstein, Leon Levy, John Lonski, Paul Macrae Montgomery, Robert Prechter, Michael Schaus, Jeremy Siegel, Jay Summerall, Victor Zarnowitz. Concerning Japan: Eugene R. Dattel and John Zwaanstra. And about gambling: Ellis Darby, Sid Diamond, Joan E. Jacka, Betty Link, Lloyd Link, Randal Putnam, Brooks Taylor.

Russell P. Pennoyer lent a helpful hand on the subject of the law of fiduciaries, as did Kevin J. Kehoe Jr. and E. Lisk Wykoff.

Librarians and archivists who rendered assistance above and beyond the call of duty included Micki Traeger of the Brooklyn Business Library and John Wheeler of the archives of the New York Stock Exchange.

Christine H. Furry copyedited the manuscript into submission.

As for Patricia, my wife, and Emily, Philip, Charles, and Alice, my children, they exhibited cheerfulness and long-suffering throughout.

Contents

Introduction

Blame for the loss of economic vitality in the 1990s has been variously assigned to the "downsizing of America," the aging of the American population, the end of the cold war, and the twisting of the screws of the federal income tax rate, among other causes. Investigations into the reasons for the slowdown in growth have focused almost entirely on what is wrong with the upside of the economic cycle. This book seeks a cause in the deficiencies of the downside.

Even before the Great Depression, the national government undertook a campaign to mitigate, if not eliminate, economic failure (passage of the Federal Reserve Act of 1913, for instance, was intended to preempt bank runs and financial panics by providing for a currency that could expand and contract with the seasons, like the population of the Hamptons). Such legislation rarely met the objection that some vital economic purpose might be served through economic destruction. However, because people in markets make mistakes, tearing down is an indispensable part of the process of building up. The errors of the up cycle must be sorted out, reorganized, or auctioned off. Cyclical white elephants must be rounded up and led away. Any social system can cope with success. One facet (and only one facet) of the genius of capitalism is that it also excels at failure.

Cycles are a natural part of the market order. Thus, there are cycles of expansion and contraction, investment and liquidation, rising prices and falling prices, optimism and pessimism. The relative scarcity of contraction, liquidation, falling prices, and pessimism (specifically, investment pessimism) has been heralded as an unalloyed blessing. However, I think, it has also contributed to the sclerotic pace of growth.

In fact, the attempted suppression of the corrective phase of the business cycle has hurt economies throughout the industrialized world. Japan, particularly, has suffered the ill effects of economic overprotectiveness. The absence of the failure of even one Japanese bank in the postwar period (that is, up until Hyogo Bank bit the dust in 1995) was long taken to be a badge of national prowess. It proved to be, instead, a root cause of the current, long-running stagnation. Banks that underwrote the notorious real estate bubble were still in business (indeed, in many cases, in denial) a decade after the lending abuses began. Recovery of the world's second largest economy from the debt-induced recession of the early 1990s is, at this writing, only just beginning.

"Where economic growth is slow and calm," pronounced the French economist Clement Juglar in 1889, "crises are less noticeable and very short; where it is rapid or feverish, violent and deep depressions upset all business for a time. It is necessary to choose one or the other of these conditions, and the latter, in spite of the risks which accompany it, still appears the more favorable." Fearing crises, the industrialized world has collectively chosen Juglar's option No. 1. Could a more robust quality of recession contribute to a better grade of expansion? The answer is yes, even if no presidential candidate this fall is likely to run on a pro-recession platform.

Error is a central theme of these pages. Indeed, the book was inspired by a howler of my own. Failing to anticipate the explosive stock market rally that started in 1991, I was unprepared for the chain of bullish events that followed, most important, the miracle cure of American banking. A half decade after Citicorp was viewed as a rank speculation because of its real estate–blighted loan portfolio, the most talked-about crisis in American banking is the crisis of excess capital; nobody seems to know what to do with it. So relentless is the stock market's rise that the idea of a cycle—a complete cycle, the downside along with the upside—has itself become a controversial proposition.

So much time has elapsed since the last shattering bear market that few active American investors have any firsthand knowledge of a full-blown decline. These pages describe the 1942 bottom, among other nadirs. In almost every particular—national morale, securities valuation, public investment participation—the 1942 low represents the mirror image of the 1996 bull-market high. Of all the consequences of sustained prosperity, none is so powerful as the delusion that markets always go up. They do not always go up. Equally (as is often forgotten during bear markets), they do not always go down.

In markets, almost no truth is permanently valid, and today's heresy may be counted as even money to become tomorrow's orthodoxy. Indeed, in recent years, heresy has been in a strong uptrend. Legalized casino gambling and paper money unballasted by gold, to name only two examples, have come into their own. Only a generation ago, each was the establishment's idea of a cardinal sin. (Perhaps it is sin that is in a new bull market. AMERICA MAKES PEACE WITH ADULTERY, *The International Herald Tribune* reported in January 1996.)

Has heresy changed, or have we? Is financial truth purely relative? Bond buyers were satisfied with a 2½ percent yield in 1946, yet they spurned a 15 percent yield in 1981. Was one idea as good as the other? It would be hard for an impartial observer to accept that the century-long evolution from the gold standard to the paper standard represents pure progress. The quarrel I have with the Federal Reserve is not so much that it creates credit as that it pretends to know the interest rate at which that credit (in the form of bank reserves) should be lent and borrowed. In the free-market world of 1996, the Fed would seem to be out of step, yet few people protest against it. In Europe there are plans to create a super, pancontinental central bank to manage a brand new currency. It is contended that this confection, the Euro, will resist "the infinite regress of value inherent in paper money itself," to borrow a phrase associated with J. S. G. Boggs, the American artist who paints pictures that look very much like dollar bills.

Perhaps the backlash against central banks awaits the end of the boom phase of the current cycle. The history of 40 Wall Street, the skyscraper next door to the offices of *Grant's Interest Rate Observer* in lower Manhattan, is a parable of the changeableness of value, markets, and monetary arrangements. So is the history of gambling and investment valuation. Booms do not merely precede busts. In some important sense, they cause them. This idea, on which so much of the analysis of these pages rests, is borrowed from the Austrian School of economics. It was the Austrians who observed that people in markets periodically miscalculate together. One important source of misjudgment is the interest rates that the central banks impose. A too-low rate provokes high spirits and speculation; a too-high rate induces morbidity and contraction. Thus, the ultralow money-market rates of 1993 not only strengthened balance sheets and reduced mortgage-interest costs, as policymakers intended. They also caused an outpouring of capital investment, as policymakers might or might not have intended. If precedent holds, these projects will be carried to extreme lengths. Like the Manhattan skyscrapers of the 1920s and the Texas oil rigs of the 1980s, the white elephants of the 1990s (coffee bars and semiconductor fabricating plants are the top candidates at this moment) will bring grief to their sponsors and drama to the next recession. Overbuilding and underbuilding constitute opposite sides of the same cyclical coin.

The history begins with 1958, with its bond market crash and stock market rally and creeping inflation. In many ways it marked the start of the modern financial age. Around the world, government spending increased and inflation stirred.

In Chapter 2, the narrative temporally doubles back on itself. In support of the theory that finance is inherently cyclical, the story of the tower at 40 Wall Street is related. If the construction of this skyscraper marked the peak of the cycle, the bear market of 1942 was the bottom. The irregular recovery of the financial neighborhood of Wall Street in the postwar years (symbolically ending with the bankruptcy of the Seamen's Bank for Savings, 30 Wall Street) constitutes another lesson in the recurrent phases of markets.

Chapter 3 lays out the Austrian theory of the business cycle and contrasts the very different cyclical experiences of the United States and Japan. In both the 1920s and 1990s, it will be seen, Japanese policymakers tried to suppress the symptoms of failure. In the

United States of the early 1920s, by notable contrast, a short and sharp depression gave way to prolonged growth; as for the America of the 1990s, a short and mild recession has yielded to grudging growth.

Chapter 4 analyzes the causes of the brilliant recovery of the American financial system from the stresses and strains of the late 1980s. The Federal Reserve is widely believed to be the agent of this transformation. However, as shall be seen, the immediate cause of the recovery of banks and overleveraged businesses was the stock market itself.

Chapter 5 is devoted to the consequences of the recent phenomenal gambling boom on the recent stupendous stock market boom. Gambling is as cyclical as anything on Wall Street could be, as we shall see, including the laws that govern the behavior of investment fiduciaries.

Not yet finished with the Federal Reserve, we compare it in Chapter 6 to the Bank of England during the years of the classical gold standard, 1880 to 1914. Through this exercise, we can see how much the earlier monetary system achieved without exactly intending to. What the contemporary banking system has achieved is, of course, a boom, and we examine one characteristic feature of it: the huge expansion of semiconductor manufacturing capacity. Next we turn to the institution of bankruptcy, without which no boom could be complete. In a sense, the modern-day central bank creates the credit that fires the booms that fill the bankruptcy courts.

THE
TROUBLE
WITH
PROSPERITY

CHAPTER ONE

HEIRS TO 1958

I N THE EARLY 1990s, the American economy could scarcely seem
to swing its legs out of bed in the morning. The debt-induced
recession of 1990–91 was neither lengthy nor strenuous in comparison to the average postwar recession (although it was lengthy and
strenuous enough to cost George Bush the 1992 presidential election). Indeed, so brief and mild was the slump that some portion of
the necessary work of clearing away the misconceived investments
of the preceding expansion—notably, surplus buildings and heavy
debts—was left undone. All in all, the body economic lacked vitality, and real economic growth over the next five years would average only 1.8 percent per annum, one of the lowest rates in postwar
annals.

Wonders filled the newspapers, but there was no visible outpouring of economic gratitude for them. No sooner had inflation
and communism been conquered, or at least knocked for a loop,
than new troubles rushed in to fill the worry void. Raises in salary
were hard to come by, technology threw some middle managers out
of work (even while throwing other people into it), some good jobs
jumped American borders (even as others jumped back over them),
and many people suffered what euphemistically came to be known
as downsizing.

Simultaneously—remarkably—Wall Street upsized. Stock and
bond prices surged and speculation took flight. The kind of unin-
hibited, unselfconscious, and headlong boom that so signally failed

to materialize in the real economy instead became a fixture of the financial one. Thus, for instance, by 1996, more than $1 trillion changed hands in the foreign exchange markets every day; it was the equivalent of one complete U.S. gross domestic product every week. (As recently as 1989, foreign exchange activity averaged a mere $620 billion a day.) The bond market, too, was hyperactive. Unable to make up their minds, investors abandoned fixed-income securities in 1994 only to reembrace them in 1995 and to cast them off again in 1996. Coming and going, they employed massive quantities of what, in the stock market, would be called margin debt. Treasury bond holdings were routinely financed with credit, even when (as in 1995) the arithmetic seemed not to favor it: that is, when one paid more for the loan than one earned in interest on the securities purchased. Bond dealers, hedge funds, and foreign central banks emerged as some of the leading buyers of the U.S. public debt in the 1990s, each and every one employing nonsavings: borrowed funds in the cases of dealers and hedge funds, freshly printed funds in the case of the central banks. At this writing, the grand total of the dealers' bond-related borrowings is $260 billion, four times greater than the volume of outstanding New York Stock Exchange margin debt. On the evidence, the financial underpinnings of the bond market were more precarious, certainly more speculative, than those of the stock market.

The seething markets reflected, among other things, a deep-seated uncertainty about the value of the dollar. On the one hand, the dollar was the world's top monetary brand name. It was the dollar in which fearful Taiwanese sought refuge in early 1996 when the People's Republic of China splashed missiles into the Formosa Strait. On the other hand, the same greenback was also in chronic surplus. The proof of this excess was the vast quantity of dollars that have come to be owned by foreign central banks. The central banks buy them because other potential holders—profit-seeking Japanese exporters, for example—habitually shun them. In other words, a weak dollar paradoxically has helped the prices of the very securities denominated in dollars.

Foreign subsidy of U.S. bond prices indirectly gave a lift to the Dow Jones Industrial Average, which in truth seemed not to need

one. Between 1991 and 1995, a supposedly careworn American public bought $470 billion worth of stock mutual funds, more than all
the preceding generations of American investors, anxious or otherwise, had purchased in the preceding 66 years. Between October
1990 and March 1996, the Standard & Poor's 500 Index returned
13.7 percent per annum. Not only did the stock market go up but
also it almost never looked back; never before had so many fiscal
quarters elapsed without even a minor setback to the S&P.

In the spring of 1996 it was possible to believe that the risk of
loss had been expunged from American financial markets. Banks
were no longer failing—they were prospering as never before. The
dollar was no longer falling—it was the yen and the deutsche mark
that were losing value in the foreign exchange market. As for the
stock market, it no longer was a source of worry—the public, and
indeed many professional investors, had come to believe that it was
destined to rise indefinitely.

A world so very nearly perfect, one apparently without financial
seasons let alone financial loss: where did this Eden come from?

IN 1958, a year not usually associated with 1929 in any way, culturally, technologically, or speculatively, the United States government
bond market crashed. People—mainly Wall Street professionals,
but also a Manhattan newsstand operator among a host of other
amateurs—sold the bonds they had bought with borrowed money.

They had liberally borrowed, paying low interest rates; the proceeds of the loans they invested at slightly higher interest rates.
Slightly was the watchword: yields on short-dated government
notes were less than 3 percent. Futures trading in government
bonds was still 20 years off in the future, most derivative securities
were not yet invented, and foreign participation in American capital markets was virtually nil. It was unthinkable that a single twenty-
eight-year-old trader could lose $1 billion in only a few short
months. Indeed, the Baring Securities employee who subsequently
did so, Nicholas William Leeson, was not then born. Even so, in
that premodern era, people undertook to do what has so often
come naturally in the history of banking and finance: they specu-

lated with a little bit more money than they could readily afford to lose.

The idea of borrowing at one rate and investing at another is a Wall Street staple. In fashion as never before in the 1990s, it produced billions of dollars in profits that signally helped to restore the American banking system to health. Then it produced billions of dollars in losses (which, however, did not destroy the banking system). In 1958, on a considerably smaller scale, people borrowed overnight at 2 percent or less, and they lent to the Treasury for seven years at 2⅝ percent. Presently, they were forced to stop, but not before the bond market had been stood on its head, the government's fiscal operations disrupted, and a senior partner of a leading money-brokerage firm publicly rebuked on the floor of the New York Stock Exchange. The record of this Eisenhower-era experience in interest-rate speculation anticipates the specific events of the 1990s, but more important, it illuminates the cyclical nature of markets. The more long-lived the investment trend, the more likely it is to appear permanent, as prosperity may appear permanent in 1996.

Late in the nineteenth century, Eugen von Böhm-Bawerk pronounced that the lower a country's interest rates, the higher its intelligence and the sounder its character. If the Austrian economist was right, the 1950s must culturally tower over every succeeding American decade.* On average over those 10 years, long-term U.S. government obligations yielded 2.99 percent. In 1958, a relatively high-yield year, New York City tax-exempt bonds fetched 2.67 percent, and blue-chip public utility bonds yielded 3.90 percent. The three-month Treasury bill rate was quoted at scarcely more than zero, five-eighths of 1 percent. A creditworthy applicant for a 30-year mortgage in 1958 could expect to pay no more than 5¾ percent (less-than-creditworthy applicants were encouraged not to apply).

It may help the cause of understanding the 1990s to study the bond market of the 1950s. Speculators in both eras responded to

---

* By the same token, the 1940s must tower over the 1950s. The moral apex of the American republic, measured in terms of short-dated government securities, would be fixed around 1940, when they were sometimes quoted at less than zero. We may take the von Böhm-Bawerk dictum at a discount from par.

much the same stimuli. Galvanizing each generation was a recession. Perceiving that short-term rates were lower than longer-term rates, they borrowed at the lower and invested at the higher.

What the recession of 1957–58 does not explain, however, is why long-term bond yields fetched little more than 3 percent in the preceding boom, or why, from 1920 through 1946, interest rates in America had mainly fallen, or why, even after this postwar low ebb, they had hardly risen. Perhaps one important contributing cause was the monetary arrangement of the day: a dollar legally defined as a weight of gold. To be sure, under the gold standard and its variations, the world had seen a variety of interest rates—some of them, as in the United States in the early 1920s, not at all low but (or so it seemed) punishingly high: 5½ percent on long-term Treasuries, for example. However, it had been a rare year in the twentieth century when Treasury obligations yielded more than 4 percent.

To most American citizens, the gold standard was a dead letter or a half-forgotten shibboleth. The right to own gold had been repealed in 1934, and no contract that specified payment in gold money was enforceable in an American court. Gold was still the official U.S. monetary collateral but, like the H-bomb, it was deemed to belong to the public sector. Foreign governments and central banks, however, not being similarly dispossessed, could (and sometimes did) exercise the old right to exchange unwanted dollars for gold at the statutory rate of $35 to the ounce. This, then, was the gold exchange standard of the Bretton Woods era, the palest copy of the gold standard in place before World War I but a setup that still retained the principal philosophical feature of the earlier day: the idea that money owed its ultimate value not to a government but to the intrinsic worth of the precious metal from which it was refined.

The second, less uplifting, reason for the low interest rates of the 1940s and very early 1950s was that the government had put them there. For years, the Treasury and the Federal Reserve Board had resisted a rising tendency in interest rates (and in wages and prices, too) with rules and regulations and financial-market intervention. From 1942 up until 1951, monetary policy was held hostage to the government's war-swollen budget. The Federal Reserve, then familiarly known as the Federal (not yet as widely, and more familiarly, as the Fed) was independent by law. It was established by Congress, and its monetary powers were delegated by Congress under the Constitution. In practice, however, it had become the bond-selling arm of the government, manipulating interest rates for the benefit of the Treasury and to the detriment of the investing public. Wishing to pay the lowest rates possible, the Treasury notified the Federal Reserve what those rates would be: three-eighths of 1 percent on short-dated Treasury bills, seven-eighths of 1 percent on certificates, and $2\frac{1}{2}$ percent on long-term bonds. These were approximately the rates at which the government financed World War II, the GI Bill, the Marshall Plan, the Berlin airlift, the containment of Soviet power in Europe, and the early years of the Korean War, among myriad other projects. Undeniably low, they were still not the kind of low rates that von Böhm-Bawerk had in mind.

An incontrovertible law of regulation holds that a government can fix the price or the supply of a certain thing, but not both at the same time. In the matter of credit over a full decade, the government chose to fix the price. Because the bond rates it fixed were sometimes below what the market would have fixed for itself, the available supply of capital fell periodically short of the crisis-inflated demand. It was then that the Federal was called upon to do its duty, purchasing securities with new money, money created just for this purpose. In effect, the central bank levied a twofold tax on the American public: first, on the savers who bought bonds at artificially low interest rates; second, on the population as a whole through the roundabout means of price inflation. Under the leadership of Marriner Eccles, a Utah banker and proponent of unorthodox ideas—for instance, of countercyclical fiscal policy years before John Maynard Keynes published his *General Theory of Employment, Interest and Money*—the Federal had enthusiastically financed the New Deal. It had financed World War II, but with privately expressed misgivings about the interest rates imposed by the Treasury; and it financed, at the same bargain-basement rates but with increasing apprehension and resentment, the early years of the cold war.

. . .

INFLATION WAS THE natural outcome of this complaisance, and consumer prices registered alarming gains in 1946–47. However, as wartime price controls were abandoned only gradually, the symptoms of suppressed inflation were almost as corrosive as the officially posted prices themselves (which, in many months of 1946 and 1947, were alarming enough). There were shortages of meat, nylon stockings, domestic help, wheat, copper, and a variety of other labor and commodities, including sugar and corn syrup, the building blocks of chewing gum. Telephone workers struck for more money and coal miners for more meat.

There were inflationary omens in real estate. In February 1946 in Ridgefield, New Jersey, an industrial property no longer needed to turn out gliders for the U.S. Army brought a record-high price: the equivalent of $7 a square foot, up from the then customary $5. In the same month, across the Hudson River, New York City apartment owners bitterly condemned the administration of rent controls by the ubiquitous Office of Price Administration, a wartime agency that stayed, like so much supposedly temporary wartime housing, well into the peace. When, in the fall of 1946, the Truman cabinet sat down to study what by then had become "the meat crisis," the OPA was ruling against a Queens, New York, steel-products manufacturer for trying to purchase 38 steers and having their slaughtered carcasses distributed as gifts to its beef-deprived employees. The officials ruled that everyone should have an equal chance to buy (or, more likely, not to buy) meat at controlled prices in the conventional channels of trade.

Governments at all levels declined to restore free markets. "If we want to be assured of adequate supplies of processed foods next fall and winter," *The New York Times* advised in March 1946, "home canning will have to take top place as the country's indoor sport this year, according to the Civilian Production Administration. The recent work stoppage in the steel mills has resulted in a loss of an estimated 450,000 tons of mill products, two-thirds of which would have gone into tin plate, which is used for commercial canning and other industrial purposes." Owing to price controls, a wheat shortage gave rise to a bread shortage and then to a White House press release suggesting a menu for bread-free lunches and dinners. In 1947, a number of New York newspapers printed a daily menu for a "low-to-moderate income" family of five drawn up by the dietitians of the municipal Department of Markets. A proposed lunch of pea soup (canned or dehydrated), a cottage-cheese-and-raisin sandwich on whole-wheat bread (bread by then being back on the shelves), grapes, and milk was condemned by the gourmet and price-control proponent A. J. Liebling as "the regimen of a well-conducted poorhouse."

Even so, in view of the monetary provocation, the inflation that didn't occur was almost as remarkable as the one that did. It may be viewed as the forerunner to the deflation-cum-bank-run that didn't occur in 1990–91, also a time of strange monetary events. A student of central banking might have expected an inflationary contagion. Between 1941 and 1945, the volume of currency and bank deposits had tripled. In the same period, the Federal Reserve System had bought, or monetized, some $20 billion worth of government securities, a tenfold increase since 1941. Except in the context of a world war, such a thing would have been unimaginable. Even so, as seen from the present day, it strains credulity. In the inflationary 1970s, analysts gasped when the rate of growth in Federal Reserve holdings of government securities reached 15 percent a year; in the early war years, these purchases climbed by more than 150 percent a year.*

It is no easy thing from a distance of decades to understand the bond market's equanimity in 1946. Inflation was rampant, yet bond yields fell; and when at last yields did stop falling, they only haltingly rose. In April 1946, long-dated Treasury issues fetched what would prove the lowest yield for the next 50 years (and counting), 2.03 percent. In that month, the consumer price index showed a year-

---

* Then as now, a Treasury bill purchased by the Fed was transformed into dollars, called bank reserves. These may be held in the form of vault cash or in an account at the Federal Reserve. The greater the supply of reserve dollars, the more easily and cheaply banks can expand, always assuming, of course, that they are not (as some were in 1946) paralyzed by memories of the Great Depression or by the dread of the next world war. The train of causation of bank reserves to the growth in money supply to the rise in consumer prices was well known, certainly by those investors who had lived through the post–World War I inflation.

over-year rise of 3.4 percent. Thus, "real," or inflation-adjusted, yields were actually less than zero. By summertime, the CPI would be rising in double digits; by Christmastime, it would be closing in on a 20 percent rate of gain. Prime corporate bond yields hardly flickered, beginning the year at about 2½ percent and ending it at about 2.6 percent. And there were income taxes to be paid. A pretax yield of 2½ percent on a corporate bond was niggardly enough for a well-to-do investor in the top 94 percent marginal income-tax bracket. After taxes (and even before inflation), it was nearly invisible. Compound interest may well be the eighth wonder of the world, but a 2½ percent reinvestment rate doubles a saver's money only after 28 diligent years (at 7 percent, to compare a more contemporary yield, the doubling time is a little more than 10 years). Yet investors willingly accepted yields of less than 2½ percent, even as they watched the cost of living spiral out of sight.*

Signs of the next inflation were everywhere except, critically, in the minds of the bond buyers. On February 20, President Harry S Truman signed the 1946 Employment Act, legislation that established the President's Council of Economic Advisers and philosophically committed the government to providing job opportunities for every American who was willing and able to work and who was actually seeking work. Truman said that the bill "gives expression to a deep-seated desire for a conscientious and positive attack upon the ever-recurring problems of mass unemployment and ruinous depression." However, the juxtaposition of the deflationary past and the inflationary future was daily more apparent. On February 25 came news that grain-futures trading had been sharply curtailed because there was so little grain on hand to be traded.[†]

* Amateur bond buyers were less willing than many professionals. "Millions of Americans are losing the thrifty habit acquired in wartime of setting aside money each week to buy government bonds," *The Wall Street Journal* reported in January 1946. The rate paid on savings bonds was 2.9 percent.

† The underlying tendency in grain prices was, of course, bullish, and among those availing themselves of the opportunity to profit was none other than President Truman's personal physician, Brig. Gen. Wallace H. Graham (a role subsequently played, with modifications, by Hillary Rodham Clinton in 1994). Disclosure of the general's substantial wheat position in the fall of 1947 brought acute, if short-lived, embarrassment to the administration, which had declared itself hostile to the futures markets.

What were bond buyers thinking about? Perhaps nothing but the observed, 25-year-long tendency of interest rates to fall. It was, of course, a given that savers needed something to invest in. Loaded with wartime wages and short of things to spend them on, Americans were more liquid than they would be for the next half century (and counting). As investors still held a collective grudge against the stock market for the losses it had meted out in 1929–32 and 1937, an obvious outlet for this reservoir of liquidity was government securities, even at the prevailing low yields. For all intents and purposes, foreign investment markets were inaccessible.

What was the alternative? It scarcely paid to buy investment-grade corporate bonds. They yielded only a little more than governments. And private businesses, unlike the Treasury could, and did—who could forget the 1930s?—default.* As for real estate, Edward J. Crawford, president of the New York State Society of Real Estate Appraisers, delivered a rousing bullish address to his colleagues in March 1946 to encourage them to take their minds off the Great Depression: "Properties are being sold at higher and higher prices each week, and opinion among the best-posted men in the real estate field is that prices will go still higher and that this condition will prevail for at least seven years."

"Grain prices naturally respond to the law of supply and demand," said Truman on October 5, "but they should not be subject to the greed of speculators who gamble on what may lie ahead in our commodity markets." When, in late December, Republican investigators forced the disclosure of Graham's trading activity (GOP presidential hopeful Harold E. Stassen charged that administration insiders were illicitly profiting in futures activity), Graham and Truman each suffered political flesh wounds.

* The Treasury, it was true, had defaulted in 1933 on its promise to redeem its bonds for gold dollars, but at least it could, and did, service its debt with paper dollars. These it could print itself, a feat that not even General Electric could duplicate. "Obviously," wrote a New York University banking professor, Raymond Rogers, in the summer of 1946, "no bank is warranted in buying even medium-grade corporate or other bonds. The higher rate cannot compensate any bank for the greater risk involved." It is revealing of those risk-averse times that Rogers chose not to qualify this blanket assertion. "Obviously," a contemporary professor of banking might counter, a medium-grade bond purchased at a low price entails less risk than a medium-grade bond purchased at a high price.

In January 1946, in the midst of the steady, counterintuitive (as a later generation would intuit) decline in interest rates, *Barron's* ruminated on a much stranger postwar shortage: the one in bonds. "Now, with huge war expenditures ended," the magazine said, "investors are bidding for available issues in anticipation of the drying up of new supplies of government bonds. Furthermore, all developments in corporate finance tend toward a reduction in the amount of industrial bonds rather than an increase."

Just 45 percent of the cost of World War II had been financed with so-called marketable debt. The rest had been paid for by taxes or through the sale of bonds that could not be readily resold, such as savings bonds or securities issued directly to the federal government itself. In 1919–20, as some of the readers of *Barron's* would never forget, bond prices had broken sharply. Three-quarters of the expense of that war had been financed with marketable securities, and in the great postwar inflation, many panicked owners remarketed them all at once. However, the argument went, the inflationary run-up of 1946 would prove as temporary as the one that had followed World War I. The more immediate risk was that the 1930s would resume, economically, at any minute.

Perhaps for this reason, the logic of the day had it, businesses would check the impulse to borrow at even 2½ or 3½ percent interest rates. Then, too, federal controls capped corporate profits and, indirectly, the demand for corporate investment as well. All in all, the *Barron's* article contended, the management of the Treasury's affairs was as artful as that of the British Exchequer in the Napoleonic Wars under William Pitt (Great Britain having emerged both victorious and solvent from that long struggle). For the time being, there would not be enough bonds to go around—and, indeed, after 1945 no new long-dated Treasuries would be issued for eight years.

However, the clinching bullish contention was that bond yields, like the price of pork chops, were controlled, and that the Federal Reserve would no more allow a rise in interest rates than the Office of Price Administration would a rise in the price of groceries. ". . . [A]s long as the public debt is anywhere near its present size," commented *Barron's* in August 1946, "it is hard to imagine any Administration in Washington abandoning an easy-money policy. The

Federal Reserve Board has pledged itself to maintain the Treasury's low borrowing rates. Every important central bank in the world is following a policy of low interest rates. Easy money is not just a passing domestic fancy; it is a strong world-wide trend."

THE PRESIDENT OF THE Equitable Life Assurance Society of the United States, Thomas I. Parkinson, did not believe a word of it. A cum laude alumnus of the University of Pennsylvania School of Law, Class of 1902 (his class rank was No. 2), Parkinson was a master legal draftsman. He had helped to investigate the disastrous Triangle Shirtwaist fire of 1911, served in the Army as Judge Advocate General in World War I (thereafter taking undisguised pleasure in being addressed by his army rank of Major), founded and presided over the Legislative Drafting Research Department at the Columbia University Law School, and served as the first Official Draftsman of the U.S. Senate. A short, heavyset man with twinkling eyes, ruddy cheeks, and a big voice, Parkinson presided regally at the Equitable from 1927 to 1954; when he arrived for work in the lobby of the company's home office in New York, the elevator starters would clear a car for him. Parkinson conceived and executed vast projects, remembered his enemies, and (when the time came) refused to groom a successor, much less to name one. Hired as a consultant by the Equitable just after World War I, Parkinson's first assignment was to shut down the Society's loss-making European businesses. The great inflation of the postwar era had been vividly impressed on him—in Germany and neighboring states, the Equitable earned less in premiums than it paid out in postage—and he was passionately opposed to what he understandably regarded as the inflationary fiscal and monetary policies of the Roosevelt and Truman administrations.

As he deplored the easy-money, low-interest-rate policies of the 1940s, he criticized the timorousness of the Life Insurance Association of America for refusing to criticize them. He led the Equitable in the search for sane, higher-yielding investments—for instance, the bonds of disgraced public utility holding companies and troubled railroads, which he bought in the mid- to late 1930s. ("We didn't have to go in search of them," said Parkinson of the railroad securities. "Institutions dumped them in our laps in great volume at unbelievably low prices. I say unbelievable in comparison with present prices.") It was well and good to buy low and sell high, but a life insurance company lived by interest rates, and in the 1940s the bond market furnished thin gruel. In 1945, the rate of return on the Equitable's assets was 2.86 percent, or 2.81 percent after tax. It was just barely enough to maintain reserves on the company's outstanding contracts. (At that, the Equitable was in a better-than-average way. For at least a decade beginning in the mid-1930s, the American life insurance industry earned a lower yield on its investments than it had promised to pay its policyholders.)

"You know," Parkinson told the Bond Club of Chicago in November 1945,

> unanimity of opinion is a danger sign. When everybody thinks that interest rates are going to remain low or go lower, look out. Maybe that is just a pious wish on my part. But in 1899—of course, that was way back in the old era—the then president of the Equitable Life addressed a letter to about 200 of the leading financiers and experts in finance in the country and asked them what rate of interest he could expect for a period of twenty years. . . .
>
> The experts were practically unanimous in the view that the low interest rates then prevailing would continue indefinitely into the future.* Lyman Gage, then Secretary of the Treasury, assured us that there could be no reasonable hope for a better rate than 3 percent. One very optimistic leading banker in New York suggested that there was a chance that rate in the following twenty years might go to 3½ percent. But August Belmont, supposed to be something of a leader of the

---

* The errant forecasts were compiled and published in book form in 1928 under the title, *A Scientific Approach to Investment Management*. The author and editor, Dwight C. Rose, drew an ominous comparison between the misguided bullishness on bond prices at the turn of the century and the widespread optimism that was then prevailing. It was a provocative point, but Rose's own implicit bearish forecast was no more accurate than the bullish one he had undertaken to lampoon. Bond prices, in fact, would continue to rise until 1946. He was exactly 18 years too early.

day, said that if the Equitable really wanted to be conservative, it had better assume a rate of less than 3 percent.

Well, you know that low-yield period lasted for only two more years. During those two years, we acquired some 3 percent corporate bonds. We still have the Altons [The Chicago & Alton Railroad, subsequently absorbed by the Baltimore & Ohio, had issued some $45 million worth of 3 percent, 50-year gold bonds around the turn of the century; no doubt they seemed an excellent investment].

During that period, second-rate [then second-rate] borrowers put out their hundred-year bonds at $3\frac{3}{4}$ percent or less. So sure was the whole investment world that there would be nothing better that they were gobbled up. You know how soon thereafter the rate went to $4\frac{1}{2}$ percent and 5 percent and higher.*

Parkinson, genially affecting an unfamiliarity with bond mathematics, said that it wasn't enough to do one's statistical homework, although his company assuredly did. "You've got to have something of the poet in you to be a good investor," he said. And a little bit of luck, too, he added. But neither luck nor poetry would avail a saver much if interest rates were going to remain under the federal thumb.

"Perhaps I am whining," Parkinson continued, "but if so it's because there is so much money seeking investment that the insurance funds for which I am responsible have to take a lower and lower interest yield. But I am also emphasizing that the long-term welfare of this country is not advanced by that abnormally low interest rate produced by that indirect and cloaked creation of money, and I am saying that there is a great source of public welfare in inspiring the thrift and saving of the people of this country by the incentive of a reasonable hire for their savings."

---

* If the 1946–81 bond bear market was heralded by passage of the Employment Act of 1946, the start of the 1899–1920 bond bear market was paradoxically marked by a very different piece of legislation, the Gold Standard Act of 1900, a law intended to anchor the value of a dollar in gold for all time. One might have expected—evidently, to judge by Parkinson's story, many did expect—that a new era of more-or-less permanently low interest rates was at hand.

In the 1980s and 1990s, Wall Street came to believe that a vigilant and powerful bond market would nip any new inflation in the bud by marking up interest rates before a government could ruin the currency. Parkinson held out no such hope for the bond market of 1945, and he urged bankers not to be the government's dupes. "If the bankers do not find a way to prevent their institutions from being used by an uncontrolled Treasury, to create more and more fictitious money under the cloak of the respectability of the Federal Reserve System," he said, "they cannot escape some share in the responsibility for consequent inflation. . . . A large supply of money has always been popular. We cannot expect the mass of the people themselves to complain that they have too much money and by the same token we cannot expect public officials who depend on the support of the people to have the courage to take the leadership in such a matter."

In the light of his views on inflation and interest rates, it could not have come as a surprise when Parkinson good-naturedly renewed the vow he had made (and subsequently broken) the prior spring not to buy any corporate bond with a coupon of less than 3 percent nor with a term of maturity of more than 20 years. Even at 3 percent, after all, as he noted, a buyer's margin for error was almost nonexistent, and he showed that the Equitable's London affiliate would have been better off in 1917 if it had done nothing with its money starting in 1896 except to stack it in a vault. Such was the risk inherent in very low interest rates.

Parkinson's analysis, although prophetic, was premature, and in the winter and spring of 1946, he must have wondered if he would ever be right. Unaccountably, bond yields continued to fall even as the inflation rate rose. For the full year, the Equitable's overall, after-tax rate of return on its assets would decline to 2.59 percent. Compounding that injury was insult: costs were rising on the Clinton Hill housing project that the company had begun to build as an investment near the Brooklyn Navy Yard. It was the worst of all worlds: bond yields down or sideways, as if there were no inflation; construction costs up, as if there were. The year-end balance sheet showed a huge portfolio of ultra-low-yielding Treasury securities: $1.6 billion out of $3.4 billion in total bonds. In the 1946 annual report, Parkinson expressed enthusiasm, even gratitude, about the 35 privately placed corporate financings in which the company was able to participate. Pathetically, the average yield on this windfall was just 2.7 percent. (In 1949, after interest rates had recovered slightly, Parkinson held out the securities of the long-bankrupt Chicago, Rock Island, and Pacific Railroad Company as an example of a successful workout investment. The annual effective yield —"including the years of depression, bankruptcy and reorganization"—was all of 3.96 percent.) As for common stocks, New York State Insurance Deputy Superintendent Shelby Cullom Davis almost pleaded with the life insurance executives to buy them in lieu of corporate bonds and governments. As we can all see now, it was a suggestion at once brilliant and obvious. Parkinson, however, who had so many forward-looking investment ideas to his credit, absolutely rejected it. Davis couldn't interest the other companies in equity investments, either, but at length he resigned from the Insurance Department to implement his own advice. Shelby Cullom Davis & Company, specialists in the industry Davis had learned inside and out, opened its doors in 1947. When, in 1994, Davis died in the home he had bought in 1947, the $100,000 of capital with which he started the firm had grown to $800 million.*

In April 1946, about the time the bond market stopped appreciating and only a few months after Parkinson had lashed out against low yields in Chicago, *Barron's* was able to report that he had apparently thrown in the towel: "A straw in the wind last week was

---

* The former insurance superintendent had a fine contempt for bonds—"certificates of confiscation" he called them both during and after the great bear market of 1946–81—but was a lifelong bull on stocks; at one time, he owned an equity position in 2,000 companies. A WASP through and through, Davis was a descendent of Mayflower passengers and Jamestown settlers and an exemplar of the cold-water philosophy of creature comforts. He got the 6 A.M. train from Tarrytown, New York, rode the subway downtown, took pride in the unrepaired holes in the bottoms of his shoes, and flew economy class. When a grandson once asked him for a dollar with which to buy a hot dog, Davis asked the young man if he realized how much better it would be to invest the money. "So in one fell swoop, he taught me three lessons," the grandson, Christopher Davis, later told the insurance analyst and journalist David Schiff: "the value of a dollar, the value of compound interest and the importance of always carrying my own money." "The first million is the hardest," Davis told his grandson, trying to encourage him (but not, with those words, succeeding).

the purchase by the yield conscious Equitable Life Assurance Society of $32 million of Philip Morris & Co. 2⅝ percent debentures at 101, to yield 2.55 percent. This suggests that the insurance company doesn't look for the coupon rates on new government bonds to be above the current yield basis of 2.25 percent." But what could Parkinson do? His company had to invest in the world as it was, not as he forecast it would turn out to be.

In his definitive *History of Interest Rates* (updated now by Richard Sylla), Sidney Homer tried to describe the mentality of the 1940s' bond buyer. "With the passage of the war years," wrote Homer, "confidence grew in the ability of the government to maintain low interest rates and bond yields. If this could and would be done, there was no reason to accept less than 2½ percent, even when investing short-term funds. Long bonds pegged at 100 were not only considered safe for short-term funds, but it was believed that, as they became shorter, they must rise in the market, first to a 2¼ percent yield and finally to a seven-eighths percent yield, because shorter bonds commanded these lower yields. Thus they would provide capital gains. This was called 'riding the yield curve'; it became a profitable sport for private and institutional investors."

They would have been well advised to ride the stock market instead. Starting from the all-time low in government yields, 2.03 percent, set in April 1946, the market moved irregularly but relentlessly lower (lower, that is, in price; higher in yield). The end of the long bear market, in September 1981, found long-term governments yielding almost 15 percent. The price of a hypothetical, constant-maturity 2½ percent bond, purchased in 1946 at a price of 101 and blindly held until 1981, would have fallen by 83 percent, to 17 inflation-shrunken cents on the dollar.

NOT ONLY DID THE wide-open monetary policies of the 1940s fail to produce a decade-long, virulent price inflation, as in the 1970s, they also incited no wide-ranging asset inflation, as in the 1980s. Neither grocery prices nor stock prices erupted as they would later do. Yields on low-rated corporate bonds were themselves wondrously low in 1946, but this fact elicited no leveraged-buyout movement or coast-to-coast real estate boom. Conservatism was ingrained more deeply than an observer of the 1990s might easily credit. "At the present time," wrote the American legal scholar George L. Clark in 1947 on the topic of what assets a fiduciary could and could not buy, "investments in government securities or in first mortgages on real estate are the only ones permitted in most states apart from statute." In such avant-garde jurisdictions as Massachusetts, a steward might, "in the exercise of sound discretion, invest a part of the trust funds in the stocks and bonds of business enterprises." Leveraged-buyout funds, Clark seemed to imply, were not on the fiduciary agenda.

Such boomlike symptoms as did present themselves were held in check by the ever present anxieties of the day. One telling measure of the public's attitude toward risk taking is that the dividend yield on common stocks was greater than the current yield on government bonds. On average in 1947, high-grade corporate bonds provided a current yield of 2.58 percent as the Standard & Poor's 500 Index fetched a dividend yield of 4.93 percent. Not until the late 1950s—August 1958, to be exact—would bonds outyield stocks. The realignment of yields was the market's belated recognition that the rising risk of inflation had rendered allegedly safe and sane bonds more hazardous than corporate equities. "My life is a failure," Parkinson declared, "if the purchasing value of the dollar in which the Equitable policies are paid decreases to the point where the policyholder and his beneficiaries cannot possibly get the things for which he bought those policies." As Parkinson was being forced out of the company in 1954 at the age of seventy-two, there was increasing reason to wonder if he had succeeded.

Concerning the transition to an inflationary age, Marriner Eccles, in the traditional way of central bankers, deplored it even as he helped to facilitate it. "If left uncontrolled," a congressional committee heard the Federal Reserve chairman solemnly testify in 1945, "the vast and rising tide of war-created liquid funds could overwhelm the markets for real estate, urban and rural, and for stocks and commodities." Such a thing "would be calamitous for Government financing. It would make a mirage out of the GI Bill of Rights." What Eccles proposed to do about this looming men-

ace was to tax it to death: to destroy the acquisitive impulse by imposing a punitively high rate on capital gains. (A glimpse into Eccles's interventionist mind, as well as into the closed and malleable
financial system of the early postwar years, is provided by his own
recollection of the Federal Reserve's attitude, circa 1951, toward
the U.S. Treasury bond market: ". . . [W]e at no time urged a
completely free market that would be subject to manipulation by
private interests . . . ," Eccles wrote in his memoirs. "[W]hat we
wanted was an *orderly* market in which the Federal Reserve maintained control, but where freedom of action would be permitted
so as to reflect more nearly the real demand by private investors.")
With the war ended, the Eccles Fed suspended its wholesale purchase of government securitics and asked to be relieved of the
emergency service of fixing the structure of interest rates. In this
it won a partial victory—the bill rate, formerly pegged at three-
eighths of 1 percent, was slowly set free, starting in 1946. However, Eccles's continued agitation against the fixing of other
interest rates had come to annoy Truman (as his regulatory pos-
ture had come to alienate Wall Street, Eccles believed), and in
1948 the president declined to reappoint him as chairman. Swal-
lowing his disappointment, Eccles chose to remain on the board
of the Fed as an ordinary governor, an unswerving rhetorical foe
of inflation (and champion of government controls) until the
end of his term, in 1951.

WITH THE OUTBREAK of war in Korea on June 25, 1950, latent inflation became manifest. Consumer prices, which had actually fallen
in 1949, began to kick up in the spring of 1950 and fairly vaulted
into 1951. From June 1950 to February 1951, wholesale prices
climbed at an annual rate of 16 percent. Appreciating prices were,
of course, the other side of the coin of a depreciating currency.
The bond market, still sedated by the Federal Reserve, betrayed no
outward alarm. The average of long-term yields in 1950 was 2.32
percent, one basis point higher than the 2.31 percent average for the
decade of the 1940s. The situation for bondholders remained just
as Parkinson had described it in the fall of 1945: minuscule yields

even before taking account of federal taxation and the upward creep of prices; all risk and no reward.

Parkinson was not alone in believing that things could not go on this way forever. The Federal Reserve, too, had begun to assert itself. By the end of 1947, the now unsuppressed bill rate was quoted at 1 percent. One of the most remarkable features about postwar finance was that bond yields were not, as might have been expected, being pushed up against the Federal's 2½ percent ceiling by the sheer demand for capital (as they had been in 1944, for instance); in no month in 1946 and 1947 did yields average even 2.4 percent. Despite all the vast monetary expansion and pent-up consumer demand of the war years, there was no spontaneous burst of inflation-induced borrowing; in fact, just the opposite. The man who seemed most to personify the postwar bond market was Sewell Avery, who hated debt and managed Montgomery Ward & Company with an eye to avoiding the next depression.*

Seen in the reflected light of the 1970s—a decade of hard times for creditors, savers, and annuitants—the interest-rate experience of the late 1940s is almost inexplicable. How could so profligate a wartime monetary policy (supplemented after the war by a heavy influx of gold) not have produced a rise in interest rates? The fact is that it didn't. Still, Eccles worried that it might, and he spoke out against "the peg." In 1949, the Federal Reserve Board went so far as to declare that it would henceforth conduct business "with primary regard for the general business and credit situation," as distinct from the perennial Treasury-deficit situation. It was an easy enough thing to say in 1949, when the economy was in recession and interest rates (following a 1948 rise) were falling again. It would prove a much harder resolution to live by in the next upswing.

The Korean War duly produced one, and businesses and families competed for credit with the government, all takers vying in the low-interest-rate environment nurtured for so long by successive

---

* Nor was Avery alone. John Kenneth Galbraith's best-selling book on 1929, *The Great Crash*, was published in 1954, just as the Dow Jones Industrial Average was surpassing its precrash high for the first time since 1929. What was on Galbraith's mind was chiefly the unprosperous past, not the unfolding bullish future. Avery and he, at least in one respect, were on the same wavelength.

administrations. Still, there was no immediate move to unfix the bond market. The obligation to maintain par value on the Treasury's debt was more than just a matter of keeping faith with investors, President Truman told an extraordinary meeting of the Federal Open Market Committee (FOMC) that he had convened at the White House in January 1951 (the only such conference in the Fed's history). It was a matter of the most urgent strategic interest. The battle against Communism had been joined, the president went on, and it was vital "to maintain the confidence of the Government's credit and in Government securities." Truman reminisced about his own unhappy experiences as a bondholder after World War I, when Liberty Loan prices collapsed in a heap before recovering to stage (what must have seemed to the neophyte bond buyers who had sold at the bottom) a galling rally. For their part, the assembled Federal Reserve officials affirmed their dedication to protecting the credit of the United States and blandly suggested that the Treasury and they stay in touch. Herbert Stein aptly called the meeting "a masterpiece of deliberate misunderstanding."

Recriminations presently followed. When the White House publicly thanked the Federal Reserve for agreeing to continue the inflation-fostering policy of pegging interest rates, something it had specifically not promised, Eccles in reprisal took it upon himself to deliver a copy of the minutes of the meeting to the press. A few days later, when the FOMC sat down to meet again (this time, of course, without the president), mass resignation and an appeal for congressional intercession were each considered and each rejected. Instead, the committee settled on a letter to Truman in which they asserted, among other things, that "in inflationary times like these, our buying of Government securities does not provide confidence. It undermines confidence."

Diplomacy at length drew the two sides back together. On March 3, 1951, the Treasury and the Fed issued a joint announcement that was as mild in its style as it was significant in its content: "The Treasury and the Federal Reserve System have reached full accord with respect to debt management and monetary policies to be pursued in furthering their common purpose to assure the successful financing of the Government's requirements and, at the same time, to minimize monetization of the public debt."

In loose translation, the Federal would no longer subordinate its mission of protecting and defending the dollar to the exigencies of the Treasury's borrowing program. For the time being, the central bank would intervene as needed to promote an "orderly" market in government debt, but it would no longer peg the Treasury bill rate and the Treasury bond rate. As a sop to long-term investors, the Treasury agreed to exchange marketable $2^{1/2}$ percent bonds for nonmarketable $2^{3/4}$ percent bonds; the new securities would fall due in 29 years. Twenty-nine years hence, as it so happened, the bond prices would still be in the coils of the generation-long bear market that had started in 1946 (Parkinson was more right than he knew). Cold comfort, then, this extra one-quarter of 1 percent in yield. Still, the Fed was free. It could do the right thing if it could only decide what the right thing was. "Dictated money rates breed dictated prices all across the board," said William McChesney Martin Jr. in a speech in 1953, two years after the signing of the peace treaty. "This is characteristic of dictatorships. It is regimentation. It is not compatible with our institutions."

MARTIN, THE THEN Federal Reserve chairman, had come to that eminent job from a succession of precocious appointments—"boy wonder of Wall Street," the first paid New York Stock Exchange president, youthful senior Treasury Department official, but in his own flamboyantly modest description, just a "bond man." He knew the 1951 accord intimately; at the Treasury he had been instrumental in negotiating it. Rewarded by Truman with the chairmanship of the Fed, he later memorably described the job of the central banker as one of leaning against the monetary winds "of deflation or inflation, whichever way they are blowing." The trouble, as Martin knew, was that winds were the hardest to read just when a banker had to read them most accurately. A little like flying an airplane, the risk in central banking was greatest not in the long hours of mid-flight, but at takeoff and landing.

Martin was still on the job as the economy began to lose cyclical altitude in 1957. The prior two years had brought profitable tailwinds to both the GNP and the stock market, and monetary policy had accordingly been taut; commercial banks, in need of dollars with which to satisfy their reserve requirements, were obliged to turn to the Fed to borrow them. Indeed, policy had remained tight even after the onset of the recession (which struck in August), as the stock market turned down, unemployment turned up, and business activity visibly weakened. In October 1957, the president of the New York Federal Reserve Bank, Alfred Hayes, warned, in what was understood to be a major policy address, that "it would be a great mistake to relax credit restraint just as we now see some hope of achieving the price stability that we have all sought so ardently." A month later, however, the New York Fed abruptly did the opposite, applying to the Federal Reserve Board for permission to lower its discount rate to 3 percent from $3\frac{1}{2}$ percent; this was the rate at which it was prepared to lend to commercial banks. The bond market drank it in (permission was granted): a new issue of American Telephone & Telegraph bonds, the 5s of 1983, unsalable before the discount-rate announcement, suddenly flew out their underwriters' windows. Explaining itself, the Federal Reserve Board said that inflation, "at least temporarily, has ceased to be the dominant factor in the economy." For bond buyers, the statement was tantamount to an all-clear siren, and prices of government securities rallied.

One might suppose that inflation-fearing creditors would always prefer a stringent monetary policy to a lenient one. However, in the late 1950s, as in the early and mid-1990s, bondholders asked for more than just a reprieve from inflation. They also seized on the opportunity to speculate on falling interest rates. Government bond yields had crept up since the 1951 monetary accord, reaching $3\frac{3}{4}$ percent by the fall of 1957, the highest since the 4 percent rates of the Calvin Coolidge era. Yet there was not much sport to be had in buying a bond for cash. If its price went to 102 from 100, the gain was hardly detectable: 2 percent if one had put up 100¢ on the dollar. If, on the other hand, the same bond could be had for little or no money down, say 5¢ on the dollar, the potential for gain was magnified. A move to 102 from 100 would be calculated not on a base of 100 but on 5; the corresponding rate of return not 2 percent but 40 percent. Conversely, the same financial leverage would also vastly enlarge a loss. The arrangement therefore satisfied the basic psychological requirement of serious speculation as set forth by Curtis Jadwin, the alpha wheat trader in Frank Norris's novel *The Pit:* the risk taker must put up more than he or she can afford to lose.

In 1958, as in 1991, 1992, or 1993, it was possible to borrow 95 percent or more of the price of Treasury bonds; then as now, the Federal Reserve's margin rules did not apply to government securities. From the point of view of leverage, the Treasury market was (and so remains today) an open city. Nothing in the federal securities laws prevented a banker from lending 100 percent of the value of a government bond. A margined Treasury bondholder would borrow in the short-term money market and invest in the longer-term bond market. In World War II, a special low discount rate—one-half of 1 percent—was available to banks on the collateral of government bonds. In 1957 and 1958, this special wartime accommodation was long gone, but such was the alignment of open-market rates that it was possible to borrow at a low rate and invest at a higher one.

Speculation in so dignified a financial instrument as a full-faith obligation of the United States of America might seem a contradiction in terms, but traders have long preferred to deal in government securities: they can be heavily mortgaged, they can be easily bought and sold, and they constitute a pure expression of interest rates (rather than, as in a corporate obligation, interest rates mixed with credit risk). For those who predicted a long recession, an obvious course of action was to lay down a bet on rising bond prices.

By late in 1957 (the peak of the business expansion was later officially fixed as August), the recession was expected to be a doozy. It would, indeed, prove to be the most fretful and publicized downturn since the 1930s, and the discount-rate cut in November 1957 seemed only to confirm that an extraordinary and grave interruption of the postwar prosperity had occurred. ("The most significant feature of the recession," wrote the economist Marcus Nadler in a postmortem, "is the fact that it did not degenerate into a serious depression, as many observers feared.") Bond prices raced higher, buyers racing after them. Long-term government yields had dropped to about 3.12 percent by April 1958, when the rally ended, from 3¾ percent in October, when Alfred Hayes was suggesting that the Federal would not do what it presently did do. When, in February 1958, the Treasury issued $1.7 billion worth of securities bearing a 3½ percent coupon and falling due in 1990, the market bestowed an affectionate nickname on them: the Gay Nineties.

But the market was grateful for the structure of rates as well as for their new level. As we have already noted, an important source of profit in the bond market is the difference between the cost of financing a portfolio of securities and the income those securities yield. If one could borrow cheaply enough, even a 3 percent bond would produce a profit all by itself. The profit would be measured by the difference between the cost of borrowing and 3 percent. One would continue to earn it for as long as the Federal Reserve remained openhanded and the recession dragged on. If bond prices rallied, of course, so much the better: a capital gain would be added to the interest income.

The bond bull market of 1957–58, like the one of the early 1990s, was sustained by idle cash. Monetary policy was easy, banks were liquid, and short-term interest rates were falling. By May 1958, short-term Treasury bills were quoted at 0.635 percent, less than one-fifth of the 3.66 percent rate seen the prior summer, and the nation's thrift institutions were weighing the first general cut in passbook interest rates (to 2½ percent or even 2 percent from 3 percent) since World War II. Concerning the opportunities for profitable lending, they were apparently vanishing. One banker described the short end of the money market as "starved" for assets, a phrase that harkened back to the 1930s.

Unlike the Great Depression, however, the Eisenhower recession caused no collapse of speculative courage. Far from it. Corporate treasurers, disdaining the low yields available on short-term bills and certificates, lent out money in what amounted to the bond market's own call-loan market, or they themselves speculated in government notes, or purchased a certain number of maturing government securities to secure the right to buy an identical number of new ones. Nor did the public hang back. Tales of the Gay Nineties inspired neophytes to participate in what had come to seem a sure thing. Brokerage firms that once refused $100,000 trades now stooped to deal in lots of $5,000 or $10,000. Banks stood prepared to lend generously against the market value of a customer's bonds, and to invest themselves, buying six-year bonds rather than one-year certificates. Like so many corporate treasurers, they did not choose to dignify yields of $1\frac{1}{2}$ percent or less with their own money.

To get in on the ground floor of the next big Treasury-note issue, an investor was advised to secure a place in the line of waiting buyers. Holders of maturing government securities automatically got a spot in the queue. Thus, the expiring securities were known as "rights"—conferring, as they did, preferential rights on their holders to renew their investment in the new Treasury borrowing—and in the hot bond market of early 1958, they were scarce. Not coincidentally, in June 1958, the volume of bank lending against securities reached a new postwar high. The Treasury Department, worried by the speculation, decided to do the public a favor by denying it all the rope it seemed to demand to hang itself. In the June refunding, holders of rights would be offered the choice of a one-year certificate (of no speculative interest whatsoever) or an intermediate-term note. Long-term bonds, the hands-down favorite of interest-rate sportsmen, would be sold only through cash subscription.

"In retrospect," recorded a joint Treasury–Federal Reserve study of the speculative debacle of that spring and summer, "it is clear that the build-up in June 'rights' reached a maximum at a time when the underlying factors making for capital gains in the government securities market had already begun to change direction"—in other words, when the market had turned, or was preparing to.

Indeed, the bond market's precious recession was already ending (the bottom of the business cycle would be fixed as April 1958). Not knowing, the owners of rights elected overwhelmingly to purchase the longer dated, and therefore riskier, of the choices on the Treasury's menu, a six-year, eight-month note: the $2\frac{5}{8}$s of 1965. All told, the holders of more than three-quarters of the $9.1 billion of publicly held maturing rights signed up for the $2\frac{5}{8}$s. Some $7 billion was thus distributed, of which about $1.2 billion was later found to be financed by credit. It came to light that one novice purchased $1 million of notes with only $1,500 down, and, indeed, it was common practice to pay no money down, deferring payment until after the new securities were issued. (It was assumed that their prices would rise and the holder could sell at a profit, without having to come up with a single cent.) "The Wall Street division of one major bank had a larger volume of loans on its books after the 2⅝s were issued than at any other time in its history," it was reported after the deluge. "Significantly, the bulk of the loans were to stock exchange firms that had never been active in the government securities market before." Nor were the 2⅝s sold exclusively to the public. Nonfinancial businesses, which customarily invested only for the short term, threw caution to the winds to buy $1 billion worth.

Still, until the middle of June, the market was in no mood to ask questions. The first loud note of skepticism was struck by *The New York Herald Tribune* on June 19. To a lay reader, the copy could hardly have seemed inflammatory. It said that the Fed would stop pushing money-market interest rates down and instead would begin nudging them up. Although there was no "inflation" as a subsequent generation would use the word or as the consumers of 1946 and 1951 could still remember it, the authorities feared that one might be in the making. "FED SEES TURNING POINT AT HAND," said the headline over the *Trib* story, "SLOWS PACE OF DRIVE FOR EASY CREDIT." Joseph R. Slevin, national economics editor, writing from Washington, led off: "The Federal Reserve System has reached a major turning point in its anti-recession drive and is slowing the pace at which it has been pressing toward easy money."

Slevin cited no authority but wrote like a man who was one.* "The Federal Reserve still is providing additional cash to the banks but it no longer is pushing out the massive supplies that marked central bank easy money efforts throughout the winter and the early spring," wrote Slevin, adding that, from where the Fed sat, the recession was ending.

---

* In 1994, still declining to name his source, he did say that his story was not the result of an intentional Federal Reserve leak. "They didn't leak it," he said. "I found it out."

Then came the passage that caused every bond speculator to stop and stare (it also caused the head of government bond trading at one leading firm to call Slevin's editor to demand a retraction): "The shift in credit policy suggests that the end of the recession decline in interest rates is in sight and perhaps is at hand. This would mean that the prices of bond and other fixed return obligations will go little if any higher."

Slevin's information proved as timely as it was accurate. The market fell to pieces immediately, as the people who never had any intention of putting up real money for the securities they bought were obliged to sell. The bond crash of 1958 had begun.

AND THEN, like the collapse of bond prices in 1994, it didn't stop. Violent liquidations are often short-lived, but the 1958 episode had staying power. Prices fell in July and August and in early September. The Treasury intervened, buying up $600 million of the new and now notorious 2⅝s in the three weeks following Slevin's scoop, but to no avail. "Blame for the rout is now being placed on the 'gamblers,'" commented an unsigned writer in *Barron's* (presumably the knowledgeable Kurt Bloch) in mid-July, "which seems like rank ingratitude, considering it was they who last fall and winter caused the rapid recovery in bond prices." The Federal Reserve, too, intervened, disclosing on July 18 that it would abandon its policy of buying bills alone to support the disorderly market in longer-dated notes. "I would not characterize market conditions today as disorderly," said Aubrey G. Lanston, eponymous head of Aubrey G. Lanston & Company, "but it was a rugged affair." It only became more so. On August 8, municipal-bond trading virtually ground to a halt. "It has been many a day since institutions, large and small, have been unable to sell bonds, regardless of price," commented H. J. Nelson, the "Trader" columnist in *Barron's*. By Labor Day, the government bond market had come full circle: it was back where it had started in November. "Because of punitive income taxes and the long-term inflationary trend," Nelson reflected, "bonds lack their old-time appeal to individuals and, to a lesser degree, to institutions."

Finally, the storm was over. For weeks on end, the bond market, so recently the government's obedient servant, had refused to obey instructions. Foreigners could not be blamed: as a group, their holdings of government securities were insignificant. Nor could the break be put down to "derivatives" (the advent of the futures market in bonds was 20 years off) or to exotic mortgage-backed securities (most of which hadn't been invented). What had happened was miscalculation by leveraged speculators. The Federal Reserve had been accommodative; therefore, they decided that it would remain accommodative. Believing the recession would deepen and interest rates would fall even below $2^5/8$ percent, a very close thing to financial sea level, the market structured itself for only the bullish outcome. When, contrary to expectations, bond prices started to fall, waves of liquidation began.

The outcry was loud and anguished: from Rep. Wright Patman, the Wall Street–hating Texas populist (who demanded that the Federal Reserve take action against the "jungle-like activities being carried on by gamblers and speculators"), to *The New York Times* (in which Edward H. Collins wrote that "speculation in the securities of one's own government is, or should be, repugnant to all responsible citizens"), to the New York Stock Exchange. On September 19, the Big Board publicly fined and suspended George K. Garvin, senior partner of Garvin Bantel, the money-brokerage firm that had facilitated a sizable portion of the low-margin speculation in government securities, for failure to follow "sound business practices," among other alleged shortcomings. Trading was interrupted for the disciplinary proceedings.

Raking through the evidence, investigators from the Treasury and Federal Reserve later arrived at two conclusions that would bear directly on the events of the early 1990s. "In the area of monetary policy," they wrote, "there is the problem as to whether easy credit conditions and accelerating monetary expansion for counter-cyclical objectives may be carried to the point where banks and other lenders respond too actively to speculative demands for credit, so that lenders, in their zeal to keep funds employed to fullest advantage, may too easily relax the credit standards which long experience has taught to be sound." In attempting to lift the country out of a recession, could the Federal inadvertently incite a speculative riot? The 1990s have furnished the answer: yes.

In a masterful use of the passive bureaucratic voice, the Treasury and Federal Reserve authors ventured one of the faint, recurring hopes that bear markets inspire: "For purchasers of marketable government securities and for lenders," they wrote, "the risks of speculation on anticipated cyclical price movements of fixed-income government securities, and particularly of speculation on slim margin, credit-financed holdings, have been widely learned." Before many years had passed, however, they would become just as widely forgotten.

TO THE SPECULATORS who bought Treasury securities with next to no money down—including a used-car dealer in Jersey City, New Jersey, who reportedly purchased $5 million worth, and a Manhattan newsstand operator—the tightening of monetary policy was both regrettable and unprofitable. In August 1957, the month the recession began, the consumer price index was rising at an annual rate of 3.7 percent. That was, in itself, unusual. The 1957–58 recession was the first postwar business downturn to be ushered in by a rising inflation rate. That, however, would prove to be the highest monthly year-over-year rise until 1966, when the Vietnam War began to overburden the nation's productive capacity. An unpredicted, nine-year inflation holiday was looming. From the Federal Reserve, the Treasury, the press, and the Congress in 1958 came an outpouring of inflationary anxiety. Was resumption of the bull stock market a wholesome thing? According to Rep. Albert M. Rains, Alabama Democrat, it was not: "The heavy buying has been clearly a hedge against inflation in my opinion." Was it advisable in those circumstances to raise the margin requirements on the purchase of common stock to 70 percent of value at cost from 50 percent? It was, said Harry F. Byrd, chairman of the Senate Finance Committee: "We're certainly faced with a period of very dangerous inflation." Was it any consolation that the less than 3 percent inflation was merely creeping—and, indeed, was what a subsequent generation would choose to call "disinflation"? Not at all, *The Wall*

Street Journal editorially answered, because Aesop's tortoise, too, just plodded along. Surveying 69 executives in August 1958, the *Journal* found that 90 percent feared inflation more than recession. "Inflation is a bigger danger than Russia, a bigger danger than recession, a bigger danger than anything this country has encountered in the last several years," declared William E. Umstattd, president of the Timken Roller Bearing Company, one of the emphatic majority. (Typically, recession and inflation were thought to be mutually exclusive. Another 15 years or so would prove that, sometimes, they were not.)

Investigating the financial condition of the United States in 1957 and 1958, Senator Byrd's conservative Finance Committee was able to produce a number of sympathetic witnesses. Bernard M. Baruch, investor and elder statesman, called inflation "the most important economic fact of our time—the single greatest peril to our economic health." Ralph Cordiner, chairman of General Electric, testified, " 'Creeping inflation' would mean runaway ruin." Like him, Professor Gottfried Haberler of Harvard University had his way with the popular inflation nomenclature: "Soon the price creep will become a trot and the trot a gallop." George Meany of the AFL-CIO and John L. Lewis of the United Mine Workers chose not to reply to the committee's questionnaires. However, it is unlikely that they were thinking along the same lines as Connecticut Senator Prescott Bush, father of the future president, who, in the fall of 1958, would tell the American Assembly that, barring a return to sound policies, the nation was in for "boom and bust, depression and panic." Nor would labor have seen eye to eye with Arthur F. Burns, the future Federal Reserve chairman (and former adviser to President Eisenhower), who prescribed an anti-inflationary amendment to the Employment Act of 1946. (In contract negotiations the next year with big steel, organized labor did respond to the companies' contention that inflation represented the nation's "No. 1 problem." David J. McDonald, the Steelworkers' president, called it a fiction and a public-relations ploy. The year-over-year inflation rate in May 1959, the month in which the verbal exchange took place, was 0.3 percent; McDonald seemed to have a point.)

What the economic and business majority found so disquieting about the inflation of the mid-1950s was its persistence. It defied the taut monetary policy of 1956 and the severe recession of 1957–58. In the 1948–49 recession, consumer prices had actually fallen. In the only other postwar recession, that of 1953–54, they had hardly risen. Now they went up defiantly.

Certainly, some observers believed, a great new inflation was long overdue. War, hot or cold, had engaged America for most of the past 20 years, and the dollar had been mobilized along with draft-age youth. Untold billions of dollars of public debt had been turned into money by an obedient Federal Reserve Board, interest rates had been suppressed, and the gold standard diluted. If that was not enough to drive up the cost of living, what was?

"The present price and cost inflation is not only conspicuously different from its earlier postwar predecessors," wrote Roy L. Reierson of Bankers Trust in the spring of 1957, before the recession began, "but differs also from the price upturns which have in the prewar past been associated with cyclical expansion of business activity, such as in 1924–26 and 1936–37. The current advance"—Reierson dated it from 1955—"has already persisted for a longer time and has been of greater magnitude than in these previous periods of prosperity. Moreover, the end is not in sight."

The decade-long respite was, of course, just around the corner. Nevertheless, as Reierson noted, the country for too long had been absorbed by the 1930s, "whereas the real economic problems of the past fifteen years have been posed by a fairly sustained business boom, repeated strains upon the supply of labor and materials, and inflation of wages, costs, and prices. Because of this concern with depression, economic policy has tended to react swiftly and forcefully to the first signs of a downturn in the business cycle but to respond only gradually and gingerly to the growing momentum and problems of an upturn."

To be sure, creeping inflation had its proponents, too. The Harvard economist Sumner Slichter argued that a gently rising price level was part and parcel of prosperity in the late twentieth century. "Inflation may or may not cause the benefits," ventured Slichter in the *Harvard Business Review* in the fall of 1957, "but, in the present state of our knowledge, it is an inseparable by-product of the processes that produce important benefits." What were those benefits? The absence of old-time deflationary panics, a rising wage level (in all industries, shrinking or growing), rapid technological progress, and a vibrant trade union movement, he replied. To those who contended that unemployment must not fall too low lest prices rise too much, Slichter said that they couldn't know what the alleged trade-off, if any, might be. And if that were indeed to be the new federal policy, he observed, someone would have to amend the 1946 Employment Act.

Ironically, one of the most impassioned denunciations of a policy of creeping inflation was heard from a senior member of the Federal Reserve System. Malcolm Bryan, a career system employee —staff economist in Washington, staff adviser to the American delegation at Bretton Woods, and finally president of the Federal Reserve Bank of Atlanta—attacked it mainly on moral grounds. "So the proposal is, on the one hand," wrote Bryan sarcastically of the Slichter school of thought, "that we take from the naive or the trusting and, on the other hand, that our defalcations be effected on the installment plan, lest doing the job all at once, we might be caught at it." Bryan went right on:

Let us be clear that what is being asked, when we are now urged to a policy of either intentional or connived-at inflation, is that we sell our honor. What altar of expediency is high enough and what bribe is great enough to absolve us from such perfidy? If this language be deemed unduly pungent, what other language shall be used? I believe that no greater delicacy of expression is warranted if we speak out of one side of our mouths to give ingratiating reassurances and out of the other side of our mouths to plan the undoing of men we have enticed and are enticing.

The integrity of our conduct is crucial. Even if we ignore past savers in money forms, which would be a great scandal, we at least have a responsibility, binding in conscience, to present and future savers in money forms. If a policy of active or permissive inflation is to be a fact, then we can rescue the shreds of our self-respect only by announcing the policy. That is the least of the canons of decency that should prevail. We should have the decency to say to the money saver, "Hold still, Little Fish! All we intend to do is to gut you!"

The Federal Reserve, of course, made no such clean breast of things. (Nor did Bryan live to see the full-blown consequences of the monetary policy he denounced; he died two years after his retirement, in 1967, just as "creeping" inflation was preparing to hop, skip, and jump. The prospect of a pure paper monetary standard, unanchored by gold, filled him with gloom. More and more, he was inclined to withdraw to his office and pace the floor. He warned of a great new inflation—accurately, as it turned out.) However, the American saver was coming to realize that the useful shelf life of his or her savings was systematically being shortened. The change in perception was expressed in a new preference for common stocks. In 1958, for the first time in 22 years, bond yields surpassed stock-dividend yields. Later in the same year, the American Telephone & Telegraph pension fund made its first investment in common stocks since its inception in 1913. Also that year, on May 29 to be exact, a landmark investment event occurred: the biggest initial public offering in the history of the mutual-fund business up until that time, a $221 million equity fund sponsored by Lehman Brothers.

The One William Street Fund, named for the sponsor's downtown Manhattan office address, overawed Wall Street's imagination and taxed its finite capital. The fund had been built around a private, rich men's investment partnership with 28 executives of Ford Motor pooling their money to invest in common stocks. Lehman had been chosen as the investment adviser, and now Lehman was selected to fold this entity, called Aurora Corporation, into a mutual fund for the masses. Lehman underestimated the masses' enthusiasm for common stocks by a factor of more than five. Expecting to sell just 3 million shares, it wound up placing 16 million. (No fewer than 640 brokerage firms were brought together to form the underwriting syndicate.) It did not immediately invest the proceeds, however. Perhaps in the back of its institutional mind were memories of the charmed life that Lehman Corporation, a One William

Street Fund forerunner, had led in the Great Depression. Launched on the eve of the crash, Lehman had been saved from disaster by good luck and conservative management. In mid-crash, no less influential a shareholder than Bernard Baruch had urged a director of the fund, Robert Lehman, to buy common stocks because the market was cheap. It was indeed cheaper than it had been, but it was not yet so cheap as it would become. Because the fund had no debt and because it resisted Baruch's advice to become fully invested, it rode out the depression with losses far less severe than those borne by other big, closed-end equity funds.

No crash occurred in 1958 (except, as we have seen, in the government bond market), but the year was anxiety-fraught all the same. The brief bear market heralding the recession was over and done with by the end of October 1957, less than four months after it began. However, as is so often the case in markets, worry grew more intense after the main danger had passed; at the close of 1957, well-informed people were asking if some out-of-the-blue bankruptcy might come crashing down on their heads. It was at the end of this deepest and most worry-laden recession of the postwar era that the investment philosophy of One William Street was codified. Management resolved to hold 25 percent of the stockholders' assets in reserve. To put that figure in contemporary context, the typical equity fund late in May 1996 let just 6.7 percent of its assets lie fallow. As of October 31, 1958, five full months after the offering date, some 30 percent of the fund's assets were still sitting motionless in cash, Treasury bills, and bonds (few of which yielded much more than 3 percent). What concerned the Lehman advisory group was not merely the risk of a bear market. They also worried that the weight of their own buying might drive up the prices of the stocks they wanted to own, thereby doing their investors a disservice. ("Whereas," the board of directors had resolved, "that the too rapid acquisition of equity securities of the desired quality and marketability in sufficient amounts to bring the portfolio to such 75 percent level might of itself affect market prices so that the acquisition cost would be higher than would otherwise prevail. . . .") The market was smaller then and the so-called momentum investing style was not widely practiced. When, from late 1957 to mid-1959, records were set in public investment in equity mutual funds, an average of $149 million a month was committed. In the early going of 1996, the monthly inflow was in excess of $20 billion.

What the professionals of both eras did share was a systematic underestimation of the public's appetite and endurance. The 1958 bull market, anticipating numerous others, rallied in defiance of certifiably bearish news: rising interest rates and the threat of war in the Middle East, among other worrisome things. "This market is like the Indian rope trick," a broker was quoted as saying in September 1958. "It goes up, but nobody can understand why."

THE QUOTATION WAS contained in a remarkable magazine article, "The People's Stock Market: Optimistic and Unpredictable Buying Baffles Wall Street's Professionals," by Ernest Havemann, which was published in—of all places—*Life* magazine. It was the perfect journalistic complement to the populist bull market. Wall Street was inclined to patronize both the public and the public's choice of newspaper and magazine reading. Taking the public's side, however, *Life* turned the tables on the professionals. New investors were streaming into the market, wrote Havemann, a longtime writer for *Life* who claimed no particular financial expertise, whose journalistic interests, in fact, had ranged from agricultural subsidies to Yogi Berra: "To an extent which our founding fathers could never have foreseen, we live today under a genuine people's capitalism, in which the stock market has become everybody's business."

A month after Havemann's article appeared, a senior man at a research meeting of Lehman Corp. reflected on the high valuation (18 times earnings) of the Dow Jones Industrial Average (at 540 or so). "He thinks [the minutes quoted him] the market is very high and with it gyrating around this level he thinks it may be in for a break. He noted that we do have some past standards by which to measure the market, and he doesn't think these can be pushed aside." The truth, just as Havemann suggested, was that they should have been pushed aside. Stocks had been going up, more or less, for a decade.

This was, however, Havemann went on presciently, no replay of the bull market of the 1920s. "In those days, most laymen who got into the market did so strictly as a gamble," he wrote. "They bought stocks on the narrow margin (down payment) of 10 percent or 20 percent and hoped to make a quick killing and get out fast. Today's man in the street usually buys stocks as he would buy insurance or make regular deposits in a savings account. He is in the market for the long pull, and temporary setbacks do not discourage him."

Old hands knew this to be fatuous. Absorbing a loss was a little like taking a punch. It was not an experience that an amateur willingly sought out or, having once absorbed, repeated. Then, too, Havemann seemed to be referring only to the confetti phase of the Coolidge market. The rise had been exactly foretold by a sober little book published just as the run-up began, *Common Stocks as Long Term Investments,* by Edgar L. Smith.

Smith's timing was, if possible, even better than Havemann's. As his book reached the stores in December 1924, the Dow Jones Industrial Average was making its first thrust above 100. It would close at 157 at the end of 1925, at 200 at the end of 1927 (it regrouped in 1926), and at 381.17 on September 3, 1929, whereupon Smith's predictive reputation would suffer a cyclical downturn. However, if the public did not get in at the very bottom, it was no fault of his. The message of *Common Stocks as Long Term Investments* was that stocks were intrinsically superior to bonds or mortgages. It was a thesis that, to a nation so long and well acquainted with bear markets, banking crises, wartime inflations, and other forms of upset and volatility, seemed not at all self-evident.

Havemann, assuring his readers that the 1958 market bore little if any resemblance to the unregulated bacchanalia of the 1920s, echoed Smith. Smith, too, had assured his readers that they lived in modern and enlightened times, proof of which included the improved financial disclosure by investor-owned companies as well as the emerging "science" of corporate management (as witness the development of the Harvard Graduate School of Business Administration). Smith's analytical case rested on both the inferiority of bonds and the built-in, all-season desirability of stocks. What made bonds a second-class investment, the book stated, was first and foremost the instability of currencies. Smith observed that the value of a dollar had been falling (that is, prices denominated in dollars had been rising) ever since 1897. The rate of inflation had accelerated mightily during the 1914–18 war, he observed, but it had been on the rise for nearly two decades before the United States took up arms. This he attributed to the inflation-prone nature of social democracies. Smith, that season, on that subject, was in distinguished company. In his Sydney Ball Lecture delivered before the University of Oxford in October 1924 (and subsequently published as a book, *The End of Laissez-Faire*), John Maynard Keynes had forecast the rise of the welfare state, with all its expansive and inflationary tendencies. "The important thing for Government," Keynes had said, "is not to do the things which individuals are doing already, and to do them a little better or a little worse; but to do those things which at present are not done at all." As for Smith, his argument would also give service in the 1950s. ". . . [T]here is a constant struggle between those who would maintain the full purchasing power of the dollar," he wrote, "and those whose interests lie in the other direction. As the latter are in the majority, and as they become increasingly well organized, there is no certainty that the dollar will recover the ground that it has steadily lost since 1897, or that it will again not suffer such radical depreciation as occurred between 1915 and 1920." Or indeed, Smith added, no assurance that it would not emulate the German mark, then astonishing the world by going up in hyperinflationary smoke. As for the protection afforded an American creditor by the lawful right to demand an ounce of gold for $20.67, Smith didn't seem to think much of it; at least, he didn't mention it. Indeed, as he was able to demonstrate, the institution of the gold standard did not prevent the gradual erosion of the value of a creditor's principal over the first two decades of the twentieth century. The inflation-reduced 1920 dollar was worth only 37 percent of the 1902-edition dollar. Inflation had, at first, crept. Then, on the wings of the wartime economy, it had flown.

Havemann wrote that stocks had entered a new era, Smith that stocks excelled in nearly every era. Smith's was a universal bull argument. Throughout virtually the entire span of years from 1837 to 1923, Smith related, stocks yielded their owners greater returns than bonds did. They outdistanced bonds in inflation-prone periods, as one might have expected, but also in deflation-prone periods (the last several decades of the nineteenth century, for example). How could it be otherwise? he asked. America's wealth was the proof of the prosperous compounding of American capital. And to whose benefit did this growth mainly accrue? Not to the creditors but to the owners. By investing and reinvesting the earnings they did not pay out as dividends, Smith observed, business corporations compounded money as a bank account did. He propounded a pair of investment hypotheses. First: "Over a period of years, the principal value of a well diversified holding of the common stocks of representative corporations, in essential industries, tends to increase in accordance with the operation of compound interest." And second: "Such stock holdings may be relied upon over a term of years to pay an average income return on such increasing values of something more than the average current rate on commercial paper." To an investment world wedded to bonds and to Brahman fiduciary ideals, Smith's ideas were novel. To subsequent generations (especially to this one), they became commonplace. What is known about the race of stocks, bonds, and cash, including commercial paper, over the period from the mid-1920s to the mid-1990s is that there was no contest. Smith's conclusions were, if anything, understated, as subsequent experience has shown. For decades on end, the winner, in a walk, has been equities.

As for Havemann, he addressed a public that still, despite its quickened interest in mutual funds and its evident indifference to valuation, vividly remembered the 21-year period in which stocks did not beat bonds. This anomalous rough patch had begun in 1929, only four years after the first edition of Smith's book showed how improbable it would be. Thus, Havemann first tried to exorcise the ghosts of the Hoover era. Just as Smith had done, he cited the improvements in financial disclosure. Compared to the Coolidge years, regulation was more encompassing and brokers were more conservative. "There are very few all-out bears at the moment," he went on, "chiefly because it is the consensus among brokers that our economy has changed so thoroughly that it is futile to try to understand it by historic analogy. Most Wall Streeters believe that we are in a New Era of business, finance and securities, and they are not at all upset by reminders that past prophecies of a New Era have always ended in bitter disappointment."

But once in a blue moon the world does change and the public does accurately take the measure of it. Havemann's contribution was to identify the fall of 1958 as one of these rare financial moments. "If we still had the old-fashioned, laissez-faire economy," he quoted an anonymous informant, "I would have expected a hell of a depression and I would have been one of the most liquid men in all Christendom." As it was, however, *Life*'s source was doing some "lazy buying" of common stocks, convinced that the soft, post-1934 edition of the gold standard and the 1946 Employment Act had introduced a powerful inflationary bias into business activity and financial markets alike. Wrote Havemann:

> One need hardly be a highbrow economist to note that wages and prices have kept right on rising despite the recession. ("If wages go up when business is bad," said one broker, "what's going to happen when business is good?") Inflation makes savings accounts and gilt-edged bonds look far less attractive . . . for while stocks are by no means a perfect hedge against inflation, they are one of the very few hedges of any kind that the average man can use. A good many stocks seem to have been bought in this spirit. "Just inflation alone," one prominent market observer said last week, "will some day carry the Dow Jones average over 1,000."*

IF ANY MARKET stood to benefit from a new inflation, it was the gold market: not the official one, but the obscure, free one. In official monetary gold dealings, the principal buyer and seller were one in

---

* One highbrow economist, at least, presently confirmed Havemann in his interpretation of the social democratic zeitgeist. Richard A. Musgrave, in *The Theory of Public Finance,* published in 1959, laid out the justification for, and the theory of, heightened government spending.

The Havemann essay anticipated by one full decade the landmark report of the Ford Foundation, *Managing Educational Endowments.* Just as Havemann had done, the foundation's panel of authors identified inflation as a postwar fact of life. They concluded, echoing Havemann, that stocks were a better class of long-term investment asset than either cash or bonds. "To be conservative today," said the Ford report in 1967, "one must protect the purchasing power of capital rather than just its dollar value. Bonds are unable to do this when the general price level is rising."

the same: the United States government. Until the devaluation of 1933, $20.67 had been the lawful equivalent of one ounce of gold. Under the Gold Reserve Act of January 30, 1934, an ounce of gold was redefined as the equivalent of $35. The value of the new, lighter dollar was reaffirmed by Congress when it ratified the Articles of Agreement of the International Monetary Fund in 1945. Individuals could, and did, set their own price for gold in private dealings, but between the United States Treasury and its official counterparts worldwide the price was a matter of law, custom, and American national honor. In the regulated portion of the gold market, stability was the greatest and highest good.

The higher the prices paid in voluntary gold transactions, of course, the greater the implied mistrust of the $35-per-ounce dollar. Now that markets are globally efficient, an ounce of gold fetches approximately the same price in New York as it does in Hong Kong. Not so in the years immediately following World War II. Rules and regulations prohibiting the movement of gold across national borders caused prices to vary substantially from one country to the next. Thus, in the same month, June 1946, the Bank of Mexico was selling gold at $40.61 per fine ounce while private buyers in Paris were paying more than $100 an ounce. During 1946, $50 an ounce or more was paid in Switzerland, Portugal, and Italy; and free-market trading was conducted, presumably at prices in excess of $35, in Tangier, Algiers, Beirut, and Macao. Almost as remarkable as the variability of quoted prices was the fact that premium prices were quoted at all. The dollar was, if anything, in short supply, and the Bretton Woods arrangements were brand new. There had been no gold hoarding to speak of, except in wartime, for a generation. From 1924 to 1941, the world's gold production had more or less been absorbed into the world's central-bank reserves; that is, it had not been absorbed into the private reserves of French peasants or Swiss bankers or Chinese speculators. Now, in 1946, commodity prices were rising and inflation was on the upswing, not least in the gold-mining industry itself. The $35 price had long since ceased to be a windfall to the miners. Wages and other production costs had continued to rise, even if the official gold price had not. Small wonder, then, that worldwide gold production peaked in 1940 and would not return to that level until 1962.

One contemporary school of monetary thought holds that the freely traded price of gold constitutes the best guide for central-bank management. In 1946, however, the authorities refused to be dictated to by a market that was variously described in official pronouncements, then and a little later, as clandestine, marginal, or parasitic. Rather than heeding the market, the IMF, in mid-1947, tried to get its member governments to suppress it. The U.S. Treasury promptly obliged by invoking wartime powers to deny export licenses to anyone who participated in the sale of gold to private overseas buyers. However, officials underestimated the tenacity of the gold bugs.

Throughout 1948, prices in the various European free markets consistently held above $50. Even in America, where the ownership of refined gold was forbidden and where, in any case, inflation seemed a less immediate threat in 1949 than a new depression, people began to buy Lucite bottles full of unrefined gold flakes at the equivalent of about $44 per refined ounce. The premium over the sanctioned $35 price presented the same kind of unflattering comparison for the dollar as did the prices paid for bullion in the exotic Eastern bazaars.

The Bank of International Settlements, the central bankers' own central bank, in its 1949 annual report expressed an almost seditious sympathy with the French gold bulls. "Among the countries in western Europe," commented the BIS, "the propensity to hoard gold has probably been strongest in France; the French people, remembering the old gold franc introduced by Napoleon in 1803 (the so-called 'franc germinal'), which maintained its value intact up to 1914 and thus withstood the strain of two lost wars—1814 and 1871—as well as a number of other vicissitudes, cannot help thinking that, compared with the paper franc which since 1914 has lost 99 percent of its purchasing power, gold, irrespective of any short-term fluctuations in the price paid for it, is in the long run a trustworthy basis for savings."

Justification for the existence of some premium to the Bretton Woods parity was promptly furnished in the autumn of 1949, when the United Kingdom devalued the pound sterling by 30.5 percent against the dollar. The British action provoked a run-up in commodity prices and gold-mining shares, and it inspired 29 other countries to devalue in their turn. It also provoked at least one anguished letter to the editor. "In the old days if people were uneasy about their country's credit, they could and did buy gold and foreign exchange," a Sussex man, critical of the monetary regimentation then prevailing in Britain as well as in many other countries, not least the United States, wrote to the *Financial Times* of London. "Natural economic forces then set up corrective action and the administration was forced to mend its ways. Today, all we have left of our liberty, with which to save ourselves, is the freedom to sell our Government Securities, Savings Certificates, etc., and buy Gold and Commodity shares and those British Industrials with overseas interests."

Before very long, however, the *Financial Times'* correspondent could only thank his intrusive government for the rules and regulations that had kept him out of the free bullion market. From its devaluation peak of a little more than $50 an ounce in 1949, gold in Europe steadily lost value against the dollar. By 1953, it would settle not far from the official $35 price. So confident was the Bank of England of the monetary situation in 1954 that it allowed the London gold market (closed since the war) to reopen. Naturally, in view of the interventionist tendencies of the times, the bank stood ready to "adjust supplies in accordance with variations in demand"—that is, to assure that the price would remain at $35, or a few cents over it. So well controlled was the market that briefly, in 1956, in the wake of the Suez crisis, the price was actually quoted at $34.90.

All around, monetary events took a turn for the better. The deutsche mark turned out to be a fine specimen of paper money, the European economy was flying high above the 1957–58 U.S. recession, and the pound was imminently to be restored to convertibility (under the Bretton Woods system, the dollar was made convertible to gold and the lesser currencies were made convertible into the dollar—not at once, but ultimately). However, a new monetary patient was in the waiting room, and it was none other than the dollar itself. When representatives of the Allied powers convened in July 1944 at the Mount Washington Hotel in Bretton Woods, New Hampshire, to plan the postwar world, almost any prospect seemed more likely than the breakdown of the dollar. An industrial power so productively intact after nearly four years of world war was hardly a candidate for devaluation. However, what the optimists of 1944 did not allow for was the tendency, so frequently observed in 1958, of prices to rise a little throughout the business cycle, or the related tendency of the United States to pay out chronically more to the world than it took in.

Yet exactly these tendencies were now coming to the fore. Not since 1933 had an American citizen been allowed to demand gold bars from the Treasury at the statutory rate in exchange for unwanted dollars. Official overseas holders, however, distressed by the American payments deficits, were perfectly willing to forgo the rock-bottom interest rates available on dollars invested in New York. As between the Treasury bill rate of less than 1 percent and the yield on a gold brick of zero percent, there seemed little enough risk in gold.

The reduction in the American gold reserve at first elicited no expression of concern in high places. "In a sense," wrote George Shea in *The Wall Street Journal* in 1957, "the present arrangement resembles the smoothly working international financial system that existed before World War I when Great Britain was the world's banker." The comparison, extravagantly flattering to Bretton Woods, was an expression of optimism. It was as much an Eisenhower-era period piece as the 1957 Chrysler New Yorker, which had eight cylinders and weighed 4,300 pounds. ". . . [W]e are a world in search of a monetary standard," said Malcolm Bryan, more aptly, in 1959. "In this country," he continued dryly, "we have had a Government bond standard in operation for a time, and we have also had very energetic propaganda for a constant depreciation standard."

When the eastbound movement of gold began to pick up in 1958, official America had a tendency to view it not as a loss for the United States (and still less as a return to the gold fever of the late 1940s), but as a gain for the rest of the world. War had tipped an outsized portion of the world's gold into American vaults—some 70 percent in 1948—and a more equitable redistribution was said to be overdue. Gold, after all, was meant to be more than a symbol of money. It was intended to be the thing itself, naturally moving around in response to the currents of trade and investment. Certainly, America had seen it come and go before. The currency upset of 1949, followed hard by the Korean War, precipitated a flight out of dollars and into gold. However, one source of worry to foreign dollar holders was assuaged when the Treasury and Federal at last shook hands in 1951, and half of the gold lost to overseas holders was returned by 1952. A second postwar decline in the American gold stock began later the same year and continued to the spring of 1955. Analysts blamed it on heavy U.S. military spending overseas and the rising prosperity in Europe (which permitted formerly straitened governments to restock their own Forts Knox). In 1957, as Shea was harking back to the good old days, gold was once more returning to the United States. But the ebb flow resumed early in 1958.

The simple truth was that many of the countries with which the United States ran deficits—Britain, Belgium, Switzerland, Italy—were demanding gold in lieu of dollars, dollars then being a "derivative" of gold (as a financial engineer of the 1990s would put it).

By the end of 1958, the United States gold reserve was at a postwar low: $20.7 billion. Nor was that the only sign of a lack of world confidence in the dollar. A new gold mutual fund, the American–South African Investment Trust, better known as ASA, was successfully opened to investors, and a new bull market in North American gold-mining stocks (including Alaska Juneau, the operating properties of which had lain dormant since 1944) got under way.* One of the big Canadian banks, Bank of Nova Scotia, advertised its services in the gold storage business, proof of a new-found interest in hoarding that had followed the lifting of government restrictions on private gold ownership in Canada in 1956.

---

* "We were all scared about the dollar," Wesley Stanger, longtime chairman of ASA, reminisced about the company's beginnings. Charles Engelhard and Dillon, Read & Co., the joint founders, had decided that inflation was the wave of the future and that investors needed an investment vehicle to protect themselves against it. Offered at $28 a share, the stock promptly plunged to $19. Righting itself, it excelled in the gold bull markets of the 1960s and 1970s, before languishing again in the disinflationary 1990s. From its offering in September 1958 to early September 1994, it generated a compound annual rate of return of 8.2 percent (before dividends), rising in price some 17-fold.

"In London," said *U.S. News & World Report* in December, "there is talk that Americans are pricing themselves out of world markets. Rumors in New York hint at a 'run' by foreigners from the American dollar. In Canada and South Africa, hope is expressed that the U.S. will be forced to raise the price of gold in terms of dollars so that gold mining will be stimulated and become more profitable." Such hope had been expressed for a dozen years or more, of course, and it would continue to be expressed for another dozen, up until the seminal 1971 dollar devaluation. Roy Harrod, Keynes's biographer, urged the United States to double the price of gold, to $70 an ounce, "as a bare minimum."

Already, Harrod observed, foreign governments had begun to queue up at the Federal Reserve gold window with surplus dollars for exchange. (He did not observe that $70 an ounce had been freely paid in markets all over the world only a few years earlier.) "To cash dollars for gold does no injury to the United States," he wrote slyly, "since she loses nothing by discharging a gold liability in gold—unless it be deemed an injury to provoke what is always a painful process, that of hard thinking."

Harrod called the devaluation inevitable, and so it was, but that was not the same as imminent. The United States gold hoard at year-end 1958 was still bigger than all the rest of the world's monetary gold put together, and it was considerably more, expressed against the relevant dollar claims against it, than the United States had possessed in the 1920s. Certainly, it was more than the country would need to satisfy its official foreign creditors in 1958. The sum of the dollars held abroad added up to only $11.7 billion, and not every foreign dollar holder was a government or central bank. By law, $11.9 billion of the $20.7 billion American hoard was earmarked as collateral against dollars held by American citizens— Americans who, since 1933, had been legally ineligible to take possession of it. Compared to the sum of these two claims, foreign and domestic, the $20.7 billion cache fell slightly short. However, it was a safe bet that not every eligible foreign holder would show up on the American doorstep with dollars in hand. The dollar was still the world's No. 1 commercial currency. Sound or not, it was eminently serviceable.

A monetary graybeard, ignorant of the new ways, might have supposed that the loss of gold would force the Federal Reserve to impose higher interest rates and thereby to force a deflation of wages. However, such policies would please almost nobody who could vote. In the house of the postwar monetary system, gold was an heirloom, esteemed but immovable. The wind into which William McChesney Martin chose to lean in the first six months of the year was that of domestic recession. The gold problem was purely a theoretical one.

"To be sure," commented the First National City Bank *Monthly Economic Letter* at the end of the year (the recession having ended but the gold outflow not), "the United States, as an international banker, owes foreigners more in dollars than it holds in excess gold reserves. But, while the U.S. is a debtor on short-term account, on long-term account it is a creditor. U.S. long-term investments abroad exceed by about $35 billion the foreign investments in this country." The bank observed, as many other analysts had done, that there had been no "run" on the dollar; in general, the dollars exchanged for gold by foreign countries were newly acquired ones, not long-standing dollar balances. "Actually," the letter added, "foreign short-term dollar holdings have continued to increase. . . . Nor has there been evidence of any sizable liquidation of the $8 billion portfolio investments held by foreigners at the end of 1957."

Looking backward, we can now see that things were not under control. The monetary aircraft was, indeed, flying straight into a mountain, but the pilot's miscalculation was so slight and the distances involved so great that no collision would occur for years. In 1960, in what proved to be the third straight year of a $3 billion–plus deficit in the U.S. balance of payments, the price of gold in the London market began to creep higher. On October 20, on the eve of a presidential election that, for all anyone knew, might deliver a young Democratic bent on devaluation, the price flared to $40 an ounce. In the event, John F. Kennedy was elected, but no such formal devaluation occurred and the gold price settled back to its official $35 floor. The dollar crisis that had loomed periodically since Bretton Woods was postponed again. Wise hands in the monetary establishment, however, did not exult. "The demonstration given that the gold price in London could substantially, and for months on end, be divorced from the official U.S. selling price was an event the consequences of which cannot yet be fully assessed," commented the Bank for International Settlements in 1961 in fine foreboding style.

But the creeping inflation so much feared by central bankers and creditors in the late 1950s didn't gallop after all. It slowed to a languorous, flaunting walk. Furthermore, it held this pace—never even reaching 2 percent—for the next six years. Fiscal and monetary policy were jointly tightened in 1959 to combat a threat that presently seemed to vanish. (The evident disappearance happened to coincide with the future president and inflation perpetrator, Lyndon B. Johnson, then a Texas senator, declaring the issue of inflation to be "second only to the issue of national survival.") Short-term interest rates rose to their highest levels since 1929, with overnight lending rates hitting 4.88 percent. A 10-month recession began in April 1960, exactly two years after the 1957–58 slump had ended. If the former recession was caused by the policymakers' attempts to forestall an actual inflation, the latter was precipitated by the attempt to head off an anticipated one.

To those who, like Allan Sproul, one-time president of the Federal Reserve Bank of New York, had gone on record with a dark prediction on price inflation, the first half of the 1960s presented an ordeal by sunshine. Much that could go right, did, and much that didn't—notably, the country's continuing balance-of-payments problems—was temporarily masked by the palliatives of the Kennedy and Johnson administrations. Was private capital leaving the United States? An interest-equalization tax on purchases of foreign stocks and bonds was proposed as a temporary measure in 1963 and implemented in 1964; it was not removed for 10 years. Were short-term interest rates too low to lure foreign dollar balances to New York bank deposits? To raise them, "Operation Twist," a gambit to lift short rates while simultaneously lowering long rates, was attempted in 1961. Was the United States not the free world's defender, and was it not, therefore, owed some fealty by the nations it guarded? West Germany agreed to refrain from converting dollars into gold in return for the protection of American forces. Would not the American position be improved by better statistics? The Treasury proceeded to deliver them by disingenuously suggesting that gold it had bought from the IMF (but was obliged to sell back on the IMF's demand) was gold that properly deserved to be counted in the permanent U.S. reserve. As for the gold price, it was held down by the weight of Russian sales, by growing mine production worldwide, and by U.S. and British intervention (presently augmented by assistance from the central banks of half-a-dozen European countries) to keep the London market in its $35-per-ounce place. By 1962, the London gold pool, as the cartel was known, was openly manipulating the international monetary system. It would sell gold into temporary, speculative strength (the authorities could not conceive that the investment demand for gold could be anything except temporary and speculative); it would buy in the inevitable periods of weakness at, or just below, the $35 official rate. But the plan failed, and the pool succeeded only when the market was objectively weak. When, after 1966, the supply-demand forces swung in favor of the bulls—Russian sales drawing to a close, private-sector demand for gold accelerating, the Vietnam War heating up—the pool drowned in its own losses.

"Something very important happened at Bretton Woods in 1944," reflected Louis Rasminsky, governor of the Bank of Canada, late in the 1960s, "and that was that the world consciously took control of the international monetary system." Indeed, by the mid-1960s, there seemed nothing left to ask for, either from the economists or the economy. The moment of perfection for the New Economics arrived in February 1966, when the Johnson administration basked in the simultaneous miracles of a 4 percent unemployment rate and a less-than-3-percent inflation rate. It is when things can get no better that they must, by definition, become worse, and worsen they presently did.

CHAPTER TWO

TALLEST BUILDING ON EARTH

THE MINIATURIZATION OF wealth made possible by the microchip, with the attendant obsolescence of bank vaults and the
downsizing of the corps of retired police officers and elderly down-
at-heel civilians who once walked Wall Street as couriers (or the
flattering misnomer "runners"), was still unimagined when
$24 billion of stocks and bonds were trucked through the deserted
streets of lower Manhattan early one Saturday morning in June
1962. Manufacturers Trust Company had merged with the Hanover Bank the year before, and the combined institution was in the
process of consolidating its downtown headquarters. The packing
and loading of some 3,166 cardboard cartons of bonds and stocks
required a draft of labor: 165 packers and movers, 54 bank officers,
57 bank guards, 22 New York City police officers, and an undisclosed number of New York City detectives, dressed incognito. A
truck left the back door of 70 Broadway, the Hanover's former
headquarters, every two minutes. To conform with insurance requirements, no single load could contain more than $55 million
worth of financial cargo. (A recent, devastating break in the stock
market had simplified matters somewhat; many more stock certificates could be loaded on a truck without tipping the cargo over the
$55 million limit.) Some trucks were therefore stacked high with
common and preferred stocks. Others bore a precious, single enve-
lope containing a handful of U.S. Treasury obligations, each valued
in the millions of dollars.

The trucks rumbled three-and-a-half blocks—north on New Street, east on Wall, north on Nassau, and east on Pine—to the back door of 40 Wall Street, the new home of the recently merged bank. It was the largest one-day shipment of stocks and bonds on record.

The vaults of 40 Wall were built for a greater prosperity than even the one attained in 1962, and they easily swallowed the wealth of the city's third-largest bank and its numerous correspondents. The two-story main vault measured 32 by 86 feet and was sealed by a 60½-ton steel door. A honeycomb of public safety-deposit boxes on the lower basement floor was protected by an 85-ton steel door. A broker or banker might visit his or her wealth by riding an elevator directly to safe-deposit-box level, a unique amenity of the year of construction, 1929.

The tower at 40 Wall Street has a rich and symbolic history. Conceived during the great Coolidge bull market, it is, at this writing, during the even greater Clinton bull market, undergoing renovation and restoration by its latest owner, none other than Donald J. Trump, famous survivor of the real estate down cycle of the early 1990s. One door west, on the ground floor of 30 Wall Street, site of the former U.S. Assay Office and one-time headquarters of the defunct Seamen's Bank for Savings, is a new health club. As we shall see, paper money rendered the Assay Office function obsolete, and volatile interest rates laid low the Seamen's. Concerning the health club, it is too soon to say. (Five floors above the stair-climbing machines and stationary bikes is the headquarters of *Grant's Interest Rate Observer;* it is thriving.)

As markets are cyclical, so is the neighborhood of Wall Street; and as stocks and bonds shuttle between extremes of optimism and pessimism, so does the real estate of lower Manhattan. The real estate story clarifies and illuminates the financial one.

IN THE SPRING OF 1930, with the newly completed skyscraper still smelling of fresh paint and with a certain number of its crash-impaired prospective tenants sliding away from their lease commitments or vanishing into bankruptcy, the real estate developer Louis

Adler made history by becoming the first individual to buy up an entire Wall Street block. The New York Stock Exchange and the National City Bank, each richer than Adler, had already accomplished this feat. Now came Adler, a 47-year-old immigrant dressmaker with a string of successful office buildings to his credit, who, in less than two months, was able to purchase 14 old, relatively stunted buildings in the block bounded by Wall, Water, Pearl, and Pine Streets. The cost was put at about $10 million (subsequently, in keeping with the deflationary tendencies, it was reestimated down to about $5 million). Satisfying a curious and admiring public, Adler vouchsafed some of his business secrets to the readers of *The New York Telegram*. One was not to skimp on price but to pay what it took to close a transaction: "You lose time fiddling around for the lowest price—and sometimes the deal," he said. If the complacency of the Wall Street sellers was itself an omen of trouble in the financial district, Adler was not alone in failing to heed it. He was still bullish: on real estate, on America, and on New York. "There will be no middle class here; no slums," he predicted for Manhattan. "The entire island will be a mountain of stone. The east side from Park Avenue an array of apartment hotels for elite tenants; the rest of the area executive office buildings for the direction of the nation's industry." As for his part in this architectural destiny, Adler proposed to make his Wall Street skyscraper no fewer than 60 stories and possibly as many as 105 stories, providing what he hopefully and inaccurately described as "much needed 'factory space' " for the brokerage community.

Adler, of course, had missed the boat; the Great Depression was already begun. (His building would never be built; when architectural plans were filed in the summer of 1930, the scale of the project had been reduced to 65 stories, five short of 40 Wall and 40 short of the ambition described in the initial press release.) Nor, as a matter of fact, would downtown office space be in short supply for any meaningful length of time from that day until this one. The depression of the 1930s would be followed by the temporary wartime prosperity of the 1940s and by a relapse of anxiety in the early 1950s, when the financial district worried about itself again. In the words of builder William Zeckendorf, Wall Street then lived "with its hat on." Its customers increasingly worked uptown, and it was there that Wall Street was obliged to meet with them. During the taxi and subway rides coming and going, the brokers, lawyers, and investment bankers could reflect on the inconvenient and anomalous fact that they worked so far from the people who paid them.

Just as no office buildings had been put up in lower Manhattan since the 1930s, few young people had chosen Wall Street careers. It was not until 1954 that the Dow Jones Industrial Average finally clawed its way back to the precrash highs. And it was in that year that Zeckendorf attempted a multicornered deal in downtown real estate with several top commercial banks—an undertaking of civic duty, as he later explained. Without some such enlightened attempt to hold together the Wall Street community, he wrote, the headquarters of capitalism would have disappeared. David Rockefeller of the Chase Manhattan Bank, whether convinced by this plea or not, decided to remain downtown (the bank in the early 1950s was headquartered at 18 Pine Street) and build Chase Manhattan Plaza at a cost of some $120 million. The new project was supposed to shore up lower Manhattan for many years to come, but less than a decade later, Nelson Rockefeller, David's brother and the governor of New York, felt obliged to undertake another vast project, the World Trade Center, to attempt to revitalize the old neighborhood all over again. Could Wall Street be saved? Zeckendorf had asked. (He might have added: Could the crossroads of capitalism be saved without public subsidy?) The question has echoed down through the past several decades, becoming more persistent as the industry named Wall Street has taken its leave from the locale of the same name. The very persistence of the question has served to underscore the cyclical nature of human affairs, of speculative financial markets, and (in particular) of New York City neighborhoods.

"Essentially," said *Fortune* magazine in 1939, "the skyscraper is a machine of commerce, geared to the centripetal forces of the age—the forces that have drawn business and professional men more and more into tightly concentrated areas." Well before the 1990s, the opposite tendency had become prevalent. Professional men—and women, too—could communicate by modem, facsimile, telephone, and computer at any distance. Except for the 27-pound bricks of monetary gold still stacked in the underground vault of the Federal Reserve Bank of New York on Liberty Street, monetary wealth in lower Manhattan was being replaced by electronic images. In 1910, a federal bank examiner found that a leading Wall Street bank, the First National Bank, was running out of vault space in which to house its money. In 1994, U.S. Trust Company, one of the great Wall Street banks that some years before had moved uptown, closed its securities vault at 770 Broadway because there was so little paper left to store in it. Financial wealth had been transmuted into photons. Centrifugal forces had scattered Wall Street not only to midtown Manhattan but far beyond the five boroughs of New York. The great irony of the financial prosperity of the 1990s is not that it occurred side by side with a steep decline in the value of the financial district's real estate—Wall Street, the neighborhood, has been leaking vitality ever since the September 1929 peak in stock prices. It was, rather, that the violent lurch down in property values, there and in so many other neighborhoods round the world, was itself an important catalyst for the decline in global interest rates. It was this decline that helped to precipitate a great bull market in stocks and the restoration of the credit of American banks. It was the silver lining of all time.

THE ACTUAL PEAK in the Coolidge bull market was accompanied by a richly symbolic milestone in the construction of 40 Wall Street, better known then as the Bank of Manhattan Building after the principal, original, ground-floor tenant. Both the market and the building were aspiring to supreme heights; the building, for the title of the world's tallest. In August, the last month of the long, speculative, stock market upswing, roofers began work—it was, in effect, a double top: the market's and the tower's. As stock prices crashed in September and October, vaults and safes were installed to house the financial wealth that was, at that very moment, disappearing. Revolving doors were fitted in February and March 1930 on the eve of the abortive rally that preceded the next stage of financial breakdown.

Similarly in the decades of the 1980s and 1990s, in its midlife, 40 Wall Street served another symbolic role. In the odd, miscellaneous company of Ferdinand and Imelda Marcos, rulers of the Philippines; Adnan Khashoggi, international arms dealer; and Citicorp, suggestible real estate lender, the building suffered a long series of indignities and reverses, from foreclosure to contested ownership to the loss of its principal tenant, Manufacturers Hanover, via another banking merger in 1991. The low estate of 40 Wall was a reflection of the international bear market in commercial real estate as well as the technological revolution in communications and money itself. For a time in the early 1990s, the bear market threatened the solvency of banks around the world.

It was the combustible mix of finance and real estate in the 1980s that helped to precipitate the banking and credit predicament. In turn, it was the protracted bear market in real estate values, Wall Street's among myriad other neighborhoods in the United States and also worldwide, that helped to bring about a healing decline in interest rates. It was a time of deflationary tendencies. Some prices fell, while others rose more slowly than they otherwise might have done. In the 1930s, too, interest rates had collapsed, but the general price level had fallen as well, so the decline in rates had done little to help the economy or the stock market. In the very different world of the 1990s, declining interest rates touched off a new bull stock market. The levitation helped to cure the sickness at some of the very banks that had financed the real estate excesses in the first place.

It is all but certain that the metaphor of financial-district real estate was not at the top of the list of H. Craig Severance, the architect of 40 Wall Street. The reigning office-building metaphor in 1929 was that of American Achievement, or of the Aerial Age—it was not yet *fin de boom*. In the race to achieve the greatest distance between sidewalk and flagstaff, Severance was set against his former partner William Van Alen. Van Alen was the architect of the Chrysler Building, and it was neck and neck as to which rising tower would become the world's tallest. In the end, Severance was a double loser, not only in the vertical phase of the competition— Van Alen, at the last minute, would triumphantly hoist a surprise,

185-foot spire, or "vertex," into place, thereby trumping Severance but falling short of the still-unfinished Empire State Building—but also in the aesthetic one. The machine-age modernism of the Chrysler Building incited passions of one kind or another (the critic Lewis Mumford condemned it as a symbol of plutocracy). Forty Wall, notwithstanding its plutocrat-laden rent roll, seemed to fire none.

The record time of construction did dazzle the building trades, however. From razing a half-dozen existing structures to putting on the finishing touches of the new building, just 363 days elapsed. Nothing approaching the scale of 40 Wall had been built in less than 2½ years or so, according to the builders, Starrett Brothers. In view of subsequent economic events, of course, there was no hurry, but so high were rents for prime downtown office space in 1929 that every month of delay implied sizable forgone income for the owners. There was another financial consideration. Most of the construction money was borrowed, as was usual in skyscraper construction of the day. The debt clock ticked day and night, thereby presenting a powerful stimulus to maximize speed and to minimize labor.

Deflation was a fact of economic life well known to Americans of the 1920s. A short, vicious fall in prices occurred in the 1920 recession, and a long decline marked the decade of the 1890s. Still, the Starretts made no allowances for a general collapse of the American price structure, let alone of the world's. Perhaps such a thing was unthinkable to a leading contestant in the race to build the tallest skyscraper, a race that the Starretts would win with the Empire State Building, the job that followed 40 Wall Street. Skyscrapers were the architectural expression of optimism, and no bookkeeper was likely to frustrate the way of progress. The cost of buying up the existing buildings (none of which rose more than 19 stories) and associated leases on the 40 Wall Street site came to $4,750,000. The developers assumed, for the purposes of planning and feasibility, that the average rent would amount to $6 a square foot, a sum of money equivalent to about $52 a foot in 1995 prices (and a rent, incidentally, higher than almost any currently obtainable on a new lease in an American office building). All of this anticipated the manic economics of the Tokyo real estate market in the late 1980s. "At first, 40 Wall was planned as a thirty-story building," reported *Fortune* magazine in a remarkable profile of that address in 1939, "but the builders soon decided that nothing less than fifty stories could meet the $675,000 ground rent and taxes of $693,000. Time and again the backers changed signals, calling for fifty-six stories, sixty-seven, and finally seventy. Because of the high land value and heavy carrying charges, speedy construction was imperative. . . ." When Bank of Manhattan Trust Company signed a 21-year lease at an annual rental of $690,000, the contract stipulated that the bank could renew for up to another 71 years (thus taking it through the year 2021). Rental for the renewal periods would be subject to arbitration. In no event, however, would it be less than the rental for the preceding term. In other words, according to the projections of the developers, prosperity loomed indefinitely.

In fact, rents fell almost immediately and the full, hoped-for $6 was obtained from only a few of the original customers. J. A. Sisto & Co., an investment banking firm that was involved with the ill-starred Cosden Oil Company, leased an entire floor at the rate of $4.575 per square foot. In 1929–30, Cosden's shares collapsed to single digits from a high of $135, a reverse gusher that ruined Sisto, too. The Sisto failure, announced from the rostrum of the New York Stock Exchange on September 30, 1930, by Richard Whitney, the president of the exchange (himself a future bankrupt and, indeed, felon), was regarded at the time as the most damaging financial bankruptcy since the crash. The firm's senior partner, Joseph A. Sisto, 41, was the son of an Italian immigrant who grew up in Newark, New Jersey, and did not learn English until he was 10. From these humble beginnings Sisto rose to become that most exotic Wall Street bird of plumage, the international financier. Dresdner Bank was an investor of his, and Benito Mussolini was his friend.

But the management of Forty Wall Street Corporation perhaps mourned his downfall most of all; J. A. Sisto & Co. never moved in. (Indeed, nine years later, the 11th floor—what was to have been Sisto's—was still in use as a storeroom; and a few years after that, in 1944, the Sisto firm was rejected for membership in the National

Association of Securities Dealers on the grounds of a pattern of self-dealing by Sisto himself.) G. L. Ohrstrom & Co., an investment bank that led the financing of the 40 Wall Street Corporation, scaled back its space requirements; or, rather, it had them scaled back by the falling market. The New York Stock Exchange, which had paid a quarter of a million dollars for an option on some ground-floor space, abandoned a contemplated clearinghouse project that would have occupied it; a portion of the unwanted real estate was finally let to Roger Kent Inc., a seller of affordable, bear-market-appropriate men's clothing.*

As was customary with major office buildings of the time, 40 Wall Street was a freestanding corporation that issued its own securities. The Forty Wall Street Corporation was a subsidiary of the Starrett Investing Corporation, which, in turn, was a subsidiary of the Starrett Corporation, builders and developers. The Starretts financed most of the building out of their own deep pockets. It was they who owned the preferred stock, second mortgage debt, and most of the common equity. Out of a capitalization of some $22 million, first and second mortgage obligations amounted to some $20 million, or 91 percent. In the argot of the 1980s, Forty Wall was highly leveraged. Public investors bought the first mortgage bonds, in the sum of $12.5 million—the "first fee and leasehold gold 6s of 1958," to use their full and dignified name. The adjective "gold" meant that the holders could elect payment in the lawful gold equivalent of United States dollars; $20.67 then was exchangeable into one ounce of bullion. A certain intangible security was afforded by the Starrett name, too. Formed in 1922 by Paul Starrett, the company had blazed to success as a builder of skyscrapers, or, as Col. William A. Starrett, Paul's partner and brother, called them, the "Mountains of Manhattan." Robert A. Lovett, a partner of Brown Brothers, Harriman & Co. and a future public servant, was a director of Starrett Corp.; and Starrett Corp., through a subsidiary, was

---

* D. M. Collins & Co., Herrick, Berg & Co., A. Iselin & Co., W. K. Johnson & Co., Munds, Winslow & Potter, F. A. Willard & Co., and Wood & Co.—New York Stock Exchange member firms and 40 Wall Street tenants—all went out of business in the 1930s.

the owner of Wall & Hanover Street Realty Corp., Brown Brothers' own headquarters building.

G. L. Ohrstrom & Co., a real estate and public-utility investment bank, the name partner of which would become chairman of the Forty Wall Street Corp., was, along with Halsey, Stuart & Co., an underwriter of the first mortgage bonds. The International Manhattan Co., the Manhattan Company's investment banking subsidiary, was an underwriter of another Starrett issue, as was Edward B. Smith & Co. All in all, the bonds seemed well and substantially sponsored. And concerning the sanctity of the gold clause of the bond indenture, there was no more reason to doubt it than there was to question the integrity of the structural steel in the building.

But disillusionment preceded even the arrival of the first tenants. An omen of the new postcrash world was the discounted price of the first mortgage bonds at their sale to the public in January 1930: 96½¢ on the dollar rather than 100 (or more). It was becoming clearer by the day that the promoters' assumptions were hugely overblown. Claims that 60 or 70 percent of the building was preleased were evidently inflated; years later, *Fortune* would put that number at 55 percent. In any case, full occupancy would be 14 years in coming.

Forty Wall Street was a losing proposition (as, indeed, were most boom-era skyscrapers) even after the Bank of Manhattan helpfully stepped forward to take up enough extra space to bump up its annual rent bill to $1 million from $690,000. The trouble lay with the world at large. Incomes were shrinking, but the skyscraper's debt-heavy capital structure was unyielding; debts assumed in good times were due and payable in bad times, too. At $6 a square foot, 40 Wall would have generated revenues of $4.7 million a year when fully occupied. It needed $3.9 million a year just to break even. It is testament to the height of the boom and the depth of the bust that $3.9 million of revenues were first earned in 1952. "The New Yorker has the feeling that he is living in a great museum as he looks around him and sees cloud-piercing towers leaping skyward on every side," wrote Elmer Davis in June 1932, only weeks away from the ultimate stock market bottom—"an unfailing refreshment and inspiration to everybody except the people who are so unfortunate as to own them."

Just as they did in the 1990s, rents seemed to fall faster than a building's operating costs. It was a curious and—to the building's owners—vexing kind of deflation. From 1932 to 1933, for instance, revenues fell from $3,031,000 to $2,959,000. On the other hand, the costs of steam, electricity, labor, etc., rose from $519,000 to $670,000. A few years later, *Fortune* enumerated the expenses in detail:

> You must buy 45,300,000 pounds of steam a year from New York Steam Corp. for $40,000; step its pressure down from 140 pounds to five pounds as you disperse it through the building, finally feeding it at .25 pounds to 3,245 radiators on days when the outside temperature falls to 65 degrees. (Each degree below 65 represents a "degree day"; the building last year used 6,040 pounds of steam per degree day.) You must buy 5,425,000 kilowatt hours of electricity for about $100,000, using about 2,000,000 yourself to run your elevators and pumps and light your corridors. Then you parcel the rest to your tenants at regular retail rates for $102,500. . . . You must keep clean 76,000 square feet of glass in 3,181 windows, working a crew of five window cleaners who start over again as soon as they finish a circuit of the building (no window cleaner has fallen at 40 Wall). . . . You must look out for 165 motors operating your forty-five elevators, and keep close watch on the 45.5 miles of cables. As soon as a cable shows six broken strands per foot, out comes the whole set—whether or not it has run its allotted 100,000 miles—and in goes a new set for $700. . . . You employ eight guards and watchmen, including a plain-clothes detective who strolls the lobby daytimes, looking so obviously like what he is that the crooks recognize him and stay away—which is exactly what you want. . . . You buy 101,000 gallons of water a day. . . . You maintain a four-bed hospital on the fifteenth floor, with a nurse in charge, handling 3,600 cases a year of colds, cuts, hangovers, indigestion, etc. . . . You operate the huge air conditioning units twenty feet below street level for the Bank of Manhattan. . . . You em-

ploy sixty-three cleaning women, fifty-five elevator operators and starters, fifteen elevator mechanics and helpers, nine engineers, a dozen painters, and sundry other staff workers to a total of 240. . . . You sell fifty-five tons of wastepaper a month at two-thirds of the market price in excess of $2 a ton (the deduction covering the cost of baling and hauling). . . . You replace 20,000 burned-out light bulbs a year. . . . You must, in short, meet the needs of a populace of 5,000 and their 15,000 visitors a day.

But the most crushing expense was interest, and the building struggled to pay it. Evidently, dividends on the preferred stock were never paid; certainly, no common dividend was paid, and the second mortgage bonds defaulted in 1935. The great bear market in stocks had ended officially on July 8, 1932, when the Dow Jones Industrial Average closed at its low of 41.22, representing a loss of 89 percent from the 1929 peak. Stupendous percentage gains were subsequently recorded from this stygian depth, and in the brief, heady days of the "alcohol market" of 1933, occupancy at 40 Wall Street climbed to 89 percent. However, for the owners and bondholders of the building corporation, it was a profitless prosperity. Rents were falling, taking profit margins with them, and money itself was an invalid. In 1933, President Roosevelt by executive order erased the gold-clause language from bond indentures; creditors of Forty Wall Street, along with those of numerous other American debtors, including the Treasury, would have to accept payment in whatever money the government chose to dispense.

This, however, was almost the least of the worries of the Starretts and their investors. In 1933, the first mortgage bonds changed hands at a price of 46¢ on the dollar; the company itself bought some of them (it had come into some cash by selling lease concessions to a tenant, by no means the sign of a vibrant real estate market). In 1934, the building absorbed a charge of almost $500,000 for canceling a contract with the United States government to acquire the land under the then vacant U.S. Assay Office at 30 Wall Street, one door directly west. The option had been acquired in expectation of future expansion by number 40, but no branching out was then indicated, or would be for at least the next 60 years. In 1935, total revenues to the Forty Wall Street Corporation fell to $2,866,000, $1 million or so below the $3,900,000 break-even mark; thus, the company failed to produce the income necessary to cover the interest expense on its senior debt. Although income fell, costs perversely rose, to $715,000 in 1935 from $656,000 in 1934.

In fits and starts, the national economy improved. Industrial production, automobile sales, retail trade, and farm income all rebounded in 1936. The exclusive Rookery Club, which served chic $2 lunches high up in 40 Wall Street, had a waiting list for membership again. Stock prices were rising, New York Stock Exchange trading volume was growing, and securities issuance was on the upswing. Charles Mitchell, the disgraced former chairman of National City Bank, was back on Wall Street as the chairman of Blyth & Co. Undoubtedly, the elite tenants of 40 Wall Street—among them, White Weld & Co., E. A. Pierce & Co., and Merrill Lynch & Co., all of which would eventually consolidate under the Merrill Lynch roof—were doing a better and more lucrative business. Yet the same could not be said for their landlord. With every passing year, leases expired at high, boom-time rates. What replaced them, if anything, were leases written at lower, depression-era rates. In the relatively prosperous year of 1936, revenues to 40 Wall Street Corporation declined again, to $2,817,000 from $2,866,000 in 1935.

IN APRIL 1937, on the eve of a sharp and particularly demoralizing stock market break, Robert Lovett crystallized the argument for cautious investing in an article in the *Saturday Evening Post*. An investment banker, intellectual, wit, and mimic, Lovett was conservative both financially and politically. He was the son of Judge Robert Lovett, a chairman of Union Pacific Railroad, and he did the right things in the correct sequence: Yale, Army service in World War I, a clerical apprenticeship at the National Bank of Commerce (one of the great New York discount banks), and then on to Brown Brothers. Unsurprisingly, in 1926 he had become a full partner of Brown Brothers (having begun, as was customary, as a runner) and a director and member of the executive committee of the Union Pacific. He was 30 years old.

Lovett's political conservatism came to the fore in 1933, when he joined James P. Warburg, chairman of the Bank of Manhattan (and occupant of one of 40 Wall Street's finest upper-story suites) in an appeal to the Roosevelt administration to turn back from the inflationary abyss. His conservative financial colors, on display to middle America in the pages of the *Post*, were apolitical, however. He contended that the deck was inherently stacked against bonds and stocks, both of which had recently enjoyed a brisk advance. It was the antithesis of the Edgar Smith argument.

Lovett first exposed the semantics of the problem. He pointed out that the very word *security*—derived from the Latin *se* meaning "without" and *cura* meaning "care"—is a gross and ironic misnomer. Bonds and stocks were anything but. "Those who have owned bonds or stocks can figure out for themselves whether the literal translation is an accurate description of the goods they bought," he wrote. In fact, as he was writing in the spring of 1937, care was fast giving way to confidence. From the depression low of July 1932, the Dow Jones Industrial Average was up by 352 percent. In another moment of financial optimism, decades later in September 1958, as we have noted, Ernest Havemann would favor the readers of *Life* with the bullish and farsighted notion that the market was only beginning to rise. Lovett, while making no forecasts and not once discussing the overarching investment issue of valuation, made a profoundly bearish argument, one that would serve the *Post*'s readers well for the next five years.

The crux of it was that capital, in capitalism, is consumed, not conserved or compounded. The fundamental reason for capital attrition is that businesses are mortal. In view of that fact, Lovett wrote, no investor should confuse the paper claims of some accident-prone business with a government bond (not that governments kept their financial promises, either). It followed that the worst investment strategy was to anticipate Warren Buffett by buying and holding. "Perhaps we have seen enough by now to concede that no investment is safe or unchanging enough 'to put away and forget,' as one is so frequently advised to do in periods of rising prices," Lovett wrote. "For our part, we are convinced that the only permanent investment is one which has become a total and irretrievable loss."

In support of this conclusion, Lovett cited the startling rate at which the leading listed companies of the past generation had reorganized themselves, declared bankruptcy, or ceased to pay dividends. Imagine the investor who bought the 20 most active dividend-paying stocks and the 20 most active bonds in a certain year of the past thirty-six, he proposed. What would have happened to the value of the portfolios? As a rule, nothing very profitable, Lovett was able to demonstrate. He assumed that dividends and interest income were spent, not reinvested, and this certainly diminished the investment results. Also, by using specific companies rather than indices or averages, Lovett confronted head-on the issue of mortality; if, in the land of investment indices, a particular company happens to fall by the wayside, its place in the average is taken by a new going concern. Corporate mortality, a real-enough problem for investors, is assumed away. Moreover, Lovett took the bleak financial experience of the 1930s on its face, anticipating no claim (such as posterity would justifiably make) that the depression era lay so far outside the pale as to render any investment lessons it seemed to teach irrelevant for normal times. Then again, by accepting his own time as normal, Lovett did only what most investors do. How many children of the 1990s will be judged guilty of projecting their own experiences—as lucky and profitable as Lovett's were grudging and mean—out into an unknowable future?

The first year chosen by Lovett for comparison was 1901. Here was a cloudless sky if ever there was one, the author observed. The West had been won, the Populist silver agitation had been quelled, and a great industrial future was dawning. All the more striking, then, as Lovett noted, that

> if an investor had purchased 100 shares of each of the twenty
> most popular dividend-paying stocks on December 31, 1901,
> and held them through 1936, adding, in the meantime, all the
> melons in the form of stock dividends, and all the plums in the
> form of stock split-ups, and had exercised all the valuable

rights to subscribe to additional stock, the aggregate market value of his total holdings at December 31, 1936, would have shown a shrinkage of 39 percent as compared with the cost of his original investment. In plain English, the average investor paid $294,911.90 for things worth $180,072.06 on December 31, 1936. That is a big disappearance of dollar value in any language.

Another bearish influence in Lovett's statistics was the lack of diversification available in the times and markets about which he wrote. In the bond market in 1901, to cite one especially extreme case, 19 out of the 20 most actively traded issues were railroad obligations. Thus, although the bond averages stood at all-time highs in 1936, the 1901 list bore the scars of mortality: five companies had gone into default. All in all, the list had lost 4 percent in market value from year-end 1901 to year-end 1936. "If our investor had followed normal practice and diversified his holdings between bonds and stocks in the interest of greater safety," Lovett went on,

> we can get some idea of what would have happened to him by combining the two lists. After having his capital at risk for 35 years of enormous industrial progress and national growth, our investor would show an aggregate loss of about 25 percent. And one out of four companies in the bond list as well as the stock list would have gone into bankruptcy. If this is a sample of what happens to the bloated bondholder, we need not feel so badly about missing the bloat.

Of the three other intervals chosen by Lovett—1910–36, 1919–36, and 1926–36—only one produced a combined bond-and-stock profit. That was the 1919–36 span. The starting year was a miserable year for bonds, but misery in investments may also spell opportunity. Precisely because prices were cheap it was a good time to buy. As Lovett wrote in 1937, long-term government securities yielded 2.65 percent; at year-end 1919, they had been priced to yield nearly 5 percent. Concerning stocks, the class of 1919 thoroughly vindicated the Lovett mortality thesis. By year-end 1936, 18 of the most popular dividend-paying issues of 1919 had suspended dividend payments, and four had gone bankrupt. However, the one no-table winner had done well enough to lift the market value of the entire 20-stock list to a gain of 17 percent over its 1919 average. That stock was General Motors. Taking one thing with another—de-faulted bonds as well as lower interest rates, the cats and dogs in the equity list as well as GM—the combined portfolio showed an 18 percent gain. Considered as an annual average compound rate of return, however, it was a feeble 0.98 percent. But at that it was bet-ter than nothing—or, as was so often the case in those years, less than nothing.

Lovett was quick to disabuse any reader who would jump to the conclusion that government financial obligations were inherently safer than private ones. He noted the long string of defaults by for-merly respectable foreign governments during the Great Depres-sion as well as the default on the gold clause of bond indentures by the United States government in the New Deal's first One Hundred Days. "There is certainly no point in getting excited about all this or falling into a fit of moral indignation," the Brown Brothers part-ner wrote urbanely.

> We merely must recognize that in dealing with people in mass or with governments, one is dealing with something very sim-ilar to a natural or elemental force. No one would consider for one moment entering into a contract with the Pacific Ocean by which it agreed to stay calm, or of accepting the promise of the North Wind to blow only once each quarter. Yet we have been taught cheerfully to accept the assurances of representa-tives of forces just as unpredictable, just as full of moods, and just as far above and beyond laws which an individual must respect.

The obvious, worrisome conclusion was that absolute safety was unavailable on Wall Street or in this life. It was not to be had in gold, which the government could seize (and indeed recently had); nor in claims of indebtedness, upon which debtors could always de-fault (a routine occurrence in the 1930s); nor still in claims of own-ership of businesses that, according to Lovett's data, dropped dead at a faster rate than the people who owned them. "Remember," Lovett wound up, "that you are buying risks and not securities. Risk in varying degrees is present in all investments. The safest bond you can buy is still only gilt-edged insecurity."

Nobody connected with the 40 Wall Street enterprise could have accused Lovett of unreasonable pessimism. In spite of the break in stock prices that almost immediately followed publication of Lovett's magazine article, the building corporation's revenues actually rose in 1937. But, because rentals were inexorably falling, relief was short-lived. The average rent reached $3.63 a square foot in 1939. Excluding the Bank of Manhattan's payment, it was on its way to about $3—all in all, about half of the $6 a square foot so hopefully projected by the Starretts in the heat of the bull-market race to the sky. In the real estate bear market of the 1990s, New York landlords routinely dispensed a year or two of free rent as an inducement to fill empty space. There is no record of exactly that in the late 1930s at 40 Wall Street. However, Charles R. Hinerman, the building manager, willingly cut rents in exchange for lease renewals. He offered free partitioning, remodeling, and repairs, and (in a sign that not everyone was poor) the services of a personal shopper for the purchase of flowers, theater tickets, and other corporate amenities.

The trouble, then as well as later, was that some rents, prices, costs, wages, and interest rates were more flexible than others. Rents, of course, were gravity-prone in the extreme. Not so the funds due to the city in property taxes, to the fee holders in ground rent, and to the bondholders in interest, and the corporation proceeded to default on each of these obligations in the spring of 1939. Formal bankruptcy proceedings were completed the next year. In reorganization, the building achieved a new distinction: the largest foreclosure-auction bid in the 80-year history of the Real Estate Auctioneers Association. Belatedly, the creditors and bankruptcy lawyers moved to introduce simplicity and flexibility into the building's finances. The common stock, the preferred stock, and the second-mortgage bonds were wiped out: the value that they represented had been deflated away. What value remained was lodged exclusively with the first-mortgage bondholders. Owners now as well as creditors, they would receive interest income as it was earned, up to a maximum of 5 percent a year. Gone was the promised protection of money defined as a weight of gold. The noncumulative 5 percent income debentures of 1966, as the new obligations of the reorganized issuer were named, were payable in dollars, and it was anybody's guess what those dollars might buy. Not coincidentally, the price paid for the building at auction, $11,489,500, represented exactly the face amount of the old first-mortgage bonds. Also not coincidentally, the 1940 value of the building was little more than half of the 1929 cost. As rents had been sawed approximately in half, so had the value of the capital. It had been consumed, in Lovett's frame of reference.

IN THE 1930s, as in the 1990s, cries of strangulation by credit prompted appeals from the White House for leniency by the federal banking regulators. The authors of the original national bank legislation of 1864 had anticipated that the comptroller of the currency would become a very powerful person, but it is doubtful that anybody foresaw the day when the comptroller might become an agent of an incumbent administration's economic policy. Exactly this, however, was the result in the Great Depression and immediate postdepression years. Comptrollers in both the Hoover and Roosevelt administrations let examiners know that considerations of safety and soundness in banking should be subordinated to the greater good of the national economic recovery program.

Could nothing be done to revive the process of borrowing and lending? Loans as a percentage of bank assets had fallen to 26 percent in 1936 from over 50 percent in 1929, and 1937 brought worse. A recession, straight from the myth of Sisyphus, struck in May, and the stone of prosperity rolled right back down the hill again. Repeatedly during the depression and postdepression years, under Presidents Hoover and Roosevelt alike, directives had gone out to the corps of bank examiners from Washington headquarters asking forbearance. Under J. F. T. O'Connor, the comptroller under Roosevelt, banking regulation was explicitly subordinated to the New Deal economic agenda. In September 1934, a conference of senior

federal banking regulators—from the OCC, the FDIC, and the
Federal Reserve—was convened by Treasury Secretary Robert
Morgenthau to get the examiners on board the presidential recovery program. In April 1938, in the midst of the recession, President
Roosevelt renewed the appeal for more lenient examination policies. Marriner Eccles, his devoted Federal Reserve chairman,
needed no convincing. In Eccles's judgment, the 1937 recession was
the result of examination policies so taut as to inhibit the expansion
of bank credit. His own inappropriately stringent monetary policy,
the cause assigned to the 1937–38 slump by some contemporary his-
torians, had played no part, he seemed to believe. Blame for this recession need not detain us here. Our business lies with the political
and financial response to recession and debt contraction: to the
economic maladies confronting (to greater or lesser degrees) the administrations of Herbert Hoover, Franklin Roosevelt, and George
Bush. As with so many other apparently discrete economic events,
meekness and boldness in banking turn out to be cyclical.

Yielding to the White House and the Federal Reserve, the
OCC and the FDIC agreed to relent on two technical examination
issues and on one philosophical one. The first narrow issue concerned a category of bank loan self-evidently described as "slow."
Some examiners deemed any and every past-due loan to be slow.
Others had applied that designation to business loans outstanding
for nine months or more; such credits were automatically criticized
and a lender's capital was docked. It didn't matter if the borrower
was solvent or if interest payments were up-to-date. According to
a banking doctrine known as "real bills," the only true business
loan was a short-dated and "self-liquidating" one. As a bank's depositors could demand their money on the spot, the thinking went,
a bank must stand ready to deliver it. Thus, a bank investment
must be the next thing to cash itself. "Term" loans, as long-dated
credits are known, obviously failed to qualify. The second technical
issue was the accounting treatment of market losses in the bond
market. The Federal Reserve was uniquely liberal on this question.
It did not deduct market losses on so-called Group I securities:
investment-grade corporates and U.S. Treasuries. The Federal Deposit Insurance Corporation and the Office of the Comptroller of

the Currency, however, did deduct them, as in 1931 and 1937, bear-market years when bond prices fell with stock prices. The bond question was vitally important, because securities portfolios comprised some 40 percent of bank assets. Some 90 percent of these securities were governments, which the Federal Reserve, if not Robert Lovett, regarded as intrinsically free from risk of default. The overriding philosophical issue was whether bank examination standards should be objective and unbending or whether they should be subordinated to the perceived political good.

The answer to the general question would depend on the disposition of the technical ones. After much debate, both issues were decided as the White House and the Federal Reserve had hoped they would be. The "slow" classification was eliminated and market-value accounting was abandoned for Group I securities and softened for Group II issues (those below investment grade but not in default). For another thing, the way was cleared for banks to buy the obscure bonds—unrated by the likes of Moody's and traded on no securities exchange—of local businesses.

Were bank examination standards objective and fixed, or should they properly be subordinated to the political and macroeconomic agenda of the incumbent administration? Jacob Viner, a distinguished economist of the day, contended for the latter point of view in 1939. Bank examiners were all too prone to share in the prevailing economic and financial ideas and moods. Thus, they were liable to encourage lending and borrowing at the peak of a business cycle, when it was needed least, and to suppress it at the bottom, when it was needed most. Echoing Eccles, Viner urged that bank examinations be centralized under Federal Reserve control, the better to coordinate "examination policy with credit-control policy."

No doubt the 1938 Uniform Agreement on Bank Supervisory Procedures played its part in preparing the ground for the thrift calamity and the near banking calamity of recent years. At least, as a pair of contemporary scholars, David G. Simonson and George H. Hempel, have written, ". . . it legitimized the dominance of transitory political and macroeconomic goals over the supervisory goal of the safety of banks and the banking system." To more than one modern American administration, it has been safer and sounder to encourage a generous flow of bank credit, at whatever long-term cost to the banking system and the economy, than not.

NONE OF THIS worked any reflationary magic on Wall Street or its unprosperous skyscrapers. When at last in March 1938 the bear market in stocks hit bottom, the Dow Jones Industrial Average had been cut almost in half (by coincidence, low ebb occurred just a month before negotiations on the new bank regulatory agreement began). The succeeding stock market rise had nothing of the old Coolidge fire, and small wonder. The outbreak of World War II in September 1939 held out sweeping vistas of everything that capital abhorred: uncertainty, taxation, and regimentation. By 1941, lower Manhattan was the financial district in name only. In the neighborhood bounded on the north by Cortlandt Street and at the south by the Battery, the securities and stock brokerage business occupied just 15 percent of the office space available in 130 buildings standing eight or more stories high. Lawyers inhabited another 15 percent; banks took 20 percent; and industrial, shipping, and utility businesses accounted for 40 percent: Bethlehem Steel, International Nickel, U.S. Steel, Anaconda Copper, Phelps Dodge, and American Water Works, among others. The federal government, already accounting for 2.5 percent of the remaining, unclassified Wall Street office space, was lurking in the wings; its space requirements would expand briskly in the very near future.

And not a moment too soon for the hard-pressed property owners of lower Manhattan. Bonds of the reorganized 40 Wall Street Corporation at their low in 1941 and 1942 were quoted at just 10¢ on the dollar. It was in February 1941 that the Westinghouse Electric & Manufacturing Co. entered into a long-term lease at 40 Wall that spoke volumes about the demoralized state of downtown real estate. To begin with, Westinghouse would pay no direct rent. The source of such compensation as 40 Wall might receive was the sublease of Westinghouse's former space at 150 Broadway. For 1942, this was projected to yield $1.29 per square foot. Conventional rent, beginning in May 1944, would be paid by Westinghouse at the rate of only $2.21 a square foot; all in all, it was a long way from $6.

. . .

EXCEPT FOR THE bond market, which had been rising since mid-1932—indeed, except for a sharp but short-lived interruption beginning in the autumn of 1931, it had been on the upswing since 1920—the well of American investment morale was dry. Nor were exceptionally low bond yields anything for a risk-taking capitalist to cheer. "It was a period when a large part of the liquid capital of the country attempted to crowd into the always limited area of riskless investment," wrote Sidney Homer of this time of financial despondency. (One of the remarkable features of the present day is the cornucopia of riskless investments. There is certainly no shortage of government securities.) Early in 1942, as the management of 40 Wall Street prepared to meet the threat of enemy air raids (the skyscraper afforded the most sweeping sea-level vista on the eastern seaboard and also, necessarily, one of the most conspicuous targets),* a New York Stock Exchange seat changed hands for $17,000. It was the lowest price since 1897 and 97 percent below the record high price of $625,000 set in 1929. The war news was unrelievedly grim. If there was any certainty, it was that Lovett had hit the nail square on the head in the *Saturday Evening Post.* Some on Wall Street called this market, with so little forced selling but a daily absence of buying, a "dry panic." The New York Stock Exchange, which in 1942 was trying to find some happy, even hopeful, note to inject into its 150th anniversary celebration, was fairly dying of starvation. On February 14, the Friday that followed the Lincoln's Birthday holiday, an entire hour of trading yielded volume of only 30,000 shares. The day itself brought forth just 320,000 shares, which, depressingly enough, was by no means a record low for that emaciated time; it was more than twice as busy as August 19, 1940, on which just 129,650 shares changed hands, the lowest daily volume since 1916. In March 1942, the New York Stock Exchange membership boosted commission rates by some 25 percent; henceforth, for instance, it would cost 15¢ a share to buy or sell a $10 stock, of which

---

* No lethal encounter with military aircraft occurred until after the war. On May 20, 1946, at 8:10 P.M., an Army transport plane, lost in the fog en route to Newark, New Jersey, crashed into the 58th floor of 40 Wall, coming to rest in the unoccupied offices of Atlas Corporation, an investment concern. All five people aboard the plane were killed; there were no casualties on the ground or in the skyscraper.

the bear market was generating more and more from the universe of formerly higher-priced issues. (Raising prices in the midst of a severe business downturn was not a form of behavior that many of the stock exchange's listed companies could engage in without fear of antitrust prosecution. What better proof that Wall Street was a cartel, or club?)

The 1942 annual report of the New York Stock Exchange was a chronicle of what posterity would learn to call "downsizing": of costs reduced, personnel eliminated (an attrition accelerated by the war), real estate taxes negotiated downward, facilities shed. Total exchange expenses had been reduced to the lowest level in 20 years. Emil Shram, who had taken over as president the year before, after serving as chairman in the New Deal's Reconstruction Finance Corporation, was able to express a certain satisfaction in the outcome: "It is gratifying to report that, although our business last year was the smallest since 1914, reaching what I am confident will prove to have been the lowest ebb of the prolonged depression through which this industry has been passing, the Exchange maintained its strong over-all financial position and increased slightly its liquid resources in spite of an operating loss of approximately $198,000 resulting from the sharp decrease in revenues."

The war had touched off an industrial boom, not to mention an eruption of federal borrowing and a gush of Federal Reserve credit creation. All these things could be chalked up as bullish for common stocks. By the same token, however, the war had given free rein to all the leveling tendencies of the Roosevelt administration. The rich were becoming fewer, and the stocks of well-to-do investors, American and British alike, were finding their way to the market. "Liquidation of large holdings has been proceeding on a scale never before witnessed," *The Exchange* magazine reported. "One only has to look at the proposals for new and added taxes to know that the trend must continue, probably in larger volume than ever before."

How high wartime tax rates would be raised was anybody's guess. The Treasury Department proposed a corporate income-tax rate of 60 percent. Compared to the previous high rate of 20 percent, also set in a wartime year, 1917, it seemed very near to confiscation. For the 1943 fiscal year alone, the administration proposed war expenditures of $56 billion, a sum that could scarcely be imagined. It was, for example, $21 billion larger than the fast-vanishing market capitalization of the New York Stock Exchange. In the event, the government spent $72 billion on the war in 1943; the budget deficit alone came in at $56 billion. Leon Henderson, the federal price administrator, did nothing to lighten the financial mood when he predicted in February that the cost of the war was bound to throw American living standards back to the levels of the Great Depression, if not in 1942, then certainly in 1943.

By the third week of February 1942, the Dow Jones Industrial Average had given up all the ground gained since March 31, 1938. From over 158, it had fallen to 105, a loss of roughly one-third. Stoical analysts seized upon the lack of trading volume as a hopeful sign ("extreme speculative lethargy is usually an outstanding characteristic, but by no means proof positive, of a sold-out market"), but volume and prices continued to fall together. Die-hard optimists could observe that stocks were cheap—arguably, in relation to bond yields, they had never been cheaper. Late in 1994, a time as ebullient as 1942 was glum, bond yields were three times greater than stock-dividend yields. At what would prove to be very near the low in 1942, stock-dividend yields were three times greater than bond yields. However, so a discouraged investor could reason, dividends would certainly be slashed, and stock prices, in consequence, would be marked down, just as they had been for most of the past five years. And even if the war did come to a quick and victorious conclusion, what then? Peace would very likely bring a deflationary relapse. Now people began to worry about the $9 dividend of American Telephone & Telegraph, which had been paid through thick and thin since 1921. Was it, too, at risk? It proved not to be (either then or later on; it only went up). However, investors were edgy enough to start at shadows as well as the objectively frightening news of the world. "The public feels that this generation is doing a staggering amount of involuntary speculation in everything else, so there is little appetite for voluntary speculation in stocks," an unnamed broker explained to *The Wall Street Journal.*

Late in March, as the valuation disparity between stocks and fixed-income securities yawned wide, the New York Stock Exchange urged the public to buy war bonds. It had preached the same public-service message in World War I, but on no other occasion had it ever explicitly recommended the purchase of any class of investment. (Tacitly, of course, the exchange stood foursquare behind common stocks at all times, but it never actually said so.) Certainly, there was no other position to be taken three months after the attack on Pearl Harbor, but bonds as a class of investment had all the friends they needed, and, taking one valuation fact with another, more than they deserved. In April, the Federal Reserve began to support the government bond market, fixing interest rates much as the City of New York was controlling residential rents. By removing the risk of price decline from the bond market, the Federal had, in effect, transformed all fixed-income securities into the equivalent of cash. The prevailing attitude toward equities was distilled by Frederick H. Ecker, chairman of the Metropolitan Life Insurance Company, in testimony he gave in 1941 concerning the revision of the New York State insurance law. As for the role of stocks in a life insurance portfolio, Ecker unequivocally stated that they had none. So saying, he lined up exactly with the influential, almost biblical, "Report of the Joint Committee of the Senate and Assembly of the State of New York Appointed to Investigate the Affairs of Life Insurance Companies, 1906," better known as the Armstrong Report. Its conclusion was that, for life insurance companies, stocks were an inherently inappropriate investment. (No life company operating in New York was allowed to own any common equity from the time of the Armstrong report until 1951, and even then not just any stock would do; a candidate had to pass various quality and earnings tests. And not even many of those undoubted blue chips were allowed. The limit was the lesser of 3 percent of assets or one-third of surplus. In 1957, the ceiling was grudgingly raised, to the lesser of 5 percent of assets or one-half of surplus. New York's regulation was the most severe of the larger states, possibly because its turn-of-the-century scandals had been more lurid.) Although, "unquestionably, many common stocks are sound investments," Ecker allowed, it was a far better thing that an insurance company owned bonds. ". . . [I]f the stock is sound," he went on, "the obligation [i.e., bond] of that company is more sound; and our belief is that we are wiser in adhering to the practice of buying the obligations rather than the equities in corporate enterprise." As he spoke, prime corporate bonds yielded all of 2¾ percent.

Not every single speculative ember was cold in 1942. Income-seeking investors ventured into junk bonds*—they needed the interest income to pay their taxes, if for no other purpose—but they had little or no use for real estate, either income-producing or residential. (Not until the early postwar years did most state life insurance regulators allow investments in income-producing real estate; New York relented in 1946.)

AS THE END of the war was unimagined in 1942, so were the twin postwar booms in incomes and population. Indeed, the arguments for "secular stagnation" (the economic equivalent to the dream-state frustration of trying to run but falling down, or of repeatedly bungling the job of dialing a number on a Touch-Tone phone) were in the process of being perfected by the leading economists. Marxists needed no convincing. They already believed that the actual breakdown of capitalism would be preceded by financial crises, falling rates of profit, and feeble expansions. The contribution of the non-Marxists was to codify and systematize the unhappy circumstances of the 1930s into a general theory of capitalist development (or lack thereof). Professor Alvin H. Hansen of Harvard, in his influential 1939 essay, "Economic Progress and Declining Population Growth," contended that the country had lost its greatest engines of growth. No new territory was available to be conquered, he noted, and the birth rate was depressed. More than that, new industries and inventions were in short supply, and big business was becoming ossified. In short, the world was running out of good investment opportunities. "It is my growing conviction," Hansen

* Or the 1942 equivalent, chiefly defaulted railroad bonds and second-tier industrial issues. In that day and age, nobody would have contemplated underwriting, much less purchasing, bonds rated speculative right out of the chute.

wrote, "that the combined effect of the decline in population growth, together with the failure of any really important innovations of a magnitude sufficient to absorb large capital outlays, weighs very heavily as an explanation for the failure of the recent recovery to reach full employment."

Joseph A. Schumpeter, also a Harvard professor, threw the considerable weight of his intellect behind the bearish school of thought in his 1942 book, *Capitalism, Socialism and Democracy.* Like his colleague Hansen, Schumpeter was preoccupied by the falling birth rate, although in an ironic footnote to his own analysis he observed that "forecasts of future populations, from those of the 17th century on, were practically always wrong." Schumpeter's own observations, therefore—"The falling birth rate seems to be one of the most significant features of our time"—may helpfully be seen in the context of a long tradition of error and wrongful extrapolation. Indeed, even as he wrote, the birth rate in the United States was rebounding sharply from its depression low. The end of the war would bring an astounding and (from the stock market point of view) ultrabullish liftoff. However, all this was some years off in the future. What was blindingly visible at that moment was the surplus of high-end residential property, the shortage of servants with whom to staff it, and the shortage of well-to-do buyers (the legacy of bear markets and steeply progressive federal tax rates). In a university town outside Chicago, a sorority house set on a hill changed hands for $10,000—$2,000 in cash and an $8,000, 4 percent mortgage. Built in 1923–24, the place once had had a $58,000 mortgage on it. Nor were mortgages always available to willing buyers. Richard Russell, longtime editor of the *Dow Theory Letters,* relates that his father, a New York City real estate investor, was unable to raise $125,000 with which to buy a hotel that earned that much a year in its bar alone. So vast a market as American real estate was not without its pockets of strength. European refugees, anticipating a postwar inflation, were buying, and speculators of whatever national origin were prepared to bid on commercial properties if the price was right. This meant, in the context of the times, that the cash return on a store or office had to cover, in just three years' time, the down payment. Commenting on the New York market, Douglas L. Elliman, a leading city real estate broker, spoke of a "creeping decay" in the entire New York economy. The huge burden of taxes and business costs, and the political and financial whipping suffered by Wall Street, he contended, had left a mark on the cityscape itself, "in vacant stores, vacant apartments and vacant loft space throughout the city, as well as in shabby neighborhoods, abnormal unemployment and even in a change in the appearance of the citizens themselves on the streets. . . ."

Certainly, few stockbrokers felt an irresistible impulse to burst into song on the way to work in the morning. The opportunities for patient long-term investors were undeniably rich, but everybody had known about them for years on end. Many of the people who, by rights, should have seized them had no doubt lost their money in the act of seizing other opportunities, apparently equally compelling, earlier on—in 1931, 1938, or 1941—opportunities that had subsequently become only more tantalizing. Faith in the ideas and institutions of capitalism had peaked with the stock market more than a dozen years earlier. Menaced by totalitarianism abroad—the Axis enemy but also, at a somewhat greater remove, the Soviet ally—and a collectivizing, financially hostile administration at home, investors held back from committing to even a historically cheap stock market, one priced, around the time of the 1942 bottom (it occurred on April 28), at seven times the prior year's earnings and offering a dividend yield of almost 9½ percent.*

Worse than the war news was the tax news, or rather—as the wartime fiscal program had not yet been finalized—the possible, worst-case tax news. The approach of the quarterly federal tax date, wrote H. J. Nelson in *Barron's*, "brought home to all men of means the extent of the draft upon financial resources necessitated

---

* Late in February, Bethlehem Steel was quoted on a 10 percent dividend basis and United States Steel common on an 8 percent basis. So ludicrously cheap were investment-grade common stocks, as we may now all see, that investors (never mind speculators) should have expanded their holdings, and boosted their returns, by employing margin debt. The cost of borrowing against the collateral of common stocks was just 3 percent. It will come as no surprise to anyone who has lived through a complete market cycle that margin debt was, at this supremely advantageous moment, out of fashion.

by the war effort. How much actual raising of money to pay taxes through the sale of securities has occurred may be open to question, but the psychological effect of the imminent payment of taxes upon the 1941 income at a time when the Government is recommending the doubling of most individual income taxes is indisputable."

In April 1942, *The Exchange* magazine published a letter from a reader in Akron, Ohio. A company that earned more than $4 per share in profit in 1941 was actually changing hands for $8 a share in 1942, observed the correspondent, who signed himself "O. T. B." "How long has this sort of thing been going on?" he wanted to know (where had he been?). "What is a man to believe after thinking for years on end that ten-times-earnings was a reasonable price for a stock?" Investigating, the magazine reported that, out of a sample of 620 New York Stock Exchange issues canvassed on April 13, 181, or 29 percent, traded at a price equivalent to 3.9 (or less) times 1941 net profits. The median price-earnings ratio in the sample was 5.3:1. And as for the reader's antediluvian notion of 10:1 as the standard valuation, the fraction of issues valued at or above that level comprised just 12 percent of the list.

W. E. Hutton & Co., finding that more than a third of all New York Stock Exchange issues were quoted at less than $11 a share, took a page from President Roosevelt's book to propose that "perhaps we ought to give more attention to the ill-housed, poorly clothed and inadequately fed third of the stock market." Some 110 issues were then quoted at between $4 and $6 a share, Hutton related. More than a third of them had paid dividends in 1941, and "quite a few" of them were selling at less than their "net quick asset value," meaning less than the cash on the balance sheet. One of these stocks, National Gypsum, a building materials company that survived the 1940s to bankrupt itself in the debt follies of the 1980s, traded as low as 3¾ a share, or just four times 1941 earnings. It wound up earning an average of 48¢ a share between 1943 and 1945 and no less than an average of $2.90 a share in 1946–48, years of the then unimagined postwar building boom (houses to be filled with then unimagined babies). From the 1942 low to the 1946 high, its stock price increased almost tenfold.

As markets become euphoric, so do they become despondent. Harry Nelson, for one, understood that 1942 was really 1929 in reverse. "Then the talk was of 10 years of prosperity, of the permanent abolition of poverty, of the road to plenty and so on," he wrote in the April 13 edition of *Barron's,* about two weeks before the April 28 low. "Industrialists and financiers, now without caste, could then see no end to the fabulous era of good times. Forecasts were glowing and frequent. Now no one in his right senses dares predict the future; the extermination of capitalism is taken for granted. In such an environment of undiluted pessimism lie the long-term profit-making potentialities of patient accumulation, not the base for shrewd liquidation.

"It is not a question," Nelson wound up, as prophetically as anyone who has ever tried to call a top or a bottom in the stock market, "from here on of whether an issue here, or another there, makes a new low or whether the stock averages dip into new low ground. The problem is whether the next big and sustained trend is to be up or down. In late 1928 and early 1929 there were those who could see the grief that lay ahead, but it seemed as if the market never would or could break. Today the logic is just as much in favor of the buyer, only it seems as though the market would never turn up."

IN THE SUMMER OF 1944, 40 Wall Street at long last reached full occupancy—all 850,000 square feet were rented for the first time since the crash-deflated grand opening in 1930—but there was one catch. The tenant that had taken the last 85,000 square feet was not a bank or a New York Stock Exchange member or a downtown luncheon club, but the Office of Special Settlement Accounts of the War Department. It was the agency that, among its other grim duties, paid the prescribed six months' worth of benefits to the families of soldiers who had died in service.

All in all, the financial prosperity of the mid- and late 1940s was grudging, anxious, and heavily taxed. When, at the end of 1945, Emil Schram was presented with a raise of more than 100 percent by the New York Stock Exchange—to $100,000 a year from $48,000, a salary more in keeping with the compensation due the chief executive of a great American business institution—his after-tax income still clung to the lower five figures: $36,872. The extra $52,000 yielded him only $15,000 in after-tax income. To anybody who would try to be rich, the tax structure presented a high hurdle.

The neighborhood of Wall Street was better off than it had been in the 1930s, but not because of strength in any locally relevant economic indicator, such as downtown office-building construction, stock prices, or trading volume. As wartime government agencies decamped from downtown offices, a prosperous corporate economy returned to the neighborhood or expanded in it, and skyscrapers continued to show high and profitable rates of occupancy. In 1948, the management of 40 Wall Street had the pleasure of re-renting the 17th floor, temporary quarters of the Office of Special Settlement Accounts, to an existing tenant at a substantial premium to the government lease. That tenant was none other than Westinghouse Electric, which had cut itself a very nearly free lease only a few years before.

Indeed, the situation in lower Manhattan was the mirror image of what it would become two generations later. In the late 1940s, financial activity was sinking as downtown commercial real estate values were rising. In the early 1990s, financial activity was resurgent while downtown commercial real estate values—commercial real estate values worldwide, as far as that goes—were collapsing.

The Dow Jones Industrial Average more than doubled from its 1942 low to its peak in the spring of 1946, but it thereupon sank, and for the next four years it loitered. By year-end 1951, three-quarters of the 893 stocks that had changed hands on the day of the 1946 high were actually lower in price than they had been at the close four years and seven months earlier, a startling and discouraging fact. Neither business activity nor corporate profits bore all the blame; each, in fact, had shown net improvement. For whatever reason, or set of reasons, investors refused to capitalize corporate profits as they had done in the 1920s, a long-distant time that shimmered in Wall Street's memory like a first love.

It was the Inconsolable Era of American finance, a mirror image to the later, more familiar Mutual Fund Era. Trading volume withered away, and the average investor from Akron, if he or she was still paying attention, continued to find price-earnings ratios in the high single digits. The price of a New York Stock Exchange seat rallied back to $97,000 in 1946, before sinking all over again to $39,000 in the fall of 1952. It was the same year that, much to the embarrassment and consternation of the New Yorkers, a seat on the much smaller Toronto Stock Exchange sold for the equivalent of $91,933. When, in 1949, the cover price of *Barron's* was raised to 35¢ from a quarter, circulation fell to about 32,000 from about 38,000.

Harry S Truman's defeat of Thomas E. Dewey in the 1948 presidential election dashed capitalist hopes and prompted Charles Merrill, founder of the nation's largest brokerage firm, to deplore the winner's assaults on a caricature of "Wall Street." "Mr. Truman knows as well as anybody that there isn't any Wall Street," said Merrill in an advertisement. "That's just legend. Wall Street is Montgomery Street in San Francisco. Seventeenth Street in Denver. Marietta Street in Atlanta. Federal Street in Boston. Main Street in Waco, Texas. And it's any spot in Independence, Missouri, where thrifty people go to invest their money, to buy and sell securities."

Fewer and fewer of them did, in point of fact. Emil Schram himself, on behalf of the stock exchange, declared that "it has been our objective to encourage the smaller investor to buy U.S. government bonds where risk is minimized." However, the risk that Schram imagined was the known danger of deflation and default, not the prospective—indeed, immediate—danger of inflation and rising interest rates.

"WHAT IS TO become of them?" asked Elmer Davis in 1932, referring to the unfilled Manhattan office buildings. "The setback skyscrapers of Babylon have crumbled into the hills of mud, but steel and concrete do not melt so easily. Of the faith that built the cathedrals of the Ile-de-France, enough has survived to keep those buildings in repair; but the faith that built the Empire State and Chrysler buildings may presently be as dead as Bel and Marduk."

If not dead, certainly overcapitalized. The skyscrapers' essential problem was financial, and the bankruptcy courts repeatedly addressed it. In case after case, ownership of the buildings passed from the stockholders to the bondholders. In reorganization, a new, hybrid security—an "income bond"—was distributed to the mortgage creditors. In exchange for a lower rate of interest, they received shares of common stock proportionate to the size of their bond holdings. The preceding stockholders were wiped out. If all went well—although, it might well have been asked: When was the last time that happened?—the new stockholders would fare better.

This time, things did go swimmingly. From their giveaway lows in the late 1930s or early 1940s, real estate bonds of the 40 Wall Street vintage multiplied in value by approximately tenfold. The 40 Wall bonds lifted from 10¢ on the dollar in 1942 to 93½¢ in 1946 to 132¢ in 1952. (It was in 1952 that the projections of the Starretts were finally vindicated: for the first time since the solid-glass automatic doors in the lobby opened, revenues topped $3.9 million, the minimum required to break even under the original plan of capitalization in 1929.) Similarly with securities of the 80 Broad Street Corporation in lower Manhattan, the Hotel Sherman in Chicago, and the Grant Building in Pittsburgh. All had appreciated by tenfold or more since the reorganization lows. In retrospect, the recovery of the real estate securities market was obvious. Construction costs were rising and vacancy rates were falling. As the country grew into the excess supply of the late 1920s and early 1930s, rents would rise and real estate bond prices would merrily follow.

The mumchance refusal of common stocks to respond to good news had become a Wall Street feature in its own right. In March 1952, *Barron's* presented a where-are-they-now analysis of the favorite stocks of the last great bull market. The Dow Jones Industrial Average closed the year 1951 at 269.23; it had closed at 273.51 on October 31, 1929. By comparing prices on the two dates—the very exercise bespoke caution—the magazine was able to show that only 15 out of 50 leading stocks of the Coolidge market had recovered their intervening losses. Standard Oil of New Jersey had more than doubled in that 22-year span, and Chrysler had more than tripled. However, many stocks were still depressed—conspicuous were utility issues, so frenetically promoted in the 1920s—and a handful had vaporized. Anaconda Copper had fetched 100 at the end of October 1929; at the end of December 1951, it was at 50½. Columbia Gramophone had gone from 29¼ to nil. The investment conclusion was that "if an investor does not convert a considerable part of his paper profits into cash profits before the current bull market is over, the consequences are apt to be unpleasant."

If, as trader lore has it, every bull market climbs a wall of worry, the anxiety of the early 1950s was not a paradox but almost a given. In a stupor of taxes, war, and deeply conditioned pessimism, investors bought and sold little more than a million shares of stock a day. It was about the same volume as that of the mid-1930s.* It was even smaller than it seemed if adjusted for the vast enlargement in the number of tradable shares since the depression. Expressed as a ratio of volume to listed shares, activity on the New York Stock Exchange had dwindled to 13 percent in the first half of 1952 from 17 percent in calendar year 1951, 25 percent in 1934, and 132 percent in long-lost 1928. At about 11 times earnings, blue-chip stocks were no longer cheap, if 1942 was the lodestar of cheapness. Certainly, they were no bargain to a dividend-minded investor in the 80 percent tax bracket, that is, to anyone earning $60,000 a year. A young John M. Templeton observed that to a person in this situation, a 4 percent dividend yield was the after-tax equivalent of no more than 0.8 percent. "In 30 years," wrote the future mutual-fund great, "this amount, compounded annually, will increase his capital by just 27 percent. If he buys a municipal bond due in 30 years, with 2 percent interest tax-free, he can increase his capital 81% by compounding." Was there no better way? Templeton did have one suggestion: channel as much income as possible through the capital gains tax rate, which then stood at 26 percent. Templeton calculated that if an investor could generate gains of just 5 percent a year, his or her capital—advantageously taxed at the relatively low rate—could very nearly triple in only 30 years.

* To put 1 million shares a day, or approximately 250 million a year, in perspective, in 1994 more than 1 billion shares of a single stock changed hands on the New York Stock Exchange, that of Telefonos de Mexico, better known as Telmex, the Mexican telephone monopoly.

Was Wall Street obsolete?* The thought certainly crossed the minds of the people who tried to make a living there. No doubt there would always be a securities market. If the public had no interest in blue chips, professionals would opportunistically find other things to invest in: the "workout" preferreds of the battered public-utility holding companies, for instance; corporate bonds with interest in arrears; obscure over-the-counter market equities; or the stocks and bonds of bankrupt, or merging, railroads. In the sense of the Charles Merrill advertisement, then, there would always be a Wall Street. However, as it seemed in the early 1950s, there did not necessarily have to be a vibrant New York Stock Exchange set down in the incongruous cityscape of lower Manhattan, with its coffee-roasting houses and ship chancellories, stevedores staggering out the doors of the 25¢-per-shot bars into the broad daylight, bankers descending the steps of the elevated train at Hanover Square on their way to work in the morning or climbing into taxicabs to visit their customers in midtown for lunch, reporters on the staff of Dow Jones shuttling to and from midtown to call on corporate headquarters (it was understood that there were no stories on Wall Street itself, there being no good financial reason to care about it).

"Many bankers visualize a return to the conditions of 150 years ago, when many sections of Wall Street and environs were residential and retailing districts," *The Journal of Commerce* ventured at a low ebb of the financial district's fortunes in 1952. "Some believe that in a relatively few years there will be garden-type apartments at Manhattan's downtown tip overlooking the Hudson and East rivers."

No doubt a certain number of discouraged brokers were prepared to support any alternative use for lower Manhattan. In those dull days, the stock exchange seemed more a "refuge of fears" (to quote Harry D. Comer, a partner of Paine, Webber, Jackson & Curtis) than the citadel of capitalism. If the shadows of coming events had ever fallen first across the exchange floor, they had evidently removed themselves to more responsive venues; certainly little or no

---

* *Fortune* magazine turned the question into a headline. As bad luck would have it, the issue in which this brooding article appeared was dated February 1954, the month after the stock market hit bottom.

inkling of the growth in the postwar economy could be inferred by the grudging rise of equity prices since 1946. Then, too, with the eclipse of margin trading, the exchange had relinquished its once-commanding monetary role. In the 1920s, the call-loan rate was the first interest rate of the New York money market, but the Federal funds rate had long since superseded it. Perhaps the basic issue was whether a capitalist institution could survive in a garrison state. Could the United States prosper as well as wage war?

THE GREAT EISENHOWER bull market was foreshadowed by a single, optimistic real estate transaction in lower Manhattan. In February 1953, the U.S. government offered to swap its historic, vacant Assay Office building at 30 Wall Street for any other suitable New York location. It received one bid.

The Assay Office was a dreadnought of a building, a three-story superstructure set down on a five-story underground vault, which was empty. Overshadowing it was an 80-foot smokestack attached to a kind of factory. Through this stack had poured the noxious vapors of melting gold. New Yorkers would take bullion-bearing dust, foreign coins, or scrap jewelry to the Assay Office ($100 minimum order required) and receive in return gold bars or United States money at the statutory rate of $20.67 to the gold ounce. All in all, the Assay Office was a structure uniquely suited for a monetary function that, by the 1950s, was already sliding into irrelevance. The building had been vacant since 1932, when the government moved its occupants and contents, including more than $1 billion in gold bullion, to new quarters at South Street and Old Slip. Its windows (some of them broken) were barred, its facade was impregnable, and its floors were reinforced up to load-bearing strength of 1,000 pounds per square foot. The underground vaults were protected by reinforced concrete sheathed with $2\frac{1}{4}$-inch sheet steel as well as by the proximity of seawater; the Treasury Department's engineers counted the Atlantic Ocean itself as a line of defense against safecrackers (or "cracksmen," in the slang of the day). Across the street, at 23 Wall, was the headquarters of Morgan Guaranty Trust Company. In front of the old Sub-

Treasury Building was the spot where George Washington had taken the oath of office as president in 1789. A few hundred feet to the west was the New York Stock Exchange. Altogether, the site had character.

It also had peerless monetary bones. A branch bank of the Second Bank of the United States, forerunner to the Federal Reserve System, was built there in 1823. It was still standing in 1841 when the parent organization, by then purely a commercial bank (President Andrew Jackson had refused to renew its central-banking charter), came a cropper as so many other banks had done. "It seems to have been sufficient to obtain money on loan," according to one postmortem of the institution, "to pledge the stock of an 'incorporated company,' however remote its operations or uncertain its prospects."

Thereupon the place was converted into a federal assay office; the first gold dust was melted there on October 9, 1854. The melting continued until 1913, when the government decided that the growth of the national monetary wealth was outstripping the places in which it might be safely stored. The invention of the oxyacetylene torch had tilted the balance of power in favor of the criminal class and against the state. Equipped with a blowtorch, a cracksman could slice through a six-inch cube of steel in less than a minute and a half. Then, too, there were possible threats of foreign invasion and domestic mob rule to be reckoned with. The old branch bank building was sadly deficient. Decrepit, cramped, and out of date, it was demolished in 1915 (but not before public-spirited people had salvaged its Greek Revival facade and had it reassembled in the American wing of the Metropolitan Museum, where it stands today). On the day four years later when the cornerstone for the bigger, mightier Assay Office was laid, Carter Glass, secretary of the Treasury, lifted the first daub of cement on a ceremonial silver trowel after reassuring his audience that the new Federal Reserve System would not displace New York as the nation's financial capital, and a military band from Governors Island struck up "The Star-Spangled Banner."

The Army reappeared in force on the afternoon of September 16, 1920, after an enormous bomb exploded on Wall Street between the Assay Office and the Morgan building. Death and devastation rained down on this richest of American intersections, with the still-unfinished Assay Office bearing the brunt of the property damage. Debris from the explosion, in the form of bits of steel window sash, scored its outside walls. The blast ruined the ornamental grillwork protecting the windows, which, like glass for blocks around, were shattered into lethal shards. It cracked the new plaster and wrenched the new marble wainscoting from the walls. The outrage was mitigated only by its timing. On that day, laborers were carrying 25-pound gold bricks from the Sub-Treasury Building next door (where they had been temporarily housed) across a wooden runway to their permanent home in the Assay Office. Breaking for lunch just before noon, the workers and the armed guard withdrew into the buildings, "clanging shut the well-barred side entrances after them," as John Brooks wrote. "Thus they escaped an almost certain death and, it is possible to speculate, prevented a spectacular raid on the Treasury." Indeed, for a moment the police speculated in just that vein, but the theory was abandoned—the bomb had detonated at a considerable distance from the safes and vaults and there had been no attempt at looting. However, as we may imagine, the power of the blast confirmed the Treasury's architects in the view that, in assay-office design, it was prudent to err on the side of strength.

A few months before the 1929 crash, the 40 Wall Street promoters had signed a contract to acquire 30 Wall from the government; the plan was to incorporate that space into the Bank of Manhattan building. Their means and appetites reduced by the depression, 40 Wall at length withdrew. Now, after a lapse of 23 years, the government decided to look for a new buyer.

The lone expression of interest was submitted by the Seamen's Bank for Savings, a Wall Street institution in its own right, founded in 1829 by, among others, the Bethel Union and the Society for Promoting the Gospel Among Seamen in the Port of New York. Except for the first two years of its existence, the bank had always made its offices on Wall Street. In one of its buildings, it had installed the Street's first elevators. It had sailed through the panic of 1857 and every subsequent financial blow, insurrection, and war, and had never missed a dividend payment. Now, on the eve of its 125th anniversary, it proposed to raze the old Assay Office and erect a nine-story headquarters building (it turned out to be twelve) in its place. "It's worth it," replied John D. Butt, executive vice president, to the question of why the bank was prepared to go to all that trouble just to move a few blocks west from its existing headquarters at 74 Wall Street. "It's like being on Fifth Avenue instead of Sixth Avenue."

In 1953, not everybody regarded a closer proximity to the New York Stock Exchange as an unalloyed benefit, much less a higher degree of glamour. "A labyrinth of gloomy and bent and inefficient streets, on some of which automobiles seldom venture and on some parts of which the sun never shines; a close-packed mass of somber, brooding buildings," said *Business Week* of the old neighborhood in 1955, when stock prices were actually rising.

In a way, it was as brash a gesture to build an office building on Wall Street in the early 1950s as it had been to buy a common stock in the early 1940s. The commercial real estate market lay almost dormant. Opportunities (as they were revealed in retrospect) were at every hand, yet capitalists refused to seize them. Across the country, businesses needed new office space, but year after year none was built. In most cities, no new commercial structures had been put up since 1930. New York was the exception—about one million square feet of new space was added on average each year from 1947 to 1951—but demand nonetheless chronically outstripped supply in midtown Manhattan, too. The Manhattan-wide occupancy rate stood at 99.3 percent in 1952, and such little space as did exist was mainly available in cut-up pieces. Casting around for reasons to explain this anomaly, journalists seized on the indelible memory of the 1930s and early 1940s: of crushing vacancy rates, falling rents, unpaid taxes, and interminable bankruptcy proceedings, that is, of histories very much like that of 40 Wall Street. Even though it was the future that stared them straight in the eye, the builders and bankers looked back to the past.*

---

* Nor was optimism in oversupply in the financial press. Robert M. Bleiberg, thirty years old, was named editor of *Barron's* in 1954, succeeding John Davenport. "They had tried everywhere," reminisced Bleiberg of the Dow Jones Company's search for a

But the Inconsolable Era was passing. In 1954, the New York Stock Exchange and the General Realty and Utilities Corporation teamed up to raze a couple of old buildings at 20–24 Broad Street and to erect on the site an air-conditioned, 27-story, steel-and-glass tower. ("The building was rented before we got to the street with the steel," a General Realty man said.) The stock exchange's new president, G. Keith Funston, was just as confident as its architect. Turning the page on the war-bond interlude of its history, the exchange began to advertise the benefits of common-stock ownership. Its slogan was "Own Your Share of American Business," and to provide the small investor with the opportunity to make regular monthly purchases of common stock, the Monthly Investment Plan was created. Such was the scale of things that a cumulative investment of $11.5 million from 28,800 individual Monthly Investment Plan participants after one year was deemed a creditable beginning. To those who still half expected the year 1931 to make a surprise reappearance, it looked like public-relations suicide. In fact, for the stock exchange and its environs, boom times were at hand.

AN OMEN OF HOW unlike 1954 and 1955 would prove to be from any preceding peacetime year since the Great Depression was neighborhood reaction to the news that the Seamen's Bank would build on the 30 Wall Street site. Even before the first wrecking ball laid into the old Assay Office, brokerage firms were on the phone with John Butt to place their orders for space in his new office building (its respectful evocation of the Assay Office exterior pleased traditionalists). Rentals in new midtown skyscrapers then ranged from $5 to $8 a square foot; there had been no new construction downtown, of course, but Butt decided, in view of the lively expressions of interest, to think big and ask for $7. Drexel & Co., Kuhn, Loeb & Co., and Wood Struthers & Co. willingly paid it.*

---

new editor. "They had tried *The Wall Street Journal.* They had tried going outside. And they weren't offering anything, really. I was a bargain, and they were going to give me a shot at it because the other alternative was to shut it down."

* It was the rent that the high-prestige skyscrapers of the early 1930s, including One Wall Street and 40 Wall, had hoped for and, in only a few cases, actually got; in more than two decades, rents had not gone very far.

"For the first time in a generation, new office buildings are rising in downtown Manhattan," *Fortune* was able to report in October 1956. "The boom has stopped the talk of Wall Street's becoming a ghost town." The only ghosts were the specters of the 1930s, so recently exorcised. As *Fortune* went to press, four new buildings had been put up in lower Manhattan, six more were under construction, and an additional eight were in the planning stage. Greatest among the latter was the Chase Manhattan Bank's projected 60-story skyscraper, the centerpiece of what was expected to become the Piazza San Marco of lower Manhattan, Chase Manhattan Plaza. There was a considered architectural similarity between David Rockefeller's planned downtown project and his father's completed uptown project, but the economic circumstances of the construction of the two ventures could not have been more different. Rockefeller Center was conceived and built in the Great Depression; Chase Manhattan Plaza, although mapped out in the dull and discouraging days of the early 1950s, was realized in the first years of the great mid-1950s bull market.

As for 40 Wall Street, it had become a gold mine. Among the top 25 tenants were the law firm of Dewey Ballantine Bushby Palmer & Wood and the New York Stock Exchange member firms of Bache & Co., Estabrook & Co., and Hornblower & Weeks. Besides the Bank of Manhattan, the building housed the Bank of China and Swiss Credit Bank. Atlas Corporation, into the 58th-floor offices of which the Army aircraft had come to rest in 1946, was still on hand, as was Westinghouse Electric. Charles R. Hinerman, who had worked so hard to make ends meet in the 1930s, was still the building agent, now having an easier time of it. One hundred percent occupied, its rental income at last above the $4 million mark (20-odd years behind the original plan), and its debts reduced, the building was at last the cash cow of which its stockholders had dreamt. Its income bonds (with two shares of stock attached), disdained at 10¢ on the dollar in 1942, now changed hands for 200¢ on the dollar. In the span from 1932 to 1957, revenue had risen by 55 percent, while operating costs had vaulted by threefold. However, more than compensating for this unprofitable trend was the collapse in interest expense. In 1932, the building corporation had paid more than $1.1 million to its creditors;

thanks to the 1940 bankruptcy (as well as to the repayment of debt in the mid-1950s), in 1957 it paid just $277,000.

On Saturday, April 2, 1955, three downtown banks picked up their money, securities, and furniture and moved themselves to new headquarters. The Bank of Manhattan left 40 Wall to join the Chase—henceforth, the Chase Manhattan Bank—at 18 Pine. The First National Bank—George F. Baker's old bank, an institution of unrivaled strength, but strength for which the world of conservative habits and federal deposit insurance had little need—pulled up stakes from 2 Wall Street to merge with the National City Bank (becoming First National City Bank and still later, of course, Citibank) at 55 Wall. And the Seamen's Bank for Savings, still independent, moved down the block to its new home at 30 Wall.

SINCE 1829, Seamen's had survived the financial equivalent of fire, flood, and pestilence, but in the 1980s it could not survive high short-term interest rates. Sailors and stevedores, thrifty and otherwise, had long ago abandoned New York for more dynamic ports. Similarly, the nation had wandered far from the kind of monetary system that once supported (or at least did not actively thwart) the habits of thrift. Creeping inflation had given way to the ambulatory kind; by the 1970s, the purchasing power of the dollar was double-timing it backward. Gold, so much a part of the history of the bank's 30 Wall Street address, played no formal monetary role after 1971, when the great inflation of the 1970s was launched like a capital ship. Why save at 6 percent a year if inflation was stealing 7 percent (and rising)? Increasingly, people decided not to.

By the early 1980s, therefore, Seamen's, like the thrift industry in general, was in trouble. Its traditional business—taking small deposits and making small residential mortgage loans out of them, paying its overhead and earning a spread—now seemed a certain route to insolvency. The long-running rise in interest rates meant that deposit rates chronically outran the yield on fixed-rate loans. Long-dated mortgages originated at low rates in the 1950s and 1960s remained on the balance sheet, earning less by the year in relation to the cost of deposits. As losses piled up, the bank withdrew from the business of making mortgages; it could no longer attract and hold the deposit dollars it needed to finance them.

What was to be done? Nothing but the worst, it developed. In the early 1980s, not only did Congress open the way for thrift institutions to enter the alien business of commercial real estate finance, it also compounded the error by boosting the maximum deposit eligible for federal insurance to $100,000 from $40,000. In effect, the lawmakers invited the owners of insolvent thrifts to heal themselves by gambling with the taxpayers' money. Along with countless other hopeful savings banks and savings and loans, Seamen's began to scour the country for likely borrowers. As usually happens with eager creditors, it found them. Seamen's discovered them not in its own backyard but in the landlocked regions of the Southwest. Loans on so-called income-producing properties—apartment buildings, shopping centers, office buildings—totaled a mere $11 million in 1982; by year-end 1984, they stood at $524 million.

Had matters continued in this vein, Seamen's might well have lent itself into oblivion. As it was, the bank was sold in 1985 to Texas investors who helped to invest it into oblivion. Jess T. Hay and Robert Ted Enloe III, chairman and president, respectively, of Lomas & Nettleton Financial Corp., the world's largest mortgage banker, and Robert K. Utley III, president of First Southwest Equity Corp., also a Dallas-headquartered real estate business, knew firsthand what a sinkhole the Southwestern property market had become. Thus, it was under their stewardship that Seamen's veered off from the Scylla of credit risk to the Charybdis of interest-rate risk. It stopped lending against the collateral of overbuilt real estate and began to invest in the mortgages of safe and sane residential properties—mortgages, however, that had been refashioned into securities. It complemented these investments with the purchase of mortgage derivatives, interest-rate swaps, and other such volatile essences. So doing, the bank was very much like one of its old seagoing depositors who, once ashore, mixed beer and whiskey and gin.

In the Seamen's, Utley and Enloe had knowingly purchased damaged goods. The bank had registered annual net losses since at least 1980; its commercial real estate portfolio was on the blink, and its tangible-capital account was less than zero (Craig Hall, a real estate syndicator who himself was on the road to bankruptcy, was one of its favorite commercial real estate borrowers). On December 31, 1979, some three months after the Federal Reserve began to raise American interest rates to unprecedented levels, the bank was able to show positive net worth of $120.4 million. Within five years, its equity capital had vanished. In truth, the only capital in the bank before the coming of Utley, Hay, and Enloe was a government fig leaf given the name of "net worth certificates"—shades of the forbearance of the 1930s. As a mutual savings bank, the Seamen's was by law the property of its own depositors. (Management was self-perpetuating: "cronyism at its best," remarked a longtime trustee, Clarence F. Michalis, the son of a former Seamen's president and chairman, Clarence G. Michalis.) Now, under the supervision of the government, it became an investor-owned corporation; to be exact, a savings and loan holding company. The existing depositors got no consideration in the change of ownership. Why should they? Their interest had been wiped out. The Texans and their fellow institutional investors—among them General Electric's pension fund and another fund represented by the Seamen's towering Wall Street neighbor, Morgan Guaranty Trust Co. of New York—put up $50 million. In the summer of 1986, public investors were prevailed upon to advance $49.5 million.

Of this sum, about $4.5 million was paid in fees to the underwriters, Bear, Stearns & Co., the First Boston Corp., and Merrill Lynch. Of the remaining $45 million, $30 million was used to redeem the nonpublic investors' preferred stock; that is, to enable the Texans, among others, to take their money out of the company. Another $6.5 million was earmarked for dividend payments to the same nonpublic investors. This left $8.5 million, the sum that was actually contributed to the bank.

That the bank could use the money was clear from even a glance at its balance sheet. A not inconsiderable component of its assets on March 31, 1986, for example, was described as "goodwill." This was the difference between the fair value of the liabilities assumed and the fair value of the assets acquired. It was, in other words, a measure of the premium paid, that is, of the buyers' enthusiasm. It requires a very great optimist to rank this kind of asset on a par with a building owned free and clear or an unmortgaged gold brick. Indeed, under standard accounting conventions, goodwill is subtracted from stockholders' equity to determine real, or tangible, capital. As goodwill totaled $217 million and stockholders' equity footed up to $59 million, it was clear that the bank had no positive tangible capital at all, not even on the day in 1985 that it was sold. That it was allowed to carry on in this state of depletion was testimony to the hopes of all concerned: regulators, buyers, and public investors.

The sale of 5.5 million shares of the common stock of the bank's newly formed holding company was accompanied by the unvarnished truth-telling mandated by federal securities laws. Among other facts disclosed was that the banking regulators were bending over backward to help in the process of resuscitation. "The capital plan approved by the regulatory authorities in con- nection with the acquisition of the bank," the prospectus related, "provides, among other things, that the bank is permitted to oper- ate at lower capital levels than would otherwise be required under regulatory guidelines and regulations." Another disclosure was that two of the three Texans had borrowed sums equivalent to the pur- chase price of their stock: $1.3 million a man. It took no great imag- ination to see that the source of the funds for repayment of their loans would be the sale of stock to the public. Then, too, for the first 11 months of the 1985 calendar year, as the prospectus brought to light, Enloe and Utley had each received $18,000 a month from the new bank holding company. The quid for this quo was not spelled out, but the document strongly suggested that it was far better to be Utley or Enloe than any unnamed prospective public buyer. The Texans and their friends controlled the board of directors (their class of common stock had 10 times the voting power of the ordi- nary, public common), and they paid a highly advantageous 40¢ a share for their stock. The public paid $9 a share, as it was asked to do. For this consideration it could lay partial claim to an institution possessing some $3 billion of assets, not quite $2.3 billion of liabili- ties, and a large deficiency in tangible net worth. At that, at the time of the sale in August 1986, things at the Seamen's were about as good as they were going to get.

Optimism infused the annual report for the first full year of public ownership. Interspersed with pictures of noble American sailing vessels at sea (manned, presumably, by thrifty depositors) was news of the bank's $27 million profit, its improved capital position, and its progress in cost control. The management's philosophy was espoused: to build a "quality, recurring income stream," to make earnings grow by 15 percent a year (year in and year out, just as Walter Wriston had hoped to make Citicorp's grow), and to burnish the long-term value of the Seamen's banking "franchise."

Whatever that franchise might be. The original one was as out of date as Jack-tar. The Texans' idea was to adapt to modern times by conducting a securities-based banking business. The Seamen's would take in deposits as it always had done, and it would apply these funds to the purchase of residential mortgages in late-twentieth-century packaging: mortgages done up as bonds. If all went according to plan, the deposits would bear a lower interest rate than the securities. Up until then, the bank had made its own mortgages, one at a time. Now, the owners decided, it would invest in mortgages wholesale. One advantage was that mortgage-backed securities could be bought and sold with a telephone call. Another was that they came ready-made; no costly origination process was required. Still another was that, as a rule, they were immune from default, because most of the issuing entities were government-sponsored agencies (for instance, the Federal National Mortgage Association). Under the management of Utley and Enloe, the Seamen's balance sheet showed fewer commercial real estate loans and more mortgage-backed securities.

Another integral part of the new Seamen's business strategy was to avoid the costly mismatching of assets and liabilities. Henceforth, management promised, one side of the balance sheet would not be significantly more sensitive to interest-rate fluctuations than the other. Thus, a rise in the general level of interest rates would constitute another manageable event, not unlike a decline in the general level of interest rates.*

---

* "Let's say," explained Lisa Hess, an investment banker who called on Seamen's, among other thrift institutions, in the 1980s, "that they went out and bought $100 million worth of Ginnie Maes that were expected to pay down at the rate of 6 percent a year. That's the left-hand side of the balance sheet. The right-hand side of the balance sheet consists of reverse repo, which is synthetically extended with a series of interest rate swaps. So there was a synthetic liability pay-down, which should, in theory, have offset the runoff in the mortgages."

It could be said of Utley, Hay, and Enloe, as it could be said of few other Americans, that the United States government was their friend. They gathered deposits with the imprimatur of the Federal Deposit Insurance Corporation. They borrowed liberally at subsidized interest rates from the Federal Home Loan Bank of New York. They invested in mortgages guaranteed (or subsidized) by the federal government. If success was in the cards, it would belong to them and to the other stockholders. If not, the loss would be largely the government's. In the event of failure, no uninsured depositor would be hurt, and they themselves (Utley and Enloe in particular) would walk away only slightly poorer. Not for nothing, as one business acquaintance of theirs recalled, "They thought they had done the greatest deal of all time."

With the government's leave, the bank undertook to grow its way out of its problems by acquiring an ever larger investment portfolio. From year-end 1985 to year-end 1988, the Seamen's assets vaulted to $4.7 billion from $3 billion. On the earlier balance-sheet date, the bank owned $379 million of mortgage-backed securities; at the later date, $3.2 billion. Interestingly, its deposits had expanded only slightly over those three years. The bank did not raise money, as it might have done years earlier, by boosting deposit rates or giving away toasters. The principal means by which it financed its growth were advances from the Federal Home Loan Bank System and borrowings secured by its own mortgage-backed securities. "The amount and percentage of the bank's portfolio in quality, liquid investments should continue to increase," the 1986 annual ventured, "while the bank's vulnerability to increases in interest rates should remain very low."

This imperial phase of the Seamen's corporate life cycle was cut short by a costly, unforeseen interest-rate development in 1988–89: short rates rose to meet, then to exceed, longer-dated ones. Like the builders of a ship that is perfect in every detail except for the one that causes it to sink, the management anticipated many financial contingencies but not the relevant one. They entered into (as a defensive measure, they imagined) interest-rate swaps, interest-only mortgage derivatives, and other financial instruments designed to protect against rising rates. They purchased other mortgage derivatives that would rise or fall in an exaggerated fashion in response to movements in interest rates. Determined not to re-create the mistakes of the prior management, the Texans instead created their own.

"Nobody on the board knew what he was talking about," remembered one trustee referring to a financial strategist whom the Texans brought in to buy and sell mortgages, mortgage-backed securities, and mortgage derivatives. The Seamen's purchased no fewer than $375 million worth of interest-only strips, or "IOs." IOs are mortgage derivatives that entitle their holders to receive the interest portion of the income from a pool of mortgage-backed securities; that is all. A corresponding principal-only portion entitles someone else to all of the principal payments. (The garden-variety mortgage, it should be remembered, is uniquely designed for the benefit of the borrower. If interest rates fall, the borrower might refinance; if rates rise, he or she will not. Falling interest rates, by stimulating a wave of refinancings, naturally cause a shrinkage in the volume outstanding in any pool of residential mortgages. It stands to reason that the interest income generated by such a pool is simultaneously reduced. This reduction is instantly reflected in a falling market price for the IOs.) On December 31, 1988, the bank's $375 million portfolio of these incendiary items was quoted in the open market at just $323 million.

"In a normal interest rate environment," said a doleful note in the 1988 Seamen's annual report, "when short-term interest rates are lower than long-term interest rates, the ownership of IOs could be expected to enhance the spread between the company's primarily long-term assets and its primarily short-term liabilities as interest rates rise. During the latter part of 1988, however, an unanticipated significant rise in short-term rates occurred that was not accompanied by a concurrent rise in long-term rates. The fact that long-term rates did not increase significantly meant that prepayments on the company's IOs did not decrease significantly and their yield did not increase materially." In other words, the management had unwittingly implemented what traders call a "Texas hedge": a defensive speculative strategy that fails to deliver the hoped-for protection and instead compounds the risk being hedged against. If the damage in IOs weren't enough, the bank had also arranged to purchase some

$68 million of "floating rate collateralized mortgage obligation residuals" (the trustees must have rubbed their eyes); as of year-end, this essence-of-mortgage investment was quoted at just $40 million.

"Throughout 1988," the report went on, "the estimated market value of many of the bank's mortgage-related securities was significantly below their book value. The continued rise in short-term rates in early 1989 has caused a further deterioration in the market value of the bank's securities."

What next? Belatedly throwing up defenses against another upward movement in short-term interest rates, the management undertook a new program of investments, entering into one kind of interest-rate swap agreement* and canceling another kind. It bought one kind of interest-rate cap† and canceled another kind. Naturally, this financial repositioning cost money. Wall Street, at least—the recipient of brokerage commissions and investment-banking fees generated by the Seamen's strenuous capital-market activities—was gratified. (So was the printer of the bank's 1988 annual report. The document went through two editions. The first, featuring full-color plates of nautical memorabilia, was—as the bank belatedly came to realize—incongruously rich. To correct the misimpression of prosperity it conveyed, management ordered it reprinted in sere black and white. The cost of this switcheroo was $18,000.)

For whatever comfort it brought the stockholders, management was able to report a decline in the volume of underwater real estate loans. However, poor lending was yesterday's crisis. On March 15, 1989, the bank entered into a "Memorandum of Understanding" with federal regulators which was, in fact, a kind of confession, or consent decree. The bank promised to suspend dividend payments, search for new capital, curtail growth, and appoint an oversight committee consisting mainly of outside directors to try to lift itself

---

* Whereby the Seamen's agreed to make payments based on a fixed rate in exchange for the right to receive payments based on a variable rate. The sum of money on which these interest rates would be paid, or owed, was in excess of $1.2 billion.

† A contract in which one party agrees to make payments to the other in case interest rates rise above an agreed-upon level.

from the shoals on which it had run aground. "As this report goes to press, the future direction of interest rates remains unclear," said the management on page 7 of the 1988 annual report in a moment of rare intellectual clarity.

"Currently," management explained in the following year's annual, which was visually unadorned, "the interest rate spread between the bank's interest-earning assets and interest-bearing liabilities is very narrow and the bank's interest-bearing liabilities are significantly greater than its interest-earning assets. As a result, the bank cannot be profitable on an ongoing basis without a significant infusion of capital." Seamen's would have needed some anyway, even if it had not borne crippling losses in 1989, by dint of some stringent new federal regulations. In any case, no capital was forthcoming, and by September 1989, the board had given up. On April 18, 1990, the government ordered the bank into receivership.

"As of June 30," said the management in its last communiqué to shareholders in the summer of 1990, "the company's remaining asset consisted of $81,000 in cash." Then it struck the only note of hope remaining to be struck: "In addition, the company is currently awaiting a refund in the amount of $27,000 from the state of Delaware for the overpayment of the Delaware franchise tax." However, it was far from enough. The stockholders and the holders of some $25 million of subordinated debt of the Seamen's Bank received not a dime in salvage. The failure cost the FDIC upward of $400 million.

Still intact, however, was the bank's 2,000-piece collection of nautical art and handicraft: paintings, scrimshaw, ship's models, barometers, posters, antique toys, and antique banks. It was in a boardroom decorated with miniature sailing vessels that the trustees (or some of them) had uncomprehendingly listened to explanations of mortgage derivatives. When, in 1991, the South Street Seaport Museum announced that it had made arrangements with the FDIC to acquire the collection, intact, for $3.4 million, competing buyers blanched. "That collection is worth $10 to $15 million," a Hyannisport (Massachusetts) auctioneer told *The New York Times*. At the high figure, the bank's art and crafts would be worth exactly three times what the Chase Manhattan Bank paid to acquire its $2.1 billion of deposits and to manage 13 of its branch offices, including the head office at 30 Wall Street, once the biggest storehouse of gold in the world.

THE DECADE OF the 1970s was subversive to the old order on Wall Street. Since time out of mind, the neighborhood had been bound together by gold, prosperity, blood, social exclusion, and the need for close physical proximity. Old money had huddled in contiguous office towers and conducted a securities business protected from outside competition by the laws and customs of the New York Stock Exchange. In the Nixon presidency, however, politics, law, technology, and necessity forced fundamental changes. In 1970, Donaldson, Lufkin & Jenrette defied precedent by raising capital from the public instead of from its own partners, issuing stock as if it were a mere industrial company. In 1971, the NASDAQ Stock Market was launched, a network of dealers connected not by a trading floor (still less by a clubby rule book) but by a network of video screens. In the same revolutionary year, as already noted, the Bretton Woods monetary system came undone, thereby relegating gold to the status of investment, or collectible, as distinct from that of money itself. In 1972, the Chicago Mercantile Exchange won regulatory approval to begin dealing in financial futures. There would come a time when bonds and stocks would resemble commodities more than the individual securities that New York Stock Exchange firms had so profitably created, sold, and traded. In 1973, the Securities and Exchange Commission voted to eliminate the age-old system of fixed brokerage commissions by which the exchange had kept competitive capitalism at bay from its own gates.

Even a minor prophet could foresee that the changes would not enrich the owners of 40 Wall Street. With the advent of the microchip, the architecture of securities trading would require spaces with fewer columns, higher ceilings, and larger floor plates than 40 Wall could offer. Similarly with the application of computer technology to banking and securities record keeping: the day was past when a New York Stock Exchange member firm had to be near the stock exchange itself, or when a bank had to clear its checks under its own stately facade rather than in some financial factory in an outlying borough or suburb. "The financial district of Manhattan will be where it is so long as the town exists," Louis Adler said in 1930 as the neighborhood was cresting. "The exigencies of banking and capital require a kernel location, and it can never spread."

Dreading the day of obsolescence, however, a seer would have worried too soon. Forty Wall Street was fully occupied throughout the decades of the 1960s and 1970s, and the people who passed through its revolving doors were just the type of broker, banker, and lawyer for whom the Starretts had laid their hopeful plans on the eve of the crash. When word leaked out in 1979 of the impending merger of the building's No. 1 tenant, Loeb Rhoades, Hornblower & Co., with Shearson Hayden Stone, a brokerage firm from outside the building, two new tenants, Morgan Guaranty Trust and Toronto Dominion Bank, promptly materialized, and Manufacturers Hanover, a tenant since 1962, signed up for more space.

Before very long, however, the supply of office space would rise up to meet demand and then to overpower it, not only in New York but also in much of the rest of the country and, indeed, throughout much of the world. In the United States, spurred on by the 1981 tax act, developers and their bankers launched another American building boom, one that gave lower Manhattan the modestly named World Financial Center, among 30 other centers, plazas, and towers. Altogether in the 1980s, some 25 million square feet of space was created in the greater Wall Street neighborhood, the equivalent of more than twenty-five 40 Wall Streets. Certainly, the original didn't need the competition.*

Nevertheless, upon sale in 1982, 40 Wall fetched a surprisingly good price. John L. Loeb and Henry Loeb, together with other partners of the no-longer-functioning firm of Loeb Rhoades, had

* Recalling the building that wasn't built by Louis Adler in 1930, Donald Trump in 1984 announced his aspiration to build the world's tallest building in lower Manhattan on a 26-acre site that was then under the East River. At 150 stories, the imagined Trump tower easily overshadowed the unbuilt, 105-floor Adler tower and even (in the tangible category of skyscraper construction) the actual 110-story Sears Tower. The Trump project, unbuilt to this day, is perhaps the tallest structure in lower Manhattan ever described in a press release.

bought the building from a British company, Transatlantic Real Estate Corporation, in 1966. ("We wanted our own home," remembered John Loeb.) Transatlantic had bought it in 1960 from the flamboyant William Zeckendorf, who in turn had bought it in 1959 at a court-sponsored auction. The Loeb partnership now sold it to a buyer representing itself as the typographically singular NYLand, which was represented to be a subsidiary of the New York Land Company, which was identified in the press with a New York developer, Joseph Bernstein. It was conspicuously not identified with the husband-and-wife dictators of the Philippines, Ferdinand and Imelda Marcos, the actual owners; nor with the noted Saudi Arabian arms merchant, Adnan Khashoggi, who claimed to be another owner. The price was $70 million; Citibank provided the mortgage financing.

Citi would be heard from again, in 1986 to be exact, when it moved to foreclose. By then the Marcoses had suffered their own political bear market, one ramification of which was a dispute over the ownership of 40 Wall Street, 8,618 miles away from Manila and so evidently out of reach for anyone, even a married couple, on a Philippine public-service income. Many vied for the title of the building, but no one, apparently, for the obligation to maintain it, and the place began to show its years. Bankrupt and cast off, it was purchased at another court-supervised auction in 1989, this time by the developer Burton Resnick of Jack Resnick & Sons. The price paid was $77 million, or $7 million more than the Bernstein-Marcos-Khashoggi combine had paid the Loebs in 1982. Just next door, the Seamen's Bank offered proof that the financial environment had taken a turn for the worse. Nevertheless, Citi provided the mortgage financing, $62 million, as well as a $50 million credit line with which Resnick could finance the necessary improvements, such as (for a start) a rehabilitation of the old elevators.

By now, however, the tide had turned against real estate generally, Wall Street particularly, and 40 Wall Street—no longer known as the Bank of Manhattan Building but, in a new marketing setback, as the Marcos Building—even more particularly. Rents in the dowager buildings of downtown Manhattan were quoted at $30 a square foot in 1989 when Resnick made his investment. By 1992, they had fluttered down to the $20-a-square-foot region. In the case of 40 Wall Street, any rent at all seemed exorbitant to the handful of remaining tenants, one of whom, Herbert Rubin, partner of the law firm of Herzfeld & Rubin, had been on the premises since 1960. "There was never a time when the building had excess space until the '80s," reminisced Rubin at a later date. "Our own experience was that we were fighting for additional space. If we could pick up a few square feet here or there, we took it, and then tried to build it into something that was contiguous. Then came the Bernstein era, and the deterioration of the building and the deterioration of the market. We finally were able to get contiguous space with seven floors." Within two years, Rubin could have had almost 56 floors out of 70 floors, that being the number unoccupied.

The final blow to Resnick was the merger of Manufacturers Hanover with the Chemical Bank in 1992, a year that happened to coincide with the 30th anniversary of the signing of Manufacturers' 30-year lease. In 1962, the combination of the Manufacturers and the Hanover banks had reduced the demand for lower Manhattan office space. So now with the merger of Manufacturers Hanover and Chemical (both of which, by then, had moved their headquarters to midtown). Without his principal tenant, Resnick was staring at a 25 percent increase in vacancy, but this time there was no Toronto Dominion Bank or Morgan Guaranty to fill the empty space. Indeed, the Morgan Bank moved out along with Chemical.

With each understanding that the building was no longer a going concern, Resnick stopped spending money and Citi stopped lending it. For the second time since 1986, the bank instituted foreclosure proceedings, but (for a change) no unreasonably optimistic bid materialized. Some $80 million of Citi's money was sunk into the premises, and the bank sought out a buyer. "People familiar with the sales effort say that Citicorp's official asking price on the debt, which effectively confers ownership of the building to the buyer, is $20 million," *The Wall Street Journal* reported in 1992, "but the bank would let it go for just $10 million." The bank let it go, in the end, for about $7 million, or only $1 million more than the annual cost of running the place.

The buyer was Kinson Properties, of Hong Kong. Kinson promised a thoroughgoing restoration but presently thought better of it. Once more the building was put up for sale. The new buyer, Donald Trump, reportedly paid less than $5 million (and only on condition that the State of New York approve a tax-incentive plan for lower Manhattan; in the event, the legislature came through). Within a year or so of the purchase, in the summer of 1996, Trump was delivering on his promised overhaul. A message affixed to a temporary construction wall bore the unmistakable touch of the master: "THIS 72 STORY BUILDING [the tower had apparently grown two stories under the prosperous Trump ownership] WILL BE THE FINEST AND MOST BEAUTIFUL BUILDING ANYWHERE IN NEW YORK WHEN COMPLETED. THE GREAT TOWER, ONCE THE TALLEST IN THE WORLD [except for the Chrysler Building], WILL AGAIN TAKE ITS PLACE AS THE CROWN JEWEL OF DOWNTOWN MANHATTAN." The imminent lapidary qualities of the tower were incorporated into a painting affixed to the same wooden wall. Trump's artist, seeming to understand the nature of the patron as well as that of the commission, took the liberty of improving the line of sight on No. 40 by removing another Wall Street building from the picture. The intrusive structure thereby obliterated was none other than the New York Stock Exchange.

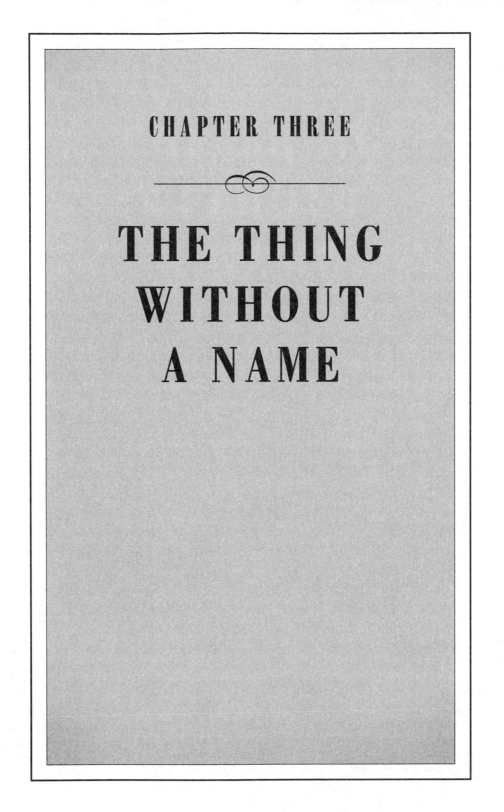

CHAPTER THREE

THE THING WITHOUT A NAME

T HE FAILURE OF the Seamen's Bank and the disposition of its nautical art was coincidentally followed by a national recession. Beginning in July 1990 and ending only 10 months later, in April 1991, the first and only downturn of the administration of George Bush was statistically unexceptional. Gross domestic product fell by just 2.9 percent from peak to trough, little more than half of the average decline of the five preceding recessions. Only the 1960–61 slump was less consequential, as measured by lost output and forgone income (if not by the worry of the cyclical victims, who in 1990–91 included a certain kind of white-collar person who was out of practice at being unemployed). Stacked up against the economic and financial snows of yesteryear—1980–82 and 1974–75, for example, never mind the Great Depression itself, or the recurring distress of the 1890s—the 1990–91 disturbance was the merest low-pressure front.

"Paradoxical as it may seem," wrote the Frenchman Clement Juglar a century before a lack of prosperity tipped the 1992 presidential election to Bill Clinton, "the riches of nations can be measured by the violence of the crises which they experience." That is, Juglar suggested, the down portion of the economic cycle serves a constructive purpose, too: undoing the mistakes and excesses of the up cycle. Paradoxical and impolitic, certainly, Juglar's idea is not so far-fetched as it might first appear. In the past 50 or 75 years, governments of the industrialized nations, along with their central banks, have gone to extraordinary lengths to stamp out crises even before they could start. Public spending—much of it in the name of income maintenance and therefore of economic crisis–prevention—has vaulted. Between 1960 and 1994, according to a pair of economists at the International Monetary Fund, expenditures by 17 governments, measured as a share of the gross domestic product of their respective economies, leapt to the equivalent of 47 percent from 27.9 percent. (In the United States alone in that period, expenditure grew to 33.5 percent from 27 percent.) Growth in outlays during those 34 years, they observe, was greater than the growth in all the preceding century.

It may not be entirely coincidental that economic growth has become less robust as governments of the same 17 countries have become more expansive. Insofar as government intervention has tended to hold back economic growth and forestall crises, to just that extent is the Juglar paradox borne out. Milder down cycles have coincided with weaker up cycles.*

"The business cycle is much more akin to fatigue than to disease," ventured the British economist G. L. S. Shackle in 1938, "in that it is not an exceptional or accidental occurrence but part of the nature of a modern industrial economy." In America in 1996, Shackle would be thought dour. The modern-day consensus of economic thought is that the symptoms of any recession can (and should) be alleviated by timely government action. Pain and suffering are alleged to be no more an integral part of the capitalist cycle than they are of human health.†

The proposition that Juglar is right and the moderns are wrong is the idea we now turn to. We have seen already that economic and

---

* Before 1933, according to the National Bureau of Economic Research, the average downturn was only a few months shorter than the average upturn. On the other hand, as it would not surprise Juglar to learn, the average expansion has become milder as the average expansion has become weaker. Booms and busts have each lost some of their elemental power.

† A pre-Keynesian view of government intervention in economic crises was expressed at the turn of the century by Theodore E. Burton. "Their disturbing effect can be greatly diminished by legislative recognition of economic laws and by wise regulations as to currency," by which Burton meant the classical gold standard; "also by higher standards of education and consequently greater wisdom in the direction of individual effort," he added, not anticipating the remainder of the twentieth century.

financial activity is inherently cyclical—that overdoing it tends to give way to underdoing it and vice versa; or that, to anticipate an argument of another school of economic thought, the Austrian one, busts are actually caused by booms.

The case for better, more robust expansions (followed, of necessity, by lustier, more dynamic contractions) is based on the conviction that failure is an integral part of the capitalist cycle. The argument is advanced in this chapter without the aid of an econometric model. Instead, the principal exhibits are historical: America and Japan in both the early 1920s and the early 1990s. In each era, inflation of one kind or another demanded a public-policy response. The most successful policy was that of the United States in the early 1920s: a short, sharp depression. The least successful policy was that of Japan in the early and mid-1990s: a chronic, lingering recession.

In a dynamic economy, adjustments take place continuously, but in the late twentieth century, with its Employment Act and its failproof banks (Credit Lyonnais in France and the Industrial Bank of Japan and no less than Citicorp in America), its burgeoning governments and ever expanding debts, adjustments have typically occurred sluggishly. In times past, inflations (and the distortions they wrought) were followed by deflations and expanding debts by contracting ones. However, not since 1948–49 has a recession in the United States been accompanied by a general fall in prices, and not since 1973–74 has the American stock market been through what might be described as a bracing bear market. The infrequency of what Juglar termed "crises"—sudden, wrenching adjustments to a new set of prices, market conditions, or production technologies—might well help to explain the characteristic torpor of the late-twentieth-century GDP.

It may be said in reply that the world must be accepted for what it is. Thus, even if the superiority of the 1920 depression to the 1990 recession were admitted by the chairman of the Federal Reserve Board himself, in open congressional testimony, the U.S. economy could not be remade to revert to its adaptable, Harding-era form. However, it might enrich the political debate to recognize that the attempted suppression of economic and financial failure, as in contemporary Japan, has costly, unanticipated side effects. Writers who condemn out of hand the destruction and waste of a business contraction would not dream of advancing their arguments without destroying the inadequately written first, second, or third drafts of the antirecession essay they had so painstakingly composed. In a world without creative destruction, the quality of creativity would be immeasurably reduced.

EVEN IN MID-RECESSION, the early 1990s were a time of wondrous material wealth. On average, Americans in the down portion of the business cycle lived more comfortably than they had in the long expansion of the 1960s. They occupied larger homes, surrounded themselves with more electronic objects, and (so one interpretation of the numbers suggests) enjoyed more leisure time than they had 20 years before. Although the rate of economic growth had declined, the rate of useful invention had accelerated. Facsimile machines, laser printers, ever smaller and more powerful personal computers, ibuprofen, cellular telephones, and the artificial pancreas were among the blessings of ingenuity that a worried American might not have had the time or inclination to stop to count.

We are not imagining things when we remember that insecurity was more palpable than wonder. What we would be imagining, however, is that insecurity is a new state of being, or that the flux of the 1990s was exclusively a by-product of the personal computer. *The Rise of David Levinsky*, a novel by Abraham Cahan published in 1917, described the hard-won cyclical business success of an immigrant cloakmaker late in the nineteenth century. The vicissitudes of the protagonist are not so different from the experiences of native-born Americans of the late twentieth century.

"People now see there is no protection against a recession of this magnitude," a Columbia University anthropology professor, Katherine Newman, told the *Los Angeles Times* in 1994, three years after the official recession had ended but long before the southern California readers of the *Times* could actually believe it. "Americans have always thought that there was no force large enough to tear down the truly motivated. But they've been sorely disappointed. The truth is, they've met their match." In this diagnosis she was joined by author Studs Terkel, who pronounced, "Saying we've been through a recession is like calling a cancer a pimple." Spiritually anticipating Terkel was corporate executive Harry Figge, who predicted national calamity in 1992 in his best-selling book, *Bankruptcy 1995*. Figge's thesis was that the public debt would consume the United States. (In the event, it was Figge International, the author's eponymous conglomerate, that underwent a debt crisis. Figge stepped down in 1994, illustrating by personal example that one is more likely to suffer a personal financial setback than to predict, accurately, a national one.)

Levinsky had seen it all. While there was no public debt to speak of in the 1890s, when Levinsky was on the rise, there was ever present business risk of prices falling, labor striking, or consumer tastes changing. In our time, it is information that has been made universally accessible. In Levinsky's time, it was blouses, dresses, and cloaks. "Foreigners ourselves," the protagonist, a Russian Jew, reflected in the novel, "and mostly unable to speak English, we had Americanized the system of providing clothes for the American woman of moderate or humble means. The ingenuity and unyielding tenacity of our managers, foremen, and operatives had introduced a thousand and one devices for making by machine garments that used to be considered possible only as the product of handwork. This—added to an increased division of labor, the invention, at our instance, of all sorts of machinery for the manufacture of trimmings, and the enormous scale upon which the production was carried on by us—had the effect of cheapening the better class of garments prodigiously. We had done away with prohibitive prices and greatly improved the popular taste." And, also of necessity, displaced, annoyed, or frightened the vested interests they succeeded, notably, German Jews.

In business in the early 1990s, "downsizing" was the order of the day. (Levinsky, although unfamiliar with the word, was intimately acquainted with the phenomenon.) Companies and their employees were "reengineered," "refocused," "de-layered," or "right-sized." "Why is the 'right' size always smaller?" asked Gary Hamel and C. K. Prahalad in 1994 in the *Harvard Business Review*. No matter. According to the late Dan Lacy, a journalist who organized and interpreted the numbers, almost one million permanent corporate staff positions were eliminated between 1989 and 1991. Creation of jobs there was, too—on balance, employment did grow—but economic necessity, technological innovation, and corporate fashion together in the 1990s favored destruction. The new management gospel taught that an employee sacked was equivalent to a unit of revenue won. Entire strata of middle management were replaced by IBMs and Apples, and a new verb entered the private vocabulary of top management: "to broom," as in to fire wholesale.

"The contemporary archetype is the redundant executive," wrote James Morgan in *The Financial Times* early in 1995. "He sets himself up as a 'consultant,' working on a casual basis for the company that laid him off and finding scraps of work elsewhere. He is the contemporary counterpart of the farm laborer, expelled from his tied cottage, but hiring himself out to his former employer at harvest time. He has no vocation, he is 'multiskilled.' He is the middle-class odd-job man, the golf-club proletarian."

"Moreover," Levinsky reflected of the uses of adversity in the late nineteenth century, "there were many among us to whom the crisis of 1893 had proved a blessing. . . . [S]ome of our tailors, being unable to obtain employment in that year, had been driven to make up a garment and to offer it for sale in the street, huckster-fashion—a venture which in many instances formed a stepping-stone to a cloak factory. Others of our workmen had achieved the same evolution by employing their days of enforced idleness in taking lessons in cloak-designing, and then setting up a small shop of their own. Newfangled manufacturers of this kind were now springing up like mushrooms."

Shuttling back to the late twentieth century, organized labor underwent its own relentless downsizing. In 1992, the proportion of American wage and salary workers belonging to unions hit a 56-year low of 15.8 percent; it had been 20.1 percent in 1983. The rise in apprehension was also reflected in the fall in strike activity. A post-1947 record was set in 1992 for the fewest number of strikes involving 1,000 or more workers: there were just 35. In the faraway, fractious, inflationary year of 1974, there had been 424. What was it all coming to? A succession of business-management catchphrases was invented to put the best face on the era of insecurity. Thus, in the late 1970s, there was Quality of Work Life movement. It was followed in the early 1980s by the Employee Participation movement. (Workers were henceforth to be thought of, if not addressed, as "associates.") Later in the 1980s came Lean Production, which was followed by a pair of 1990s' concepts: Total Quality Management and Reengineering. Perhaps the epitome of the reengineered American corporation of the 1990s was a Texas-based maker of plastic hair gadgets, TopsyTail Company. Including the founder, Tomima Edmark, the company employed three persons. The author of not one but two books on the art of kissing, Edmark poured the royalties from these literary works into the purchase of the first TopsyTail mold, and parlayed her own downsizing experience—a $25,000 "individual transition" check from IBM—into the first boffo, two-minute TopsyTail TV spot. One hallmark of the Edmark method is to "outsource" virtually every standard corporate function, from manufacturing and accounting to public relations. With a full-time staff of two plus the founder, TopsyTail was able to generate revenues of some $80 million a year.

One by one in the early 1990s, the familiar landmarks of the postwar economy fell away. One such fixture was price inflation. In the United States since the mid-1950s, inflation had been successively creeping, dormant, virulent, and receding. Now it seemed to be vanishing. In 1990, consumer prices rose by 5.4 percent; in 1994 and 1995, they scarcely rose by that much in both years put together. Indeed, no less an authority on the subject of inflation than the chairman of the Federal Reserve Board, Alan Greenspan, declared in 1995 that the truth was even better than the statistical fact; the real inflation rate was probably less than 1 percent, he said. Southwood J. "Woody" Moreott, chairman of Dana Corp., $5.5 billion maker of automobile parts and other industrial products, flatly told *Business Week* in November 1993: "We are in a period of low to no inflation that we may live with till the year 2000. That means you have to get productivity improvements forever."

Usually, in the early going of a business recovery, prices do not rise significantly. What was extraordinary about 1991 and 1992 was the deepening belief that, this time around, they would not rise at all. There was, to begin with, a vital change in monetary affairs. The banking systems of the leading industrial countries stopped creating credit at the familiar, brisk, postwar pace. In the 1970s, for perspective, the basic United States money stock—M-2, to initiates—grew by as much as 13.9 percent a year. In 1993 and 1994, it scarcely grew at all. So, too, with the national supplies of yen, French francs, and (eventually, after the unification of the two Germanies) deutsche marks. The throbbing pulse of monetary expansion in the industrial world virtually stopped. It did so, moreover, in the context of a universal paper-money system that was, in theory, infinitely expandable.

As national banking systems created less money, so cartels fixed fewer prices. In the 1970s, the Organization of Petroleum Exporting Countries had lorded it over the oil-consuming world. With the advent of free oil markets, however, the power to set prices moved from the sheikhs to the traders, notably to the New York Mercantile Exchange. On a given day in 1996, the NYMEX priced more than 1,000 percent more crude oil than did OPEC. So, too, with the other cartels, oligopolies, and tight little clubs of yesteryear. From brokerage-house commission rates to interest rates to automobile prices to the cost of a long-distance telephone call, competition had ventilated not only the American economy but also the world's. At this writing, a new futures market in electricity—a commodity long priced by regulated monopolies—was taking shape.

The cold war, like television or price inflation, was an everyday American institution, but now it, too, was gone. The collapse of Communism and the Soviet Union dealt a blow to America's own shadow brand of socialism, the defense business. Cold war–related expenditures by the federal government grew by leaps and bounds in the 1980s. In the 1990s, they began to contract. The downsizing of the Defense Department budget symbolized the triumph of free markets and democratic institutions. However, simultaneously, it cast defense-dependent regions of the United States, notably Southern California, into their own particular recessions, no less punishing to the victims because the source of the slump was a famous victory. Then, too, the economists observed, the opening of China and Russia to the world economy expanded the world's workforce by more than one billion souls. If, as seemed likely, the newly enfranchised masses were prepared to work for less than the comfortable American (or the plush German) manufacturing wage, how could American or European workers continue to live in their accustomed capitalist style?*

"Four years after the fall of the Berlin Wall and the ultimate triumph of capitalism," reflected a man on *The International Herald Tribune* early in 1994, "the victors and their vaunted system find themselves in a creeping crisis. Long accustomed to economic cycles in which the ebb tides of recession are more than reversed by strong surges of recovery, the industrial world is seeing something new: the rising tide that fails to lift all ships."

Finance was recast, along with geopolitics, but one of the pillars of the regulated postwar American economy was allowed to stand. This was a banking system warranted against collapse. As mass unemployment had been stricken from the list of macroeconomic possibilities, so had the risk of a serial bank run. All in all, as *Life* magazine had so cogently observed in 1958, the 1930s was the decade least likely to be repeated in the postwar era. The price level would not be allowed to fall, debts to contract, or the gross national product to fall in on itself.

Periodic symptoms of contraction, deflation, or depression there had been, but they were very far from being the real things. Inflation became the characteristic American monetary condition. In gold-standard days, overexpansion of bank credit had frequently been followed by outright contraction: not merely a falling off in the rate of growth of banking activity but an outright shrinkage. At

---

* The swords-to-plowshares movement had its direct beneficiaries, of course. U.S. Banknote Company, which lost a major portion of its domestic stock-and-bond-certificate business to computer technology, found new outlets in the central banks and stock exchanges of Eastern Europe. "The best thing that ever happened to us was the disintegration of the Soviet Union," said Paul Amatucci, Banknote's vice president, commercial sales, in 1994.

As for Southern California, 1995 marked the first year since before Pearl Harbor in which the entertainment industry employed more people than the aerospace industry. "At a cost of $45 million," *Weekly Variety* reported in its March 18, 1996, edition, "Disney is turning the former drab gray home of Lockheed's Stealth aircraft design facility into an animation studio."

the least, prices and wages had fallen in the bad years after having risen in the booms. Under the post-1933 dollar, for better or worse, as we have seen, no deflationary contractions were allowed to occur. When the banking system did seem to come unstuck—as in 1974, with the failure of the Herstatt Bank in Germany, or in 1982, with the Mexican default—it had promptly been stuck back together again.

However, as a corollary to the law that no good deed goes unpunished, no vast subsidy goes unexploited. The institution of the federal banking "safety net," intended to protect innocent depositors from the consequences of bad banking, had the unintended consequence of promoting bad banking. In the United States, but also in Japan, most of the Nordic countries, Britain, and Australia, scenes of competitive bank wrecking and fabulous real estate inflation were played out in the 1980s. Part of what made the recession of 1991–92 considerably more dangerous than its statistical profile were the credit policies of the upswing. The risk of a banking crisis, at all times and places, is that bad banks topple good ones and that failure snowballs. What made the aftermath of this particular crisis unique was that recovery snowballed; the banking system was rolled back up to the top of the hill from which it had fallen.

IF BUSINESS CYCLE data of many years ago can be taken at face value, the U.S. economic climate has been gradually warming. As recessionary winters have become shorter and milder, so have the expansionary summers become longer. Thus, the 22 American recessions from 1854 to 1948 averaged 21 months in duration, while all but three ran in excess of 10 months. However, the nine recessions from 1948 to date had an average span of 11 months, and none lasted for more than 16 months. In consequence, however, expansions have not also become stronger. The theory of "secular stagnation," so popular in the early 1940s and so irrelevant beginning in the late 1940s, has been vindicated on this one count, at least. The annual rate of real growth in the American economy has averaged only 1.8 percent in the 1990s to date. It is a weaker showing than the 2.8 percent registered in the 1980s, the 3.2 percent in the 1970s (stagflation, malaise, and all), and the 4.4 percent in the 1960s.

Why this persistent loss of economic energy? Crisis suppression is one underappreciated source of weakness. What ails the country is not only the quality of its expansions but also the caliber of its recessions. A more purposeful kind of slump might, perhaps, contribute to a heartier grade of prosperity. Adjustments that now drag on for years could take place in months or in fiscal quarters. Nobody can doubt that economic expansions serve a good and constructive purpose. It is the bad times that need more attention.

"Where economic growth is slow and calm," Juglar pronounced in 1889, "crises are less noticeable and very short; where it is rapid or feverish, violent and deep depressions upset all business for a time. It is necessary to choose one or the other of these conditions, and the latter, in spite of the risks which accompany it, still appears the more favorable."

Not to the twentieth century, which has seen for itself, as Juglar did not, the Great Depression of the 1930s. That event alone would disprove the proposition that a severe downturn must bring forth a brisk upturn. Certainly, in America, the 1930s did not. "The present generation of economists," wrote Schumpeter in 1942, "has witnessed not only a world-wide depression of unusual severity and duration but also a subsequent period of halting and unsatisfactory recovery." "Halting and unsatisfactory" might also describe the worldwide economic recovery of the past few years, in Europe, Japan, and the United States alike.

Schumpeter's generation of economists included the giants of the Austrian school, a contingent that congregated in Vienna before the birth of Kurt Waldheim. Among its leading lights were Carl Menger, Eugen von Böhm-Bawerk, Ludwig von Mises, and Friedrich A. von Hayek, as well as the non-Austrians Knut Wicksell (a Swede) and Lionel Robbins (an Englishman). The Austrians (of all nationalities) proposed that the seeds of every downturn are sown in the preceding upturn. This fun-starved idea informs an insightful and illuminating body of cyclical thought, one that sheds considerable light on the millennium (a rare accomplishment in economic thought; will contemporary theorists speak so clearly to their great-grandchildren?).

We may all agree that people miscalculate. A vital Austrian observation was that investors err together. In the heat of the moment, they will build too many skyscrapers, semiconductor fabricating plants, shopping malls, or commercial aircraft. The weight of these white elephants—"malinvestments," or in the native tongue *Fehlanlagen*—reaches a critical mass during the downturn, depression, or crisis. Many projects stand unfinished, pending a return to prosperity. "We should always expect some mistakes to be made somewhere," noted Lionel Robbins in the error-rich year of 1934. "But in the absence of special information, we should expect a random distribution. We should not expect this peculiar cluster of errors."

In the Austrians' judgment, there is one principal source of collective error: interest rates. Set them too low and people will overreach. They will borrow to excess and, with every good intention, build the marginal, redundant capital project. Set them too high and people will underdo it. At what interest rate would people be led to do just enough and not one thing more? The Austrians had an answer: the rate at which the demand for loans exactly equals the supply of loans. That is, a rate of interest so well founded that, if set by the Federal Reserve, it would cause no disturbance in the general price level, either to the upside or to the downside. This is the "natural" rate.

Yet, as might be imagined, the natural rate is all too rarely the rate that an imperfect world actually gets. The rate it does get—the "money" rate, in Austrian nomenclature—is one often distorted by the policies of banks and central banks. If the money rate were set lower than the natural rate, the pace of credit creation would quicken: seeing that it paid to borrow—that the cost of credit was less than what might be earned on a new investment—corporations, partnerships, and sole proprietorships would apply for a loan.* If the discount persisted, borrowers and lenders would go

---

* In real life, there are many natural rates. Each is conceived by a fallible human being hazarding a guess about the future rate of return on capital. Like any good theory, the Austrian capital theory simplifies the world in order to try to explain it. It does not incorporate every important financial influence or contingency, but—such are its merits—it inspires creative thinking about non-interest-rate subjects. Concerning currency values, for example, an Austrian-minded observer may draw a parallel between a too-high central bank rate, on the one hand, and an overvalued foreign exchange rate, on the other. Each is a macroeconomic depressant.

too far. They would jointly create too much credit. Many useful and necessary things would thereby be financed, but also many dubious ones. Prices would rise, and white elephants would proliferate. The upswing would continue only so long as the banks continued to finance it. On the day the lending stopped, so would the boom.

Wilhelm Röpke, although not, strictly speaking, a member of the Austrian school (his economics genus is that of German neoliberal), helped to advance the Austrian capital theory by the clarity of his exposition. A political refugee from Adolf Hitler who, in the mid-1930s, alighted neither in Geneva nor in New York but in Istanbul, Röpke observed that there was more than one way to engineer a credit expansion. "A credit inflation . . . ," he wrote in *Crises and Cycles* in 1936, a work made accessible to English-speaking readers by the translation of Vera C. Smith, "can very well arise by the fact that the banks leave their interest rate unchanged or do not raise it far enough at a moment when the equilibrium rate in the economic system—which is only a fictitious figure reflecting roughly the average rate of profits anticipated from capital investment—has risen. This is, however, exactly what regularly happens in the boom period. If at the commencement of the boom, the profit expectations of the economic system rise but the banks maintain their previous rate for credit advances or do not raise it sufficiently, then the automatic consequence is an increase in the demand for credit, owing to the widening of the gap between the rate of interest and profits on capital."

This very process was acted out in America in the early 1990s, as the "profit expectations of the economic system" rose—one sign was that stock prices rose—whereas money rates fell. One downward influence on money interest rates was speculation itself. Already, as the 1990–91 recession was ending, money rates were lower than the expected return on capital in the workaday world; businessmen and businesswomen were thereby encouraged to borrow. That they did not immediately avail themselves of the opportunity was a sign that they had not recovered their courage. Also, and more inflammably, money rates were lower than the prevailing rate of return available in short-dated Treasury notes. In the early 1990s, as we shall get around to exploring further, people were able to borrow at a low overnight interest rate and invest at a higher, longer-term interest rate. They borrowed at the federal funds rate (or a first cousin, the overnight repurchase rate) and invested the proceeds of their loans in government securities. As in 1958, they could borrow virtually every dollar they invested. All in all, the 1991–93 bull bond market was a faithful reenactment of the 1958 speculation but with a vastly larger cast of characters set upon a larger stage, the actors throwing around hundreds of billions of dollars instead of the Eisenhower-era tens of millions. Thus, the structure of interest rates in the early 1990s was enticingly low. In the first place, the natural rate was above the money rate. In the second place, the financial rate* was above the money rate.

Even if businesspeople were slow to resume borrowing, speculators were not. Bidding up bond prices, they simultaneously offered down yields. Thus, they themselves became a force for lower interest rates, perhaps as potent a force in 1991 and 1992 as the Federal Reserve itself.

What is wrong with such a festive and profitable state of affairs? Röpke did not condemn every case of monetary accommodation out of hand. Indeed, to combat high unemployment attendant on depressions, there was nothing else to do except to push down interest rates and promote the resumption of lending and borrowing. To which we may add that credit is a lubricant, an accelerator, and a necessity. Immoderate consumption brings unwanted and painful side effects, of course: inflation, for example, and (a subtler problem) distortion of the structure of production. The characteristic distortion introduced by mispriced credit is excessive investment in capital goods. The Austrians described this trap as the misconceived "deepening" of the productive process, that is, the overbuilding of tools, plant, and equipment. Without a shot of monetary stimulus, Röpke postulated, no disruption of the productive process would occur. In the Austrians' idea of a state of nature, every investment undertaken voluntarily out of saving would be matched by a decrease in consumption. Buying 500 shares of Microsoft, for instance, a person would refrain from buying a new car. In the world as we know it—a

---

* Is there room for one more piece of jargon? If so, let the *financial rate* be defined as that rate of interest prevailing on short-dated government securities.

world in which the Federal Reserve is trying to get the economic ball rolling, or credit-card companies are calling American consumers at home at dinnertime to remind them not to forget to borrow—an investor might buy Microsoft stock and borrow the price of a car and get away for a weekend in the Bahamas, all at once. Nor would that be the end of it. Continued monetary stimulus would tend to raise the price of our investor's stock, causing a rise in his or her self-esteem. The investor may reflect upon his or her impending wealth and, in the context of this strongly felt financial destiny, wonder: *Of what consequence is a small loan?* The psychological stimulus of a prolonged bull market might (other things being the same) prompt more spending and borrowing, a virtuous cycle that would presently produce one key problem. That is, the price of a car (or of other consumer goods) would rise in relation to producers' goods. Those whose incomes failed to keep up with the rise in prices would be forced to consume less.

This part of the Austrian dialectic has been overtaken by the VISA card. If, in old Vienna, interest rates mainly influenced the structure of production, in contemporary America they also influence the patterns of consumption. Insofar as a central bank subsidizes lending and borrowing in 1996, it also gives a lift to shopping.

But far more remarkable than the partial obsolescence of the Austrian model is its continued vitality. Thus, the elegant theory of the natural rate, conceived in the days of the slide rule, allowed a latter-day Austrian practitioner to understand the dynamics of the boom in computer investment and to anticipate its probable windup.

Similarly, Austrian theory has shed a helpful, unconventional light on the persistent lack of reported price inflation. The 1990s, like the 1920s, are innovative, and the 1990s, also like the 1920s, are disinflationary. So innovative was the decade of the 1920s, in fact, as Röpke and others observed, that prices might well have fallen. The inflation issue was not so much about the stability of prices as about their integrity. Did they or did they not convey accurate information? Acting on them, would investors and consumers make the right choices? Or, misled, would they perpetrate the "malinvestments" that weigh so heavily on one and all after the boom ends? A central bank could take no pride in price stability as that idea is conventionally defined. A perfectly stable Consumer Price Index might mask a distortion in the relationship of prices within the index. As for the 1920s, the Austrian theorists wrote, so great were the strides in production that prices actually should have declined. That they did not was the proof of an overly lenient monetary policy. From 1923 to 1929, the broad-based money supply, M-2, rose by 27 percent; bank loans and investments expanded by 35 percent. Wrote Röpke:

> A rise in the general price level did not occur in spite of this enormous credit expansion, for the reason that at the same time the prices of commodities were being pressed downwards by the fall in costs due to the progress of technique and organization. In other words: if at that time enormous amounts of borrowing had not taken place, prices would have fallen. The fall of average production costs in industry and agriculture realized in that period was so large that a rise in the price level was all the time prevented in spite of the fact that additional credits were always being pumped into circulation. The opinion that the credit inflation would thereby be rendered harmless turned out to be fatal. . . . The important point is then not that the general price level rises, but simply the circumstance that additional quantities of money and credit are supplied to the economic system, calling forth dangerous disturbances in the structure of production.

So we may see, as the Austrians saw, that the seeds of every bust are sown in the preceding boom. It is a cinch that Ludwig von Mises, Wilhelm Röpke, Friedrich A. von Hayek, or Knut Wicksell, if they had read the rueful literature on the unoccupied New York skyscrapers in the 1930s, would have felt that they understood. What drove the Starretts and the Adlers was, technically speaking, an inflation-inducing subsidy in the money rate of interest. Naturally, this led to an enlargement of investment, a process that continued until the lending stopped, at which point the economy was left with a brilliant new skyline, marred only by the fact that it was unpaid for. The rub was that a good deal of the new investment was undertaken to serve not the economy as it was then constituted, but the economy as it was expected to grow in the years ahead. Thus, the mere lack of future expansion was enough to nullify the profit forecasts on which the decision to borrow money had depended.

What then? A depression, of course. Slumps follow booms, because booms cause slumps. If one were bound and determined to eliminate the downside, one would first have to prevent the upside. In the Austrian construct, the cardinal flaw of prosperity is the "elongation" of productive processes. Thus, the economic purpose of a slump is to shorten, or—a nontechnical term—squish, the structure back to the appropriate length, redirecting labor and capital out of the overdeveloped industries and back to the needful ones.

WE MAY BRING this discussion down to earth by considering that salient boomlike phenomenon of real estate speculation. The descendants of the Adlers and Starretts in the 1980s were scattered near and far. Builders and bankers went overboard in Japan, Britain, Canada, Australia, the United States, and most of the Nordic countries. Short-term interest rates, adjusted for inflation, were high: an odd thing at first glance, inasmuch as it is beckoningly low market rates of interest that are known to incite overinvestment.

However, there was one important offsetting tendency in the 1980s: a general, worldwide relaxation in the terms and conditions of lending. The Austrians wrote in a time of more or less austere banking practices. The liberalizing spirit of the 1980s brought with it an inclination of lending officers to say yes. Then, too, as the Austrians taught, the level of market interest rates must be considered in relation to the natural rate, or the expected rate of profit.* One of the leading contemporary American lenders to growing busi-

---

* Admittedly, there is something circular about this idea. Almost every business borrows in the expectation of making a profit. That is, in Austrian argot, people borrow because the natural rate is profitably above the money rate. If so, it would stand to reason that the best and simplest test of the element of subsidy in monetary policy is the volume of business-related borrowing. The more borrowing, one might infer, the greater the subsidy. Similarly, the weaker the rate of borrowing, the lower the subsidy. An outright shrinkage in the volume of business borrowing, as occurred in 1991 and 1992, would suggest that the natural rate is lower than the money rate, i.e., that monetary policy is punitive. However, this is not quite satisfying. Business loans have their own cyclical ebb and flow. Does a rise in the demand for inventory finance constitute

ness, David Gladstone, chairman of Allied Capital Corp., Washington, D.C., has found that there is almost no rate at which an entrepreneur will not borrow. The enthusiasm of the fledgling capitalist is almost irrepressible.

Be that as it may, the real estate boom proceeded until the money ran out. What followed, true to form, was a depression (the euphemistic "recession" fails to convey the depth of the losses to developers and their lenders). Individual real estate operators filed for bankruptcy protection, but to the economy fell the job of redeploying labor out of real estate speculation and writing off the sunk capital.

In Austrian terms, it was an excellent depression, inflicting damage only incidentally to the process of wringing out distortions in the structure of production. Röpke and his colleagues were at pains to distinguish between good depressions and bad. The Great Depression, for instance, according to Röpke, was a good depression gone bad. It got off to a good, wholesome start, but veered off into wanton destruction. He suggested matter-of-factly that the reason for this disaster was the Hoover administration's attempt to thwart a necessary and inevitable deflation by propping up the boom-time structure of wages and prices. Röpke delivered this verdict with the air of a man repeating the obvious. The current authorized interpretation of these events, of course, is very far from that. Rather than doing too much, the historical consensus of opinion has it, Hoover did too little, and that too late. (The late Murray Rothbard, an American economist in the same Austrian tradition, developed the unconventional argument in his provocative history, *America's Great Depression.* Instead of being a paragon of laissez-faire, Rothbard showed, Hoover in truth anticipated the Roosevelt New

---

certain evidence of a misalignment of rates? Or is it merely a sign that the business expansion has reached a certain point of maturity?

Nor does the Austrian emphasis on business borrowing address the commanding role of mortgage and consumer debt in the contemporary capital markets. Consumers borrow for any number of reasons, but not because the money rate is below the natural rate. Installment interest rates, in fact, have chronically been in the mid- and high teens. People borrow on their credit cards because they need the money; they borrow to buy a house or—a more up-to-the-minute example—a few thousand shares of Micron Technology.

Deal. By the time Rothbard had got around to uttering this thesis in 1963, it had become heretical.)

"The severity of the decline," wrote Gottfried Haberler in 1937, "is no longer believed to vary rigidly with the degree of the structural maladjustments which gave rise to it. There is no longer the same confidence in the inevitability or the curative function of the depression." If the Austrians' belief in the existence of a purely salutary depression was shaken, it was no wonder. Bankruptcy had lost whatever friends it might have claimed in the days when many fewer people were bankrupt. So, too, with child labor, foreclosure auctions, bank runs, bankruptcy, and mass unemployment: it was harder and harder to make the case that suffering was the handmaiden of economic betterment. Still, Röpke tried to draw clear, unemotional distinctions. "In a crisis," he reiterated, "what has been sown during the boom has to be reaped; a readjustment of the disjointed economic system cannot be avoided." Yet there was no guarantee that a curative deflation would not pick up its own momentum, becoming a locomotive running in reverse. Indeed, it had done so in America only a few years before. "Instead of restoring the economic equilibrium disrupted by the boom," he went on, "the depression may lead, after a while, to a new disequilibrium which, caused by the process of the chronic depression itself, has nothing to do with the old set of disturbing factors."

"Secondary depression" was Röpke's name for a runaway, futile deflation. The great question was how to distinguish that kind of slump from the constructive kind. Alas, Röpke admitted, there was no foolproof method. One sign of a secondary depression was its excessive length, although not eating for even one day will seem excessive to the one not doing the eating. "More conclusive," the economist ventured, "is the symptom of persistent mass unemployment, which may be taken as an indication that the primary depression has quite outgrown the dimensions imposed by its function of readjustment, and most conclusive of all will be the fact that the depression has also engulfed the industries producing consumption goods."

In the waning years of the twentieth century, we may be sure, no such collapse would be allowed to occur. (Röpke himself, who became an influential adviser to Minister Ludwig Erhard and one of the creators of Germany's postwar "Social Market Economy," would have opposed it himself, to the death.) It was to forestall the possibility of even a primary depression in the United States that the Employment Act of 1946 and the Full Employment and Balanced Growth Act of 1978 were passed into law. As for a secondary depression, the surest sign of its coming would not be mass unemployment or the bankruptcy of a leading consumer products' company, but the overthrow of the federal government.

HAS THIS SUPPRESSION of deflationary tendencies come without cost? The answer is no. How could it have? However, credit must go to the United States for evolving creative solutions to the unintended side effects of its own crisis-suppressing policies. To a striking degree, structural adjustments have been carried out one by one, rather than in the context of a general depression. For instance, in need of shrinkage in the mid-1980s, the Oil Patch was duly shrunk. The Rust Belt underwent a "rolling recession," which was followed by a rollicking recovery.* There was a rolling depression in commercial real estate and a chronic, headlong deflation in computer prices. (Prices fell as innovation raced on.) Downsizing came to Wall Street in 1994 and 1995, as it had earlier come to banking and to so many nonfinancial fields, including the cold war industry. In the teeth of rising global competition, American wage rates did not recover in the post-1991 expansion as they had done in the past. However, thanks to the operation of a free labor market, new jobs were created even as old ones were eliminated. Endings and beginnings together pushed through the same dynamic revolving door. "The churn," as the Federal Reserve Bank of Dallas redesignated Joseph Schumpeter's process of creative destruction, "continues during an expan-

---

* Late in 1995, *Forbes* magazine, taking note of labor shortages in Flint, Michigan, backdrop for the anti–General Motors documentary of 1989, *Roger and Me*, proposed that a new, feel-good movie be produced, *Restructuring and Me.* "It would demonstrate," the magazine said, "that efficient, profitable factories create more dependable jobs than do inefficient, unprofitable factories." Also, one might add, that a cheap dollar exchange rate is a powerful lubricant for export sales.

sion, although its most visible effect—job layoffs—is far more common during recessions, when industries come under stress. . . . The process frees labor in declining industries to produce new and better goods in new industries. This facet of the churn goes on almost invisibly as new jobs are added, a few at a time, as thousands of new enterprises in areas that are geographically dispersed."

All of these necessary accommodations—to the information age, to the age of one big, integrated, global financial market, and to a brand-new geopolitical map—took place without a domestic depression, benign or malignant. The capitalist system of the late 1980s and early 1990s was a paragon of market-driven adaptability, with one conspicuous exception: the Bush administration, with help from the Federal Reserve Board, intervened to suppress the nascent crisis of banking and debt.

As we have seen, an axiom of the modern economy is that prices might be inflated but never deflated. Debts might be amassed but never (in the context of a national depression) wiped out. Big banks might be allowed to overlend but never to collapse; certainly, failure must never take the form of a financial chain reaction, as occurred in 1933 or 1907. The structure of production might change—as indeed it must—and the financial system might evolve, but the Federal Reserve must defend and protect its banking charges, and if a neighboring country should suffer a financial crisis that seems to threaten the U.S. economy, as Mexico did in 1995, that country should be temporarily annexed, in the monetary sense.

Even under the classical gold standard, central banks sometimes served as lenders of last resort, and secondary depressions were unpopular with some of the very theorists who found no objection to primary ones. However, the welfare state of credit, conceived in the 1930s and still building in the 1990s, represents a profound change in the scale of intervention. What is new since Hoover is the widely shared assumption that the government ought to try to keep the macroeconomic thermostat at room temperature. Contemporary banking policy is dedicated to checking the recurrence not only of 1931–33, the tragic years of secondary depression, but also of 1930, the year, according to Austrian doctrine, in which Herbert Hoover inadvertently put the "Great" in Great Depression, and even of 1920–21, the very model of the short-lived but productive depression.

"The belief in the desirability of central-bank organization is universal," wrote Vera Smith, a nonbeliever in that arrangement, in 1936. The ideological transformation of the past 60 or so years has been nearly complete—capitalism now advancing, collectivism retreating—but Smith's observation is no less valid at this writing than it was at the time of the New Deal. Belief in the desirability of central-bank organization is now somehow more than universal. Paul A. Volcker, former Federal Reserve chairman, remarked in the spring of 1994 that central banking had never been more popular, and he admitted that he was puzzled by the fact. (What he did not say was that central-bank prestige was approximately at its nadir when he arrived at the Fed in 1979. Thanks in large part to his own policies, it has been increasing ever since. One was left to wonder if the faith of 1994 was as exaggerated as the skepticism of 1979.)

Central banking was indeed in a bull market, but its deeds were less dazzling than its press. True, inflation was under siege in virtually all the industrialized countries, but a student was led to wonder if that was a thoroughly wholesome development. In 1992, the European Rate Mechanism, a contrivance for coordinating the management of European currencies, went to smash. In 1993, speculators bid up prices on the world's bond markets, but in 1994—hurt by rising short-term interest rates in America—they sold them down again, in a heap. Smith had observed that central banking under the gold standard was governed by objective rules. However, under the newfangled system, rules were replaced by discretion, a style that, at the Federal Reserve Board in the 1990s, seemed very close to guesswork. There was almost nothing that the Fed was not expected to do. It was held accountable for economic growth (not too much and not too little), the rate of inflation, the level of interest rates, the solvency of the nation's banks, and, in conjunction with the Treasury Department, the state of the dollar and the complementary condition of the Mexican peso. Looking back over the 1920s, Wilhelm Röpke had contended that stability in consumer prices was not an end-all. It could be (and in 1920s' America, in his judgment, was) a mask for distortions introduced by easy money—in the relationships between consumption and saving on the one hand, and between present consumption and future investment projects on the other. In other words, perfection as the central bankers defined perfection was nothing more than fresh paint over cracked plaster. To be sure, that was another world—prices were allowed to fall and banks to fail, for better or worse—but the analysis has applicability in the 1990s, a time of deflationary cracks that have also been obscured by central-bank policies. Vera Smith understood how this seeming boon to humanity could bring about new problems. "It is not unlikely," she wrote, understanding matters, "that the bolstering up of banking systems by their governments is a factor which makes for instability."

THE YEAR 1920 saw prices leap, then crash—not only stock and bond prices, which are expected to move around in a sporting, volatile fashion, but also the prices of agricultural commodities, clothing, and everyday necessities. Much to the gratification of the architects of the Federal Reserve System, there was no money panic or generalized bank run, as in 1907, but in other respects the disaster was everything that the Federal had been created to prevent. Yet the deflationary crash under Warren G. Harding should not be condemned for that reason alone. Foremost among its admirable and redeeming features was the speed with which the economy adjusted to severe dislocation. In the 1980s, America was years in weaning itself from the consequences of the inflation of the 1970s. In the 1920s, the nation was able to purge itself of the inflationary toxins of World War I in a matter of fiscal quarters. (To be sure, country banking and agriculture suffered for years on end, but the urban economy recovered in relatively short order.) Comparisons to the plodding economic gait of 1989–96 are not entirely flattering to the latter day.

The monetary drama of 1920 encompassed the industrialized world, and the Japanese experience complemented the American one. Seeking to mitigate the deflationary damage of its wartime boom, Japan instead compounded it, just as it would do in similar, if not identical, circumstances in the 1990s.

What commends the 1920–21 episode to students of financial and cyclical excess is, in the first place, its universality. Boom-and-bust is one of the great capitalist themes, fully the equal of work-and-save and greed-and-fear. Wartime shortages, and expansive wartime fiscal and monetary policies, had lifted agricultural prices, industrial commodity prices, retail prices, and speculative spirits in the United States. Collapse duly followed. From peak to trough (i.e., from January 1920 to September 1921), the gross national product declined by 4 percent in inflation-adjusted terms. Wholesale prices, however, fell by no less than 56 percent, most of the decline taking place in only six months. There was a staggering reversal in fiscal policy. In the war, the government had spent billions more than it took in; starting in late 1919, it began to take in more than it spent. ("Within the space of little more than a year . . . ," wrote George Soule in *Prosperity Decade,* "the American economy had to absorb a net decline in purchasing power stemming from governmental sources that amounted to approximately one quarter of the total national income.")

In May 1920, the department-store merchant John Wana-maker, sensing a turn in the tide, cut his prices by 20 percent. Wanamaker's competitors gasped. Up until that moment, inflation had been the ruling state of mind in American retailing. Now there was the possibility of deflation, which indeed promptly material-ized. (True to form, economists and intellectuals were taken aback by the change. A poll of economists, bankers, and government offi-cials in the *New York Evening Post* at year-end 1919 had found deep-rooted optimism. In June 1920, a month or so after the deflation had begun in earnest, an unsigned editorial in *The New Republic* as-serted that there would be no deflation; the tone of the essay strongly suggested omniscience.) Commodity prices, more sensitive than retail prices to changes in the monetary and cyclical environ-ment, registered their sharpest plunge in American history. One index fell to 142 from 227 in only 13 months.

The cost of the break in the tissue of war-induced inflation was enormous. Labor relations were poisoned, politics were radicalized, and record numbers of businesses were consigned to bankruptcy. Farmers were caught by the drop in cotton prices, and merchants by the collapse in the value of their inventory. Banks not so fortunate as to belong to the Federal Reserve System failed in near-record numbers. In 1921, the unemployment rate hit 11.7 percent. "It is not a pleasant thing to see well-meaning but relatively ineffective men lose their capital and lose control of their companies and see their companies put into stronger hands through bankruptcy and informal reorganization," wrote Benjamin M. Anderson, long-time economist at the Chase National Bank (later the Chase Manhattan) of the 1920–21 slump. "And it was certainly not a pleasant thing to see 4,754,000 workmen unemployed, as was the case in 1921. But there are many worse things." There was not a worse thing for Harry S Truman, then a Kansas City (Missouri) haberdasher. Any chance that Truman might adopt an open-minded view on the uses of failure in capitalism was materially reduced when Truman & Jacobson, the clothing business of which he was a partner, failed in April 1922. The closeout sale, held almost two years after John Wanamaker had had his revelation, featured fixtures, cases, and lighting as well as ties, shirts, and belts, all sharply reduced. If, as Truman biographer Robert H. Ferrell writes, the ordeal made the future president a fiscal conservative, it also undoubtedly made him a business-cycle liberal. The depression had taken his money and his optimism. What "worse things" could an economic historian have in mind?

The Great Depression was one. The chronic post–World War I stagnation in Britain and Japan was another. The strength of the American economy, as Anderson persuasively argued, was its resilience. Confronted by the abrupt end of a false, war-bloated boom, lenders and borrowers combined to effect the necessary, painful adjustments. "Businessmen and bankers both did a very thorough job in cleaning up the weak spots and in making readjustments in prices, costs, methods and the proportions of industrial activity," wrote Anderson, who was there. "By early spring 1921 the credit weak spots were mapped and charted. The banks knew what businesses could survive and what businesses must go under or at all events have a readjustment of their financial setup. It was clear that the general credit situation was impregnably strong, and that the credit system would survive the shock."

That it did, even if A. Barton Hepburn, head of the Chase National, lubricated the natural processes by organizing a secret pool in December 1920 to support the stock market. ("The term *pool* is one which suggests a great deal of iniquity," wrote Anderson, a Chase employee now slipping on his company necktie, "but the present writer is unregenerate enough to believe that this was an act of financial statesmanship.") "Costs were rapidly readjusted," Anderson's narrative continued. "Raw materials, of course, had fallen drastically. Rentals were in many cases readjusted, often by voluntary negotiations. . . . Wages declined, although nothing like so much as commodity prices."

One reason the work of the 1920–21 depression was as brisk and orderly as it was, Anderson contended, was the unique organization of the American banking system. Some 20,000 banks, most small, each obliged to meet its obligations or else, saw to it that unsuccessful experiments in business enterprise like Harry Truman's were brought to a timely (and devastating and heartrending) end. "It was not possible for us to maintain stale and hopeless situations by means of bank credit," wrote Anderson. "Each bank had to clean up in order to keep itself solvent. Certain of the great British banks, as late as 1925, had still uncollected loans to the cotton industry in Manchester, carried over from 1920, and other commitments of a similar sort, stale and frozen. The forbearance of the British banks had not saved these industries. It had, on the other hand, prevented their passing into stronger hands and into the hands of more alert and flexible management. It had prevented their freeing themselves through bankruptcy from impossible financial burdens. It had prevented their becoming effective again."

True, although precious little gratitude was expressed to the forces of supply and demand. "Notwithstanding [the] absence in 1920 of the spectacular phenomena of a financial crisis," recorded Alexander Dana Noyes, a financial journalist of the day, "the scope of forced economic readjustment which followed was possibly wider than in any American 'panic period' since 1873." And the disappointment was surely keener. Working people had gladly acclimated themselves to the higher scale of wartime wages, farmers to the brilliant, inflated crop prices, and bankers and industrialists to the fetching proposition that the new Federal Reserve Board would make booms and busts obsolete. Now it was back to the drawing board. Perhaps, many suggested, it would be better if the economic system were taken apart and put back together again, but without so strong a reliance on the profit motive.

UNDERSTANDABLY, the blessings of the downside are appreciated most of all in retrospect, but the American system owed much to the respect it paid to failure. Less so the British and—of particular contemporary interest—the Japanese systems. A nonbelligerent, Japan had gaily ridden the inflationary wartime boom. Its economy had grown by leaps and bounds, but so, too, had its inflation, both the conventional and Austrian varieties. Japan's inflation, indeed, was even greater than that of its main trading partners. From 1914 through 1919, its bank deposits rose by almost threefold. The bubble was burst in April 1920 by the failure of a single Osaka bank. In the deflationary aftermath, common stocks broke, and the price of a bale of silk fell to $1,800 from $2,500. The Japanese authorities, anticipating the policies of the 1990s, intervened to restore what they might have viewed as sanity. "The government," reported *The Economist* reprovingly, "proposes to throw some 200,000,000 yen on the market for the relief of the stock exchanges and exchange banks, but this, it is feared, will only tend to keep up abnormal prices as well as promote further speculation."

In consequence, perhaps, the average Japanese wholesale price index fell by only 20 percent from 1920 and 1921. To realign Japan's price level with the rest of the world's, by one historian's reckoning, prices would have had to fall by another 20 percent (no doubt causing the ruination of many more people, businesses, and banks). But at least, wrote Hugh T. Patrick, a student of the period, "it would have cleared the slate for a renewed emphasis on growth." Many Japanese must have been grateful with the policy of half measures that the government did adopt. The trouble, however, was that Japan (not alone among nations, then or later) liked its bank credit. G. C. Allen, in his *Short Economic History of Modern Japan,* described the institutional setting: "The expansion of business during the war and the post-war boom had been made possible by the heavy extension of credit on the part of the ordinary banks of the country. The collapse of the boom in 1920 meant the 'freezing' of many of these advances, and further deflation would have increased the crop of industrial and banking failures to the point of economic disaster." So violent was the collapse that it stunned American observers.* Up until that moment, the Japanese and American stock markets had been moving in tandem. "The government," Allen continued, "reluctant to push things through to a crisis, preferred to temporize rather than to incur the social consequences of a violent, deliberate deflation. Moreover, it had to take account not merely of the general public reaction to such a policy, but also of the influence of powerful organized groups," namely, the *zaibatsu,* or "money cliques." If the public was frightened, it was no wonder: in only five or six weeks, the prices of staple Japanese commodities had fallen between 17 and 35 percent.

Heavy debts, an overvalued yen (the government had seen to that as well), and a suppressed deflation: when the Tokyo-Yokohama earthquake struck in September 1923, the Japanese financial system was not at its best. The yen exchange rate, at least, was rectified by that disaster; the currency was allowed to depreciate. Altogether, the country needed more credit, and this the authorities presently delivered. "The Bank of Japan adopted an easy credit policy," Allen recorded, "and, in order to relieve financial institutions whose loans had become frozen as a result of the earthquake, it was authorized to discount specified bills (earthquake bills) under a government guarantee. . . . Further, the Industrial Bank of Japan and the Hypothec Bank made loans on easy terms to facilitate reconstruction. Government expenditure

* And, on the evidence, confused them, too. AFFAIRS IN JAPAN MYSTIFY WALL ST., was the headline over a story in *The New York Times* on April 20, 1920, about the deflationary set-to. The *Times,* which conducted its research from New York, cited rumor and a week-old cable to the New York branch of a Japanese bank. The second-day follow-up FINANCIAL PANIC SHAKES JAPAN was given over, in part, to retracting the factual errors of the first day's story. As the main source for this installment was a State Department communiqué, the story was datelined Washington, D.C., a listening post no closer to the scene of the action than was midtown Manhattan. If the world has become no wiser in the intervening 75 years, it has certainly become better informed.

also increased as a result of the earthquake, and this was financed mainly by borrowing."

On the other hand, the world was bound and determined to reclaim at least a portion of the prewar rigor. In 1925, Great Britain returned to the gold standard at the old exchange rate,* and Japan, an admirer of British monetary institutions and a gold-standard[†] nation itself from 1897 until 1917 (it suspended convertibility just days after America did), proceeded to follow. In 1925, in preparation for an eventual return to the old money, the Japanese government took steps to raise taxes and reduce expenditures. These policies, bracing and very British, had the deflationary effect of boosting the yen exchange rate and depressing exports. The silk interests were hard hit, and so, in short order, were the banks, some of which were still overburdened with the financial debris of the preceding boom. Confidence in the banking system did not survive a springtime 1927 debate in the Diet over the necessity of postponing settlement of some still-outstanding earthquake bills. Only about 10 percent of the 2.1 billion yen's worth of this issuance was still unpaid, but the prospects of recovering this hardened kernel of debt were dim.

Among the top repositories of the bad loans was the Bank of Taiwan, a semiofficial institution that held the banknote-issuing monopoly for what was then a Japanese colony. Like so many other banks that have strayed from the straight and narrow, both before and since, the Taiwan bank had passed through a growth spurt (venturing from Taiwan to lend extensively in Japan itself, especially to Suzuki Shōten, a sprawling company with interests in, among other deflation-prone commodities, sugar). It had funded this expansion not with stable deposits, but with call loans,

---

* Not the classical, prewar version of the gold standard, but a "gold exchange" standard, in which financial adjustments between trading partners might be postponed and in which the public was not allowed to exchange its government-issue money for gold coins.

[†] Japan had been on its own gold-exchange standard even before the general slippage in rigor after World War I. Instead of taking delivery of its foreign exchange earnings in the form of gold bars or coins, it invested them, or some of them, in the form of short-dated assets in New York or London.

credits from banks that could be, and presently would be, summarily withdrawn. Not only did the bank borrow short; also, fatally, it lent long.

Bank examinations were little used in Japan at that time, and the law imposed no limit on how much a bank might lend to a single borrower. Unit, or one-office banks, undiversified as to both assets and liabilities, were common, and there was no government deposit insurance plan. There was, indeed, no government beginning mid-April 1927, following the resignation of the cabinet of Reijiro Wakatsuki to protest the privy council's rejection of the prime minister's request to organize a rescue of the Bank of Taiwan. Now the public wanted cash, and only cash. The Bank of Taiwan could not accommodate its breathless depositors. Neither could the giant Fifteen Bank, nicknamed the "Aristocratic Bank" by dint of the lofty birth of its owners. All told, 12 banks failed in only four days. It was the worst upset in Japanese financial history.

The panic brought about a temporary healing of the body financial. Losses that had not been admitted to years before were recognized and dealt with. "Unsound industrial and trading concerns were weeded out," Allen wrote, "or passed, after decapitalization, under new and more efficient control; many of the Suzuki interests, for instance, passed to Mitsui. The same is true of the banking system. The 18 months after June 1927 were a period of consolidation, during which the number of ordinary banks was reduced from 1,359 to 1,030. This period saw the beginning of efforts to improve the efficiency in the textile industries which were later to bear fruit."

Now the forces of financial orthodoxy took control. With the return to power of the Minseito Party in the summer of 1929, Junnosuke Inouye, a former Bank of Japan governor—he had run the bank during the 1927 panic—assumed the nation's finance portfolio. In America, 40 Wall Street and the Dow Jones Industrial Average were peaking simultaneously; in Japan, Inouye pressed for a prompt return to the gold standard. Japan had never returned the yen to convertibility, as the leading Western nations had done by 1928. Inouye, an old-fashioned European-style liberal devoted to balanced budgets, the gold standard, and the sanctity of financial promises—the kind of Japanese of whom a Morgan banker could say, approvingly, he "spoke the same language"—insisted that the restoration of the yen to its old-time value of almost 50¢ (U.S.$) would pay handsome dividends.

Half of the Japanese population was then engaged in farming (silk was Japan's top export), but Inouye rejected the claims that a deflationary monetary policy would go hard on them. A "depreciating exchange," he said, lacking the common touch, "while it means increased business for the man who is selling silk abroad, goes heavily against the man who is getting raw cotton from abroad, and if it goes against the latter, it means, gentlemen, higher tailors' bills for you and me."

In truth, not many Japanese were then in a position to have a tailor's bill to pay, and many fewer would be so fortunate during the Inouye tenure as finance minister. Sound money and free markets were not, and had not been, a Japanese policy staple. When, late in the nineteenth century, the occidental world had suffered through its gold-standard deflation, Japan had enjoyed a lilting, silver-backed prosperity. When, in 1897, after its war with China, Japan did join the greater gold-standard family, the occidental world was entering one of its periodic inflationary cycles; Japan participated in that, too. Indeed, as the American financial analyst David Asher has written, "The Japanese economy had been built on a platform of protectionism and inflation." As for Inouye, he rejected this statist tradition in favor of the doctrines for so long espoused by Anglo-Saxon financiers. The canons of this orthodoxy have been endlessly debated, but there can be no dispute about the finance minister's market timing. It was unlucky.

American prosperity, which was just then ending, had been the silk market's best friend, and the robust state of world trade had sustained the Japanese merchant marine. The stock market crash soon reduced the American demand for silk (as it would, at length, for cotton and burlap), and the Smoot-Hawley tariff, death knell to world trade, holed the market in merchant shipping. On January 11, 1930, only six months before Herbert Hoover signed the infamous tariff legislation, Inouye's long-cherished dream came true: the yen was restored to the value of 45¢ (U.S.$), very near the 1917 rate. In effect, Japan undertook to roll back the price history of a dozen years, some of those years—1919 and 1920, for example—highly inflationary ones. It brought to mind a middle-aged man who tries to slip into his old Army uniform and button every button.

To prepare for the great day, the government reduced its expenditures and the Bank of Japan reduced its loans; to encourage the necessary shrinkage in costs, the government assisted industries that were (as the world has learned to say) downsizing. The wholesale price index fell by 6 percent in only six months. As it turned out, the decline had hardly begun.

"It is generally recognized," wrote Allen, "that Japanese prices before 1929 were too high in relation to American prices to make it possible for her to maintain dollar parity without exporting gold or borrowing abroad. Thus, even had the world prosperity continued after 1929, it is likely that some fall of domestic prices would have been necessary in order to maintain the yen at par. This fall would have placed a strain on the economic system, since price- and cost-relations had, for a long period, been consolidated at a level well above that in the rest of the world. The onset of the depression, just when the yen had been restored to par, and the consequent heavy fall in world prices, greatly increased the difficulties of adjustment." Now Japanese markets demonstrated a fearful flexibility on the downside. Silk prices fell by 50 percent in 1930; the overall Japanese wholesale price index dropped by 30 percent from 1929 to 1931. American wholesale prices, by contrast, declined by a slightly less wrenching 23 percent in the same period.

No sooner did Japan embrace the gold standard than Europe began to abandon it. Britain, Japan's monetary light and beacon, made its exit in September 1931. Inouye must have been heartsick. Japanese banks suffered immediate losses on their sterling deposits in London, and Japanese exporters faced stiff new competition in world markets from cheaper British merchandise. Was the yen really as good as gold? The world had reason to doubt it. In the brief span of months that Japan stood ready to exchange the yen for gold bullion, it lost more than half of its gold and foreign exchange. In December 1931, Japan stopped trying; the yen was set free to sink.

Inouye's personal humiliation was still not complete, however. What happened next was not collapse—an outcome that a patriotic Japanese hard-money man might have equitably borne—but rather an inflationary revival. "And on the following day," recorded the monetary historian Hiroshi Shinjo concerning the start of the nongold era, "the stock market showed such an abnormal rise in prices that the session was stopped." It was a full-throated celebration of everything that Inouye, 62 years old, and the Morgan Bank and the City of London regarded as unsound. On February 9, 1932, Inouye was shot dead by a member of the *Ketsumeidan*, or Blood Oath Association. The killer was a young rustic, a member of the peasantry for whom Inouye had come to represent a cruel and alien capitalism. Nor did the farmers monopolize national resentment. Small business owners could not bring themselves to believe that policies so gratuitously harmful were, in fact, going to be carried out.

A decade of ineffectual measures to quash the Japanese price level now gave way to a kind of anticipatory Keynesianism. In the decade of the 1920s, real Japanese economic growth averaged little more than 2 percent a year. The preceding decade had produced an average of 4.6 percent; the following one, that of the truculent 1930s, would generate an average of almost 6 percent. In relative terms—in comparison to what might have been as well as what preceded and followed—the Japanese economy in the 1920s scarcely made headway.

A new finance minister, Korekiyo Takahashi, octogenarian financier of the Russo-Japanese war of 1905, presided over a vast increase in government expenditures, almost all of them financed through borrowing and a sizable proportion earmarked for armaments. Interest rates were reduced, the yen was devalued, and credit was created. It was Takahashi's idea to pull up short of an outright inflation. In his judgment of where this might be, however, he collided with the militarists, who assassinated him in 1936. At the time of his death, the Japanese economy was humming, as both he and Inouye had intended it should, but the engine of growth was the coming Pacific war.

DO RECESSIONS PLAY A constructive role in the business cycle, always assuming that there is a business cycle? "Yes" is the correct, counterintuitive answer. Thus, it follows that some recessions are better than others and that the very finest may not necessarily be the shortest. On the contrary, a too-brief recession may not expunge the errors of the preceding up cycle. It might not force enough labor and capital out of the skyscraper construction or aircraft manufacturing businesses, for example, or enough banks out of the unsafe lending field. No less than an expansion, a recession might prove to be subpar, foreshortened, or unproductive. It is easy to see how a boom could be nipped in the bud by an act of state: war, tariff, taxes, inflation. No less, by the same logic, a recession might be prematurely cut short by a government's well-intended intervention; say, by an aggressive cut in interest rates just as the boom time's misshapen crop of *Fehlanlagen* is about to wiped out. A recession, we would have to conclude, should be purposeful, not any more brutal than it has to be but not any less, either.

It must be admitted that the theory of the silver lining has rarely been an electoral winner. Some politicians have caused recessions after their election, but almost invariably they promised prosperity beforehand. Patiently awaiting the correction of the collective economic error, a citizen is prone to vote for the candidate who promises to bring the adjustment to an early, possibly untimely, end. Wives and husbands of the maladjusting capitalists or the misallocated employees are particularly ill-disposed to vote a recession ticket, not believing that long-suffering is a more desirable state of being than the possession of a market-distorting government income. Could a boldly worded platform favoring the return of business depressions appeal to even a remnant of free thinkers?

Men and women of the world may doubt it. Certainly, no one brought it up as the recession of 1990 began. President Bush, choosing not to invoke the authority of the ancient economists, even the estimable Juglar, did not ask the nation to trust in the curative powers of a good (although not excessive) depression. As bank stocks fell, he did not propose that the process of credit contraction be allowed to proceed up to the point of diminishing returns, or that, one thing taken with another, the gradual phasing out of federal deposit insurance would go a long way to preventing the clustering of error so suspiciously endemic in modern banking systems. ". . . [I]t seems not improbable," Vera Smith observed while not running for office, "that the tendencies to misdirection are magnified by the form of the system, in particular that part of it which entrusts the determination of the volume of credit to a single authority, between which and the government there exist reciprocal tendencies toward paternalism." Just so: the chief executives of the government and of the Federal Reserve each wanted to keep his job.

Understandably, the Bush administration was inclined to favor the cyclical outcome that was even then taking form. The stock market, which peaked in July, would decline into the early autumn. Then it would stop going down and would resume going up, exploding in January 1991 along with hostilities in the Persian Gulf. By every conventional, non-Austrian measure, the recession was as good as a recession could be. In the five American downturns from 1957–58 through 1980–82, inventory investment had fallen by an average of 1.4 percent; in 1990–91, the decline amounted to just 0.7 percent. In the same five preceding recessions, final sales had fallen by 4.3 percent; in 1990–91, the decline came to only 2.2 percent. At low ebb in 1991, the U.S. unemployment rate was 7.1 percent, or 2.6 percentage points less than the annual rate generated in the worst postwar year, 1982.

Altogether, 1990–91 was an era of firsts. As a matter of course since 1945, the Federal Reserve had precipitated business downturns by raising short-term interest rates. As we have seen, the business of banking is grounded in the risk-fraught practice of borrowing short and lending long. By lifting short rates above long rates, the Fed could stymie new lending and therefore starve the economy of credit. What was different about the 1990–91 recession was that short-term interest rates did not peak, as they usually did, with the onset of the business expansion. Uniquely, they topped out a full 16 months before the peaking of growth. Up until this episode, short-term rates had crested no more than four months before the peak of the economy (as in 1960 and 1969). The early 1990s were different in that the agent inhibiting bank-credit expansion was not so much the Fed as the banks themselves. What caused them to expand more slowly (or in some cases to contract) was the state of their own balance sheets.*

Watching short-term interest rates, the shape of the yield curve, and the rise of the stock market, a form bettor was led to conclude that no recession was beginning, or could begin. In fact, it was not until the economy had actually begun to recede that the average economist got around to forecasting that it would, thus resembling a weather forecaster who predicts a rainstorm while standing under a dripping umbrella.

To the eclectic observer, each recession is different because each has its own apparent, proximate cause. Thus, the recession of 1990 was ascribed to war, the 1980 recession to a misunderstood presidential address on the role of credit cards in promoting inflation, and the 1974 recession to rising oil prices. The trouble with the theory of the external shock, however, is that on many occasions the country has not been plunged into recession by war (1898, 1917, 1941, 1950, 1967), presidential rhetoric (e.g., Harry Truman's attack on the commodity futures markets in 1948 or John F. Kennedy's criticism of the steel companies in 1961), or oil-price gyrations (e.g., the collapse of 1985–86).

Neither has the theory of the internal, central-bank-induced shock proven fail-safe. As we have already noted, the decade-long suppression of interest rates in the United States up until 1951 did not unleash the kind of inflation that an Austrian theorist would have expected of it. Nevertheless, the theory of interest rates laid down by Röpke and others has given long and reliable service. In understanding the booms and busts of contemporary Japan and America, in fact, it has been indispensable.

---

* It was the structure of rates, as we have seen, that sunk the Seamen's. Early in 1989, three-month Treasury-bill rates temporarily moved to a premium over longer-term rates, i.e., the yield curve became negatively sloped. This has been a relatively rare occurrence in America since the days of the full-strength gold standard before World War I. As a matter of course, short rates have been set lower than longer-term ones, i.e., the yield curve has been positively sloped. When the yield curve does invert, unprosperous things almost always happen. What was so unusual about the Bush era of finance was the sequence of events.

. . .

JAPAN HAS EXCITED the admiration of many Westerners precisely because it does not pursue financial policies that a capitalist would immediately recognize as capitalistic. As much as or more than any
leading industrial country in the 1980s, Japan turned its back on all
that the Austrians wrote, thought, or said. Perhaps no country enjoyed the experience so richly until it ended. When, in 1985, the
United States (itself no bastion of classical thought or deed in
money and deficits) demanded that the yen be revalued against the
dollar, the Japanese revalued. Almost simultaneously, Japanese exporters demanded relief from the higher yen-dollar exchange rate.
The Japanese authorities duly reduced yen-denominated money-
market interest rates, holding them to 5 percent or less from the
spring of 1986 through the spring of 1989. Undoubtedly, the
money-market interest rates posted by the Bank of Japan were
consistently lower than the "natural" rate, or the rate of return con-
fidently expected by Japanese manufacturers, traders, and speculators. A splendid boom was launched.

Was it inflationary? It was not, people were led to believe, because the prices of goods and services denominated in yen did not
materially rise. They had risen in the past, from 1976 to 1985, for
example. In that span of years, consumer prices in Japan climbed
by an average of 4.4 percent per annum. In 1986, the Japanese
consumer price index rose by just 0.6 percent. It rose by 0.1 percent in 1987—heaven on earth, in the central banker's perception—by 0.7 percent in 1988, and by 2.3 percent in 1989.
However, as we have seen, there is more than one kind of inflation. The prices of stocks, bonds, land, and buildings jumped as
consumer prices steadied. There was a boom in capital investment, an expansion that many deemed a certain national blessing.
Rarely in postwar Japan had capital spending amounted to more
than 15 percent of any year's gross domestic product; by 1990,
buoyed by low interest rates, it had bubbled up to more than 24
percent.*

* One important cause of the boom was the obvious Austrian one. Starting late in
1985, the cost of a loan declined as the rate of return on capital increased; as it paid
to go into debt, corporations borrowed. The capital spending boom proceeded be-

The sight of the vaulting new Japan filled the Japanese with pride, and their neighbors and trading partners with envy and dread. On Wall Street, as David Asher relates, some economists "were known to express Japanese growth in terms of the GNP of certain developing countries—i.e., the 'Nikkei may appreciate by an Argentina next month,' 'Japanese capital expenditure increased by nearly one Mexico last quarter' . . ." Admiring authors wrote in praise of Japanese business management, Japanese manufacturing techniques, and Japanese finance. A Japanese neurologist flattered his compatriots by laying out the theory of the alleged uniqueness of the Japanese brain. "The quality of Japan's financial regulators is unsurpassed," wrote a non-Japanese essayist in the *Harvard Business Review* in 1989, the year before the Japanese bubble burst; "they are recruited from the top ranks of the best universities and they average decades of training and experience."*

However, proof was soon forthcoming that the Japanese bureaucrats were no more all-seeing than their non–Tokyo University–educated American counterparts. Inspired by excess optimism, a typical by-product of superabundant bank credit, the people whom the regulators regulated kicked up their heels. The misallocations of capital in the boom years took the conventional, exuberant forms: overbuilding of real estate, overexpansion of manufacturing capacity, overbuying of bonds, and stocks that had nothing to recommend them in the matter of price except that their prices had been rising. In 1987, to pick one illustrative bubble year, big Japanese companies could borrow at 1 or 2 percent and invest the proceeds in

---

yond the point of diminishing returns, as it so often does: projects committed to in boom times came to fruition during the downturn. Indeed, Japanese capital spending, expressed as a percentage of GDP, did not peak until 1991, more than a year after the top of the stock market.

* Upon leaving the Bank of Japan or the Ministry of Finance, the anointed ones often went to work in the top echelons of the banks they formerly regulated. There, during the late 1980s and early 1990s, they helped to make the banking debacle even worse than it might have been without them. It has been shown that the regional banks headed by former Ministry of Finance bureaucrats between 1976 and 1993 earned significantly lower returns than the banks that had not been so honored by the presence of former officials. "I think that because of the presence of [retired] bureaucrats," said the author of the study, Adrian van Rixtel, a Ph.D. candidate at the Free University of Amsterdam, "banks engaged in more risky behavior and consequently show worse performance."

government bonds at 6 percent. Alternatively, they could invest in common stocks through tax-advantaged *tokkin* accounts at a profit of some hoped-for vast multiple of 6 percent; or they could buy some fast-compounding Tokyo real estate (in the three years ended 1987, quoted property values in central Tokyo would nearly triple). When Tateho Chemical Industries reported a loss of the equivalent of $197 million in 1987 because its bond traders had zigged when they should have zagged, the market was briefly stunned. However, Japanese corporate executives were not so stunned as to stop the practice of extracurricular speculation. Demonstrably, the returns on buying low and selling high in the great bull markets were hugely in excess of anything available in any legal line of industry. *Zaitech*, meaning "financial engineering," the name given to this corporate sideline, conveyed the erroneous impression that a speculative market resembled a computer.

It cost as little as 1 or 2 percent to borrow because the bonds were linked (through warrants) to the fortunes of the issuing company's stock. And as it could not be repeated too often, stock prices only went up. "Foreigners can't seem to grasp the depth of the bullishness here," said a Japanese stock market analyst in early 1989, a year when the Nikkei 225 stock average would vault to about 39,000 from about 30,000, but then suddenly stop vaulting. In November 1989, within months of what would prove to be the Nikkei's all-time peak of 38,915, Nomura Securities ventured a forecast for the middle of the next decade: the Nikkei would hit 81,700. In fact, by the end of 1995, the Nikkei would be quoted at only a little more than 20,000, a predictive deficit of some 60,000 points.

The bubble did not occur by accident but by a combination of governmental design and inadvertence. It began with the Plaza Accord, so-called for its venue at the hotel of the same name at Fifth Avenue and 60th Street in Manhattan. In September 1985, the G-5 countries, the United States first and foremost, decided to reduce the foreign exchange value of the dollar. From the Japanese viewpoint, this was identical to ordering an increase in the foreign exchange value of the yen. The change went down hard on Japan's exporters; as the yen rose, their profits sank. In the fiscal years ended March 1986 and March 1987, operating profits for all listed Japanese companies fell by 8 percent and 14.5 percent, respectively.

Trying to compensate for the loss of business vitality, the Bank of Japan attempted to create some speculative effervescence. From 5 percent in January 1986, the Official Discount Rate was reduced to 2½ percent by February 1987. Early in 1988, an unnamed functionary of the Bank of Japan explained the grand design. "We intended first to boost both the stock and property markets," he said.

> Supported by this safety net—rising markets—export-oriented industries were supposed to reshape themselves so they could adapt to a domestic-led economy. This step was then supposed to bring about enormous growth of assets over every economic sector. This wealth effect would in turn touch off personal consumption and residential investment, followed by an increase of investment in plant and equipment. In the end, loosened monetary policy would boost real economic growth.

However, the central bank reckoned on neither the thoughts of Wilhelm Röpke nor the deeds of Nui Onoue. A former bar hostess turned restaurateur, Onoue had become the Hetty Green of Osaka: the holder, by year-end 1990, of roughly $800 million of common stocks, including what was said to be the largest stake by any individual investor in the Industrial Bank of Japan. Why Onoue would choose to invest in IBJ rather than in some other prestigious Japanese lender was a deep mystery. She was intimately acquainted with its pliable lending policies, having succeeded in borrowing $2 billion from it (or its local leasing affiliate). Later, in the contraction phase of the cycle, after she was charged with fraud, accused of running up debts on the order of $3 billion (secured by phony collateral), arrested, and brought to trial, Onoue would be known as the "Bubble Lady."

In August 1993, *The Washington Post* reported on the testimony of a desolated former lender of Onoue's, Eiichiro Hayata, during the Bubble Lady's trial at an Osaka district court. He had been charged as an accessory in her alleged fraud, and he tearfully described the shame of it. "When she asked him to keep extending credit to her while swapping one piece of collateral for another," the *Post* reported, "he said he knew it went against company policy, but had

no idea what was really going on. He recalled how 'Nui's Gang,' a group of about 40 elite brokers and bankers, had celebrated her birthday at her restaurant. How could a woman with such connections be a fake? Now an employee at his brother-in-law's small factory two hours away from his home, Hayata sobbed: 'I will live the rest of my life for my children.' "

More than a bull market, Japan invented what enthusiasts believed was a perpetual bull-market system. Japanese companies bought each others' stocks, and Japanese banks bought their clients' stocks. These "cross-holdings," so the argument went, would never be sold, so the shares that did remain outstanding were all the more valuable. The most expansive element of the bull-market system was that banks were able to count a percentage of their stocks as a contribution to their own capital. Thus, as the stock market rose, so did the banks' capital and so did their lending capacity. The more the banks lent, the greater the prosperity in the markets in which the proceeds of the loans were spent. It came to dawn on Americans that the Japanese did not think at all like the legendary value investors Benjamin Graham or David Dodd. (Later, in the speculative phase of the American bull market, it would come to light how very few Americans thought like Graham or Dodd, either.)

As investors, the Japanese seemed to like high valuations even better than low ones. In the real estate market, like Donald Trump, they preferred big, splashy properties at big, splashy prices. In bonds, they seemed not to care if a particular security was a senior debenture, a subordinated debenture, or a junior subordinated debenture. In boom times, the overriding concern was that it yield decently more than the interest cost of the corresponding liability on the buyer's balance sheet.* Eugene Dattel, an American who wrote a book about his experiences in Tokyo during the 1980s, de-

---

* Banks had no choice but to lend to a riskier grade of borrower. Not only were their blue-chip corporate customers abandoning them for the securities markets, but also they were under regulatory pressure to earn more capital. By lending to companies that actually needed to borrow, they could charge a higher interest rate than they had been able to get from companies that were under no such compulsion. Higher rates would contribute to higher earnings, the argument went, and therefore to the goal of better balance sheets. The unhappy ending to this story has been often told. By trying to earn more money by taking more credit risk, the banks earned less money. Their balance sheets notoriously weakened.

scribed the Japanese preference for "wet" investment analysis over "dry." "Simply put," Dattel explained, " 'dry' is a pure, analytical approach deemed to be Western; whereas 'wet' is a more personal, human relationship–oriented style. Performance measurement was never taken seriously because market prices were improving. Precise calculation of results and comparison of results among Japanese financial institutions was considered a 'dry' Western concept."

As it does in all countries, the rising bull-market tide covered up errors and imbued the participating capitalists with a sense of invincibility. The Japanese were all the more susceptible to positive, new-era feelings because of the structure of Japanese finance. Most major financial institutions, to start with, belonged to a *keiretsu*, or a Japanese corporate family. The *keiretsu* tended to insulate its members against the full force of outside competition. Another layer of perceived security was provided by the Japanese bureaucracy, notably the Ministry of Finance. "The MoF granted the Japanese financial institutions a franchise and protection," Dattel observed. "In return, the MoF demanded obedience, homage and the hiring of retired officials."

"Unlike the Americans," wrote Daniel Burstein, author of *Yen! Japan's New Financial Empire and Its Threat to America*, "the Japanese have evolved planning capabilities and procedures to carry out systematic structural economic readjustments to new conditions." Burstein wrote in the late 1980s, a time when many Americans feared that Japan would buy the United States whole before Trump could get around to it. Adaptable the Japanese industrial economy may have been, but profoundly inflexible the Japanese financial economy proved to be. Japan itself, as some on Wall Street have noticed, bore a close resemblance to the pre-reformed IBM, with its lifetime employment practices, its protected businesses (allowing cross-subsidization of subsidiary businesses), and its dark suits and white shirts. As IBM persistently failed to adapt to a changing world, so did Japan.

For more than two bubbly years, from February 1987 to May 1989, the Official Discount Rate was stuck at 2½ percent. In June 1989, with a rise to 3¼ percent, it came unstuck. This unfriendly act the stock market seemed not to notice; nor did the Nikkei average react when the rate was raised again in October of 1989. When, however, under the new, hard-horse leadership of Yasushi Mieno, the rate was raised to 4¼ percent on Christmas Day 1989, the market was badly jolted; stock prices peaked a few days later.

Not only did the government raise interest rates in 1989, but it also invented new taxes: on consumption, real estate transactions, and capital gains. The boom was over, it was increasingly plain to see. The issue was what to do with the herds of white elephants that the boom had coaxed into being. It was the government's decision not to shoot them, but to conserve and protect them—in effect, to deny their existence as white elephants. Stock prices fell by half, it is true, but by no more. Even at the bear-market lows in 1992, they presented no bargain. In Japan in 1966 as in America in 1974, culminating years of long-running declines, values had been objectively compelling. Admittedly, there was precious little money and courage to grasp the bargains thereby offered, but there they were. At low ebb in Tokyo in 1992, there were (in the "dry" American perspective) no bargains to be had.* The Nikkei 225 stock average was quoted at 30 or so times earnings. It had peaked in 1989 at about 70 times earnings. "[T]rusting their brokers and the financial system," Dattel wrote, "Japanese investors felt secure that they would be cared for and prices would rise."

The Japanese authorities did their best to smooth things over. In boom years, the Tokyo market had been baldly manipulated by the brokers, notably by the behemoth Nomura. Abuses were legendary, but they were not (at least as far as a foreign observer could ascertain) officially sponsored. Beginning in the fall of 1992, however, the government itself took the market in hand. Determined to forestall a panic, the Ministry of Finance directed that various pools of government-controlled capital—the Postal Savings deposits, the Postal Life Insurance, and part of the State Pension Funds—buy common stocks, even at the still-high prevailing valuations. (This official action was not officially acknowledged.) That the average dividend yield could be scarcely 1 percent even after the market had given up half its value from the 1989 peak was proof positive that something was wrong. In 1966, another Japanese gov-

---

* Nor, as we shall see, did the U.S. stock market get cheap, as the word cheap was used in 1942, 1974, or 1982.

ernment had entered the market to buy stocks, but every capitalist in that distressed year should have done the same; the average dividend yield of stocks listed on the first section of the Tokyo Stock Exchange was 4.45 percent. It proved to be one of the great opportunities of a lifetime, and the government subsequently turned a handsome profit on its investment. (Shelby Cullum Davis, the one-time New York State Insurance Commissioner who was so forehandedly bearish on U.S. government bonds in the mid-1940s, was one of the earliest American bulls on Japan. He bought Japanese insurance stocks after visiting the country in the late 1950s. The stocks sold for the value of the headquarters buildings alone, Davis marveled. He could hardly believe his good luck.)

The 1992 "Price Keeping Operation," which at this writing was still extravagantly in force, has cost the government the annual equivalent of as much as $60 billion. As a government can regulate either the price of a given commodity or its supply, but not both at once, the Finance Ministry was obliged to restrict the listing of new issues at the sky-high valuations that it had caused to be created. "It has been a matter of some delicacy and skilled management to ensure that the selling pressure from domestic investors did not overwhelm the sources of demand," wrote Andrew Smithers, a British economist who has made a specialty of Japan, in November 1994. "The situation is similar to that of any cartel operation, in which it is in the interests of all members that the price level should be maintained above its competitive clearing level. Such cartels are difficult to maintain, however, as it is also in the interests of individual members to sell as much as possible at these prices and the market cannot absorb all the potential supply. It is perhaps a credit to the abiding discipline of the Japanese consensus that the present situation has continued for two years." Or to the kind of mass delusion that made long-dated $2\frac{1}{4}$ percent Treasury bonds appear irresistible to American investors in the inflationary year of 1946.

Unlike the isolated essay in "financial statesmanship" by the Chase National Bank in 1920, the Japanese government's intervention in the early 1990s was all-encompassing. Stopgap was piled on stopgap, the consequences of the first such intervention making necessary a second, third, and nth. For example, the government asked banks not to reduce their dividends, not to acknowledge anything like the true dimension of their losses, and not to dump their sizable portfolios of common stocks on to a weakened market. The cost of these measures—delaying, as they did, the correction of error and the resumption of growth—was incalculable, but there was one small mitigating side effect. In 1991 and again in 1994, foreign buying of common stocks offset heavy domestic selling. For the Japanese, whose investment blunders had become the butt of countless Wall Street jokes in the 1980s and 1990s, the credulity of occidental buyers must have been a welcome tonic. For credulity it certainly was. Although stock prices were propped up, corporate earnings continued to fall. The decline in earnings produced the inevitable arithmetic result, a massive rise in the ratio of stock prices to earnings. From 1992 and 1994, price-earnings ratios on the Tokyo market vaulted to 80 from 30, that is, to out-of-sight from merely high.

"The financial crises of the 1920s and 1930s were more severe in Japan than elsewhere," The *Financial Times* related in October 1994, "and there are many in the MoF who believe that any threat of a repeat, however small, should be avoided." Plainly, the Harry Truman interpretation of the early 1920s had won the day over the Benjamin Anderson interpretation. What Japan faced was something new in the memory of middle-aged people: an outright contraction of credit and prices. As it chronicled the deflationary tendencies, *The Nikkei Weekly* more and more came to evoke the 1930s.* Readers were left to wonder which era Japan inhabited.

---

* The *Nikkei Weekly* of January 17, 1994, which I have saved like an heirloom because of the density of its deflationary coverage, helps to convey the texture of the times. The domestic wholesale price index had fallen by 2.1 percent in 1993, and the government had spent no less than 8 trillion yen, or the equivalent of $70.8 billion, on the stock market "price keeping operations" in the preceding two years, the paper said. Ryuchiro Tachi, a member of an advisory panel that had the ear of the Finance Ministry, proposed that banks should, after all, make a clean breast of their problems. This suggestion the chairman of the Federation of Bankers Associations received as if it were a long-dead fish. Investors had begun to pay more discriminating attention to the credit risk attached to the bonds of Japanese financial institutions (a far cry from the willful unconsciousness of the boom days). Other savers were flocking to the safe haven of the call-loan market, despite then prevailing yields of 2.37 percent. It appeared to be "one of the few safe investments channels" said the paper. By early 1996, the call rate had fallen to less than one-half of one percent.

Here was the law of unintended consequences run riot. By simultaneously inflating stock prices and suppressing the volume of new issuance, the government had stymied the ability of debt-laden companies to recapitalize. It had, indeed, turned the stock market into a kind of public works' project. "There is no mechanism to mobilize the capital that exists within Japan," a senior vice president of Prudential Securities, James Walsh, told *The Wall Street Journal* in the autumn of 1994. By causing the banks to temporize, the authorities suppressed the chain reaction of self-help that honest accounting would have imposed on lenders and borrowers alike. As in the early 1920s, a short, sharp deflation would have pleased no one, but its long-term cost might have been lower than the slow, relentless leak created by the Japanese bureaucracy. "At home," reported James Sterngold of *The New York Times* in January 1994, "the banks have undermined their futures by continuing to support, often with loans at nominal interest rates, dozens of companies that became badly overstretched through reckless property and stock speculation in the boom years." It was the 1920s all over again, but on a vastly larger, hugely more frightening scale.

Plainly, Japan was a country in need of a deflationary depression. Just as clearly, it would get one over the dead bodies of its protective regulators. What the bureaucrats wanted least—a sharp, sudden collapse in the prices of inflated assets and a liquidation of superfluous investment—was what the country needed most. The American devotees had it exactly wrong. Japan was unadaptable. It could not allow itself to face that most essential capitalistic state of being: failure.

CHAPTER FOUR

MIRACLE CURE

I F DENIAL WAS A root cause of Japanese financial decline in the
1990s, truth-telling was a prime source of American revival.
Both countries had offended against the laws of banking and liquidity. However, only the United States made effective postboom
amends. For the most part, insolvent banks and thrifts were allowed
to fail, and slow loans and loss-making real estate to be revalued. It
is true that federal regulators were lenient when the largest American banks needed it most, and that Citicorp, the very largest, would
not have been allowed to fail, even if (as seemed possible in 1990
and 1991) the capital markets chose to stop taking its credit. It is no
less true that the Federal Reserve Board was instrumental in pro-
longing the healing period of low interest rates that set in during
the early 1990s. However, in comparison to Japan, where no bank,
big or small, had been allowed to fail in more than a half century,
regardless of merit, the United States was a model of unrecon-
structed laissez-faire. In Japan, financial error was prolonged by
denying that it had ever been perpetrated.

The optimistic American imagination in 1990 and 1991 was another cause of the financial revival, a greater cause even than the
Federal Reserve Board. Americans conceived bullish thoughts, and
they gave them expression with money. Higher stock prices, the ma-
terialization of those ideas, allowed financial repairs to be conducted
with a minimum of economic disruption. The economic facts thus
became harmonious with the speculative thoughts. In Japan, where

speculation had been a national pastime in the mid- and late 1980s, people came to entertain bearish thoughts. They forswore the stock market in favor of low-yielding savings accounts.

The conventional interpretation of events in America is that the market followed the economy, the noncrash of 1990 anticipating the nondepression of 1990–91. However, it is even more plausible that the economy followed the market; or, more exactly, that the optimism implicit in the stock market rally helped to support the economy. It was the financial liftoff of 1991 that delivered the nation from the financial crisis that had daily taken shape in 1990 and that continued to threaten in 1991. The economic and financial facts are always subject to the vagaries of perception. In America, financial perception became unstintingly bullish.

If a panic had actually occurred, no journalist or historian would have been at a loss to explain why. The content of an average issue of the *American Banker* in 1991 might have caused a coast-to-coast bank run in the days before deposit insurance and the doctrine that some banks were too big to fail. The objective state of the top New York banks late in 1990 was worse than it had been at the bottom of the Great Depression.* However, condemningly, there was no Great Depression to explain it. What could explain it, in part, was federally inspired complacency. The existence of government guarantees inspired the bankers to take greater risks than their unsocialized forebears could have afforded to take. When some of those risks turned out badly, the depositors were calmed by the knowledge that the government and the biggest banks were partners in all but name. The knowledge prevented the kind of run that led to the creation of the FDIC in the first place.

---

* At year-end 1932, in the throes of the Great Depression, the National City Bank, forerunner to Citicorp, showed equity capital equivalent to 12.7 percent of its total assets; 58 years later, during the 1990 recession, Citi could show equity capital equivalent to only 3.4 percent of its total assets. In 1932, National City earned 9.2 percent on its equity; in 1990, Citi earned just 4.4 percent on its equity. In 1932, loans amounted to 47 percent of National City Bank's deposits; in 1990, loans amounted to 106 percent of Citi's deposits. Even managed as conservatively as it was, the National City Bank had no easy time of it in the Great Depression. Managed unconservatively, it might well have failed.

Similarly with Chemical Banking Corp. (recently absorbed into Chase Manhattan): its 1990 financial condition was considerably less robust than its 1932 condition.

In the spring of 1942, American investors could imagine almost nothing but the worst. Beginning in January 1991, they chose to conceive of little besides the best. Their attention was diverted from the issue of losing their money in an unsound bank to the risk of not participating in the unfolding bull market. Deeming money-market yields too low, they reached for higher yields, the banking and monetary dilemma notwithstanding.

Speculation has sometimes precipitated financial crises. In America in the 1990s, it helped to forestall a crisis, or at least to facilitate a cure. The great bull markets that erupted after the outbreak of the Persian Gulf war reversed the sinking fortunes of American debtors and of the United States dollar. Overleveraged companies were given the opportunity to issue common stock and real estate–freighted banks to buy government bonds. Venturesome investors could buy some of the very buildings that the banks and savings and loan associations (both living and dead) had been forced to dispose of. Ordinary rich people bought two-year Treasury notes with no money down, helping themselves, their brokers, and (in the form of lower governmental borrowing costs) their country. High securities prices presently canceled the bearish effects of low securities prices and helped to restore liquidity to seized-up markets. The public extended the maturity of its investments by migrating from money-market instruments, which mature in days, into bonds, which mature in years, and finally into stocks, which never mature at all. Buying low and selling high became, de facto, a successful national economic policy.

"WE ALL WENT TO BED New Year's Eve 1989 [as] geniuses," remembered Jay Chiat, who built and then, through overborrowing, unbuilt, the Chiat/Day advertising agency, "and we woke up the next morning and we were fools."

Similarly in finance. Many bankers, too, regretted that 1989 (itself no unbroken span of prosperity) ever stopped. The new year brought a deeper bear market in global real estate, a domestic recession, the beginning of what would prove to be a protracted bear market in Japan, the closing of the American junk-bond market to new issuance, a steep decline in the foreign exchange value of the dollar and a brush with disaster in the United States banking system, the closest such encounter since the 1930s. However, this ominous train of events did not ring down a depression. Nor, indeed, was it caused by a depression. What followed next, in 1991, after an ordinary business downturn gave way to a mild recovery, was a gaudy speculative revival. Stock prices rallied, interest rates declined, and the recession (as its dates were subsequently established by the National Bureau of Economic Research) stopped. The banking system staged a mighty recovery. There was no panic, no brutalizing bear market, no currency crisis, and no protracted sorting out of the crop of boom-time errors. Presented with the very low interest rates that usually accompany debt contractions, recessions, and depressions, people did what they so often used to do. They withdrew a portion of their funds from banks. What they did with that money, however, bore no resemblance to any bank run of yesteryear. The public began to invest it in mutual funds.

No proper appreciation of the miracle cure of American credit in 1991 and 1992 is possible without an understanding of why it was miraculous. It was, in fact, a double miracle: first, the lightning-quick healing itself; and second, the lack of allergic reaction to the course of treatment. Although overnight interest rates fell from 8 percent in 1990 to 3 percent late in 1992, the lowest level since the 1960s, and then stayed there for the next year, no harmful monetary repercussions were immediately visible. The dollar exchange rate did not collapse, nor did the domestic inflation rate erupt. According to Austrian theory, ultralow interest rates usually stimulate an ill-founded investment boom, but there was nobody to deplore the boom as it unfolded in the United States. Röpke himself might not have condemned every aspect of it, for he allowed that a little monetary stimulus was not amiss in a time of high unemployment. Even if the unemployment rate was not shockingly high in 1991, the Thing Without a Name—downsizing, debt, technological revolution, the end of the cold war, and associated dislocating events— cast a pall of near recession, or of recessionlike anxiety. Down through the years, banks have overlent, corporations have overborrowed, and nations have consumed more than they produced. In the United States, all of these tendencies were on display. What was new was their happy resolution. Dollar-denominated interest rates fell, short rates falling more quickly and steeply than long-term ones. Both the level and the structure of rates constituted a standing invitation to invest and speculate, and this the nation energetically did. There were times when it had refused to put its money at risk, as in the 1930s, despite nominal Treasury-bill yields of less than 1 percent. Nor did the Japanese public plunge back into stocks in the 1990s, despite interest rates almost as close to zero as dollar rates had come in the Great Depression. Not least miraculously, the world did not reject the dollar as the de facto universal money. Rather, it demanded more of it.

If people did not fall down on their knees in thanks for the new bull market, it was in part because they had come to expect it. The public understood that the hoped-for and desirable resolution of financial problems was usually the one that came to pass. They could see that things worked out for the best. For decades, the country had been distancing itself from monetary orthodoxy, but this transformation seemed all for the best (if, indeed, it excited any discussion at all). The improvised monetary arrangements of the late 1980s and early 1990s produced wild extremes of currency valuation and the occasional recondite European monetary crisis. However, they did not produce domestic inconvenience. Currency rates floated or sank, but the consequences of these gyrations seemed to have no bearing on everyday life in the United States. Although American officials were expected to declare in favor of a strong and stable dollar exchange rate, they were equally expected not to let any international consideration intrude on their monetary policy-making. It was literally inconceivable that the Fed would raise interest rates to influence the dollar–deutsche mark exchange rate, or the dollar-yen exchange rate, for instance, as it had once raised rates to conserve gold, or as other, smaller nations—Italy and Britain, for instance—had continued to raise rates to defend their foreign exchange reserves. When, as in the mid-1970s or the early 1980s, the wheels had seemed to come off the banking system, the Federal Reserve retightened them. Indeed, insofar as threatened crises caused the Fed to push down interest rates and otherwise to stimulate credit expansion, Wall Street had become pro-crisis.

The bears had to reach back farther and farther in financial history for examples of crises that had not been dextrously managed away, or for theories, like Röpke's, to explain why downturns of one kind of another served a positive capitalist purpose, or why, more broadly, failure is just as vital a feature of the capitalist process as is success. In the spring of 1995, with the Dow Jones Industrial Average bumping up against 4,500, the last preceding great bear market was as distant in memory as World War II had been from the experience of Americans during the Johnson administration. Bond prices had been going up since the early 1980s. There had been no severe recession since 1982, no truly devastating bear market since 1974 (the Standard & Poor's 500 Index actually registered a small net gain for the crash year of 1987), and no domestic commercial banking panic since 1933. The arguments marshaled against stocks and bonds by Robert A. Lovett in 1937—namely, that an investor was all too likely to outlive the corporation in which he or she put money—no longer seemed to apply. By 1991, the superior long-term investment results of common stocks were clearly established, although not so clearly as they would later be by 1996. Gold bullion, the monetary substance displaced in 1971 by floating exchange rates and the element that stood most to benefit from any breakdown of the new order, had been depreciating against the dollar most of the time since 1980. "Real money," as conservatives were wont to refer to gold, had proven no hedge against anything except, as the expression went, capital gains. Thus, feelings of wonder or gratitude about the bullish turn of financial events were rarely expressed. The deliverance of the American banking system from crisis was not a miraculous outcome, in Wall Street's opinion, but the conventional one.

When, in May 1995, Alan Blinder, vice chairman of the Federal Reserve Board, reflected on monetary policy in the prior year or two—it had truly given the United States the golden mean, neither too much growth nor too little, and scarcely any inflation, he said— he added a historical afterthought. Perhaps with a little luck, there would not have been a recession in 1990, either. What had tipped the cyclical balance in that year was neither the debt predicament nor any of its manifestations, in his opinion. It was rather the war against Saddam Hussein. Thus, Blinder implied that the Federal Reserve had both the means and the foresight to iron out the business cycle as well as the credit cycle. Central economic planning had been repudiated in the Soviet Union and Eastern Europe, but to listen to Blinder, the Fed was capable of imposing a form of monetary control not so very far from the ambitions of the newly unemployed technicians of the Soviet Gosplan. If Röpke was right, Blinder was wrong; and if Blinder was right, Röpke was (and remains) obsolete. At all events, as the mainstream saw the world, the miracle was not that things worked out for the best: it would have been a miracle had they not.

No new wonder drugs could account for the turn of events in the 1990s. The medicine chest of policy was no bigger in 1991 and 1992 than it had been during earlier crises of money and banking. Interest rates could be depressed, regulatory forbearance could be vouchsafed, reserve requirements could be reduced, and the dollar exchange rate could be devalued. All these treatments were duly administered. Floating exchange rates permitted greater freedom of action in the international monetary realm, and the institution of federal deposit insurance reduced the chances, almost to the vanishing point, of a systemwide run. However, it was also the rubber dollar and the partial socialization of banking risk that had allowed the debt predicament to proceed to such a ripe stage of development. No coast-to-coast bank run occurred in the wake of the 1984 failure of the nation's eighth-largest bank, Continental Illinois Bank & Trust Co., for example. The government scooped up the institution and its creditors, not only the depositors but also the holders of the parent company's bonds and preferred stock; in exchange for the transfer of 80 percent of its common stock to the FDIC, the government allowed the bank and its balance sheet to remain in one piece. This noncollapse, a boon to depositors everywhere as well as to the stock market, the real estate market, and to the gross domestic product, surely entailed its own long-term costs. There were two unintended consequences, at least, of the federal government's intervention. First was the perpetuation of the tendency toward too many banks making too many loans at too little profit to the lenders; and second, the demonstration that harebrained lending practices did not necessarily threaten the lender with oblivion. Had the Continental Bank not been rescued, many innocent depositors' dollars would have been lost. FDIC officials feared that a chain reaction of failure might have threatened the FDIC fund itself. On the other hand, many new, redundant office buildings would not have been built, and the worldwide credit bacchanalia might not have occurred. Just possibly, Japan might not have lent itself into a great asset inflation and into the subsequent, long-running stagnation-cum-deflation.

If the tools of monetary policymaking were the same tools, the human recipients of policymaking were different. The threshold of financial worry, let alone panic, among Americans had risen markedly. The children and grandchildren of the people who had run on the banks in March 1933—the depression at that moment having substantively run its course, the stock market having bottomed more than six months before, in general the time for capitulation having passed—refused to run in 1990 and 1991, when, from an objective, balance-sheet viewpoint, there was arguably more to worry about. They were not necessarily braver or wiser than their forebears but, rather, better subsidized. If investors in 1942 and 1974 were prone to doubt, the class of 1990-91 was inclined to believe. Their greatest article of faith was that the government had enough money.

The troubles that preceded the great levitation have long since been forgotten, finance representing an exception to the general rule about the victors writing history. In financial markets, it is the vanquished who frequently write historical works, the winners having the means to forgo the pleasure of writing anything for publication. What is remembered best about late 1990 and early 1991 is the rally in stocks and bonds. The reasons not to buy them, being irrelevant, have been filed away in obscurity along with other lost financial causes, including the reasons to be bullish on bonds in 1946, the reasons to sell stocks in 1974, or the reasons to queue up outside a gold dealer's office in January 1980 to purchase a shiny new coin.

The many crises that did not occur in 1991—the collapse of the dollar and the closing of Citicorp, for instance—were preceded by one that did: the real estate breakdown of the 1980s. Old-time bankers disapproved of real estate collateral on the ground that it was hard to sell a building at the very moment the depositors might demand their money back. However, this scruple, like so many other traditional banking doctrines, had been overtaken by events, technology, or perception. In the first place, bankers had decided, the age of systemwide runs was over; the money market would never be closed to solvent institutions. If some of the creditors wanted out, others would want in, or could be induced to enter by rising deposit rates. Then, too, the field of available lending opportunities was narrowing all the time. The storied blue-chip corporate borrower had left the banks for cheaper alternatives—in bonds or commercial paper—many years before. Even if a banker had dressed in morning clothes, imported a rolltop desk, and resolved to revert to the old, solvent ways, it is unlikely that he or she could have found enough of the old, short-dated, solvency-promoting kind of banking asset to lend against. The source of the banker's competitive advantage in years gone by was knowledge. What was changing in the 1980s and 1990s, thanks to the personal computer, was that the financial secrets were out; now, almost anybody could know them. Nor could a modern banker afford to let money lie fallow in safe and sane money-market instruments; the cost of the deposits too often exceeded the rate of return on Treasury bills. The banker was, truly, compelled to lend.

But to whom? To real estate developers, first and foremost, and also to corporate dealmakers and sub-investment-grade corporations. The formerly irreproachable big-city banks had been much reduced by their misadventures in the Third World. No longer themselves possessing a topflight credit rating, they were obliged to go slumming; and if, as often happened, the experience of reaching for the extra increment of yield cost them further losses and a weaker credit rating, they were bound to reach even farther into the barrel of credit the next time. It was not only the banks that said no to their loan applicants. Over the span of many years, the investment-grade business borrower also said no to its bank.

Thus, the bankers had turned to real estate, expanding those credits by threefold in the 1980s, to $750 billion from $248 billion. Furthermore, between 1984 and the middle of 1990, no less than 72 percent of all loan growth at commercial banks was provided by real estate. By late 1990, the concentration of real estate assets on the balance sheets of banks of all sizes had reached alarming proportions. As a rule of thumb, real estate loans at the larger banks—those with $1 billion or more of assets—accounted for something on the order of one-third of all loans. Among banks with $1 billion or less in assets, approximately half of all loans were real estate loans. What would become of the banks, their depositors, and the economy itself if the national real estate market went the way of the shrinking Texas market?

ALTHOUGH THE Dow Jones Industrial Average and the economy peaked together, in July 1990, the Bush recession did not take Wall Street completely unawares. Through the spring and early summer, bank stocks and junk bonds were in daily, visible decline, and bank lending officers, who had spent the preceding decade mainly saying yes, especially to real estate propositions, were now saying no again. From the bearish point of view, God was in his heaven.

One vital structural support to the prosperity of the 1980s was easy credit. Not only in America but also in Japan, the Nordic countries, and almost any other country where English was spoken as a first language, the marginal loan applicant had been able to find the accommodating lender. Now that circumstance was changing. Japan was embarked on what would prove to be a full-scale credit contraction, and real estate values were falling around the world.*

As usual, those not in clear need of a loan could find one. What changed in America in 1989 and 1990 was that the solvent, but needy, applicant was sometimes denied. The collapse of the junk-bond market had pushed up average yields of speculative-grade

---

* In Texas, scene of the formative period of the American real estate boom, desperate times inspired creative acts. "They scatter a few dead birds and dogs around their property and tell the lender that they have no idea what's killing the poor little critters," related Frederick E. "Shad" Rowe, a Dallas investor, of some hard-up Texas developers. "But if the lenders want to take on a potential billion-dollar liability, they are welcome to the place."

dcbt to 20 percent, an interest rate so punitively high as all but to
foreclose new issuance. In 1989, $29.5 billion worth of bonds had
been sold for corporations that did not possess an investment-grade
rating; in 1990, the year Drexel Burnham Lambert failed, issuance
shrank to $3.6 billion. The blame for the contraction in business
lending was sometimes put down to a government-sponsored, anti-
entrepreneurial vendetta. No doubt, in the specific case of junk
bonds, regulatory overreaction to the savings and loan calamity
caused the forced sale of junk bonds that would otherwise have remained off the market, but no government ukase was responsible
for the contraction in auto credit, or for the record number of defaults by the issuers of junk bonds, or for the record number of personal bankruptcies and bank failures. As for commercial real estate,
if the 1986 tax law was a depressing influence on the American
market, that did not explain the simultaneous decline in overseas
property markets. Neither did the regulators put a gun to the heads
of commercial bankers to force them to continue making real estate
loans long after the anti–real estate tax legislation was passed. And
it was a general loss of courage (or rise in prudence) that shut down
the speculative-grade tier of the commercial-paper market: by
1989–90, buyers of the unsecured promissory notes of speculative-
grade companies had decided that the quoted short-term yields
were no longer worth the potential risk.

Many had warned that the next recession would cut a swath
through leveraged finance, not only through the companies that
had borrowed in the junk-bond market but also through the banks
that had lent extensively (collectively, in the sum of $32 billion) to
facilitate the debt-heavy corporate takeovers. What precipitated the
contraction, in fact, was a bear market; what preceded the bear
market was a change in outlook. Each preceded the 1990 recession
itself. One milestone in the deleveraging movement was the June
1989 failure of Integrated Resources, a debt-heavy real estate syn-
dication and "financial services" company that had done its extensive junk-bond business—as an issuer and a buyer—through
Drexel Burnham Lambert. Overnight, Integrated ran out of borrowed money. Up until it found it could not renew its commercial-
paper borrowings, its senior debt was still rated investment-grade

by Standard & Poor's. It filed for bankruptcy protection in June. "The capital structure requires some type of continued confidence," an officer of the company admitted in the hour of need. "In retrospect, it was a fragile capital structure."

"The traditional bearish view was that a recession would cause some LBOs to default, which would start the downward cycle," observed Christopher T. Mahoney, a vice president of Moody's Investors Service, in March 1990. "But instead, the psychology changed without a recession—and the change in psychology alone has had and will have devastating consequences (which may include a recession). A changed attitude toward leverage is dangerous for leveraged borrowers; a bearish environment is bad for refinancing and it is bad for asset values. It may turn out that a recession won't be needed to put a lot of LBOs in the tank."

The country itself was more deeply in debt in relation to national output than it had ever been in the postwar era. Nonfederal debt amounted to 148 percent of gross domestic product in 1990, one percentage point below the record 149 percent set two years earlier. On average, in the decade of the 1950s, nonfederal borrowing had totaled 77 percent of GDP. It had reached 104 percent in the 1960s, 114 percent in the 1970s, 131 percent in the 1980s overall, and 140 percent in the boom portion of the 1980s, from 1984 to 1989. Excessive borrowing had had a long running start.

The optimistic interpretation of the growth in debt was that borrowing records had been set in successive decades ever since the 1950s and that the country survived each and every one of them. Why should 148 percent prove to be any more ruinous than 138 percent, 128 percent, or 100 percent had been? It would not be. Indeed, after a brief, dramatic interval in 1990–91, the nation would be financially improved. What filled the interval was a spectacle unseen since the 1970s, a near brush with disaster by a succession of eminent banking institutions. In fact, nothing like it had occurred even during the 1930s, as the failed banks of the Great Depression were principally small institutions. In the 1990s, on the other hand, it was the big-city, or "money-center," banks that suffered the biggest losses. Not a few regional or superregional institutions profitably sailed through the blow. In the 1970s, on average, two banks per year had failed. From 1982 to 1991, the average annual toll was 130. Granted that capitalism was ever changing, that more and more lending and borrowing were taking place outside the banking system, and that the state of the banking business, per se, was no longer as vital to the health of the economy as it once had been. Nevertheless, a generalized contraction of credit was taking shape. At the margin—in banking, insurance, and the securities markets— loans were becoming scarcer. The marginal applicant, denied the extra dollar of credit, could not contribute the needed unit of additional spending.

CITICORP, THE NATION's only truly international bank, had a closer brush with financial oblivion in the one-horse Bush recession than in all of the Great Depression. In 1992, it signed a "Memorandum of Understanding" to placate its federal regulators, one of only 41 banks so stigmatized that year. Although there was nothing in such a document to connote insolvency, actual or imminent, Citi pledged to make no big decisions without the permission of the Federal Reserve and the Office of the Comptroller of the Currency. Furthermore, as the bank said in making a clean breast of these arrangements in its 1992 annual report, "the memorandum of understanding provides that Citicorp will not transfer, bid for, acquire, or enter into agreements to acquire significant bank or nonbank entities or asset or liability portfolios or expand its consolidated assets without first consulting with the Reserve Bank and the OCC." Here was a bitter pill: Citi had been a most acquisitive institution. "In this respect," the bank continued, putting a vaguely cheery face on things, "the memorandum of understanding memorializes a closer working relationship which has evolved with Citicorp's primary regulators over the last two years."

The seeds of this "relationship" were sown in the late 1980s, when Citi couldn't say no to anyone, not even to Robert Campeau, the Canadian developer, Donald Trump, the American developer, a motley of Australian promoters, or First Capital Holdings, a bankruptcy-bound life insurance company. Already hurt by its write-downs of Third World loans (in 1987, the bank had taken a gleeful lead in owning up to its losses, embarrassing its competitors in the process and enlarging its already considerable and well-founded reputation for arrogance), Citi barged into the contraction of 1989–90 with an undiminished enthusiasm for real estate lending. In the summer of 1990, a Wall Street analyst happened to ask a Citicorp investor-relations officer what the chairman, John S. Reed, was up to. "Johnny's out trying to make real-estate loans," the man replied. By year-end 1990, what would prove to be the low ebb of the industry's fortunes (though not yet of the biggest American bank's), Citi showed nonperforming assets amounting to more than 6 percent of total assets, easily the highest among money-center banks. Yet its loan-loss reserves amounted to less than 34 percent of nonperforming assets, easily the lowest among the money centers.* It was a conceit of Citicorp's that a great bank—that is, specifically, itself—could operate with only trace amounts of capital and with the bare minimum allowance for bad debts. In 1991, an undercapitalized and underreserved Citi possessed a portfolio of high-risk (or at least out-of-favor) loans almost 400 percent greater than the shareholders' equity. It required no leap of faith to imagine how the bad assets might engulf the balance sheet.

Certainly, the stockholders had every reason to worry. In the early 1930s, the predecessor to Citicorp had lobbied against federal deposit insurance on the ground that it would tend to subsidize bad banking. The National City Bank had been as right as rain about that; it was insured consumer deposits that tended to subsidize and perpetuate Citicorp, its feckless corporate descendant, in the early 1990s. In its $217 billion balance sheet, Citicorp had both its greatest asset and greatest liability. The quality of its assets was a fright, but their sheer size was a lifeline. If any bank was too big to fail, that bank was Citi, and if it could only survive the crisis in one piece, it might well become a wonderful moneymaking business again (as it indeed went on to do). However, in mid–bear market, only visionaries could bring themselves to believe it.

---

* For the 50 American banks in the Salomon Brothers analytical universe at year-end 1990, nonperforming assets averaged 3.07 percent of total assets; loan-loss reserves amounted to 61.6 percent of nonperforming assets. Citi was truly a nonpareil.

Week by week in the fall of 1990, the capital markets delivered a critique of Citi in the form of a condemningly high yield on its auction-rate preferred stock. The stock was a peculiar hybrid: nominally a form of equity, but functionally a kind of money-market instrument. Each share, new, cost $100,000. Its yield was adjusted in periodic auctions. In theory, a buyer could enjoy liquidity, a reasonably steady market price, and an always-current yield. In practice, in the fall of 1990, what a buyer suffered was illiquidity, volatility, and worry. Because so much Citi auction-rate preferred was outstanding—about $950 million worth—some of it was repriced every week.

It became a weekly vote of no-confidence. The yield was expressed as a percentage of the 60-day commercial paper rate. The market had settled for less than 80 percent of that yield as recently as August. As the sell-off in bank stocks deepened, however, buyers demanded a greater return. By mid-August, they were insisting on more than 100 percent of the commercial paper rate. They recalled the unhappy history of the auction-rate preferred of MCorp, the bankrupt Texas bank holding company. Its preferred had become worthless.

That the Citicorp auctions did not fail was largely thanks to the Wall Street dealers who managed them. When too few actual investors showed up to bid, the underwriters themselves bought. "The senior management would talk to Citi in the morning," recalled a former brokerage-house trader of preferred stock who was on hand at the time. "The lead underwriters would essentially divvy up the issue, whether it was for customers or whether it was for their own account. . . . 'We're taking $25 million today,' " the man recalled of the instructions that came down from the highest echelons of his firm. It was all in the cause of keeping up a decent financial front for the nation's leading bank—and, of course, of the participating investment banks protecting their own reputations.

However, it became harder and harder to pretend. Matters came to a head on October 24, when Citicorp bowed to the market's low opinion of its credit. It did this by raising the "fail rate" on a certain $100 million preferred issue to be auctioned that day. Heretofore, the fine print allowed Citi to pay no more than 120 percent of the 60-day commercial paper rate. Now it raised the limit to 200 percent. In the event, the market demanded 154 percent, equivalent to $12\frac{1}{2}$ percent per annum. Except for this 11th-hour adjustment of the terms of the issue, Citi would have been faced with a technically "failed" auction (that is, by the market's demand for a yield higher than the maximum Citi was allowed to pay under the terms of the issue). The salvage of the auction seemed scant consolation to the reputation of a bank that had almost discredited itself, but two weeks later Citi moved to put itself, its dealers, and its preferred-stock buyers out of their collective misery by announcing the redemption, for cash, of a substantial portion of its auction-rate securities.

It proved to be the high-water mark of anxiety. At that very moment, the story of the decline and fall of the American banking system was reaching the end of its useful investment life.* Abutting the news of the Citicorp auction results on the front page of the *American Banker* on October 25 was a report that Warren Buffett had been investing in Wells Fargo. Such a thing had been rumored for months, but Buffett, even though he possessed a supernatural net worth, was himself a mere mortal, and Wells was at risk in California real estate. The bears were unperturbed.

BANK STOCKS EXTEND RALLY BUT ANALYSTS REMAIN WARY, the *Banker* reported on November 6 in what turned out to be, very nearly to the day, the bottom. In the way of markets, no clear objective evidence of the turn was available. Investors who had underestimated the depths of the country's (indeed, the world's) credit problems had long ago purchased bank stocks, insurance stocks, "stub stocks" (the equities of highly indebted companies), and junk bonds. They now read the newspapers, if they could stand to pick them up in the morning, with a frustration bordering on despair. They were as wary as anybody.

---

* *Grant's* memorialized it with a drawing depicting the starting line of the New York City Marathon race. "Hey, let's make it a bank run!" yelled a voice in the crowd. Perhaps this cartoon caused the subsequent bull market.

From the fall of 1990, the crisis receded, bank stocks appreciated, and interest rates fell. However, the dramatic, political, and journalistic life of the banking story lived on and on. Two years after the bottom, in the 1992 presidential campaign, Ross Perot, quoting from a new, calamity-conjuring study by a pair of college professors, forecast an epidemic of bank failures. Perot, a proven moneymaker when wearing his capitalistic hat, on this occasion illustrated the truism that an investment idea never seems so compelling as when it is over the hill. In 1933, 1942, or 1974, the idea that an investor could most profitably have doubted was the very idea that seemed irresistible: national disaster. Similarly in the bond market in 1946: deflation appeared self-evident just as inflation was coming into its own. It was at the frothing, hysterical peak of the gold market in January 1980 that inflation became an excellent short sale.

The analytical issue is why the 1990 bottom was so different from the other watersheds of pessimism in American finance. Always before, investors could rue having given in to fears that proved unfounded or overblown. The remarkable feature of the 1990 downturn was how little fear there was to surrender to. Either the investing public saw no ghost or, seeing one, coolly decided not to believe its own eyes. The financial fact that could explain the downturn—the great rip in the fabric of credit—was exactly the kind of fact that had once caused panics. Yet the stock market's verdict on abuses of credit amounted to a suspended sentence, pronounced with the wink of an eye. The Standard & Poor's 500 Index, after peaking in July, hit bottom in October. It was a decline of 20 percent, recorded in only 12½ weeks. Moreover, when the market did strike low ebb, its valuation bore no resemblance to the nadirs of the two preceding bear markets. In the matter of price-earnings ratio, the 1990 bear market bottomed out at 14 times. In the 1974 and 1982 bear markets, low ebb was seven times. Similarly as to book value or dividend yield: the S&P 500 at its worst was almost a study in optimism.

The bulls, carrying the day, contended that even if the financial problems were exaggerated, the Federal Reserve could fix them by reducing interest rates. The bulls' trillion-dollar perception was that nothing stood in the way of lower American rates: not inflation, not renewed dollar depreciation, and not (least of all) the cautionary theories of the classical Austrian economists.

The bears leapt to unprofitable conclusions. More was involved than a squadron of unwell New York City commercial banks, they could see. They noted, for example, that the Japanese banks were paying substantial interest-rate premiums to hold short-term overseas deposits, that the common stock of Britain's fifth-largest bank, the Standard Chartered Bank, was priced to yield an exhorbitant 18 percent, and that an Australian Bank, Metway, was offering a $10,000 reward for information about the source of rumors that had started a run on it. Back in the United States, money-market mutual funds, under orders to put safety first, were purging their portfolios of second-tier commercial paper. "We are not dealing with a rational process right now," an exasperated trader said.

In its 1990 annual report, Citicorp would suggest that it was really nobody's fault. Neither the market nor the regulators had anticipated the "adjustment of asset values or the drop in U.S. real estate values." The "corporation was essentially in no worse shape than the market" and "[to] an important degree, we are in the hands of the economy, and nobody is very secure in predicting its performance." The cumulative salary that Citi's senior management earned for not anticipating the performance of the national economy, of which it believed itself to be a virtual prisoner, was $18,285,000.

The bulls, who had watched bank stocks and junk bonds depreciate for upward of two years, saw the great truth that the government would allow no engulfing, systemwide crisis. They knew that pessimism about banking and credit could be carried to only a certain point, for beyond loomed the disasters of yesteryear. As for the source of this pessimism, it was only partly grounded in the objective facts of banking itself, they contended. Much of it was a rote reaction to the savings and loan calamity. More particularly, the bulls understood that the pool of bad loans in most banks was not getting bigger; or at least the rate of growth in bad loans was getting smaller. Furthermore, they saw that the salvage value of a bad real estate loan was not zero, as the market seemed to imply, and a slow bank loan to a highly indebted corporation was a more senior, and therefore more creditworthy, claim than the particular kind of junior loan called a junk bond. If all this were so (as indeed it proved to be), bank earnings must eventually recover. And if a bank's profitability were restored, so would be the value of its business franchise (in many cases from a level that the market had valued almost at zero). In the obsessive concern about credit, the bulls believed, the market had lost sight of the banks' earning power. Costs would be cut, and profits would continue to be earned on activities having nothing to do with lending a dollar and getting it back again: on securities trading, for instance.

Ever since the 1930s, federal policy had sought to protect the banking system against systemwide runs by depositors. However, no federal agency insured deposits above $100,000, and none guaranteed the various obligations—commercial paper, subordinated debentures, common stock—of the bank holding companies. Through the fall of 1990 and into the new year, the prices of these obligations weakened. In September, the 10-year notes of Southeast Banking Corp. were quoted at a price to yield about 18$\frac{1}{2}$ percent. Southeast would fail, but Chemical Banking Corp. would not. Its debentures were priced to yield almost 14 percent, only 4$\frac{1}{2}$ percentage points less condemning. Citicorp's yielded 13$\frac{3}{4}$ percent. The slump in bank bond prices was demoralizing in the extreme. If the bonds of the bank holding companies were of dubious merit, what hope was there for the preferred and the common?

IN SEPTEMBER 1990, at the annual meeting of the International Monetary Fund and the World Bank in Washington, D.C., a Deutsche Bank officer pronounced judgment on the bear market in U.S. bank obligations. "There is . . . very little interest in U.S. bank holding company paper in Europe, and only a little more for the banks themselves," the man said. "Why, you might as well buy *junk* bonds."

Many institutions, including the Equitable Life Assurance Society of the United States, owned enough high-yield debt as it was. Now the interest-rate crisis that Thomas Parkinson had faced in the

1940s returned with a twist. The yield famine was relative, not absolute, and the cause was not the Federal Reserve's interest-rate policy but the Equitable's. The company had overpromised by writing
contracts that guaranteed payments to its policyholders at the ul-
trahigh interest rates prevailing early in the decade. When interest
rates fell, the Equitable found it lacked the secure investments necessary to deliver the yields it had guaranteed. To obtain those
yields, it reached: into junk bonds, commercial mortgages, and real
estate itself. Parkinson had despaired of the monetary policies that
kept government bond rates in the neighborhood of 3 percent.
How surprised he would have been to see his company go to pot in
an era of 9 percent government rates.

The Equitable had been losing financial buoyancy throughout
the late 1980s, and rumors of its troubles reached Europe in the
fall of 1990. Late in November, in what was admittedly a hurried
sale of an illiquid security by a worried seller (or sellers), reportedly
of Swiss nationality, a short-dated Equitable debenture changed
hands at the bankruptcy-like yield of 32.7 percent. It was an even
more distressing rate than the junk-bond yields attached to the subordinated debt of the leading money-center banks.

In this one yield, an imaginative bear could find clinching evidence of the theory of greater calamity. What had stricken banks
and thrifts was now going to work on the life insurance industry as
well. Who could tell how far the contraction would carry?* The low
estate of the uninsured liabilities of the once-great American banks
(and of the once-great Equitable) suggested that it would not end
without heroic measures.

Auto finance, many miles distant from high finance, stalled in
its own way. In the midst of the 1990 recession, no fewer than 40
percent of would-be American car buyers had no automotive eq-

* Not much farther, as things developed, although, in fairness, the Equitable's balance
sheet was objectively weak. "In 1991, only 33 percent of the $422 million of mortgage
maturities owed to Equitable were paid as due, and during the first quarter of 1992 just
7.2 percent of scheduled mortgage maturities were paid as due," subsequently observed the insurance analyst David Schiff. "This non-payment poses a potential liquidity problem for Equitable because, by the end of 1995, it must redeem $5.8 billion
of the [guaranteed investment contracts] it issued."

uity. That is, they owed more on the car they were driving than they could realize on that vehicle in a trade-in. In auto-dealer lingo, they were "upside down." In 1982, by contrast, during the previous recession, only 15 percent of the universe of auto customers had been so embarrassed. The source of the rise in upside-downness was the advent of five-year loans and easier terms, culminating (as so many credit experiments did) in 1986–88. Here was a pure example of the ripening of the credit cycle. There were no regulators or overzealous government prosecutors to blame for the problems. Saddam Hussein had had nothing to do with them. Banks and finance companies simply lent until the arithmetic didn't work.

When, in September, it was disclosed that FLF Partners (for Four Lucky Fellows, the self-deprecating name given by the sons of Lawrence Tisch to the fund that held a portion of their family capital) was buying the cast-off shares of regional banks, and indeed had been for a long time, the market took only small solace in the news. Up until that time the Tisches, excellent investors though they were, had been wrong. It did not dawn on the market how right they would become in the very near future. There was other cause for optimism. MOODY'S DONE DOWNGRADING MONEY-CENTERS, the *American Banker* reported in a headline, and ANALYSTS SAY BANK STOCKS SOON MAY HAVE NOWHERE TO GO BUT UP.

A good many other analysts had come to believe that a short sale of bank shares was the easiest money to be had in capitalism. By the tenets of contrary opinion, the newfound popularity of this idea could only be interpreted as bullish, because it revealed a shift in the financial odds. The idea of a collapse of banking, the most distant of long shots in 1989, was by the fall of 1990 being touted as a sensible, short-odds investment, like IBM. Ordinarily bullish employees of brokerage houses unguardedly talked about which bank stocks to sell short. Late in 1990, the Feshbach brothers, California-based short sellers with almost $1 billion under management, bought themselves an airplane in which to fly from client to client to deliver what they had reason to believe would be the good news about the stock market: its collapse, or, failing that, the collapse of the shares of which they were short, including certain bank stocks. This, too, was an omen. At about the same time, members of the

Denton, Texas, fire department asked the noted Dallas bear Frederick E. "Shad" Rowe to address them on the art of short selling. (Rowe declined, later deciding that pessimism itself had become a short sale. The Feshbachs, too, eventually reoriented themselves to the long side.)

In markets, both the bulls and bears receive a measure of vindication, but only one side is vindicated with money. The other, temporarily, finds encouragement in the newspapers. In the short term, an investor holding the wrong idea is likely to open *The Wall Street Journal* to read about how right he or she is; the press has not caught up with the news.

In the fall of 1990, in keeping with the theories of the speculator-metaphysician George Soros, the markets supplanted the news as the proximate cause of financial events. It was the action of prices, or the structure of markets, that more and more dragged the news in its wake. Thus, the multiyear decline in the federal funds rate, from 10 percent in early 1989 to 3 percent in late 1992, constituted a national elixir: it was a balm to the banking system, Wall Street, and the economy at large. In the late 1980s, speculative-grade debtors had promised to pay very high interest rates, but the collateral values and the income streams on which the promises depended sometimes fell short. The result in those cases was a period of adjustment that took the form of bankruptcies, restructurings, and—presently, in a sharp break from historical precedent—a great, healing burst of speculation.

What was so winning about the collapse of interest rates from 1989 to 1993 was that it was all-encompassing. Not only was their level reduced but also their alignment was improved. The 1989 inversion of the yield curve was over in three months; beginning in August, short-term rates resumed their conventional place below long-term rates, and the gap between them profitably widened. How profitably became a matter of Wall Street legend. Borrowing short and lending long became one of the great American growth industries.

DAVID BRAVER WAS A Wall Street beginner in 1958 when the very same technique caused far-reaching losses just after it had delivered excellent gains. What had temporarily been the year's best bond-market investment idea—buying the Treasury's $2\frac{5}{8}$ percent seven-year note with the proceeds of a broker's loan—suddenly became its worst. It is often said that a professional's investment personality is formed by his or her first formative Wall Street experience, but Braver might as well have arrived in 1951, 1961, or any other year in which a bond bear market did not devastate Wall Street. For in 1994, he and his partner, Steven Stern, were managing some $20 billion in fixed-income securities, applying the techniques that had scalded the people to whom Braver applied for a job as a young man of twenty-four.

The Braver technique was to borrow at the overnight rate, or at the two- or three-month rate, and invest at a long-term rate. His preferred investment medium was mortgage-backed securities. It was profitable to buy them so as long as the spread between short-term rates and mortgage rates remained advantageously wide. Year in and year out, the spread might as well have been drawn to Braver's personal specifications.

Fresh out of Columbia University with a master's degree in mathematics, he applied for a job with Garvin Bantel, the firm that would hear itself rebuked on the floor of the New York Stock Exchange for helping to incite the 1958 liquidation. Braver's application was refused. ("They were too white-shoe," Braver later said of the firm that didn't hire him. "I could never have fit in there.") Raised in Crown Heights, Brooklyn, Braver attended the prestigious Stuyvesant High School in Manhattan. He would ride the subway to the top of the upper East Side and walk down Fifth Avenue, taking in the possibilities. Sometimes, to vary the opulent view, he would walk along Madison.

He began his career in accounting, but quit on the advice of a client. "You'll never make any money doing this," the man told him. Applying to Wall Street, he was hired by D. H. Blair & Co. His field was (and remains today) bonds.

Although he became rich, even by the standards of his adopted borough of Manhattan, and although he does not shrink from making big declarations on big subjects, and although he wears monogrammed, custom-tailored shirts and summers in Southampton, Braver is given to striking biographical understatement. "Since

I wasn't as smart as anybody else, I couldn't compete in the equity market," is a recent sample. Becoming a bond broker, he specialized in convertibles.

Embedded in every convertible bond are a certain number of shares of the issuing company's common stock. As in cryogenic storage, the shares are dormant. They are released, or converted, when the stock achieves a certain price. Until the point of conversion—typically, at a share price 25 percent higher than the price prevailing at the time of issuance—the bond is only a bond. It pays a fixed rate of interest in semiannual installments. Until March of 1968, convertibles enjoyed one unique advantage over garden-variety common stock: no margin requirement was levied on them. In theory, an investor could borrow 100 percent of the purchase price. The buyer of common stock could borrow no more than 50 percent of the purchase price. Almost always, the cost of a bank loan was lower than the yield on the bond. Furthermore, the stock market usually went up (thereby lifting the prices of bonds that could be converted into stock). It followed that buying a convertible on margin was mostly a winning proposition. Braver became an enthusiast.

This special margin dispensation on convertibles was repealed in 1968. "When the government outlawed convertible bonds," is Braver's hyperbolic recollection of the change in margin rules that did not, in fact, outlaw any class of security, but that did deprive him of an excellent personal brokerage income. Adapting, he moved into Treasury securities, federal-agency securities, and prototypical junk, or "story," bonds: securities with a past. Recalling one such story with special fondness—a Philippine bond that enjoyed the implicit, little-understood backing of an agency of the U.S. government—Braver said, "The fact of the matter is that we wound up making a zillion dollars."

Sometimes he has lost a zillion, too. One such setback occurred in 1979, the year that Paul A. Volcker began to administer interest-rate shock therapy to the U.S. economy. Another was 1981, the year the bond market hit its all-time North American low and when, to compound the misery of the creditors, short-term rates towered over even the record-high 15 percent bond yields. The upended yield curve made it unprofitable to buy bonds with borrowed money. A third setback was 1994, in which an unexpected rise in short-term rates caused the reenactment of the losses of 1958, but on a vastly larger scale.

On the whole, however, the 1990s have been make-a-zillion years, not only for Braver, but also for the many who implemented the fundamental Braver idea. In 1991, hedge funds, banks, and others undertook to borrow short and lend long. They borrowed in the overnight market at 6 percent or so, and they purchased two-year Treasury notes at 6½ or 7 percent. (They renewed the loans day by day for as long as they held their notes.) The difference in interest rates provided a measure of profit; the size of the purchases provided a measure of risk. In the government securities market, no margin rules limit a purchaser's borrowings. He or she can obtain as much as a lender will stand for. In this, the market in the solemn obligations of the United States government resembles the used-car market, or a nothing-down-and-zero-percent-financing-until-Labor-Day sale, or the old convertible-bond market before the Federal Reserve turned out the lights.

In mid-May 1991, I was invited to lunch in the downtown offices of one of the top mysterious Wall Street speculators. My host stared over my shoulder at one of the electronic monitors on the wall, and his left knee danced nervously under the table. He asked me if I knew how much of the U.S. public debt was being financed with hot, or speculative, money. I did not. Perhaps $50 billion, he ventured, a sum to which he added he himself had materially contributed. Although not naming a number, he said that his holdings, which he was able to finance entirely with borrowed money, yielded him $300,000 in interest income over just one weekend. With the use of a pocket calculator, it was possible to determine that he owned about $769 million worth of government securities, a calculation corroborated (at least to the extent of its order of magnitude) by his dancing foot. (Another source of his agitation, as I later realized, was the ongoing federal investigation into Treasury-market financing practices, specifically into the claims of bid rigging and collusion in the springtime auctions of two-year notes; he himself emerged unindicted and unfined, but his name was publicly mentioned, which he deplored.) He confessed that it gave him the willies. Yet he could hardly pass up the chance to participate, given the alignment of interest rates and the availability of cheap credit. On the other hand, none of his peers in the upper reaches of finance could afford to pass up this obvious moneymaking opportunity, either. It was plainly a fad and would therefore come to a bad end. However, on form, it would last longer than anyone attempting to make book on the outcome in mid-fad could imagine. Probably, it would stop at the first sign of a rise in short-term interest rates. Such an event would raise a speculator's cost of financing as it lowered the value of the securities being financed. The hot money would fly away to the next temporarily great investment idea. The hasty selling would cause the sincere, long-term holders of Treasury obligations to wonder what had hit them.* *When* was the great unknown.

What neither he nor I suspected was that the next increase in short-term interest rates would be nearly three years away. Almost nobody, not even David Braver, was bullish enough on the bond market in the spring of 1991. The few true optimists, by the lights of the Justice Department and Securities and Exchange Commission, were bullish to a fault. The government would charge that a pair of hedge funds engaged in a scheme to corner an issue of United States government securities, $12 billion worth of two-year Treasury notes. Two of the alleged perpetrators, funds owned by Michael Steinhardt and Bruce Kovner, would later pay $76 million in fines to settle charges that they had bought all the notes there were to buy, and then some, thereby squeezing extra profits from the hides of the shorts and bringing the government securities market into crisis and disrepute. (The fines were merely an annoyance. Steinhardt is believed to have made several billion dollars in the trade. In 1991, he

---

* On the page facing the interview with this unnamed grandee, *Grant's* published an illustrated fanciful history of the Dow Jones Industrial Average, in which the market never fell because the Federal Reserve was always easing, or was about to ease, policy. Whatever this send-up contributed to humor, it lost in timing. Interest rates were indeed embarked on a long decline, a trend that the Fed would ratify and perpetuate and that would last until February 1994. The net outcome was even more bullish than the most compulsively optimistic broker could have imagined.

told Kurt Feshbach, one of the short-selling Feshbachs, that stocks would go down and bonds would go up. In the event, Steinhardt was only half right—stocks, too, would go up—but in speculation, being only half right can very often be stupendous. Steinhardt delivered this forecast aboard the Feshbach jet. Because stocks would also go up, the jet would be sold.) Salomon Brothers, which helped to engineer the corner and which had been cheating in the Treasury market on its own behalf since the summer of 1990, suffered twin blows to its self-confidence and its income statement. The loss of some of its customers was compounded by the loss of some of its top employees, and not even the legendary Warren Buffett could restore the firm to its old lucrative ways.

WHERE THE GOVERNMENT had swung wide was in its charge that the conspirators had "hurt confidence in the markets." On the mounting evidence, confidence was shatterproof. By the end of 1991, the Treasury-bond market resembled a vast construction project. Its growth dazzled the sidewalk superintendents who stopped to stare and worried the kibitzers who doubted the soundness of the underlying physics. The structure was built on the yield curve: borrowing at a low rate, an investor was able to earn a slightly higher rate. In the fall of 1991, the numbers fell out this way: For $10 million down, a well-to-do speculator was able to purchase $500 million of two-year Treasury notes. His or her bank or broker would lend the $490 million difference. The cost of the loan was 5.125 percent. The yield on the notes was 5.89 percent. The difference between the yield and cost worked out to approximately $4 million per annum. Thus, the rate of return on the speculator's down payment amounted to approximately 40 percent. Nothing like it—in risk or return or leverage—was available in the stock market. Edgar Lawrence Smith would have been slack-jawed.

Borrowing short and lending long was a long-standing bankers' taboo. However, as we have seen before and will have occasion to observe again, there are no permanent financial truths. The nature of established belief in markets is itself perverse; believing in the intrinsic merit of a certain class of securities, for instance, people will

bid up its value, finally causing it to become overvalued and therefore unmeritorious. So with beliefs in credit risk or interest-rate risk.
In the 1990s, the banks found deliverance by employing roughly the
same techniques that had sunk the savings and loans in the 1970s
and early 1980s. They borrowed for days, weeks, or months (that is,
short); and they invested the proceeds in government securities maturing in years (that is, *long*). Bank purchases of government securities presently shattered every standing record, rising by $109.6
billion in 1991, by $101.6 billion in 1992, and by $67.1 billion in 1993.
Brokerage-firm balance sheets expanded, and the "carry trade"
became a multi-billion-dollar hedge-fund annuity. A Pennsylvania
banker told *The Wall Street Journal* how it was done in Harrisburg.
One hires "some bright, well-paid people" and surrounds them with
"lots of electronic technology," the man said, adding that the bond-
speculation department "takes up little floor space, has low overhead
and obviously no credit risk." The *Journal's* reporter continued: "It's
not unusual for an investment portfolio, comprising government securities and the like, to produce returns of 35 percent on risk-based
equity, he maintains."

In an economy starved of growth, and in a banking industry
deprived of loan demand, 35 percent returns were almost certain to
be fleeting. They would melt away under the heat of the competition, as so many other brilliant rates of return in market economies
disappear. As the banker from Harrisburg marveled at the achievements of his bond corps, a senior managing director of Bear
Stearns & Co., William Michaelcheck, reflected on the inevitable
speculative denouement. Michaelcheck spoke from rich personal
experience. In 1976, he contributed $10,000 to the founding capital
of J. F. Eckstein & Co., money-market brokers; by early 1979, his
share of the firm's burgeoning net worth was more than $3 million.
It was a good thing that he did not get around to spending any of
this money, Michaelcheck later reflected, because by May of the
same year it was gone. An errant, leveraged trade in Treasury-bill
futures—a "classic textbook margin squeeze," as Michaelcheck remembered it—swept away nearly every cent of the firm's capital.
(There was just enough left to discharge obligations, close the
doors, and turn out the lights.) Now in 1991, Bear Stearns was a fa-

cilitator of a far bigger leveraged interest-rate trade: It lent to the speculators who bought the notes and bonds. "You've got your famous speculators and your not-so-famous speculators buying two-year notes," Michaelcheck related in October 1991. "There are, well, not hundreds, but tens and twenties of little, not-so-famous speculators all over the place. A billion here and a billion there, and pretty soon you're talking about real money. We think that there has got to be $100 billion to $200 billion of this right now, of investment partnerships, going from the biggest to the smallest, buying one-, two- and three-year Treasuries and financing them day to day, speculating on interest rates. And the people who have done this over the past year have made a fortune." He did not mention Braver, but he clearly had him in his mind.

So, Michaelcheck was asked, a meaningful percentage of the public debt of the United States of America is being financed by hot money?

"It's not being financed by hot money," he replied. "It is owned by hot money. It is financed by money-market funds, pension funds and governmental bodies—people who invest in the repo [i.e., repurchase] market. So what's happened is that a partnership acts to buy $10 billion in Treasuries, comes to Wall Street and does a repo. We turn around and give them the money. We in turn take these bonds to the State of New York or the World Bank, borrow the money from them, and they use the money that the public has in their money-market funds or their short-term cash."

As in the 1958 bond market, this happy situation would probably be brought to a close when the economy mended, Michaelcheck ventured. A succession of unexpectedly strong readings on business activity would interrupt the continuity of bullish thought. All at once, the market would decide that the Federal Reserve was going to tighten, or at least that it was no longer going to ease. This realization would produce a cascade of selling, and the bond market at that moment would resemble the soybean market after a much needed rainfall in Illinois.

However, the economy did not mend itself, and the competition to borrow short and lend long did not destroy the carry trade. On the contrary, the industry of bond speculation only grew. By the summer of 1992, the arithmetic had actually become more appealing. Buying $1 billion of two-year notes with $20 million of earnest money, a speculator would have earned 5.05 percent; the cost of borrowing would have been 3½ percent. The difference, over the course of the 12 months, would have produced a return of 81 percent on the $20 million down payment (even without a capital gain on the purchased securities). The Fed had eased no fewer than 20 times since the start of the 1990 recession, and there was no end in sight. It would, indeed, ease 24 times in succession by the time Gordon W. Ringoen, a businessman turned professional investor, invited an audience of financial skeptics to imagine the scene at the Mirage in Las Vegas on New Year's Eve. At the crap table, a patron takes the dice in hand and goes for 24 straight passes. "Can you imagine how much money would be on the table on the 24th consecutive pass?" He paused for dramatic effect. "That's exactly what we have experienced in the debt market. We have had a one-way bet." Not in a lifetime, he ventured, could one have expected to see 24 consecutive anything in the essentially random process of interest-rate oscillation.

The carry trade, considered as a monetary phenomenon, was out of the pages of Röpke. It was a boom instigated by interest rates. One of these rates was central-bank-administered; the other was market-determined. The central-bank rate was lower than the market rate. People seized the speculative opportunity (borrowing at the one, investing at the other), thereby lighting the fuse of a boom. Because the object of speculative desire was Treasury notes, not skyscrapers, factories, or oil tankers, the structure of production was not obviously distorted. The distortion was, for the time being, mainly financial: the yield curve steepened, meaning that the difference between overnight rates and long-dated rates widened, and the general level fell. In sympathy, the stock market rose. Treasury notes were not what leveraged speculators had chosen to buy in the 1970s (then the preferred asset was capital equipment) or the 1980s (people chose operating business and real estate). However, just as Ringoen suggested, times and tastes change. In 1992, bankers and brokers devoutly believed in the safety of soundness of margin debt (for that is what it was) secured by Treasury obligations. "Everybody is playing this game," Ringoen wound up—this was October 1992, a year and a half after the speculator with the dancing foot had marveled at the improbability of earning $300,000 over a single weekend, seemingly without risk. "Interest rates are going to go up, we're going to see a huge unwinding of this entire debt process. These Treasuries will be sold. What will happen then? As Ross Perot says, we will hear that great sucking sound . . ." Ringoen was vindicated—as was Michaelcheck and another perceptive student of the carry trade, James A. Bianco. When, 16 months later, on February 4, 1994, the federal funds rate was moved up by just one quarter of one percentage point, the bond market was shattered. Speculators were driven to sell, and their selling created more selling (caused in part by margin calls, in part by the rapid depreciation in the value of mortgages and mortgage derivatives). It came in waves. In the fall of 1993, the 30-year Treasury bond had yielded less than 6 percent; a year later, it yielded more than 8 percent. (Late in 1994, Robert L. Citron, treasurer of Orange County, California, was unmasked as one of the not-so-famous speculators; the $7.4 billion investment portflio he oversaw was shot through with $2 billion of losses; soon he became one of the famous speculators.) According to the record book, it was the worst 12 months in government securities. Braver, who survived it, called it his second-worst year, behind the year of the coming of Paul Volcker, 1979. But then, in 1995, forced selling abated and lusty buying resumed and the market recovered nearly all of its losses. "You scc," Braver said in the heat of the rally, "I was right all along!"

THE STOCK MARKET, which had stopped going down in the fall of 1990, went straight up beginning in January 1991. It may be seen to have discounted the end of the mild recession, but its liftoff was only in part effect. At some deeper level, the rising market itself became a fundamental economic cause. It precipitated events (notably, the healing of balance sheets, both in and out of the banking system) as much as it anticipated them. When Whitney Houston sang the National Anthem at the Super Bowl in January 1991, raising transcontinental goose pimples, the national mood was clarified. It was optimistic, patriotic, and bullish. "Yes, there are terrible problems," a sagacious investor wrote to his clients shortly afterward, "but they're old news. . . . The market's heard, digested and absorbed enough melancholia to last a lifetime."*

On Wall Street nothing dispels melancholic vapors like a drop in interest rates, and the rate of decline of money-market rates steepened in 1991. The Federal Reserve was credited for this fall, as it is customarily praised or blamed for every fall or rise in interest rates. Possibly there is a need to believe that so vital a financial event is caused by one or more people who can be named and haled in to testify before a congressional committee. The same people who would explain a fall in the price of tomatoes in terms of supply and demand are inclined to impute Federal Reserve causation to a fall in the price of a loan. The Fed, being human, is itself inclined to encourage this belief, taking more credit than the facts would fairly seem to allow. In testimony before the Senate Banking Committee in May 1994, Alan Greenspan all but claimed that the Fed had acted alone. "In the spring of 1989," Greenspan led off, "we began to ease monetary conditions as we observed the consequence of balance-sheet strains resulting from increased debt. Households and businesses became much more reluctant to borrow and spend, and lenders to extend credit—a phenomenon often referred to as the 'credit crunch.' In an endeavor to defuse these financial strains, we moved short-term rates lower in a long series of steps through the summer of 1992, and we held them at unusually low levels through the end of 1993—both absolutely, and, importantly, relative to inflation. These actions, together with those to reduce budget deficits, facilitated a significant decline in long-term rates as well."

Students of the Greenspan record, listening to the chairman claim credit for the restoration of American solvency, were left to wonder what they had missed. Interest rates had fallen, of course, and the broken financial economy had knitted. However, it was the first they had heard of this commendable and forehanded course of action by the Federal Reserve. Greenspan went on:

* Patriotic demonstrations were just as bracing for the American bicentennial on July 4, 1976, as they were for the outbreak of the Gulf War in 1991, yet there was no great Gerald Ford bull market. What there was, instead, was a great Ford and Carter commodity bull market, a very different proposition.

Lower interest rates fostered a dramatic improvement in the financial condition of borrowers and lenders. Households rolled outstanding mortgages and consumer loans into much lower rate debt. Business firms were able to pay down high-cost debt by issuing bonds and stocks on very favorable terms. And banks, which had cut back on credit availability partly because of their own balance sheet problems, were able to strengthen their capital positions by issuing a substantial volume of equity shares and other capital instruments and by retaining much of their improved flow of earnings. Moreover, the lower interest rates, together with expanding economic activity, recently have bolstered the commercial real estate market, stemming the losses on the collateral underlying some of the largest problem credits of banks and other intermediaries and, in some cases, permitting them to find purchasers for these assets.

A search of the literature for examples of the personal and institutional foresight to which the chairman had alluded was unavailing. When the majority of the financial world was complacent, so was he. It was not until October 1991 that the phrase "economic headwinds" entered the Greenspan repertory. He used the metaphor to describe the unprosperous gusts that were buffeting the aircraft GNP, the source of which he identified as the debt predicament. However, it was a historic observation rather than a predictive one. Bank stocks had reached low ebb fully one year before Greenspan favored a Rhode Island audience with this aperçu; the stock market–assisted recapitalization of the banking system was already long under way. In the midst of the overbuilding of real estate and the overleveraging of corporate balance sheets in 1988–90, Greenspan had been inclined not to dwell on the issue of credit, possibly because it had not yet, to him, become an issue. In remarks titled "Innovation and Regulation of Banks in the 1990s" before the American Bankers Association in October 1988, for example, he did not mention the excessive lending against real estate that was being carried out by members of his audience even as he spoke to them, and that would be featured as one of the great regulatory issues in the decade under examination. In his semiannual

Humphrey-Hawkins testimony in July 1989, the subject of excessive debt came up in only one context, that being the technical matter of the effect of the woes of the thrift industry on the growth of M-2 money supply.* In testimony before the Joint Economic Committee in January 1990, on the eve of the failure of Drexel Burnham Lambert, a signal event in the credit contraction of 1989–92, Greenspan did not dwell on junk bonds, junk loans, failing banks, or in general on "the consequence of balance-sheet strains resulting from increased debt," as he would put it in 1994. Although he did mention commercial real estate, among other macroeconomic trouble spots, he did not let on that interest rates would be progressively lowered to reduce the "financial strains" he would see so clearly four years later, while looking backward: "But such imbalances and dislocations as we see in the economy today probably do not suggest anything more than a temporary hesitation in the continuing expansion of the economy," he wound up in that 1990 appearance. The messy default by Washington Bancorp on its unrated commercial paper came only one week after a pronouncement by the Federal Reserve Board, also based in Washington, D.C., that no generalized credit contraction was under way.

Nor was Greenspan's the only deficit in acuity in the highest policymaking reaches of the Federal Reserve System. "I think the real estate market, with the exception of northern New Jersey, is probably not going to be any significant drag in terms of the overall national picture of the real estate sector [*sic*]," pronounced Gerald Corrigan, president of the Federal Reserve Bank of New York and vice chairman of the Federal Reserve Board, in a closed meeting of the Federal Open Market Committee in early February 1990 (a time when Donald Trump was just beginning to come under well-founded financial suspicion). Corrigan could see no real estate thunderheads six months later, either (as the market was beginning

---

* Greenspan sounded a warning note in a speech on October 16, 1989, the Monday following the "minicrash" of the preceding Friday. Addressing the American Bankers Association, the chairman described the 150-year odyssey by which the association's members had become more leveraged and less liquid. "[A] review of the composition of both on- and off-balance sheet exposures," he said in summary, "suggests that the level of risk in banking today may, if anything, be higher than it has generally been in the recent past." It was a theme that warranted another speech, at a minimum.

to perceive that not all was well with the office-building empire of the Canadian developer Paul Reichman). "I would say," Corrigan ventured in October 1990, just as the problem was cystallized— bank stocks, indeed, had stopped going down—"that by far the greatest risk of further deterioration in asset quality is in the real estate area."*

As for Greenspan, who showed no great understanding behind closed doors, either, the debt financial predicament began to figure more prominently in his public utterances in the summer of 1990. He warmed to it in 1991, the year that began with the failure of Bank of New England and ended with the morbid decline in the price of the shares of Citicorp. In 1992, now joined by the third-party presidential candidate Ross Perot, college professors, and newspaper readers, he delved more deeply into the crisis of indebtedness, a crisis that by that late date had been transformed into a crisis (among professional investors) of not owning enough bank stocks.

THE FEDERAL RESERVE'S 24 consecutive cuts in short-term interest rates from 1989 to 1992 brought to mind the 24 major printings of a runaway best-seller whose publisher had initially expected to sell only 2,000 copies. It did not burnish the publisher's reputation for commercial judgment. Similarly, a skeptical market might have wondered if the Federal Reserve was any more capable of seeing into the financial future than the Central Intelligence Agency had been into the Soviet one. The market was not, however, skeptical. On Wall Street, the central bank was credited with powers exceeding even those of the turn-of-the-century Money Trust over which J. P. Morgan was thought to have presided. One Federal Reserve employee, however, Daniel L. Thornton, an economist at the Federal Reserve Bank of St. Louis, asked the fundamental question. Was the Fed, posed Thornton, the cause of movements in money-

* Martha Seger, a Reagan appointee resigned as governor of the Federal Reserve Board in March 1991, seemed to see what Corrigan and Greenspan missed; at FOMC meetings in 1990, she consistently (if unsuccessfully) argued for a lower federal funds rate. Among the other reasons she cited was the credit contraction.

market interest rates between 1983 and 1994? He found no evidence to support the conventional answer, which is yes.

From time to time, it is helpful to visualize an economic trend, an idea, or a governmental institution as if it were a common stock. Imagined in such as way, the Fed had hit rock bottom during the early tenure of Paul Volcker. In this period, the central bank of the United States was figuratively selling below book value. The proof of its low standing were the high interest rates that investors demanded to hold dollar-denominated securities, or, a mirror image of this distrust, the high prices assigned to the asset with which paper money and the institution of credit most directly competes: gold bullion. It was at this moment of maximum distrust when a clairvoyant would have bought dollars, bonds, and (had they been available in the open market) shares in the Federal Reserve System.

In 1995, Volcker could remark that central banks stood "at a pinnacle of influence and respect," not having to add that from a pinnacle it is impossible not to come down in the world. "By and large," the ex-Fed chairman conceded, "if the overriding objective is price stability, we did a better job with the nineteenth century gold standard and passive central banks, with currency boards or even 'free banking.'"

However, not even so high a priest as Volcker could deliver a convincing sermon of doubt. In 1981, the public had refused to credit him even when it was offered 15 percent bond yields in the bargain. Believing devoutly in his successor, however, the market in 1993 settled, briefly, for a $5\frac{7}{8}$ percent Treasury-bond yield. In the same spirit of piety, investors purchased some of the 100-year debentures issued by American corporations.* The buyers of these novelties consigned their principal to the ultimate care of the great-great-grandchildren of the incumbent Federal Reserve Board. What was different about this demonstration of enthusiasm for fixed-income securities was that it took place in the absence of any legal certainty about what a dollar was, or could become. In 1900, following passage of the Gold Standard Act, and in 1946, following

---

* Paul Isaac, Wall Street thinker and doer, observed that at the bonds' maturity in 2093, Mickey Mouse would be older than the characters in "Uncle Tom's Cabin" were in 1993. Like Lovett, Isaac believed in the mortality of corporate collateral.

enactment of the postwar Bretton Woods arrangements, a bond-holder could draw confidence—the longer-dated portion of this faith misplaced, as it happened—in the monetary institutions of the day. The optimists of 1995 bet purely on faith.

The 1996 Morgan Stanley Central Bank Directory listed 171 central banks (in just that many countries), of which 22 banks had come into existence in the prior five years. Evidently, no self-respecting government was complete without one. Even more than a prison, a bank of issue had become an indispensable appendage to national sovereignty. The 1994 devaluation of the Mexican peso was distinguished from the earlier peso devaluations in that it was preceded, also in 1994, by the ostentatious separation of the Bank of Mexico from the governing Mexican political party. The im-provement in the stature of the Mexican central bank did not pre-vent the devastating collapse of the peso late in the year, but it was a welcome observance of the modern forms.

As with religious faith, the source of belief in central banking was not revealed to a pure rationalist. The federal funds rate, the systemwide balance sheet, the Washington headquarters building, the prose style of the minutes of the Federal Open Market Com-mittee, the members of the Federal Open Market Committee themselves, and the congressional testimony of the chairman of the Federal Reserve Board were, when taken one at a time, only a little more imposing than the personnel, operating methods, and real es-tate of the Department of Agriculture.

To the nonbeliever, the Fed's balance sheet suggested a nearly half-trillion leveraged bond fund. It contained assets, mainly Treasury securities, and liabilities, mainly currency, the latter balanced on a trace amount of capital. The profits produced by the assets were siz-able; the Fed turned over $23.4 billion worth to the Treasury in 1995.

The principal source of these earnings was the Fed's privileged exemption from the ordinary requirement of a bank to pay interest on its liabilities. Currency, of course, was non-interest-bearing, and so, too, were the deposits called reserves that banks were obliged to leave with the relevant Federal Reserve bank. (The vision of the founders of the Federal Reserve System was that reserve balances, massed in the regional Reserve banks, could be bundled on a train and sent to the scene of a bank run to forestall a recurrence of the Panic of 1907. One dark day, the reasoning went, depositors might want their money back again.) The Federal Reserve's shareholders, some 3,965 commercial banks, earned a 6 percent dividend. However, the stock, which could not be bought or sold in the open market, entitled them to no voice in the system's management. In theory, the Fed answered only to Congress, a nonstockholder.

The central bank's greatest power was the power of suggestion. Besides this hypnotic instrument, it had three other tools of monetary control: the federal funds rate, which influenced the shape of the yield curve and the availability and the cost of bank reserves; the discount rate, at which a bank might, in theory, borrow from a Federal Reserve Bank; and bank-reserve requirements, which determined the number of reserve cents that a bank was required for each dollar of deposits—specifically, of demand deposits—it held. Of these three, the most potent, by far, was the power to jigger the funds rate.

The basic theory of monetary control holds that the Fed determines the monetary base, that is, the sum of currency and bank reserves. Thereby it determines the money supply, and thereby the inflation rate. Let us say that the members of the Federal Open Market Committee, the Fed's policymaking arm, determine that the nation could use a little pick-me-up. To start with, one or more members might slip the news of this intention to a friendly journalist (and which recipient of a feed-box tip would not be friendly?). Depending on the state of financial morale, the disclosure itself might cause a decline in interest rates; expecting the Fed to act, the market might act first.

To lower the federal funds rate, the Fed would augment its enormous securities portfolio by buying Treasuries in the open market. The purchases inject new funds into the banking system. By enlarging the supply of reserve dollars, the Fed thereby tends to reduce their cost; that is, it lowers the federal funds rate. To bring about higher interest rates, the Fed does these things in reverse, selling instead of buying.

The theory brings to mind dogs on a leash. At one end is the chairman of the Federal Reserve Board; at the other are the straining banks: money centers, regionals, thrifts, community banks, and the lesser breeds of depository institution. A longer leash—more and cheaper reserve dollars, or lower reserve requirements—means more financial running room, more exuberant lending, and more opportunity for the animals to wrap themselves around financial tree trunks or to race in front of the cyclical traffic. In another way, the structure of monetary affairs resembles an acrobatic act, with the lighter members of the troupe, the banks, ultimately resting on the shoulders of the understander, the central bank. The bottom dollar is the Federal Reserve's. The inadequacy of the metaphors is almost identical to the demerits of the monetary theory. Sometimes the dogs, as in the 1930s or, less dramatically, in the 1990s, refuse to run but instead lie down. The leash goes slack. The Federal pays out more leash, encouragingly, but the animals slumber. The persistence of this condition describes a state of stagnation, or contraction. An especially severe case describes an outright deflation.

The process by which control is supposed to be exerted is more plausible the farther away from the schematic one stands; it is the details that corrupt faith. At most, the Fed can control one key interest rate, the federal funds rate. The rest it may influence. Like the mother who finds her child becoming more headstrong with every passing year, the Fed's influence is weakest at the longest reaches of the maturity spectrum. The funds rate is the rate at which banks lend and borrow among themselves over days, weeks, or months. The needful banks borrow from the flush ones, or from flush non-banks, like the Federal National Mortgage Association. The reason that banks lend and borrow is to settle up their reserve accounts at the Fed. Every two weeks, a bank must produce the required number of dollars. Coming up short, it must borrow them; alternatively, finding itself overprovisioned, it may lend them. The federal funds rate, therefore, is the going rent for spare cash in the banking system.

So far, so good. The exact technique by which the Fed exercises control and dominion over this one interest rate is the purchase and sale of government securities in the open market. Buying Treasuries, it creates credit; selling them, it destroys it. Doing either, it directly influences another vital interest rate, the repurchase rate. The repurchase, or "repo," rate is the interest rate at which a loan can be floated against the collateral of securities. It, too, is a short-term rate. Via the funds rate and the repo rate, the Fed can influence the cost of cash to the wholesale financial economy.

The significance of the repurchase rate is that borrowed money (as we have already seen) finances a sizable portion of the public debt. The principal equity capital beneath this debt belongs to the banks and the bond dealers. They are enormously leveraged as a matter of course. Salomon Brothers, for instance, had common stockholders' equity of $2.82 billion at year-end 1990; the rest of its capital, totaling $98.1 billion,* was borrowed. The bulk of this debt, borrowed at the repurchase, or repo, rate, financed government securities. The securities on Salomon's balance sheet totaled $48.8 billion.† Salomon, of course, was only one leveraged financial institution among dozens. On the same year-end 1990 statement date, the sum total of borrowing by the principal government-securities dealers totaled $77.9 billion.

As mentioned, it is not merely the level of interest rates that makes the sun come up in the morning on Wall Street, but also their structure. The alignment preferred by the dealers and speculators in government securities is positively sloped. This means that the lowest rate on the spectrum is the funds rate. The three-month Treasury-bill rate is higher than the funds rate, and the two-year rate is higher than the one-year bill rate. So it goes out to 30 years, with yields ascending by maturity. The lower the repo rate in relation to the yields on longer-dated securities, the more profitable the business of owning and financing notes and bonds. Thus the Fed, as the arbiter of the funds rate and, indirectly, of the repo rate, is also the silent partner of David Braver, of Salomon Brothers, and of all the other Braver- and Salomon-like aspirants who assisted in the great transformation of American banking and credit in the years 1991–93. The Fed played to the market and the market to the Fed in a kind of double concerto grosso.

THE FAILURE OF THE Bank of New England, with $22 billion of assets, over the first weekend of 1991 was an event out of the pages

---

* Including short-term borrowings, financial instruments sold but not yet purchased, collateralized mortgage obligations, and term debt.

† The sum of U.S. government and agency securities and securities purchased under agreements to resell.

of the first Roosevelt administration. So, too, was the proposal by William Seidman that the FDIC, of which Seidman was chairman, should be allowed to buy stock in blighted bank holding companies. And so, again, was the bear market in commercial real estate that had settled in to stay on Wall Street itself, among countless other American neighborhoods. It was not the 1930s that the Federal Reserve faced in late 1990, but the modern age in toto: failing banks, rising consumer prices, and a receding economy on one side of the ledger; the promise of the unfolding computer age, the partial socialization of banking risk, and the famous resiliency of the American enterprise on the other. The rate of growth in the broad money supply was declining and the dollar exchange rate was weakening. As the Fed was expected to protect the banking system, suppress the inflation rate, and sustain the national economy (all in the context of a looming war in the Persian Gulf), it was perhaps no wonder that the chairman seemed to speak in tongues. Direct and plainspoken attention to one situation might have undermined that aura of mystery without which the Fed would be hard put to conduct its ordinary business.

In December 1990, the Fed took three-pronged accommodative action. It cut the federal funds rate, in two quarter-point stages, to 7 percent from $7\frac{1}{2}$ percent; it dropped the discount rate to $6\frac{1}{2}$ percent from 7 percent (the first such reduction in almost two years); and it eliminated reserve requirements on certain bank liabilities. The change in reserve requirements, the most rarely used and therefore the most exotic of the monetary-policy devices at the Fed's disposal, released $3 out of every $100 in so-called nonpersonal CDs, time deposits, and Eurocurrency from enforced idleness in bank vaults or in non-interest-bearing reserve accounts at the Fed. Approximately $13.6 billion was thereby liberated throughout the banking system. In the scheme of things, it was no vast sum. (Furthermore, it was a savings that would be largely neutralized by an imminent rise in the assessments to be levied on the same banks by the FDIC.) Yet the buyers of bank stocks, so recently despairing, now recovered their courage. Nothing that the Federal Reserve press release said could have accounted for the change of heart. Perhaps the buyers were reading between the lines:

The Board took action at this time also in response to mounting evidence that commercial banks have been tightening
their standards of creditworthiness and the terms and conditions for many types of loans [the statement said in part].
While much of this tightening has been welcome from the
standpoint of safety and soundness, it has in recent months
begun to exert a contractionary influence on the economy.
This influence has been reflected in slow growth in the broad
monetary aggregates and in bank credit.

The evidence to which the release alluded had, in fact, been
mounting since 1989, when Integrated Resources failed for the
want of its maturing commercial paper, and United Air Lines was
unable to win the financing to complete its proposed leveraged buy-
out. The prices of junk bonds were falling and the availability of
real estate credit was shrinking. As recently as December 1989,
Treasury-bill yields had exceeded 30-year bond yields, the contractionary circumstance that speeded the ruin of the Seamen's Bank
and almost always discourages the process of credit creation. The
yield curve had reverted to a more bullish shape in early 1990, but
the dogs at the end of the monetary leash were listless.

AMONG THE UNUSUAL features of the war that began on January 17,
1991, was that steel production actually declined in the principal belligerent country, the United States. Another was that the principal
belligerent's rate of inflation did not turn higher, but fell. Still another was that the chairman of the Federal Reserve Board and
countless other interested parties were able to observe the stunning
financial accompaniment to the opening American bombardment
of Baghdad in the comfort of their own computer-equipped homes.
What they saw was a first-round knockout: stocks and bonds over oil
and gold.

If the outcome of the war was never in doubt (not, at least,
to the spectators), the domestic financial suspense continued for
months on end. On January 24, Robert Van Buren, chairman of
Midlantic Bank in Edison, New Jersey, the self-styled "Hungry

Banker" of regional television advertising fame, resigned, with the FDIC warning as the door closed behind him that, barring improvement, the real estate–bedecked bank would roll up a loss of $4 billion by the end of 1992. (So many improvements were subsequently effected that in July 1995 the bank would be sold for $3 billion.) In February, Moody's warned that defaults by junk-bond issuers might ricochet through the banking system. In March, the *American Banker* contributed a headline to the permanent annals of American financial and social relations: WEALTHY SHOW CONCERN FOR DEPOSIT SAFETY. Also in March, authorities quoted in the *Banker* warned that hundreds of billions of dollars of real estate loans would be falling due in the next few years, "ballooning the demand for refinancing at a time when it is difficult to underwrite any real estate loan." And in the same month, the Chase Manhattan Bank offered praise for the monetary and regulatory initiatives that were, in fact, contributing to the bank's own resuscitation: "Although the effect of these actions cannot be quantified, it is possible that their effect could be positive," the bank grudgingly allowed.

"There's a nervousness out there that I haven't seen in my 25 years in the organization . . . ," Nicholas J. Ketcha, director of supervision for the New York Region of the FDIC, said in March. "We are running our businesses on the assumption that next year will be difficult," John Reed, chairman of Citicorp, said in April.

May brought news of rising delinquencies in Citicorp's consumer-loan portfolio, and in June came a gloomy prediction by William Seidman on the future of the banking system. "This year could soon shape up as the grimmest for dividend cuts since the Great Depression by major banks . . . ," declared the firm of Keefe, Bruyette & Woods in July. A sign of the market's fragile confidence, Whitney Houston notwithstanding, was revealed in August with a report on the continuing difficulties faced by weak banks in borrowing fed funds. ("A fed funds trader at one large bank recalled contacting about 20 banks without finding one that was willing to sell," according to the *Banker*. " 'We literally could not get any money out of the market,' the trader said.")

Chase Manhattan Bank got out of the junk-bond business in September; Citicorp suspended its dividend in October; and Don-

ald Trump, pleading for a tax break for himself and other former
real estate moguls, warned of a "deep recession-slash-depression,"
in November. Citicorp common closed below $10 a share (for the
first time in 11 years) in December.

It was on the day of the low trade in Citicorp, in fact, that the
Fed uncharacteristically took a big step instead of a little one. On
December 20, it lowered the federal funds rate by 100 basis points,
to $3\frac{1}{2}$ percent. In a monetary trompe l'oeil, it reduced the discount
rate by one percentage point. It did not escape the market's notice
that the Fed's action corresponded with a new sinking spell in the
stock market and—most suggestively—with a new low price in the
common stock of the nation's biggest bank. It was a short inferential hop to the conclusion that the Fed was running monetary policy for the express purpose of bailing out Citi in particular, the
banking system in general, and Wall Street in toto.

BEFORE THE CREATION of the Federal Reserve, monetary cranks
could blame J. P. Morgan, George F. Baker, or one of the Rocke-
fellers for deflation and hard times. Late in the twentieth century,
bears could blame the Fed for bull markets and preternaturally
good times. The impulse to blame someone in a position of authority for an unprofitable financial outcome is a Wall Street ever-
green. With the advent of derivative securities and futures markets,
it was not inconceivable that a well-timed purchase of some high-
octane financial instrument could cause a falling market to recover
or a banking crisis to subside. Speculation abounded that the Fed,
by purchasing stock-index futures or by causing them to be purchased in ways left undisclosed, had prevented a pit from opening
up in the market on October 20, 1987, the day after the crash. The
conspiratorial thought was that the Fed in 1987 had played the role
of the so-called bankers' pool in 1929, but that its intervention had
succeeded whereas the bankers' had (except in the very short term)
failed. No evidence has been adduced to support this idea; it has
just as much historical standing as the canard that J. P. Morgan
robbed the country by lending assistance to the administration of
Grover Cleveland in the gold market in 1895. However, in the wake

of the 190-point collapse of the Dow Jones Industrial Average on Friday, October 13, 1989, H. Robert Heller, an ex-governor of the Fed, draped the idea in a retrospective plausibility by advocating that the Fed do exactly what some people suspected it had already done. He proposed that, in moments of crisis, the central bank should intervene directly in the stock market. Better to intervene directly, the argument went, than to compromise monetary policy by intervening indirectly; if the Fed wanted stock prices to rise, it should buy stocks, not Treasury bills. The Heller proposal, if it accomplished nothing else, served to remind the public that the Fed was already in the business of market rigging. Its everyday modus operandi was the manipulation of the money market to produce a certain federal funds rate. When called upon by the Treasury, it intervened to manipulate the currency market. Like armed force, it was a kind of behavior that governments reserved for themselves but refused to allow for their citizens.

Was monetary policy in the early 1990s subordinated to the banking dilemma? Did the Federal Reserve ride to the rescue of the banks when it ought to have ridden off in another direction? My conclusion is no, it did not. In which alternative direction might it have ridden? To the currency market to rescue the dollar. But in international finance, too, America was blessed. Under the classical rules, it is the deficit country on which the burden of adjustment rightly falls. In January 1991, the United States was that maladjusted deficit country. Proof was that the dollar exchange rate was setting new post–World War II lows. However, on February 1, 1991, only a day after the Bundesbank raised a pair of German interest rates, the Federal Reserve reduced a pair of U.S. interest rates. Germany was then reunifying itself; America was leading a coalition against Saddam Hussein. Each enterprise entailed vast expense (in the case of the United States, partially reimbursed by coalition partners). Here was a test of the durability of the dollar brand name. The issue before the currency market was whether the decisive, extra, unwanted dollar had at last been emitted into the world's monetary channels. The reason to believe that it had was that more and more dollars were winding up in the custody of foreign central banks. (Among the other participants in the dollar's semipermanent international rescue party were the central banks of Norway and Greece; things had come to a pretty pass indeed.) Had the dollar been deemed good value, it would have been seized upon and invested in by profit-seeking private parties. As it was, it was moving from strong hands to weak. Said *Grant's* in some heat:

> By spitting in the eye of the Bundesbank on February 1, the Federal Reserve served notice that its No. 1 priority was not the dollar but the recession (and related domestic topics, e.g., Citicorp). Super bulls on the stock market have said that the Fed can virtually push the funds rate to zero, at which level, certainly, someone would want a loan [a reference to the tendency of people then not to want one]. The past three weeks have provided indelible proof that a lower funds rate is good for common stocks. What remains to be seen is its long-term effect on the dollar and interest rates.
>
> That there has been no dollar crisis this year is testament both to the enduring appeal of America and to the brilliant manipulative record of successive American governments. Literally for decades (since the 1950s), the United States has run deficit positions with the rest of the world. What has changed is the accepted method of paying for them. Under the Bretton Woods system, the dollar was the world's "reserve currency." It was convertible into gold, and the other currencies (the planets, moons and asteroids of the monetary system) were convertible into dollars. Presently, however, the foreign liabilities of the United States outstripped the gold that backed them. In a formative episode of eye-spitting, the Nixon administration in 1971 abandoned the last pretense that the dollar had any objective definition in gold or anything else.

In the 1960s, the French economist Jacques Rueff had condemned the Bretton Woods monetary system for permitting "deficits without tears." So-called reserve-currency countries could live like gigolos, he suggested, as the United States was doing and as Britain had done. The economic trouble with this indulgence was that it permitted the cumulation of error. Deficits (and surpluses) piled up, economies became distorted and the world's central banks became overloaded with depreciating alien currencies, specifically, in his time and later, dollars. In the 1980s and early 1990s, policies by which the United States would have righted its payments imbalance were not undertaken because America's creditors did not force the issue. In the late 1960s, France, under de Gaulle, had demanded gold in exchange for its unwanted dollars. So much gold left the United States at the statutory, $35-per-ounce rate that Washington changed the rules. After August 15, 1971, no official dollar-for-gold withdrawals would be allowed at any rate. Henceforth the dollar, being convertible into nothing except other currencies at market exchange rates, was run-proof in the particular sense that there was nothing to run on. The monetary system in its pure paper state was comparable to the insured banking system: in both cases, the modern rules discouraged panicked withdrawals of funds. The cost of this improvement was that a certain kind of conservative financial behavior was discouraged. It couldn't be said that foreign central banks did not behave in a conservative fashion. They had become the conservators of the dollar by dint of owning so many of them. A "run on the currency"—in the shape of emotional selling of the dollars that they themselves had accumulated—would be almost as costly to them as it would be to the United States. Indeed, insofar as the United States officially, if tacitly, favored a weaker currency, a sharp reduction in the dollar exchange rate would hurt only them. Thus, the United States continued to emit dollars, the central banks (in lieu of genuine, private-sector demand) continued to accumulate them, and the dollar exchange rate continued to drift lower. However, no disaster-causing supersaturation was to occur in 1991 (or in any year up until this writing). That the Federal Reserve was able to cut interest rates early in 1991 at the lowest postwar ebb of the dollar exchange rate must be counted one of the great feats of the American empire.

ON SEPTEMBER 22, 1994, in a committee room of the Dirksen Senate Office Building, Donald W. Riegle Jr., nearing the end of a 17-year Senate career, six of them as chairman of the Banking Committee and three of them as a member of the so-called Keating Five, received hearty bipartisan congratulations. The name of Charles Keating, the savings and loan felon from whom Riegle had accepted campaign contributions (not breaking the law, the Senate Ethics Committee delicately found, but exhibiting "insensitivity and poor judgment"), was not once mentioned, least of all by the chairman, who was himself, in his private capacity as a consulting economist, the recipient of a Keating fee. (Greenspan, in 1985, had pronounced that the management of the Keating thrift enterprise was "seasoned and expert," with a "record of outstanding success in making sound and profitable direct investments.") Alan Greenspan, witness and well-wisher, reflecting on the cure of banking during the preceding few years, pronounced it "truly amazing," as indeed it was. But who or what was behind it? Did the central bank knowingly rescue the banks by lowering dollar-denominated interest rates?

Perhaps Greenspan, being bound by the central banker's vow of ambiguity, might have kept his brilliant, innermost thoughts to himself. But in no contemporary utterance did he indicate any deep understanding of the situation. What he said for the record on the subject of money and banking prior to the middle of 1990, as we have already seen, was nothing that a regular viewer of *Wall Street Week* would not have said. He became more concerned, as did the television audience, but he was bound to stay concerned longer than it was because the exultant rise in stock prices in 1991 did not, on its face, seem to constitute an immediate healing of the lenders and borrowers who had overindulged in the boom. The surprise was that the speculative gush brought deliverance. From the moment the bull market began, the eventual restoration of balance sheets was a certainty. The bull market became the most important financial fact in America, more important even than the federal funds rate or the Federal Reserve Board's forecast of the year's gross domestic product. However, what is obvious in 1996 was subtle in 1991.

The Fed facilitated and nourished the bull market, but it did not knowingly create it. I would say that the central bank was "lucky" if that word did not seem to imply that those of us who missed the boat were merely unlucky. Not one of the top banking and central-banking figures of that day to whom I have spoken was prepared to claim that monetary policy was managed for the salvation of the banking system or, even less, of a particular bank, even a very large one.*

The mainstream Wall Street view of 1990–91 is that the banking restoration was a production, jointly and severally, of Federal Reserve policy, economic recovery, and speculative revival, in that order. I would put the bull market—or, rather, markets, in stocks and bonds—at the top of the list. According to the early-twentieth-century theories of Robert Rhea and William Hamilton, the stock market discounts future financial events. According to the late-twentieth-century theory of George Soros—he calls it "reflexivity"—financial markets may, at times, themselves constitute an independent source of causation of future financial events. The 1990–91 episode is out of the pages of Soros. For reasons that we may never entirely understand, the financial markets levitated. Salvation—for many a lush year—followed.

* "If that was going on," said Robert Clarke, comptroller of the currency at the time, speaking both on interest-rate reductions of December 19, 1991, and of a general, central-bank-driven relaxation of policy, "it was done totally without my knowledge and certainly was not discussed in any of the meetings we had." Senior officials in the Federal Reserve System, as well as a former senior Treasury official, have seconded this view.

CHAPTER FIVE

THE
CANFIELD
MARKET

IN THE EARLY 1990s, in the midst of a worldwide real estate bear market, there was a telltale, incongruous boom. Tunica County, Mississippi, a soybean and cotton backwater and longtime low achiever in the national economic and social rankings, became a gambling mecca.

Americans had gambled under the gold standard as well as under the paper standard, in prosperity and depression, in bull markets and bear markets, on riverboats and dry land. Now—with a business expansion and a bull market under way and with a paper dollar in circulation—they gambled even more. In 1982, when the bull stock market began, the amalgamated businesses of poker, craps, roulette, slots, etc. (along with their associated restaurants, bars, and hotels) generated revenue of about $10.4 billion. In 1994, they produced almost $40 billion. Was it purely accidental that the Tunica County renaissance coincided with hedge fund speculating in bonds on flyspeck margins, with novice public investors turning to mutual funds and away from money in the bank, with resurgent initial public offerings, and with state legislatures moving to liberalize the old inhibiting rules governing the investment behavior of fiduciaries? Almost certainly, it was not. In ways large and small, America was becoming financially bolder. It was coming around to the philosophy that there was more to be feared in not making money than in risking its loss. Such, of course, is the psychological hallmark of every boom. The spectacle of possibly undeserving people getting rich with little or no apparent effort has made bull markets through the ages seem, to some, like gambling enterprises, and the controversy over the gambling aspects of derivatives is recurrent.* On top of the other innumerable bullish influences in the early years of the decade was the weight of conditioned experience as well as a shared faith in the competence of central banks. It was not that investors intentionally began to gamble away their savings. It was, rather, that they began to reevaluate the odds on losing them: increasingly, these seemed to lengthen. If, in 1974, an investment in any blue-chip common stock was regarded as the height of recklessness, in 1996 it was held to be just the opposite. Neither was it gambling to buy the stock of an unseasoned company priced at the equivalent of 75 times earnings, people had come to decide, because equities always appreciated over the span of decades. Thus, gradually and by degree, the downside was stricken from the list of realistic potential financial outcomes.

IN THE BULL-MARKET year of 1964, Nicholas Darvas, professional dancer turned successful lay speculator, wrote *Wall Street: The Other Las Vegas* as an exposé of the stock market. Although the book was not overly long, the gambling metaphor died of exhaustion long before the denouement in chapter 8, "Figuring My Winnings." What was wrong with Darvas's rendering of the Las Vegas analogy is what has been wrong with every other attack on "stock gambling," both before and since. The stock market is not the kind of game in which one party loses what another wins. It is the kind of game in which, over certain periods of time, nearly everyone may win, or

---

* Around the turn of the century, the elders of the New York Stock Exchange equated gambling with derivatives activity, or a kind of derivatives activity known as bucketing. In it, the house, or bucket shop, took bets on the short-term movement of stock prices: no actual shares changed hands. The modern-day equivalent of bucketing is options trading, over which the establishment is now proud to claim paternity. It was not born so much as reincarnated, however. The Wall Street establishment at the turn of the nineteenth century was all in favor of "time bargains," which, because they did not involve the transfer of actual securities, were unenforceable in court. In the eyes of the law, they were no better than common gambling.

nearly everyone may lose. A participant may invest or speculate or gamble on geopolitics, corporate earnings, or interest rates, but a high incidence of outright gambling would not by itself transform the stock market into "the other Las Vegas." It would still be Wall Street, in which the value of businesses is continuously appraised. What had changed during the great bull market of the 1990s were the points of reference of the appraisal.

The acceptance of long, or longer, odds on Wall Street was undeniable. The symptoms included the rationalization of high stock market valuations, the popularity of "momentum" investing, the proliferation of laudatory biographies of leading speculators (including, in 1995, the life story of the 17-year-old flash from Troy, Michigan, Matt Seto), and the unmistakable signs of mutual-fund addiction. This last pathology was first reported by Reed Abelson in an article in the Sunday *New York Times* on April 30, 1995, the headline over which was STOP ME BEFORE I INVEST AGAIN. The experience of rising stock and bond prices had become as deeply imbued in Americans in the mid-1990s as the experience of falling or stagnant securities prices was for Americans of the early 1940s.

The nation would find much to like in this sea change. As we have seen, it was the rise of the stock market that was instrumental both in the cure of the banking system and in the flowering of entrepreneurial capitalism, most visibly in high technology. Tunica Countians, certainly, could find little to regret about the changes in investment doctrine, or in the legitimization of casino gambling. The county seat, also called Tunica (an Indian name for "the people"), was inoculated against the characteristic real estate excesses of the big cities by both its geology and its poverty. Even if someone flush with bank credit priced below the natural rate of interest and oblivious to the shortage of potential tenants had got it into his or her head to build a skyscraper on Magnolia Street, the sodden Delta soil would not have supported it; about five feet below the surface, a man with a shovel struck water. The county's principal industry was agriculture, and agricultural employment had been falling at least since the commercial introduction of the cotton picker during World War II. ("When I took over the farm in Hollywood [Mississippi] in 1936," a longtime Tunican, the late Bard Edrington Selden, reminisced, "I had 385 sharecroppers tilling my 1,200 acres. In 1965, my last year of farming, I was cultivating the same land, but with only four workers.") The high-water mark in the county's postwar population was the census of 1950, at 21,664; the loss up until 1990 measured 62.3 percent. What Tunica had, however, was close proximity to Memphis, in which casino gambling was not allowed. So endowed, it became the card-and-dice capital of the Mississippi Delta.

Before the advent of gambling, the county's leading point of interest was its poverty. Some black families in the county seat lived on an alley that ran alongside the Sugar Ditch, an open sewer. The sewer meandered on to the White Oak Bayou, then to the Coldwater River, then to the Yazoo River, and finally to the mighty Mississippi. It spilled onto the national television screen in 1985, when Jesse Jackson, streaming reporters and photographers, toured the ramshackle, roach-infested dwellings along the ditch and condemned the squalor of their inhabitants as the emblem of a misgoverned nation. A pre-outraged *60 Minutes* followed Jackson, and delegations of pre- pre-outraged out-of-town press followed *60 Minutes*. The county seat awoke from its slumber to be designated (by Jackson) as "the new America's Ethiopia."*

RIVERBOAT GAMBLING was legalized by the Mississippi legislature in 1991. It had been ubiquitous on the old, explosion-prone antebellum sidewheelers, and romantic images still persisted of deckhands playing at chuck-a-luck as sharps crimped cards or cheated the passengers at faro. The late-twentieth-century kind of riverboat was intended to be safe, nonpredatory, and stationary. The craft was tied up at river's edge or in a ditch adjacent to the river. Some casi-

---

* In 1995, *The Tunica Times* published a two-part, 10th anniversary retrospective of this mortification. THE PRESS HOWLS AT TUNICA, said the headline over the first installment, sounding a siege theme. SOME NEWSPAPERS CAME TO TUNICA'S SUPPORT, said the second, restoring balance. Mainly, it was the Mississippi press that rallied round, wrote William Russell of *The Tunica Times*. "After all," Russell reflected, "other towns have some Sugar Ditches of their own to conceal."

nos, abandoning any pretext of naval architecture, were almost indistinguishable from buildings. Even the seaworthy boats would cast off lines no more frequently than a destroyer tender.

In the fall of 1991, as the push for casino gambling in Tunica gathered momentum, Paul Battle Jr., president of the Board of Supervisors, ventured that 90 percent of the county's population welcomed the new developers. None of the reasons that the holdouts might adduce—religious opposition to gambling, for example, or the possible trampling underfoot of favorite hunting or fishing spots by construction workers or by lost or drunken casino patrons— seemed as urgent as the need to reopen the Tunica County Hospital, to staff the Sheriff's Department, or to maintain the county's roads. The riverboat gambling industry was almost certain to provide a tax windfall.

The promoters, in presenting their projections of revenue to the Tunica planners, did not discourage the vision of a new, golden Mississippi River, "El Rio d'Oro." Some, for emphasis, likened themselves to Columbus and Tunica to the New World, and predicted that the 458-square-mile county, like the land that the Admiral of the Ocean Sea beheld in 1492, was on the verge of greatness. The county fathers smiled on the promoters, whom they affectionately called "Boat Folks."

Animal spirits, which even then were reviving American credit, quickly entered the Tunicans' bloodstreams. People optimistically put their money at risk: investors backed the developers in the expectation that gamblers would come from nearby Memphis to patronize the floating slot machines. The promoters issued stock, raised loans, or sold junk bonds. In Tunica, real estate transactions were simplified by the fact that only two men, Dutch Parker and Dick Flowers, owned most of the land. Local husband-and-wife representatives of GE Capital, the huge multinational finance company, explained the texture of the negotiations with them. Lloyd Link: "Dutch Parker and Mr. Flowers are super nice people. . . ." Betty Link: "Couldn't ask for nicer people. . . ." Lloyd: "The first piece of property that we bought from them, we never wrote a contract on it. We negotiated a price. We shook hands, and that bound the deal." Betty added, "Of course, you never do that in real estate. We've been in real estate for twenty-some years, and you just never do that."

In Tunica, as elsewhere, it was no easy matter to distinguish investing from gambling from speculating.* Was an investment in a gambling den an investment or a speculation? "Any attempted definition," a legal commentator ventured in 1952, "must be based chiefly on the attitude of the person making the investment. If he buys for the purpose of selling at a later day at an expected profit, he is speculating." In the modern view, no such clear distinction is possible. The eminent Depression-era authors, Benjamin Graham and David Dodd, anticipated the modernists by showing that safety was not a fixed investment attribute but a relative one. Thus, a bond judged to be a rank speculation at 100¢ on the dollar might well be considered a sound investment at 50¢. Then as now, margin debt was regarded as inherently speculative, and yet, as the authors observed, penny mining stocks could not be margined because no prudent banker would lend against them. "Conversely," they wrote, "when the American public was urged during the war [i.e., World War I] to buy Liberty Bonds with borrowed money, such purchases were nonetheless universally classed as investments." Their trusting citizens suffered speculative-caliber losses in the postwar bear bond market.

An investor is always a buyer and always, therefore, a bull. The person from whom the investor purchases 100 shares of stock could be the issuing corporation, in which case the interests of buyer and seller would be identical. They would each wish the other health and prosperity. Alternatively, the seller might be a disillusioned former bull. Selling, he or she may believe that the price of the stock will go down but not have a vested interest in that outcome. Thus, in the investment arena, the interests of the buyer and seller are typically not antagonistic.

A speculator, on the other hand, is sometimes a bull and sometimes a bear. In either case, he or she serves the function of a finan-

---

* In Japanese law, according to the editor of the *Grant's Asia Observer*, Jeff Uscher, it is written that lottery tickets are "negotiable securities" (*yuuka shooken*) and, as such, must "be handled by banks." Thus, observes Uscher, lottery tickets in Japan are the legal, if not moral, equivalent of stocks and bonds, even if stocks and bonds are not the legal equivalent of lottery tickets.

cial impact attenuator. If the speculator is a seller of cotton futures, the buyer could be a cotton mill. The mill, being a consumer of cotton, has a vested interest in falling prices. Buying futures contracts, it is able to protect itself in the event that prices go up instead of down. It is therefore able to shift some of that risk to the speculator.

Or perhaps the speculator is a buyer—for instance, a Tunica cotton farmer. The farmer is occupationally bullish, but he is also realistic, and he sees that the price of cotton for October delivery is quoted at a price substantially above his cost of production. It is now the Fourth of July, and long weeks of uncertainty stand between him and his harvest. By selling forward an unharvested portion of his crop, he is able to lock in a profitable price. This he does with the self-interested help of the speculator. Once again, the speculator bears risk for pay.

Speculation is frequently conducted with borrowed money, and the time horizon of the speculator is often shorter than that for an investor. For both of these reasons, a speculation is often more fragile than an investment. It is more susceptible to destruction by the forces of financial or economic wind and tide than is an unleveraged, long-term purchase of a bond, annuity, or mutual fund. However, the main distinction between the investor and speculator is not so much the durability of their respective operations, but the social function they respectively serve. The speculator, knowingly or not, is in the business of risk dispersal. An investor may bear just as much risk as a speculator, but the risk is incidental to the end in view: that of obtaining a stream of income, dividends, or rents.

Harold Smith, namesake of Harolds Club, a formative Reno casino, was a busy, self-destructive gambler, and it annoyed him to hear his father preach against the sins of dice and cards. He was especially inflamed when his father launched upon one of his recurrent, often futile, investments in oil exploration or mining. Then who was the gambler? Smith demanded.

Our Tunica farmer, taking his chances with insects, weather, and crop prices, might well identify professionally with a visiting dice player. (GROWERS GAMBLE ON 1996 COTTON, was the way the *Tunica Times* expressed this idea in headline form.) In the sense that he forgoes current consumption by putting his capital at risk in the expectation of earning a future stream of income, the farmer is an investor. To the extent that his livelihood depends on the unfathomable outcome of a set of future events, he is a gambler. The farmer is more of an investor and less of a gambler insofar as he reduces his vulnerability to chance. This he can do by embarking on what seems, at first glance, a speculation, namely, the forward sale of a portion of an unmade crop. In such a transaction, however, the farmer is not the speculator; the speculating party is the buyer.

What chiefly distinguishes a speculator from a gambler is that the risk he or she bears comes into existence independently of the speculator's decision to bear it.* Thus, the risk of falling cotton prices antedated the decision of the cotton speculator to enter the futures market. In a world without speculators, every farmer would have to hedge his or her own crops, every banker his or her own securities, and every insurer his or her own promises to underwrite the next natural disaster. In gambling, no risk of loss exists before a casino patron sits down to try his luck. The risk borne by the gambler, like that by the skier, is created specifically by the participant for the occasion. In a world without gambling, people would find other amusements, temporarily.

Such a world, the world imagined by Horace Greeley of the New York Association for the Suppression of Gambling, by Fiorello La Guardia, the anti-slot-machine mayor of the City of New York, or by Henry G. Blasdel, the nineteenth-century antiwagering governor of Nevada, seems very distant now that legalized gambling outearns every other leisure industry in the United States.† Even though gambling, investment, and speculation are separate and distinct lines of endeavor, still the question must be asked: How does one affect the other? If Americans gambled less, would they invest more? If they gambled less, would they invest differently? Is the rise of gambling in the past decade wholly unrelated to the rise of the

---

* Keith Bronstein, a professional Chicago speculator, is the author of this excellent distinction, the merit of which was partially demonstrated by the refusal of Bronstein's economics professor to validate it, circa 1968, and by Bronstein's own subsequent lucrative career in the futures markets.

† "After the capture by us Spaniards of a Moorish ship in the Mediterranean had produced much booty," related a Spanish soldier of fortune, Alonso de Contreras, about an aborted attempt to suppress gambling during the Thirty Years' War, "the commander of the victorious galleon, knowing well the predilections of his men, strictly

stock market averages? Does the gambling impulse occupy a unique region of the human brain, or does it share neurological quarters with the buy-low-and-sell-high regions? The questions become more pertinent as the United States becomes less risk averse. The outpouring of public money into mutual funds and pension funds may not, after all, be unrelated to the outpouring of public money into lotteries, casino gambling, and the other great aleatory pastimes.

Perhaps, as some authorities contend, the popularity of long-dated financial assets is a demographic phenomenon, pure and simple. The greater the share of workers over the age of thirty-five, so it can be shown, the greater the share of household assets committed to stocks and bonds (assets of inherently greater risk than short-term money-market instruments and cash). This line of argument, so soothing to investors and promoters, would suggest that the inflow of money into the public markets holds none of the risks so frequently (and, to date in this cycle, fruitlessly) adduced by the bears. The demographic school of market analysis implies that there is scarcely anything else to know about markets except the age of the workforce: not valuation, not interest rates, not the shape of the yield curve. As to the fear that the newcomers to Wall Street might be driven to sell in a panic, the theorists refute it, first by insisting that a public in search of long-term financial stability would hardly panic and, second, by reminding the alarmists that the new breed of investor, middle-aged and well-educated, wasn't born yesterday. "Such investors seem unlikely to behave in a manner that would destabilize financial markets," one economist has written.

Inasmuch as the working population is getting no younger, we may never find out. It might well be that the baby-boom generation, which has done so many other things to excess and gotten

---

forbade gambling, so that each soldier would preserve his share and return to Malta a wealthy man. To enforce this order, he had all dice and cards thrown overboard. But the urge to gambling among his men was not to be so easily denied. They drew a chalk circle on the deck and each concurrently placed a louse near its center, the winner to be whose louse first crossed the line and left the circle. Great sums were wagered on this basis. When the commander learned of this, he let his men have their way, recognizing that this vice of gambling cannot be suppressed among soldiers," or, as American experience has amply demonstrated, among civilians.

away with them, will now save itself into a perpetual bull market. However, there are reasons to doubt it, and there are nondemographic explanations for the decline in American prudence. Much of the change in temperament can be explained by government policies and by the habits of long experience. Thanks to federal deposit insurance, for example, the population of fearful depositors has shrunk. Owing to the recent absence of devastating bear stock markets, the population of hopeful investors has expanded. Insofar as the rise in gambling is related to the rise in mutual-fund buying, the comparisons revolve chiefly around probability.

Odds are the reason that Herbert Asbury titled his charming history of gambling in America, *Sucker's Progress*. Not only does the slot-machine addict contribute no capital to the betterment of America, he or she also bets against the house. The stock market enthusiast, on the other hand, not only commits capital to a presumably constructive end but also bets intelligently with the house. The investor is betting (to use the word that J. P. Morgan loathed) on the demonstrated tendency of common stocks to appreciate over time because the businesses that issue the stocks earn money and reinvest a portion of it.

As at the track, the odds on Wall Street tend to fluctuate with the volume of money wagered. Massive flows of funds into the market cause stock prices to rise. So flowing, the money disturbs the arithmetic of valuation. If stock prices rise faster than corporate earnings (leaving aside interest rates for a moment), certain processes are launched. One of these is the underwriting cycle. Watching the capitalized value of a business enterprise go up, entrepreneurs and investment bankers team up to issue common stock. In time, the public runs out of money to buy it, but only in time. The nature of a great bull market is that the reservoir of investable capital seems limitless. To say that stock prices rise faster than corporate dividends is to say that the price of a dollar of dividend income rises. As the price of a dollar of dividend income goes up, so does the likelihood of a new bear market. To understand the risk attendant on high prices, it is only necessary to understand the opportunity associated with low ones. Thus, in 1933, 1942, or 1974, infamous bear market years, investment risk was paradoxically low because stocks were terminally cheap. (We may all see this in retrospect; at the time, investment risk seemed mythically large, because the great arrow of trend was supposedly pointing down.) The lower the market and the more generally hopeless the financial situation, in other words, the better the odds on an ultimately happy investment outcome. And vice versa: the higher the market and the bluer the skies, the greater the odds of an accident. Thus, the higher the price of a dollar of dividend income, the greater the resemblance of Wall Street to a Tunica riverboat (as considered from the patron's point of view).

EARLY ON IN THE Tunica renaissance, local landowners were treated to a payoff so hugely improbable as to straddle the philosophical ground between gambling and investment. Overnight, the value of their assets climbed tenfold or more. The realization of a long-shot investment furnishes some of the same thrill as winning the lottery. The home run investment is not "something for nothing," however, as the winning lottery ticket may be said to be. It is something in exchange for an idea, as distinct from something in exchange for a guess or a hunch. What the winning investment shares with the winning lottery ticket is a soaring, exulting pleasure; the greater the odds conquered, the greater the joy. It is a feeling worlds apart from the laudatory satisfaction of earning a weekly paycheck.

Before the developers arrived, cotton land along the levee near Moon Landing in Tunica was valued at $3,000 to $4,000 per acre. Leased for the mooring of gambling barges, it promptly fetched $300,000 to $400,000 per acre. ("You can call it valuable if you want to," William B. Webb, longtime county tax assessor, told *The Commercial Appeal* of Memphis in November 1993. "It wasn't valuable a year ago.") Dutch Parker, septuagenarian farmer, John Deere dealer, sportsman, and grandfather, was one of the landholding beneficiaries. Parker, a big, trim man who has hunted throughout the United States and twice in Africa, has seen cycles come and go before. Once he farmed 10,000 acres belonging to Nelson Bunker Hunt, scion of the oil titan H. L. Hunt. Bunker's key misperception, conceived in the 1970s, was that inflation would never end and that the price of silver would not stop at $40 or so an ounce (where he and his confederates had put it), but would keep going up. No-toriously, it did not. Parker came up $200 per acre short in bidding for the Hunt farm at auction, but there was no shame in losing. He was outbid by the Prudential Insurance Company.

Just as the visionaries promised, people came to Tunica. A church organist from Memphis enrolled in a casino-sponsored dealers' school, and patrons drove bumper-to-bumper to the open-ing of the first casino, Splash. Traffic accidents increased on "Death Highway," U.S. 61, but the people kept coming, many from Memphis, 35 miles to the north. By 1993, there were not enough casino employees to go around. (In early 1992, Tunica had had the state's highest unemployment rate, at 19.1 percent; now there were jobs for everybody who wanted them.) Business blossomed. The mainstay downtown Tunica restaurant, the Blue and White, ex-panded by converting an auto repair shop into the "Grease Rack Lounge." A pawnshop, Hock It to Me, was opened, and construc-tion workers, perhaps as many as 4,000, poured into the county. A year before, 4,000 had approximately constituted the county's pop-ulation.

In 1993, so poor was the cotton crop and so rich was the casino season that the principled opponents of gambling were sorely tested. The $2.5 million in casino-generated tax revenues for Tu-nica County in that year very nearly equaled the county's revenues from all sources in 1992. The county's incomes rose and its assessed valuations doubled. It received a new telephone prefix. The eco-nomic impact of casino gambling on Dutch Parker was unquali-fiedly bullish. "I'll tell you this," he said in response to a question about the impact on others, "they're paying their gas bill, and they're paying their electric bill. They're getting better Christmas, but they're also getting better housing." It was hard to argue against the sin of gambling solely on the ground of facts and figures.

A second casino, Lady Luck, opened alongside Splash in September 1993. All told, within nine months the casino population along El Rio d'Oro had risen to eight. They included Harrah's Casino (done up in a Margaret Mitchell theme), Bally's Saloon and Gambling Hall (bland outside, Old West inside), President Casino (Mississippi riverboat—not a theme but a replica), Southern Belle Casino (Margaret Mitchell in pastels), Treasury Bay Casino (stationary, eighteenth-century pirate ship), Sam's Town Hall and Gambling Hall (Wild West, outside and in), and Fitzgerald's Casino (Irish castle, Irish music piped into the parking lot). Lady Luck, a woebegone barge, was done up à la Elvis, but the Presley estate forced it to redecorate. In October 1992, gross gambling revenues for the state of Mississippi totaled $27 million; in May 1994, they were almost $125 million.

Opponents of gambling did the best with the few resources at their disposal. "Some things are simply wrong, and shouldn't be legalized or promoted," wrote Matt Friedman, a columnist for *The Tunica Times*. "And casino gambling happens to be one of those 'things.'" In the spring, Tunica farmers complained that they couldn't move their machinery through the congestion of the casino traffic. ("My wife and I," a man had complained a few months before, "we like to walk to the post office, and it takes us four hours to get across the highway.") There was a boom in the caseload of the county courts, and a 50 percent rise in the number of county telephone lines, calculated from 1991. George Perry, a fourth-generation Tunica farmer, chafed at the possibility of losing a part of his farm and most of his peace to a new road. "The first week Splash opened, some fellow pulled up here in my front yard and passed out," he told the *Times*. "Things like that get under your skin. All we want is to be left alone." ("Situations ranging from passersby shouting obscenities and making rude gestures, to drivers losing control of their vehicles and running off the road were reported to have occurred," the *Times* went on. "In addition, one young woman was allegedly raped in front of her home, and another incident occurred when an intoxicated person used his yard as a rest stop.")

The opening of Sam's Town, the county's biggest gambling emporium, in May 1994 brought Mississippi's total casino space up to 1 million square feet, more than Atlantic City and second only to the state of Nevada, which had had a multidecade head start.

IN 1869, NEVADA s first elected territorial governor, H. G. Blasdcl, opposed gambling as a sin and a blight. The Nevada legislature refused to outlaw it, but the Blasdel line was successfully taken up by the women's clubs of Reno and the president of the University of Nevada, Joseph Stubbs, after the turn of the century. A law to prohibit gambling was passed in 1909. The legislature loosened the law in 1911, tightened it in 1913, and loosened it again in 1915, working it like a lug nut. Gambling, untaxed, flourished nevertheless. The official attitude of disapproval turned to envy after the 1929 stock market crash and (even more relevantly to the mining economy of the Silver State) the silver market crash; in 1932, the white metal would be quoted at 24½¢ per ounce, a twentieth-century low. The search for economic diversification began.

In 1913, in another burst of moralism, the Nevada legislature had doubled the residency requirement for obtaining a divorce, to a year from six months. In 1915, observing the subsequent decline in business activity and church attendance in Reno, the state's divorce capital, the lawmakers had again returned to six months. In 1931, in mid-depression, they compressed six months to six weeks. Simultaneously and historically, they legalized casino gambling.

The combination of divorce and gambling helped the needy Nevada economy, but it was as nothing compared to the stimulus to come in the shape of gambling, alcohol, and child care. (Nevada was also able to offer 90-second, $5 marriages, with no blood test required. Its attitude toward Prohibition was sardonic. In 1927, the state's governor, Fred D. Balzar, was able to claim that Nevada was the "only free state in the Union.") Just as Tunica would draw its clientele from Memphis, and Atlantic City would find its market in and around New York City and Philadelphia, Las Vegas began to attract visitors from Los Angeles and San Diego.

The city got rich slowly. When, in 1935, Harold Smith visited Reno to scout business opportunities in gambling, he found that the limit on dice games was $25. He said he had seen better action in Miami in the pocket-turned-out year of 1931. Fittingly for the 1930s, the principal tourist attraction in Las Vegas was a federal public works project, the 726-foot-high Hoover Dam. The population of the future Atomic City was 5,165 in 1930, not much greater than the population of Tunica County before the arrival of legalized gambling in 1991. *The WPA Guide to 1930s Nevada*, published in 1940, described Las Vegas before the full flower of neon: "Relatively little emphasis is being placed on the gambling clubs and divorce facilities—and much effort is being made to build up cultural attractions." The greatest casino success in Nevada in the 1930s was not, in fact, in Las Vegas but on Virginia Street in Reno. It was Harolds Club, the creation of a visionary New England carnival man, Raymond I. (Pappy) Smith, who did not personally gamble, and of his son Harold, who (as we have noted) did. The Smiths, who had previously operated bingo games at Chutes-at-the-Beach, San Francisco, had been driven out of California by the zealous antigambling attorney general and future Supreme Court justice, Earl Warren. As Arthur J. Morris democratized consumer credit and Henry Ford popularized the automobile, so Smith opened the doors of casino gambling to Mr. and Mrs. America. "He substituted female dealers for men at the twenty-one tables," recorded the historian Gilman O. Ostrander, "and also employed female shills, inexpensively acquired and quickly trained from the floating population of divorcees." The female dealers were under instructions not to challenge the customers, but to tutor and embolden them. This nurturing environment, along with an unprecedented mass advertising campaign—HAROLDS CLUB OR BUST, said the famous roadside signs—brought in women to the tables and slot machines as never before. Inspirationally, Smith also introduced a baby-sitting service, "so that children would not be left alone in motels, while their mothers were cranking the handles on the slot machines."* In this, and in his museum of Western Americana, he anticipated the Disney-style "family entertainment" at the Lexor or MGM Grand in fabulous, contemporary Las Vegas. (The dark side of the family experience with gambling was exemplified by the club's namesake. In the late 1940s and early 1950s, both Harolds, the club and the man, went into a decline; the eponymous one, by his own account, drinking himself sick and gambling away his money at neighboring casinos, including the nearby one managed by the relentlessly sober William Harrah, whose business legacy has

---

* Smith's only error was in not capitalizing it. Late in 1995, Kids Quest (no apostrophe, please), a company specializing in day care for the children of gamblers, did go public. It was promptly capitalized at $25 million, the equivalent of 5.7 times sales. It did not then earn a profit.

survived him, even in Tunica. As for Harolds Club, it went through a succession of owners after its sale to Howard Hughes in 1970; it was closed for good in 1995, 10 years after the death of Harold Smith.)

As Nevada preceded Mississippi in the history of American gambling, so did numerous colonial governments anticipate Nevada. In the seventeenth century, the Virginia Company, short of working capital, organized a series of lotteries to finance the temporarily unproductive settlers it had transported to the New World. In the eighteenth century, one lottery financed the construction of coast defenses in Massachusetts, another built churches in Pennsylvania, and a third endowed Princeton University. The most needful government of all, the Continental Congress, exhorted its citizens to buy a chance in the United States Lottery to contribute to the "great and glorious cause" of the rebellion against King George III. Thomas Jefferson, although sometimes censorious of gambling, was open-minded enough to find the time to take a flutter in bingo and backgammon.

ONE MIGHT SUPPOSE that the recurrent up cycles in American gambling would correspond to bull-market cycles in common stocks, one strain of animal spirits reinforcing and inflaming the other. Gambling flourished during the 1920s, and so did the stock market. However, gambling outlasted Wall Street during the 1930s. Seeing the times for what they were, Raymond Smith offered penny roulette at his Reno emporium at a time when the competition required a quarter. Harold, who had scorned a $25 dice game in 1935, the next year set a $5 limit on both "21" and dice at Harolds Club. You could roll dice for a dime. Smith thereby bore the derision of his less perceptive competitors, who hooted at "Smith's Honkey-Tonk" or "Harolds Penny Arcade." Little did they know. By 1940, almost a quarter of the American population was betting on church lotteries. At about the same time, one in ten was playing the numbers.

It was in a bear-market year, 1946, when Benjamin "Bugsy" Siegel built the Flamingo, one of the first casinos on the Las Vegas

Strip. (Although not a prime year for common stocks, it was an excellent year for borrowing money; ultralow interest rates prevailed in the government bond market, although not, perhaps, in the credit market in which Siegel operated, borrowing $6 million out of his initial $7 million capitalization.) In 1963, a bull-market year, New Hampshire revived the institution of the state lottery, dormant since the last of the nineteenth-century state lotteries, Louisiana's, was felled by a corruption scandal in 1894. It was in a bear-market year, 1970, that New York State created Offtrack Betting. In 1974, an estimated 61 percent of all adult Americans placed a bet for money; curiously, almost nobody had the heart to bet on common stocks, which were being given away. The Atlantic City casino-gambling industry got off the ground in 1978, a mediocre year in the inflation-stymied Carter market.

Sometimes in American history, gambling has fallen victim to a bear market even as stocks, bonds, or speculative enterprise flourished. One such wagering blackout occurred in the several decades preceding the Civil War. By 1830, racing, card games, dice games, and lotteries had entered the American mainstream. What shattered this idyll was a succession of scandals: one by one, trusted games of chance were revealed to be crooked. The professional gambling fraternity came in for disgrace and rough handling, notably in Vicksburg, Mississippi, on July 6, 1835, when the leading citizens tore down casinos, burned playing cards, faro boxes, and roulette wheels, and hanged five professional gamblers who had failed to heed an earlier order to get out and stay out. All along the frontier, news of the Vicksburg lynching helped to embolden the reformers. Thereafter, they and the gamblers changed places, the former coming aboveground, the latter disappearing below.

Gambling outlasted reform, as history taught that it would. Policy, in particular (a forerunner of keno and numbers) returned after the Civil War to become a late-nineteenth-century American urban staple. (In search of authoritative guidance on selecting winning numbers, policy players boosted such volumes as *Old Aunt Dinah's Policy Dream Book* to bestsellerdom.) Such was the improved postwar status of racing that a joint session of the United States Congress adjourned one October day in 1877 to spend a day at the Pimlico

Race Track near Baltimore, to watch Parole beat Ten Broeck and Tom Ochiltree in the rain.

When reform again roused itself, this time at the turn of the century, the battle cry was not so much the corruption of the professional gamblers as the sinfulness of the pastime itself and the corruption of the police who were paid to look the other way. The same tide of uplift and temperance on which the Volstead Act floated into law also bore a series of statutes banning policy, casinos, and racing. Now indignant, Congress ejected racing from the District of Columbia and the California legislature voted it out of the Golden State. The antiracing movement spread even to Tennessee, home state of the fondly remembered Rev. Hardy M. Cryer, who had devoted himself to the improvement of Andrew Jackson's racing stable when not preaching from the Methodist pulpit. By 1911, 95 tracks were closed and the number of states that allowed racing had dwindled to six.

IN NEW YORK CITY, the cyclical collision between sin and uplift claimed the lucrative and beautiful gambling operations of Richard A. Canfield. On December 31, 1901, the Saratoga Club closed its great bronze doors for what would prove to be the only time (except for police raids and the routine coming and going of the proprietor, his discreet staff, and his lawyer). The club was a brownstone house at 5th Avenue and 44th Street, next door to Delmonico's Restaurant. It was fitted out, it was said, with Whistler paintings and etchings, Chinese Chippendale furniture, peachblow vases, rare Barye bronze groups, and delicate Chinese porcelains. An excellent supper was served every night at 11, at no extra charge, the menu supplemented as necessary with takeout from Delmonico's; the best cigars were available for the asking, and the wine cellar was heaven. The proprietor easily recovered the cost of these amenities, and then some, from the single faro box and a pair of roulette wheels at which a rich clientele willingly lost income that was not yet taxed at the federal level.

The great Whistler was one of Canfield's friends, and it was Canfield who sat for the painter's last portrait. The artist ironically titled it *His Reverence.* The unprepossessing subject was fat, gray-eyed, and serene, his hands folded ecclesiastically in his lap. He was sober, by the looks of him, almost certain proof that Canfield had posed in the daytime. With his hair parted straight down the middle, Canfield looked like a bartender, but his talk gave him away for the bibliophile that he was. He read Edward Gibbon with particular pleasure, having discovered the great books during a formative stint in prison. As his wealth grew, Canfield assembled one of the city's finest private libraries. His collection of Whistlers, which he sold in 1914, fetched $300,000. "Such a passion for the rare and beautiful," marveled Leonard Jerome. This Jerome was the uncle of William Travers Jerome, the reforming district attorney who would prosecute Canfield as a common gambler, forcing him into a new line of endeavor, one that would almost bankrupt him: the stock market.

The newspapers called Canfield "the prince of gamblers," but that was a libel. Anticipating both Raymond Smith of Nevada and, many years later, the even more brilliantly successful Stanley Ho of Macao, Canfield didn't gamble, and he asked his employees to abstain as well. He could see, from the progress of his own net worth, that the odds lay with the house. "I have always told a loser his loss was to be expected," Canfield said, "and that if he played again with the hope of recouping it, the chances were that he would lose still more."

At the height of his fortune before the Panic of 1907, Canfield was worth as much as $12.4 million. The provenance of this wealth included the Eden on East 44th Street ($1.5 million), other establishments in New York and Newport ($900,000), and the Club-House casino in Saratoga, New York, with its legendary, loss-leading restaurant ($2.5 million). The source of the remaining $7.5 million was the stock market. According to his biographer, Alexander Gardiner, "His operations in a single stock, that of the Reading Railroad, which he bought at 40 in 1903 and sold when it touched 150 three years later, netted him a profit of more than two millions."

The scale of Canfield's stock market operations had grown from 100 or fewer shares in the early 1890s to 10,000 or more shares in the prosperity preceding 1907. "The sagacious gambler never counts on luck's lasting and prepares for adversity amidst good fortune," adjured the Spanish moralist Baltasar de Gracián y Morales, in 1647. "When they were losing," recorded Gardiner about Canfield's gambling clientele, "the players almost invariably pushed their luck; when they were winning, they were conservative." Not so Canfield on Wall Street. On the evidence, he, like so many others then and later, became less risk averse as the market went higher. Furthermore, he used margin debt, borrowing 60¢ or 70¢ of every dollar he invested. It was possible to borrow as much as 90¢ in those days, but even the amounts Canfield did borrow increased his vulnerability to a price decline. (Canfield had a professional affinity for credit. He advanced loans to his gentlemen gamblers, the first gambling-house operator in America to accept IOUs as a matter of business policy. Now, in 1995, banks are putting automatic teller machines in casinos. Financial progress appears limitless.)

Or perhaps he heard so many authoritative-sounding tips in the course of an evening's entertainment that he allowed himself to misjudge the odds. Arthur A. Housman, the senior partner of Bernard M. Baruch, was a full-strength, Manifest Destiny bull, and he might have inculcated the dangerous idea that the cyclical prosperity of the time would be uninterrupted. On Wall Street, there is no exact analogue to "the house," unless it is the market itself. Because, over decades, common stocks have tended to appreciate, it cannot be said that the odds lie with "the house" and against the investor. However, over relatively short investment intervals and, indeed, over a number of fairly long, unprosperous intervals, the market has exhibited a tendency to take the money of anyone who would presume on its generosity. It is this side of the market that has inspired a number of rueful Wall Street aphorisms, which the current bull market has robbed of any but antique interest. For example, "The purpose of a bear market is to return money to its rightful owners."

With the rise of incorruptible Jerome, the odds decisively shifted against the house, and 5 East 44th Street was closed like any common gambling hell. Canfield, narrowly averting another jail sentence, quit the gambling field, except for stock market gambling (as he chose to regard that field of endeavor). In the panic of 1907, he gave back most of the small fortune he had previously won. Reduced in wealth, but surrounded by his books and paintings, he died in 1914; the value of his estate was in the neighborhood of $1 million.

Although Canfield did not live to see it, the tide of reform again ran out, and gambling made a prosperous return after World War I, just as it had after Appomattox. As the evangelists had foretold, liquor formed an alliance with dice and cards, each illicit activity largely indulged by society and law enforcement. In the Great Depression, the state of Florida, sorely in need of new sources of revenue, undertook a two-year trial in legalized slot machines. The financial experiment succeeded but the political one failed; church groups howled it down. Nevertheless, Colonel Bradley's splendid Palm Beach Casino Club, serving the financial descendants of the Canfield market, operated as an open, prosperous secret in Florida, even during the long bear market in investment securities.

What is unique about the 1990s, therefore, is not that gambling is popular, or that, for the house, it is profitable, but that it is legitimate. A generation ago, when the Del E. Webb Corporation disclosed a huge rise in the profits it derived from Las Vegas gambling, it almost felt obliged to apologize for them. "The casino itself does not gamble, but functions as a service organization," said Webb, which the public still associated with real estate development, in its 1964 annual report. "While certain customers wager that certain chance combinations will occur, others wager that they will not occur. The casino handles these transactions for a fee, much as a bank charges a fee for participation in cash transactions." No apologies were needed in 1987,* when Jackpot Enterprises was admitted for trading on the New York Stock Exchange under the ancient ticket symbol "J," the letter that had formerly identified the Standard Oil Company of New Jersey, the life's work of John D. Rockefeller. Inferentially, gambling had become the investment equivalent of oil refining. As recently as 1990, only three states suffered casino gambling (outside the precincts of Indian reservations); at this writing, there are nine. At the beginning of 1990, just

---

* Of all days, Black Monday, October 19.

32 states sponsored lotteries; now there are 38. When New Hampshire, in need of revenues, instituted a lottery in 1964, it held biennial drawings. When New York State, also pressed to close a fiscal deficit, authorized a lottery in 1966, it held monthly drawings. "The long intervals between drawings caused interest to wane and participation to fall off," wrote John Rosecrance, a historian of gambling. "In addition, the waiting for drawings was passive; the lack of active participation further discouraged players." The interval gap was easily closed. Weekly drawings were introduced in New Jersey in 1970. Daily drawings followed, also in New Jersey, in 1975. When in 1995, Quick Draw furnished the equivalent of continuous five-minute drawings, Donald Trump, the real estate developer and gambling promoter, filed suit contending that the people of the State of New York would be fleeced.

ONLY A FEW MONTHS earlier, Trump had raised $155 million in the bond market to finance the expansion of Trump Hotels & Casino Resorts, Atlantic City. It was a transaction ripe in heresy: a gambling enterprise borrowing unsecured paper dollars on the thinnest of margins. However, it was a transaction that also pointed up the strengths of postclassical finance. The market, in its self-confidence, did not proscribe a questionable credit but rather charged what it took to be an appropriately high interest rate. (It did this in consumer finance, too; speculative-grade people could, and did, get a loan from an aboveboard financial institution more readily than they ever had before.) A bond is held to be an investment, but not all bonds are equally investment-like. Even a Treasury bond, which is a promise to pay dollars by the very government that prints them, contains speculative elements. A creditor of the Treasury is necessarily a speculator in the value of the government's currency. Because the value of money is free-floating, the level of long-term interest rates is volatile. Thus bond prices move freely, even the prices of bonds deemed free of the risk of default.

The obligations of Donald Trump were anything but. ("If we were a credit card company, we wouldn't let him fill out an application," one fixed-income investor told the Bloomberg news service in

June 1995, explaining his investment decision vis-à-vis the Trump deal; it was, however, a minority opinion.) Three of the Trump Atlantic City properties had defaulted in 1991 and 1992, and the company that would issue the new securities, Trump Hotels & Casino Resorts Holdings, itself exhibited signs of wear and tear in 1995. In keeping with the requirements of the federal securities laws, the new prospectus listed the good reasons (24 in all) not to invest in the Trump enterprise, including poor financial results, the need for additional financing, crippling indebtedness, intense competition within the Atlantic City market, and the risks related to a contemplated Trump assault on the virginal riverboat gambling market of Gary, Indiana. In the preceding 12 months, Trump Hotels had generated $308 million in revenues, of which the gambling patrons contributed $273 million. On the other side of the ledger, operating expenses had come to $260 million, of which the expenses associated with gambling amounted to only $145 million. Comparing gambling income with outgo, an analyst could see why Canfield got rich and why he advised his employees not to emulate his customers. So far, it seemed clear sailing.

However, the creditors, too, would have to be paid, and interest expense in the latest 12-month period had come to almost $50 million. It was a sum slightly larger than the company's pretax cash flow. On paper, therefore, Trump Resorts would not easily be able to pay the creditors who were even then supposedly reaching into their pockets for new money. Moody's Investors Service rated the bonds B3, meaning junklike. Offsetting those considerations, just as the prospectus suggested, was the "widespread recognition of the 'Trump' name and its associations with high-quality amenities and first-class service." It went without saying that Trump's reputation was sui generis, especially among his former creditors.

However, this unique attribute was not the bonds' principal selling point. Tilting the balance was the interest rate offered, $15\frac{1}{2}$ percent, some nine full percentage points higher than the yield available on a 10-year Treasury note (and one full percentage point more than Trump had expected to pay). Thus, an investor in the Trump debentures was speculating not so much on interest rates, on which bond buyers down through the ages have been at risk, nor on the currency, on which every buyer of dollar-denominated debt securities has speculated at least since the gold-based monetary system fell apart in 1971, and even before that time. The investor's greatest worry was that the highly leveraged Trump business would be unable to pay the promised 15½ percent. His second-greatest risk was that gambling, at long last legalized, would attract enough legitimate investment capital to force a decline in the existing profit margins of the existing casinos, Trump's included.

Tunica County, a living laboratory in creative destruction, continued to grow. In 1995, the catfish harvest was prime, property taxes were low, and the price of cotton was quoted at more than $1 a pound for the first time since the Civil War (a conflict to which *The Tunica Times* continued to give thorough, retrospective coverage in its feature pages). Splash, the county's first casino, closed in July 1995. For 11 lucrative months, Splash had had the gamblers to itself, but the market moved closer to Memphis, and Splash was left behind. Even at that, however, there was little enough to regret. The casino's initial $21 million investment had been repaid in only three months.

"In a landmark vote last week," *The Tunica Times* was able to report on June 8, 1995, "Tunica County Supervisors lifted almost $4 million of debt from the backs of local taxpayers." That was all the debt there was; all six outstanding municipal bond issues were defeased; the county became debt-free. Armed robberies, it was true, had become more prevalent; there was more to rob in the county than ever before. But through the institution of gambling, the county, at least, had balanced its budget. Through sin, it achieved orthodoxy.

"NINETEEN NINETY-THREE will be remembered as the greatest year Wall Street has ever seen," pronounced Securities Data Company in a review of the year's financing achievements. "The stock market hit new highs and huge increases in securities issuance occurred in every domestic arena: common stock, initial public offerings, investment-grade debt, junk debt, etc. In almost all cases, full-year records were set by the end of the third quarter. For the year, total domestic new issuance of debt and equity topped out at just above $1 trillion, shattering the previous record of $856 billion set in all of 1992."

The principal source of these feats was the low cost of borrowing. All year long, the federal funds rate was quoted at 3 percent, the lowest in three decades. Longer-term rates ascended according to maturity, with the highest yield attached to the 30-year bond. The practical significance of the shape of the yield curve was that a banker or speculator could profitably borrow at a short rate and lend at a long one. By the autumn, the Treasury's 30-year bond rate had fallen below 6 percent, a level at which an ordinary, bill-paying American family could find a 7 percent fixed-rate mortgage loan. The government itself throughout the late 1980s had borrowed at 8 percent and up.

Wall Street enthusiastically adjusted to this textbook case of interest-rate-induced levitation. It was the heresy described by Röpke. The "natural" rate of interest, a concept closely related to the expected rate of return on capital investment, was hugely in excess of the 3 percent bank rate. The bull stock market was proof of it. People were buying stocks in anticipation of bigger and better corporate earnings. In 1992, American manufacturing corporations had generated after-tax profits equivalent to just 2.2 percent on their invested equity; they would earn 8.1 percent in 1993 and more than 15 percent through the first nine months of 1994. The bank rate's discount from the natural rate was a tonic. The nation's banks were direct beneficiaries of low-cost credit. Not only did their costs decline, but also the value of their real estate assets increased. The stock market, too, jumped on the springboard of interest rates. To yield-hungry investors, it seemed like Mecca. (Inferential evidence that money-market interest rates were artificially low was the fact that the Federal Reserve worked so hard to suppress them. Throughout the 1993 calendar year, the Fed expanded the size of its portfolio of government securities by 11.7 percent. It created the credit with which it bought the bills, notes, and bonds; the new credit augmented the supply in the market, and thereby tended to hold down money rates. Almost nothing else in the American economy in that sluggish year rose at such a vibrant rate. The stock market did, of course—it was up by 7 percent—but that was a related phenomenon.)

The boom did more than improve investment profits. It also salvaged debts. Bank failures stopped cold, and the real estate market was repriced and refinanced. The real estate investment trust, or REIT, a structure that became popular in the late 1960s and then just as unpopular in the mid-1970s, enjoyed a new lease on life. In the main, from the Great Depression up until the 1990s, real estate had been financed with nonpublic money. Insurance companies, pension funds, and banks had backed builders and developers. During the long postwar inflation, the borrowers had had the upper hand, as the value of bricks and mortar tended to appreciate, and rising prices concealed a builder's mistakes. The developer Sam Zell, reflecting on this history in 1995, called the cycle of lending and building a process of mutual deception. "The developer would lie to the lender," he said, "and the lender would lie to himself, and the two of them would, therefore, be able to justify what they were doing. In most cases, the lender was sure that by the time the loan came due, he would have another job. . . . The whole process prior to 1980 of borrowing long-term, fixed-rate, self-amortizing, nonrecourse debt at 90 percent to 100 percent of value was nothing more than a massive wealth transfer from the lender to the owner— a very convenient process, particularly if you were an owner."

The bear market of the late 1980s and early 1990s threatened the old lenders and, through bankruptcy, created new owners. Now the lack of inflation exposed the preceding self-delusion. What saved the day was not only low interest rates but also Yankee ingenuity. Wall Street proceeded to refashion real estate, and the illiquid claims against real estate, into tradable securities. It was, in Zell's well-chosen words, "the greatest clearing process and recognition of losses certainly since World War II and probably since the Depression."

At the height of the first REIT boom (1969–72), no more than $2 billion of real estate–backed stocks and bonds were issued in a single year. In 1993, the grand total was $18.3 billion. Although scarcely visible when set alongside the $3 trillion national real estate market, the new securities helped to unfreeze the iceberg of commercial mortgage debt. Through REITs, banks and insurance companies could sell the properties they had acquired in bankruptcy proceedings. Developers could sell their buildings before they lost them in bankruptcy proceedings. Fully half of the public money raised for REITs in 1993 was equity capital, and this $9 billion represented no less than 22 percent of all the initial public offerings floated in the United States that year. In effect, the stock market became the new lender of last resort. In need of funds, leveraged corporations and real estate–clogged banks successfully turned to investors.*

Just as a 3 percent interest rate attracted borrowers, so it repelled savers, and the public's nest eggs were increasingly carried to Wall Street. The year 1993 was the best on record for the mutual-fund industry and for the allied enterprise of minting the securities that the mutual-fund industry bought. Some 700 new funds opened for business in this one bell-ringing year; as recently as 1981, the entire population of funds had totaled 665. (Since about that year, by coincidence, the number of mutual funds in existence—stock, bond, and money-market—has run neck and neck with the level of the Dow Jones Industrial Average.) The amount of money invested in the nation's stock market mutual funds in 1993 came to no less than $226.2 billion, which, needless to say, was also a record. From the inception of the first modern American mutual fund, Massachusetts Investors Trust, in 1924, until August 1990, a grand total of $150.7 billion was invested in equity mutual funds; between September 1990 and March 1996, more than three times that sum—$531.5 billion—poured in. The excitement was widely chronicled. Of all the magazine articles to be published on the topic of mutual funds between 1971 and the close of 1993, almost a third saw the light of day in 1993 alone.

It was a far cry from the underpopulated markets of the early 1980s (let alone the early 1940s or early 1950s), when bargains seemed to outnumber investors. In 1981, when net new investments in equity and bond funds had totaled just $2.2 billion, Trea-

---

* In Japan, a 1988 law in effect prohibited the reconstitution of mortgages into securities. Ostensibly enacted to protect investors against fraud, it also helped to protect the economy against recovery.

sury bonds yielded as much as 15 percent and the stock market was priced at less than 10 times earnings. The partners of Salomon Brothers, sharing the pitch-black mood, merged with the commodity house of Phibro, a marriage that was consummated on October 1, 1981, within a day of the postwar low ebb of the American bond market. A month later, the partners of Goldman, Sachs & Co., also passing up the cheapest bond market in American history, paid the equivalent of 30 percent of their capital to acquire the assets of another commodity-based business, J. Aron & Co., in one of the most expensive commodity markets in American history. In vivid contrast to the bleak, value-laden year of 1981, 1993 offered hope without value, or at least value as conventionally defined: bond yields of just 6 percent and a stock market priced at more than 20 times earnings. Nevertheless, the public's net purchases of equity, bond, and income funds were 127 times greater than the 1981 total. The precise number came to $280.2 billion.

Americans flew away from 3 percent, but they didn't fly toward 6 percent (the yield available in stodgy utility stocks, for instance). What people sought was not yield exclusively but a higher return from all available sources: capital gains, currency appreciation, or valuation. The most popular types of equity mutual fund in the greatest mutual fund year were the ones that paid the lowest dividends. International funds and growth funds, the people's choices, yielded 0.6 and 0.9 percent, respectively, significantly less than the available miserable money-market instruments. In 1982, the morning of the Reagan bull market, the share of American household wealth committed to money-market funds and bank accounts totaled 61 percent; caution, after the 1970s inflation, was deeply conditioned. By the end of 1993, however, the share of low-risk assets in the American family's portfolio had fallen to 46 percent; caution, following a decade of rising markets, had become less deeply conditioned. Appraising these trends early in 1994, John Bogle, president of the Vanguard Group of mutual funds, the nation's second-largest fund enterprise, observed that more and more investors had been "pulling out" their horns. "It may be only coincidence," added Bogle, a man professionally inclined toward bullishness, "but the family risk profile looks almost identical to that of 1972, immediately before a sharp two-year market decline of 50 percent (from high to low)."

HOWEVER, RISK WAS still in the back of the American investment mind. Gain had had the orchestra section to itself for years, despite such brief, sharp setbacks as the 1987 crash or the 1990 bear market. The 1993 stock market upswing, like the rally of 1958, was a people's market. In response to warnings that dividend yields were too low, or that price-earnings yields were too high, the public only invested more, thereby sending yields even lower and price-earnings multiples higher. As seen from the windows of the rushing train of the bull market, the valuations that had originally caused worry looked quaintly modest in the receding distance. Ahead loomed new, putatively excessive valuations, but they, too, based on experience, would be validated by falling interest rates, higher profits, or both simultaneously.

In the way of great bull markets, money seemed to materialize; it apparently replicated itself. Early in 1992, a Georgia high school economics class learned about investing in the stock market according to the momentum method. "They generally ignore a company's earnings," the *Atlanta Journal and Constitution* reported. "Their strategy: Darting in and out of low-priced stocks, especially those with heavier than usual volume coupled with rising prices." One group of quick studies turned an imaginary $100,000 into a more impressively imaginary $972,760 in only 10 weeks.

At midyear, a cover of *Fortune* magazine pictured a beaming Charles Schwab, the entrepreneurial stockbroker, along with the potentially unlucky headline, CHARLES SCHWAB WINS INVESTORS. THEY'RE RUSHING BACK TO STOCKS IN A BIG WAY. Professionals knew that any such strong journalistic verdict on the direction of a market (implicit or explicit) usually presaged a change of direction, but this time the trend did not waver. Stock prices only rose.

Rising, they came to constitute a powerful and constructive macroeconomic stimulus in their own right. What the United States needed in 1991 and 1992 was the opportunity to pay down

debt, to dispose of redundant investment, and to heal (and also reduce) the population of overextended financial institutions. No less,
it needed the capital with which to expand its production of semiconductors, to devise new software, and to fire up America Online.
All of these agendas the stock market meaningfully helped to move
forward. StrataCom, a pioneer in computer switching (or frame-
relay) technology, went public in July 1992 at a split-adjusted price
of $1.75 a share. Four years later, following a buyout proposal by
Cisco Systems, its stock was quoted at more than $50 a share. A
cluster of education and entertainment software companies also
went public in the early 1990s. Broderbund Software, Learning
Company, and Davidson, to name just three, advanced the information revolution as they enriched their investors.

The big 1993 crop of new equity issuance was testimony not
only to the potency of low interest rates but also to the diversity of
the American economy. Among other endeavors described in a
random sampling of prospectuses collected at midyear was the development and commercialization of high-energy-density, recharge-
able, zinc air batteries (AER Energy Resources), food and drug
retailing in Alaska (Carr-Gottstein Foods), and the breeding, production, and marketing of cotton planting seed (Delta & Pine Land
Co.). In Huntco, of Town and Country, Missouri, a leading proces-
sor of intermediate steel, the recent history of the U.S. economy
was miniaturized. Although its steel prices had been steadily falling,
the prospectus disclosed, Huntco had just as steadily been bettering
itself. It was, to start with, a net beneficiary of lower interest rates.
It had also reduced its operating costs, not by firing employees but
by spreading more steel volume over its substantial fixed costs.
Thanks to greater efficiency (achieved, in part, through the construction of a new plant in Blytheville, Arkansas), it had sold more
steel, even at the prevailing low prices; since 1989, its annual steel
shipments had risen by no less than 74 percent. Like so many other
American businesses, Huntco had been on a self-improvement campaign, diversifying its customer base, stepping up its production efficiency, and clawing its way back to profitability. In the Federal
Reserve Board, its management had had a helpmate, and now the
stock market was able to render its verdict. The new Huntco shares

were priced at $17 each, representing 32 times the profits that had only resumed (following two years of loss-making or break-even operations) in the 1993 fiscal year.

In one more way was Huntco a typical corporate specimen of the 1993 season: the principal use of the equity capital it raised was the redemption of debt and the retirement of preferred stock. By reducing the cost of borrowing and facilitating the issuance of equity in place of debt, the decline in interest rates was a double blessing for overleveraged American companies. So potent was the assistance thereby rendered that the incidence of rated corporate-bond defaults in 1993 declined to the lowest level in nine years. In each of the three years of the miracle cure, 1991–93, net corporate interest expense declined from the preceding year; nothing like it had been seen for at least three decades. As for the leveraged American consumer, interest-rate relief permitted a coast-to-coast mortgage trade-in. No less than $1.16 trillion of high-cost loans were exchanged for lower-cost loans. The estimated annual savings to households in the 1993 period alone was put in the neighborhood of $5.5 billion.

THE MOST ALLEGORICAL feature of the 1992–93 equity-issuance boom was the gambling aspect. Shuffle Master, Lady Luck, Primadonna Resorts, and Argosy Gaming, among other gambling-related businesses, availed themselves of the public capital markets in broad daylight. Bugsy Siegel could never have gone public in 1946 even though Las Vegas was a brilliant, long-term investment and interest rates were as low as they were going to get, at least up until this writing. Indeed, the Wall Street establishment probably would not have countenanced a public gambling company even if the chairman and chief executive officer were not a gangster. In the 1990s, with the decline in orthodoxy and the rise in heresy in so many venues, Wall Street was purely nonjudgmental; gambling institutions, in fact, were more profitable than thrift institutions. (The runaway success of the Foxwoods Resort and Casino, in Mashantucket, Connecticut, is credited with revitalizing a handful of small, southeastern Connecticut savings and loan associations, another case of sin holding out a helping hand to virtue.)

There is a lottery-like element in any initial financing. An un-seasoned company presenting itself to the public market is usually a bull-market creation. Besides a standard measure of entrepreneurial optimism, it may also assay a high promotional content. It is the job of the underwriter to protect its investment clientele against ventures in which promotion is the principal business product. In a bear market, skepticism is the natural turn of mind. Falling prices heighten the propensity to doubt until, at the moment when prices can fall no more, average investors are likely to doubt themselves, the market, and the institution of capitalism.

By the same token, rising markets bring out good feelings. The steeper the market's angle of ascent, the greater the bonhomie; the stronger the lift, the deeper the faith in continued appreciation. As we have seen, cold-blooded operators will try to summon up confidence at the bottom of markets and doubt at the top, but only the chosen few can identify either extreme. What ordinary mortals can understand is that the very hospitality of a market toward new ventures is, by its nature, proof of a certain speculative ripeness. (Perhaps, as a reforming measure, the capital markets could henceforth underwrite new ventures at the nadir of bear markets rather than at the peak of bull markets. The reversal of standard practice would deliver helpful Keynesian jolts to the national economy in moments of the greatest need.) A hearty new-issue market is likely to be the kind of market in which investors do not read the fine print. Nothing is more subversive to the habits of caution than a gaudy bout of prosperity. The inevitable consequence is that, at such confetti-speckled moments, the investment odds quietly tilt against long-term success.

An investigation of the 1960s new-issue market by Roger G. Ibbotson had, for many years, stood as the last word on the subject of initial public offerings. The study showed that new issues were actually priced at a discount to the overall market in which they were sold. However, subsequent studies have cast doubt on this proposition, and a new school of scholarly thought has convincingly upheld the opposite thesis. The successor idea is that IPOs tend to be richly valued. It is clear enough that they are extravagantly overvalued in comparison with the polar opposite investment proposition:

namely, a seasoned corporate equity purchased at the bottom of a bear market.

We may all imagine the consummate anti-IPO moment: a bear market in progress; a buyer, acting without brokerage-house instigation, hesitantly buying 1,000 shares of a former $50 stock, now quoted at $5; everyone despairing for the future; the national passion for mutual funds giving way to a reverse migration into passbook savings accounts.

Thus, paradoxically for the investor, what seems the easiest part of the underwriting cycle is, in fact, the most risk-fraught. The new scholarship, reinforcing the prejudices of older investors, holds that IPOs tend to be priced at a premium, even to the lofty valuations that prevail in times of the highest IPO issuance. The new scholarship notwithstanding, the Standard & Poor's new-issue index was up by 570 percent from January 1990 through December 1995, easily outdistancing the S&P 500 Index, which was up by a mere 87.2 percent.

"THE FRENCH ARE naturally thrifty," wrote Andrew Dickson White, chronicler of the great inflation of the French Revolution, "but, with such masses of money and with such uncertainty as to its future value, the ordinary motives for saving and care diminished, and a loose luxury spread throughout the country. A still worse outgrowth was in the increase in speculation and gambling." There was no certainty about the value of money in the United States two centuries later, but there was no price inflation to speak of, either. Instead (ever so much more agreeably), there was an inflation in values. White might have seen it as a double debauch that a resurgence of investment and speculation took place in the shares of gambling companies.

Video Lottery Technology, a maker of electronic poker paraphernalia, owed some part of its soaring prosperity to sheer luck. Late in 1990, it had agreed to sell out. The price was $13.6 million, representing approximately four times net income and one-half annual revenues. Then, just before the stock market lifted off in the smoke and haze of Operation Desert Storm, the deal fell through. Later in

1991, Video Lottery itself went public. A little more than a year after the sale, in March 1992, the company stood transformed. It was still making the monitors and software with which a contestant could play poker, blackjack, bingo, or keno, for $2.50 a fling (an inflation-adjusted bet not much different from the upper limits first set at Harolds Club). What was profoundly different, however, was the stock market's capitalization of Video Lottery's earning power. The new, revised, bull market judgment put the company's value at $318 million, or 38 times 1992 net income, that is, roughly 23 times more than the price the company had providentially not accepted in 1990.

Shuffle Master Incorporated was another star of the 1992 new-issue market, profitably marrying two of the decade's leading investment concepts: technological innovation and gambling. Shuffle Master, of Eden Prairie, Minnesota, invented, manufactured, and distributed the automatic card-shuffling machine. (It had taken Shuffle Master's founding entrepreneur, John Breeding, a year to develop his card-shuffling machine and almost another decade to sell it. In the interim, he was forced into personal bankruptcy. Today, judged solely by the market value of his stock holdings, he is spectacularly solvent. He says that he does not now, and did not then, gamble.) With this device, leased at a rate of approximately $500 a month, the hourly productivity of a dealer of blackjack, California aces, Caribbean stud, five-card draw, or Texas hold'em, among other games, might be increased by as much as 60 percent. It would be the equivalent of adding another seven months to the house's already lucrative calendar year. By producing an absolutely reliable random shuffle, furthermore, Shuffle Master not only improved the productivity of the house, but it also, and simultaneously, reduced the productivity of sharps, card trackers, and other undesirables. The stock market, as hopeful and patient as it has sometimes been morose and shortsighted, capitalized Shuffle Master's $4 million or so in revenues at no less than $150 million at the peak in 1995. At that moment, the company had not turned a profit.

In February 1993, Argosy Gaming, the owner of a single Mississippi riverboat, sold its first shares in the public stock market. In 1991, it had cost just $13.8 million to buy and outfit the *Alton Belle*, Argosy's triple-deck, 150-foot, Mark Twain–conjuring gambling craft. In 1992, it required 2,232 patrons a day to generate revenues of $58 million (and net income of $7.4 million) aboard the very same *Belle*. In 1993, it required just five million shares of Argosy stock, priced at a hopeful valuation, to uplift the *Belle* (along with three barges and a successor riverboat that was under construction) to a capitalized value of $440 million. The difference between the 1991 cost and the 1993 value was the great bull market.

Returning from the dead, Canfield would not have believed his eyes: the audited financial statements disclosed the payment of not one dollar in police tribute. One key difference between his era and the modern one was that the very legitimization of gambling had cleared the way for well-financed competition. In its entire 17 months of operation up until the time of the 1993 initial public offering, the *Alton Belle* had had the market on the Illinois side of the Mississippi River (near Alton, of course) to itself. In 1992, the company's pretax margins were greater than 47 percent; it would be hard to improve upon them, as the prospectus admitted: ". . . [I]t is possible that substantial competition will arise that could have a material adverse effect on the company's existing and proposed operations."

Projecting bigger things itself, Argosy had already laid the keel for the *Alton Belle Casino II:* "The proposed interior design for the new cruise liner is that of a Las Vegas–style casino, combining contemporary elements with Roman antiquity motifs," said the prospectus. "The proposed interior design uses contemporary lighting combined with brightly colored carpeting, polished stone and mirrored surfaces and elements from Roman antiquity, such as Ionic columns and replicas of ancient coins, to create a unique and exciting gaming environment."

THE GAMING ENVIRONMENT on Wall Street was also unique and exciting, and compensation for the absence of mirrored surfaces and elements from Roman antiquity was provided in the form of superior returns. From 1926 until the end of 1992, the Standard & Poor's 500 had delivered annual compound growth (including dividend reinvestment) of 10.3 percent, far in excess of the returns available in cash (3.7 percent) or bonds (4.8 percent). As for gold, between 1974 and 1992, it had appreciated by just 4.1 percent a year. The excellence of the long-term equity record was hardly a secret: Smith's encomium to common stocks had been published in 1924. One of the distinguishing features of the 1990s was how well the long-term bullish arguments were understood and how thoroughly they were aired. Another was the benign interest-rate environment. Understanding that common stocks excelled, people bought them; buying them, they drove their prices up; watching their prices rise, they bought more. (Furthermore, just as some economists had observed, the population had entered an equity-buying stage of life. The demographic winds were prosperous.)

The reason stocks could not rise uninterruptedly was the certainty of failure, in both the specific case and the general. If nothing else, the wrong bank rate would sooner or later help to produce a surplus of investment, to be followed by a drought. Success, once achieved, presents no insurmountable problems to any social system. Where the free enterprise system shines is in its treatment of failure. Individuals, as individuals, are always error-prone, and they register their failures in bankruptcies, fresh starts, and the write-off of investments they wish they had never heard of. Acting under the influence of central-bank-administered interest rates, as we have seen, individuals also make collective mistakes. They overinvest, then underinvest. The underinvestment portion of the cycle is dealt with constructively: with new business formations, bull markets, and initial public offerings. The overinvestment problem is also dealt with constructively, but with the emphasis on demolition: with bankruptcies, bear markets, consolidations, and liquidations. To presume that the stock market would continue to deliver its historically observed 12 percent annual rate of return, year in and year out, without a discouraging lapse, would be to believe that the Federal Reserve would never miscalculate, that people would never be swept away by emotion, or that the fact of a great bull market would itself create no countervailing tendencies. (Without miscalculation, there would be no price action, no capital gains, no losses, and no commissions. Determining the ideal price, the market would sit on it, preening. As it is, one set of errors produces another.)

In the stock market, as in the Oil Patch, rising prices contain the germ of falling prices. As prices and valuations increase, entrepreneurs create more companies and sell more stock. At length, the supply of common equity saturates the demand. More fundamentally, the new competitive enterprise that the investment brings forth begins to meet competition; its profit margins become the worse for it. (From a 47 percent pretax profit margin before it went public in 1993, Argosy Gaming had attracted enough competition by early 1995 to drive down its margin to 4.2 percent. The stock price, having soared to a high of $35\frac{1}{4}$ in the first few months after its 1993 offering, declined to the high single digits.) Ultimately, if the resulting downturn were severe enough, business school professors would be able to show that common stocks can, and frequently do, deliver poor results over the short to medium term.

A quite specific form of inflation infected the stock market in 1993, a year, like 1946, in which low interest rates and superabundant credit caused one kind of price to rise but not another (it will be remembered that meat prices, but not stock prices, went up in 1946; in 1993, it was the other way around). Almost no one objected to it. The companies that issued the stock at previously unimagined valuations had no reason to object, naturally. Nor did the investment bankers who were paid by them. However, curiously enough, neither did the investors who paid the fancy prices, commissions, and fees. Not one of these investors, presumably, would have felt any better if the price of a coveted refrigerator was suddenly marked up by 100 percent. Yet they staged no buyers' strike when a half-billion-dollar corporation was offered for sale at $1 billion.

In the stock market in 1993, two successful, ozone-bound computer software companies, Intuit and PeopleSoft, could have been purchased together for less than $1 billion. (In the spring of 1996, the two commanded a market capitalization in excess of $5 billion.) Quantum Corp., an up-and-coming supplier of data storage products, was available for less than $650 million (it would double by the middle of 1995). Alternatively, for slightly more than $1 billion, an investor could have bought Primadonna Resorts, a gambling enterprise situated on Interstate 15 at the Nevada and California state line, 40 miles from Las Vegas. At the time of its public-market debut, Primadonna's corporate assets consisted of a pair of casinos connected over the highway by a monorail. The Bonnie and Clyde Death Car was on permanent display at one of them, Whiskey

Pete's Hotel & Casino, but the company otherwise lacked destination appeal. Its greatest existing claim to fame was that it afforded motorists their first and last chance to gamble as they entered and exited Nevada by way of California. Usually, the patrons were just passing through, and the company's oceanic parking lot was frequently filled with 18-wheelers. The style of the Primadonna properties was not the Canfield style. A room cost $18 on weekdays, and the patrons could bet no more than $500. To enhance the excitement, management proposed to build a new, Wild West–theme casino at a cost of $90 million, and to connect the new place with the others via a robber-baron-style railroad. Riding it, a patron would be able to imagine a 100-year issue of 3 percent gold first mortgage bonds underwritten by Kuhn Loeb & Co. (When Buffalo Bill's Resort and Casino was completed, it also featured the "Desperado," the world's tallest, fastest, and most sickening roller coaster. Later, in the bull market, it would be threatened by the construction of an even taller and more sickening ride, in Las Vegas.) All of this, actual and prospective, was offered in the market for $1 billion, a sum representing 33 times earnings, seven times book value, and nearly seven times revenues. In the excitement of the moment, the market valued Primadonna even stephen with Circus Circus, which had seven casinos, two hotels, recreational-vehicle parking, and expansion plans of its own in the shape of the imminently fabulous Luxor in downtown Las Vegas (not 40 miles away but in the place itself). The Luxor would be done up in an Egyptian theme, up to and including the pyramid and a fake river. In keeping with the traditional send-off accorded new issues in a hot market, Primadonna common rocketed to $34 from about $20 before returning to about $20. Two years after the initial public offering, the market's revised opinion was that the billion-dollar corporation was actually worth about $620 million.

A MARKET THAT would invest in gambling at these valuations was a market that would not scruple to take a chance on other lines of industry. The tendency to do so was already well established. It was manifest in March 1992 in the selection of a stable of speculative corporations to fill out the American Stock Exchange's new Emerging Company Marketplace. More than half of the 22 allegedly dynamic, entrepreneurial businesses on the list were shells. They were companies that themselves had no operating history. Their plan was to go out and buy a business; its identity would be revealed to the outside investors in the fullness of time. Because of this central issue of uncertainty, a shell was sometimes called a blind pool. It was an appelation that, down through market history, had spelled trouble, but even professionally risk-averse people could find nothing worrisome about it in 1992. One of the well-wishers on hand to send off the Emerging Company Marketplace on its opening day of trading (red, white, and blue balloons had been tumbled onto the trading floor to emphasize "only in America") was none other than the chairman of the Securities and Exchange Commission, Richard C. Breeden. Asked if the prevalence of shell companies concerned him, as a regulator, Breeden replied, "Any company can evolve rather substantially. I care less about what they were than about what they have become."

Only a few weeks passed before *The Wall Street Journal* unmasked Alfred Avasso, the largest shareholder of one of the 22 emerging companies, PNF Industries, a maker of flame retardants, as a convicted arsonist. Subsequently, *Business Week* disclosed that Eleanor Schuler, chairman of Printron, another one of the emerging 22, had been sued by the SEC in connection with companies she previously ran when her name was John Huminik (a sex-change operation had intervened). Three years later, as Floyd Norris of *The New York Times* reported, a few of these green shoots had indeed sprouted. Colonial Data Technologies, a maker of telephone ID equipment, was one shining example; its stock price appreciated more than eightfold. However, the majority of the companies had fallen flat. Eighteen were quoted below their original offering prices and a number had become worthless. Robert Lovett, the theorist of corporate pathology, might have predicted as much.

Lovett, however, conceived his theories in 1937, when the demonstrated direction of securities prices was down (or, in a fair stretch, sideways). By the start of the 1990s, the prevailing direction was seen to be up. Amazement overcame the Atlanta investment banking community early in 1992 when copies of a letter addressed, "To my friends in health care," were circulated over the signature of Thomas E. Haire, widely known as the chairman of an exponentially growing home-infusion-therapy company, T^2 Medical. The letter was attached to a prospectus for the common stock of a new, Haire-sponsored medical enterprise, Radiation Care. Founded in November 1990, the company owned and operated radiation-therapy centers for cancer patients. Its first center had been opened in June of 1991; it had eight in operation and three under development by March of 1992. "To my friends in health care," Haire led off:

> About a year ago, I started a new company to own and operate outpatient radiation therapy centers. We are pleased with its progress and have decided to proceed with a public offering of its stock. I thought you might be interested in making an investment and am enclosing a copy of the preliminary prospectus. . . .
>
> If, after reviewing this document, you wish to be contacted as the offering proceeds, please complete the attached form and fax it . . . or call . . . to indicate your level of interest. If you choose to call the office, please ask for Investor Relations. The offices of Radiation Care only have eight incoming lines, so please bear with us if the lines are busy.
>
> Very truly yours.

The prospectus contained a number of startling, prophetic, and damaging admissions, for instance: "Substantially all of the company's revenue to date has been derived from cancer patients referred to the company's centers by physicians who are stockholders of the company, and loss of such referrals would materially adversely effect [sic] the financial condition of the company." Not only did the company not have a proofreader, but it also lacked an underwriter; it sold the stock itself. Concerning the lack of professional banking help, the prospectus said, "No independent due diligence has been performed by an underwriter, and this prospectus has not been reviewed by underwriter's counsel."

On the evidence, the document was not reviewed by prospective investors, either, because they proceeded to send money in exchange for share certificates. At the peak of its fortunes in March 1992, the company boasted a stock market capitalization of $223 million, or the equivalent of 68 times its meager annual revenues. It was quoted at $14.75 a share. When in March 1995, Radiation Care was acquired by Oncology Therapies, the stockholders received the grand total of $2.625 a share.

The Haire method, the merger of Wall Street and Hippocrates, had earlier produced T^2 Medical. A purveyor of home-infusion therapies—for instance, antibiotic therapy, chemotherapy, and pain-management therapy—T^2 went public in 1989. By the fall of 1991, in the heat of the biotechnology and medical-stock boom, it had achieved a $1 billion market capitalization. Haire, both chairman and chief executive, took the occasion of the 1991 annual report to pay the management's respects to Wall Street: "We believe this billion-dollar market capitalization shows tremendous confidence in T^2 on the part of the financial community." In point of fact, the bull market had already rendered that message obsolete. By the time the grateful shareholders could read it, T^2's market capitalization had cleanly pierced $2 billion. The annual report broke new ground in investor relations by publishing, on page 4, the picture of a Wall Street analyst who had recommended the stock. Pictures of the chairman, president, and chief operating officer appeared as well, but on page 5. The text that accompanied the analyst's picture consisted of questions and the management's answers. The most pertinent question went unasked, however: Could this moment approximately represent the all-time high of the stock? (The answer proved to be yes.) "So this is the face of the 1990s," mused Michael J. Harkins, a New York investor who was short the stock even before it attained its first $1 billion market capitalization—"the analyst staring out at you from the annual." Within 15 months, the price of a share of T^2 had fallen to about $10 a share from more than $60; in July 1994, the company was acquired, in a four-way merger, by Coram Healthcare Corp., for $9.056 a share. By the summer of 1995, Coram itself was losing altitude. In a press release, management explained the failure, in part, on its overattention to "external growth" and its inattention to day-to-day operations.

ANOTHER TEMPORARY favorite in the 1992 medical science market, was the manufacturer of the L-D-X System, a device to measure blood cholesterol on the spot, just after the patient stuck out a finger. From $5 a share at the time of its public debut in June 1992, the price of a share of Cholestech had climbed to $15 by mid-autumn. Stocks in general were going up, but none so fast as biotechnology, health care, and gambling. (Reuters reported from Tehran in November that an Iranian foundation was able to increase the reward it had placed on Salman Rushdie's head because of the shrewd investment of the original $2 million bounty; it was apparently impossible to miss.) Electing to take some profits, Cholestech that fall announced a secondary offering: 2.5 million shares would be sold, half of them by officers and directors. Reading the prospectus, a would-be purchaser could take encouragement from the general medical backdrop: 100 million Americans had high, or borderline high, cholesterol. Also, to quote the prospectus, "Among competitors, only Cholestech's L-D-X system can measure total cholesterol, high-density lipoproteins and triglycerides from a single drop of untreated whole blood within five minutes." And yet, there was the undeniable fact that the people who knew the company best were selling rather than buying. Among the specific enumerated risks was that one customer, Warner Lambert, had accounted for 77 percent of total product sales since test marketing began in the summer of 1991. Also, "the company's ability to manufacture consistently sufficient volumes of cassettes remains uncertain," and "the company has experienced difficulties achieving acceptable manufacturing yields on cassettes." Then, too, there was the matter of profitability, or the lack of it: as against the $38 million of capital that the company had raised, it had run up losses of $28 million (and counting; through this writing, in late 1995, it has never shown a profit). Finally, of course, there was the unstated investment consideration that 3 percent is a very low rate on a certificate of deposit. Weighing the risks

and the rewards, the stock market rendered its verdict: almost from the moment of the secondary sale, in December of 1992, it pushed the value of this loss-making company lower. The latest available quotation: $3 a share.

By giving Cholestech, temporarily, the benefit of the doubt, the market was only being consistent. It had vouchsafed its verdict of approval (only to withdraw it on further reflection) throughout the 1993 new-issue boom. Master Glazier's Karate International (ticker symbol: KICKU), a chain of four martial arts centers with $1 million in revenue and an $879,000 net loss, came public at a capitalized value of $50 million. NationsMart Corp., a conglomeration of dry-cleaning, shoe-repair, and laundry businesses stuck into vestibules at Wal-Mart and Kmart stores, which also showed a net loss on small revenues (less than $3 million in 1993), was capitalized at $54 million. And Discovery Zone, a small, loss-making chain of indoor children's playgrounds, was valued at $1.3 billion.

Nothing was wrong with Discovery Zone's corporate lineage. Conceived by an entrepreneur in a Kansas City basement in 1989, it had come to the attention of Donald F. Flynn, former chief executive officer of Waste Management (subsequently WMX Technologies), in 1992. Flynn invested $12.1 million. The company then consisted of 39 Fun Centers, two owned outright, 37 franchised. Each Fun Center was a climate-controlled romper room equipped with child-size gerbil tunnels, foam mountains, spiderweb bridges, ball baths, moon walks, trapezes, and obstacle courses. Conspicuously, there were no video games, as the corporation wanted every child to get his or her exercise by running around in stocking feet, yelling. Then, in April 1993, Blockbuster Entertainment invested $10.3 million for some 21 percent of a slightly bigger business; thus, the implied market value of Discovery Zone vaulted to about $49 million.

It was not through vaulting. In June 1993, the company went public, in the process raising an additional $55 million. Instantly, in keeping with the antigravitational forces then prevailing, the stock price surged. At the highest pitch of excitement, in September, the implied capitalization of Discovery Zone passed the billion-dollar barrier. What an investor could hope for was the proliferation of

Fun Centers from the Atlantic to the Pacific. Hope was in the air. It lifted the company's shares to the equivalent of 655 times forecast 1993 earnings and 69 times forecast 1994 earnings. (In 1993, in fact, the company wound up earning all of $3.3 million; in 1994, it showed a loss of $24.9 million.) In Japan, valuations like that didn't last, and neither did Discovery Zone's. In 1996, the company filed for bankruptcy protection.

DISCOVERY ZONE's apex coincided with the bond market's explorations of the yields below 6 percent and with a warning about asset inflation delivered not in *The Quarterly Journal of Austrian Economics* but in the pages of *Rolling Stone*. William Greider, whose approach to the Fed (as laid out in his book, *Secrets of the Temple*) resembled that of William Jennings Bryan toward the House of Morgan, contended that Alan Greenspan's oft-expressed worries about the consumer price index were a smokescreen. What actually worried the chairman was the well-being of the bloated bondholders. Sooner or later the Fed would have to raise interest rates, if only by a hair, to remind the bulls, especially the stock market bulls, that markets do go down as well as up. By so acting, it hoped to forestall a repetition of the 1987 panic. Next to this preoccupation, Greider contended, the Federal Reserve's interest in that portion of the national economy concerned with human beings (e.g., employment and production) was negligible. It was said that Hillary Clinton had seduced the Fed on the night of the 1993 State of the Union Address when the chairman was unexpectedly seated to the left of the First Lady. However, Greider concluded, it was just possible that it was Greenspan who had seduced the administration.

"I cannot prove that this is the case," Greider wrote in mid-September, "since Fed governors do not share their innermost thoughts with me." One of them, however—none other than the vice chairman of the board, David W. Mullins Jr.—presently unburdened himself to *The New York Times*. For a full year, observed Mullins, Greenspan's second in command, Fed-administered interest rates had been remarkably low, lower even than the rate of inflation. Further interest-rate reductions would risk a speculative

inflammation. "Some people are concerned about the possibility that excess liquidity will create imbalance, such as a bubble in asset prices," said Mullins, who denied that stock and bond prices were then inflated.

As the Federal Reserve was trying to locate the one correct interest rate (the one that would restore financial balance), the trust and estates bar was seeking to modernize the "prudent man," a legal creature whose attributes were memorably described by Judge Samuel Putnam of the Massachusetts Supreme Court in 1831. A case had come before the court involving the estate of a rich Boston capitalist, one John McClean, "a man of extraordinary forecast and discretion," in Putnam's estimation. McClean had left his wife $50,000 in trust. She would live on the income; after her death, the principal would be distributed, half to the Massachusetts General Hospital, half to Harvard College to endow a chair in ancient and modern history. McLean, who himself invested in common stocks, instructed the trustees of this estate, Jonathan Amory and Francis Amory, to choose "safe and productive stock, either in the public funds, bank shares or other stock, according to their best judgment and discretion. . . ."

The Amorys invested in a bank, an insurance company, and a pair of manufacturing businesses. Not every one of these investments prospered, however, and when the trustees' account was presented for settlement in 1829, the principal amounted to roughly $12,000 less than the original $50,000. The Amorys described an "accidental and temporary depression" in value; Harvard claimed a loss "occasioned by injudicious and improper investment." The college sued the Amorys personally (they happened to be the widow's blood relatives) for the restoration of the original value.

"Insurance and manufacturing stocks are not safe," Harvard contended in arguments, because "the principal is put at hazard. It is otherwise with bank stock, the money being lent on good security. . . ." Judge Putnam slapped the argument away. "Do what you will," he wrote in his opinion, anticipating modern portfolio theory, "the capital is at hazard." As for the idea that the Amorys should have bought government securities, Putnam recalled the deplorable state of the public credit at the end of the War of 1812. "[I]t may well be doubted," he wrote, "if more confidence should be reposed in the engagements of the public, than in the promises and conduct of private corporations which are managed by substantial and prudent directors. There is one consideration much in favor of investing in the stock of private corporations. They are amenable to the law. The holder may pursue his legal remedy and compel them or their officers to do justice. But the government can only be supplicated." (The Comte de Mirabeau had expressed the same idea more succinctly. "I would rather have a mortgage on a garden than a kingdom," he said.)

Banks and insurance companies may fail, Putnam noted, and mortgages may fluctuate. "[T]he title to real estate, after the most careful investigation, may be involved," he went on, "and ultimately fail, and so the capital, which was originally supposed to be as firm as the earth itself, will be dissolved." In short, concluded the judge, anticipating Lovett, there is no such thing as absolute safety. "All that can be required of a trustee, is, that he shall conduct himself faithfully and exercise a sound discretion," wrote Putnam in an oft-quoted passage. "He is to observe how men of prudence, discretion and intelligence manage their own affairs, not in regard to speculation, but in regard to the permanent disposition of their funds, considering the probable income, as well as probable safety of the capital to be invested." (In the Putnam clan, the application of these ideas awaited the judge's great-great-grandson, who founded The George Putnam Fund of Boston in 1937. If George had read Lovett's piece in the *Saturday Evening Post* the same year, he fortunately did not let it discourage him. At this writing, the Putnam organization manages $110 billion.)

What followed the Amory decision was, as the modern financial theorist would see it, retrogression. Courts and regulators presumed to define and delineate the field of assets appropriate to trust investment as if they could foretell the future. Prudence (and intelligence and discretion) would be stipulated by higher authority—namely, themselves. Thus, in 1869, a New York State appeals court found that common stocks were imprudent: all stocks. At the turn of the century, state regulatory authorities drew up "legal lists" of eligible bond investments. In 1939, Harvard professor Austin Wakeman Scott admonished what would prove to be two generations of trust lawyers. "[C]ertain investments are universally condemned," he wrote, not forseeing that, within a few years, Paul Cabot, Harvard's own treasurer, would worry and astonish the fiduciary world by committing a significant portion of the Harvard endowment to common stocks, or that in 1995 *Forbes* would describe the university's endowment as being "knee-deep" in derivatives, or that *Forbes* would mean it as a compliment. "It is improper for a trustee to purchase securities for the purpose of speculation, although the line between what constitutes speculation and what constitutes a businessman's risk and what constitutes a prudent investment is drawn differently in different courts," Scott went on. "It is clear, of course, that a trustee cannot purchase securities on margin; nor can he properly purchase speculative shares of stock or bonds selling at a large discount because of the uncertainty as to whether they will be repaid at maturity. A trustee cannot purchase shares in untried enterprises."

However, as financial markets have phases, so do financial ideas. In keeping with the resurgent, one-way markets of the 1990s, Wall Street and the American Law Institute made their intellectual peace with modern portfolio theory. A new Prudent Investor rule, legislation intended to reform state trust law as ERISA had enlightened the federal government's approach to pension regulation, was drafted and submitted for consideration in New York, among 15 other states. In 1996, it was sweeping the field.

"Under the new Prudent Investor rule," New York University professor Harvey P. Dale explained, "directors and trustees cannot find protection merely by putting all of the charity's assets into certificates of deposit or U.S. Treasury obligations. Not only is no investment, taken alone, per se imprudent, but no investment, taken alone, is per se prudent." Out was hypercaution; in was sensible risk taking (it being widely believed that risk and reward are opposite sides of the same coin). Because risk could not be avoided, the new way taught, it must be managed. Under the old state law, a fiduciary could be attacked for the failure of a single investment, even if the one loser were lost among dozens of winners; now it was the portfolio that mattered. In the old days, certain classes of assets were deemed intrinsically unsuitable for a trust account; no longer. In the old days, a trustee could not delegate investment authority; the new rule allows it. In place of a single-minded focus on the preservation of capital, the reform movement urged an emphasis on total return (that is, dividend income and capital appreciation together).

Who could object to the new ideas? Was there anyone still living to stand up for the old ones? In New York, it seemed, there was not. The Prudent Investor Act was passed by the state Assembly in July 1994 by a vote of 147–0; it squeaked through the state Senate, 55–1. Consent was galvanized not only by the urgent desire of the law-makers to get out of Albany—the vote came near the close of the leg-islative session—but also by the force of the theoretical arguments, by the example of the wealth produced by rising markets and by the de-termination of the mutual-fund industry to get its hands on some of the $600 billion of personal trust money that was then entrusted to bank management. Could anyone in 1994 doubt that more money had been lost in American financial markets over the past half cen-tury because of too much caution rather than too little? "Investment products or techniques are essentially neutral," Bevis Longstreth had written in his highly regarded *Modern Investment Management and the Prudent Man Rule* in 1986; "none should be classified prudent or im-prudent per se." To which he added, "Prudence is not self-evident."

Contrarians ached with anxiety. Were these the conclusions of enlightened science or of bullish scientists? As recently as the late 1960s, the Ford Foundation felt obliged to make a case that educa-tional endowments could, in fact, invest in common stocks without risking disgrace, or worse; the idea was regarded as controversial. (Its appearance on the eve of the 1969–74 bear market made it no less controversial.) It was only in 1970 that the New York State legal list of eligible bond investments was retired. As recently as 1983, the Federal Reserve Board was warning the trust companies it regu-lated not to involve themselves in futures or options: "Any invest-ment transaction involving a high degree of risk, or producing no income yield, [is] considered per se speculative and therefore im-proper," the Fed declared. Had the world become so much wiser?

PAPER MONEY, legalized gambling and chronic deficits on current ac-count elicited no shock in 1996 even though each and every one of them had been condemned as heretical only a generation or so beforc. When Paul Wick, world-beating manager of the Seligman Communications & Information mutual fund, told *SmartMoney* magazine in the fall of 1995 that some of his competitors "never do anything dangerous, so their return numbers are mediocre," the earth did not open underneath him. No derision met Nationsbank when it sponsored a new equity mutual fund that proposed to buy shares in companies that exhibited "earnings momentum." (The brochure that described this wonder-fund did not mention the businesses that issued the stocks, the mortality rate of those businesses, the yield, if any, of the stocks they issued, the concept of value, or many of the other ideas that filled the four editions of Graham and Dodd.) Borrowing from Longstreth, therefore, one could say, "Heresy is not self-evident." Like an overdressed guest at a dinner party, modern finance removed its necktie and slipped off its jacket.

In the fall of 1995, a California mutual-fund manager, William "Beau" Duncan Jr. was asked why he was not a value investor (buying stocks when they are cheap and down) instead of a momentum investor (buying them when they are dear and up). "Because you are buying companies where positive things are happening," Duncan replied, "and I am basically an optimist, I guess. That just fits my personality."

Optimism has generally fit the American personality. The nation was no less optimistic in 1995 than it was when the Donner party set out for Oregon in covered wagons, or when men built a transcontinental railroad with sledgehammers. Yet the intellectual and legal structure of financial stewardship was built on a high degree of caution. If the courts and regulators made mistakes, as they surely did, they were not so remarkable in view of the periodic destruction of risk capital through bank run, depression, and bear market.

The striking recent change in the law has mirrored the equally striking change in the financial cycle. The age of bull markets has encouraged the bulls and the legal progressives just as it has discouraged the bears and the legal conservatives. It would be an all-time first if the cycle did not, at some future date, swing all the way back again. At such a time, based on precedent, the return of the unenlightened old ideas will be heralded by a frightened and vengeful public as not only necessary but also as forward-looking.

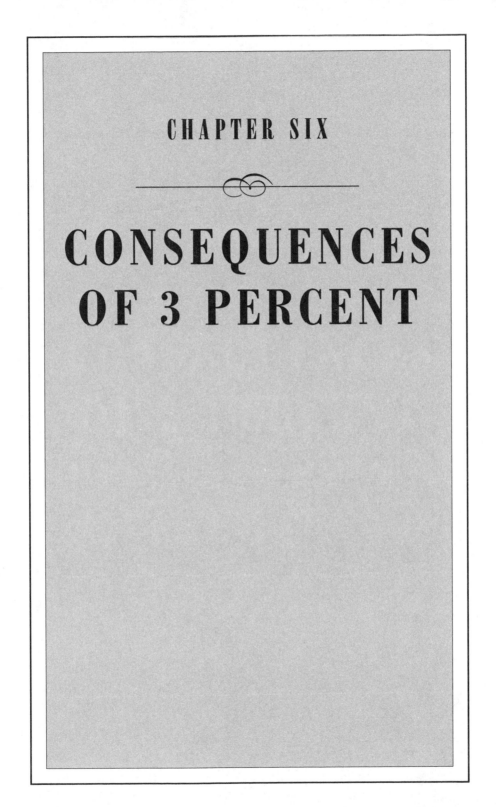

CHAPTER SIX

CONSEQUENCES OF 3 PERCENT

E ARLY IN 1996, the tallest freestanding observation tower in America was under construction in Las Vegas. Stratosphere, rising to a height of 1,149 feet, 165 feet higher than the Eiffel Tower, was the distant cyclical echo of 40 Wall Street: a boom-time capital project coaxed into being by hospitable securities markets and a low bank rate as well as by an entrepreneur's inspiration. The vision of the builders of Stratosphere—besides the tower, an 118,500-square-foot casino, 2,500 hotel rooms and suites, an entertainment complex with seven restaurants, including a Rainforest Cafe, either under construction or on the drawing board—was that Americans would gamble in the clouds as well as at sea level. They would not only willingly lose at games of chance, the builders decided, but also they would pay good money to board a fantasy spacecraft that would hurtle them, at approximately four times the force of gravity, 160 feet straight up in the mast of the tower; this amusement would take place 100 stories above the Las Vegas Strip. Like 40 Wall Street, Stratosphere got bigger as it went; a $6 million King Kong elevator was added to the attractions that an acrophobe would travel any horizontal distance not to experience. A passenger car rendered to look like Fay Wray's leading man would climb the tower's 1,149-foot exterior in fits and starts, as King Kong ascended the Empire State Building in the contraction of the 1930s. Plainly, this was not yet the contraction phase of the cycle of the 1990s: preceding a 10-million-share secondary offering in December 1995 was a $210 million sale of high-yield first-mortgage bonds in March and a $51 million initial public offering in February 1994. Early in 1996, Stratosphere was capitalized at a grand total of $450 million.

The Austrians had described the theory of credit inflation and the process by which a too-low bank rate would incite a capital-investment boom and, inevitably, a bust. A too-low bank rate there had been, and the expansion was under way. Capital spending and the stock market were setting new records on the upside. Semiconductor fabricating plants were mushrooming, and the equity capital of American banks was fructifying. The missing link was the bust. Companies failed, to be sure, but many continued to operate in bankruptcy as if they hadn't. The stock market faltered from time to time, but it continued to set records for the greatest number of consecutive months without a 10 percent correction (from October 11, 1990 to April 30, 1996, the Standard & Poor's 500 Index delivered a string of 2,027 days; the prior record set between June 26, 1962, and February 9, 1966, was 1,324 days). The dollar had bouts of weakness, but the foreign central banks always intervened to prop it up. It is true that the bond market went to pieces in 1994 and that the number of consumer bankruptcies leapt in 1995 (to 874,642, just 26,232 shy of the record set in the postrecession year of 1992). However, there was no generalized correction of error. To listen to the most bullish voices on Wall Street, none was necessary. In effect, the argument ran, systemwide error had been eliminated by technology and enlightened central banking. The season of finance had been replaced by perpetual springtime.

A student of cycles, having read many variations on the theme of the end of cycles (in 1942 or 1974, people expected that the only phase would be winter), was prepared to doubt it. There would always be cycles—and the more intent a government was on denying the downside, the greater the ultimate cost. In the spring of 1996, the stock market was climbing, the economy was growing, and complacency was reigning. Yet the chronic loss of economic vitality—in Japan and Western Europe even more than in the United States—went unexplained. An observer was led to wonder if a cause of this sclerosis might not be the suppression of failure.

. . .

THE 300TH BIRTHDAY of the Bank of England in 1994 was the occasion for scholarship, celebration, a newly commissioned choral work, and devout thanksgiving (a service at St. Paul's Cathedral was attended by Queen Elizabeth and the Duke of Edinburgh). The scholarship included a monograph on the development of central banking by a trio of British scholars. "So, currently," the three wound up their survey of monetary evolution from the gold standard to the paper standard, "at the end of this historical journey, the international monetary system remains as disordered as at any intervening time, and the way forward unclear." In this developmental sense, the birthday proceedings presented cause to regret as well as to celebrate. Regret could be read between the lines of the economists' essay. It could be inferred that the world had moved backward from the simplicity of the international gold standard. The objective evidence of a wrong historical turn was stamped in the lamentable record of the birthday central bank's own currency. The pound sterling had lost 98 percent of its purchasing power in terms of gold in the 80 years since the close of the end of the classical gold standard in 1914.

CERTAINLY, the central bankers who gathered to wish the Old Lady of Threadneedle Street a happy 300th birthday cut a poor figure in comparison to the long-departed celebrants of the bicentennial birthday year. It could not be denied that the modern-day bankers led more interesting professional lives than their gold-standard forbears. Equally, however, it had to be admitted that the moderns were less successful at what they did, if success were reckoned by the lack of inflation, either of the price or credit variety. In the late nineteenth century, a central banker was not required to hold an opinion about the economic future, much less to implement one. Not held accountable for economic growth, the banker was not expected to testify about it, to deaden it, or to stimulate it. (For those reasons, among others, the central banker was unlikely to become a household name, as Alan Greenspan, chairman of the Federal Reserve Board, has become.) What central bankers were duty-bound to do, under the gold standard, was to exchange gold for bank notes, and bank notes for gold, each at the legal rate. They were expected to conduct a conventional banking business to earn a rate of return for their shareholders (the typical central bank then being an investor-owned institution). They were expected to manage their government's finances but not to monetize its debt.

"It was almost unbelievably soothing to sit in a quiet upper room with walls about two feet thick, looking into a soundless inner court, with nothing to do but lay out bank-notes in patterns like Patience cards, learning all about the little marks on them, crossing them up in piles like card-houses, sorting them into numerical order, counting them in sixties and finally entering their numbers in beautiful ledgers made of the very best paper, as if intended to last out the ages." So recalled one of the first women employees of the Bank, Janet Courtney, who joined the staff in the bicentennial year, 1894.

Naturally, it was not always so serene in Europe's central banks. At great intervals, war or financial panic would force the suspension of the convertibility of currency into gold. For the duration of the emergency, the particular central bank's money would resemble that of a bank from a barbarous, "scrap-of-paper economy" (to borrow a nineteenth century epithet). Then, too, a central bank, even in a noncrisis, might wish to discourage the export of gold from its vaults. In times of stringency, the Bank of England, for example, would sift through its piles of sovereigns to find the oldest and most worn, and therefore the lightest, coins; these it would pass through the teller's window to anyone who wished to export gold from the kingdom when the bank preferred that he didn't. Or, to encourage a gold inflow, the bank might extend interest-free loans to bullion importers. As for Germany, the legal right to import or export gold might be temporarily abridged by a word from on high, a form of communication known as a "frown from the Director of the Reichsbank." However, such gambits, called "gold devices," did not change the fundamental fact about the capital flows that balanced international payments under the international gold standard. They were "disproportionately of a private nature: i.e., private bank loans, individuals investing in foreign securities, and

banks and houses discounting in the international market for bills,"
relates a contemporary historian of the gold-standard era, Giulio
M. Gallarotti. ". . . Official balance-of-payments financing (i.e., advances from international lending agencies and consortiums of
central banks) was rare, and nations allowed fairly unrestricted
movement of capital flows that financed deficits (capital controls
being few). Whatever public manipulation of capital flows occurred—the use of gold devices and discount rates to attract gold to
central banks—indirectly impacted on adjustment. The principal
public goal of central bankers was to maintain sufficient public gold
to preserve national and international convertibility." It was a far
cry from the system that has evolved in this, the post–Bretton
Woods era, in which the Bank of Japan, for example, buys dollars
for the sake of forestalling a domestic depression that was very
nearly brought on by the preceding credit inflation. The old way
was simpler, at least.

In 1887, the Bank of England employed 1,160 persons, of whom
two—the chief accountant and chief cashier—actually lived on the
premises. The pay of the average employee was £250 a year. The
staff administered the public debt, conducted the government's
banking business, printed banknotes, created the dies on which the
water marks were made as well as the plates on which the notes were
printed, exchanged gold coins for notes and notes for gold coins,
counted and weighed the coins and bullion (making use of a steam-
powered scale invented by a director of the bank for the very purpose), discounted bills of exchange, administered the accounts of
private banking clients, and paid dividends on the national debt as
well as on the stock of the Bank of England itself and a number of
colonial and Indian enterprises. The number of employees required
to carry out the most basic gold-standard transaction—exchanging
gold for currency and vice versa—was approximately nine. No
branch of the bank was yet devoted to economic or econometric
forecasting: until 1930, the macroeconomic future went unforecast.
The clerks wore black (as, indeed, did nearly everyone else in the
City of London), and they were expected to do their duty without let
or hindrance. "The most complete subordination and the strictest
discipline are insisted upon amongst the body of clerks," a contem-

porary inside description of the bank held forth. "Their work is not excessive, but is generally expected that it will be (and, indeed, it generally is) performed with punctuality, zeal and gentlemanly behavior. Should occasional instances arise to the contrary, and fortunately they are few, the system of administration is so judiciously arranged, that upon the first appearance of irregularity it is promptly and resolutely suppressed." A library of some 18,000 volumes, accessible to the staff, was situated over the gold-weighing room overlooking the bullion yard. Many of the books were donated by the directors.

As to whether the Bank of England should serve as a lender of last resort in time of crisis, debate raged. The view that it should not, championed in England by Thomson Hankey, governor of the Bank of England from 1851 to 1852, did not withstand the critical attack of the eminent Walter Bagehot, editor of *The Economist*. Bagehot famously contended that in time of panic a central bank should lend unstintingly against good collateral at a high rate of interest. At this writing, Hankey's argument looks better than it has in more than a century, having anticipated some of the unintended consequences of federal deposit insurance in America and, more broadly, the costs of the socialization of credit worldwide. Hankey, a West India merchant and Member of Parliament, contended that every financial institution should be held responsible for its own balance sheet, even in a pinch. "I am no advocate for any legislative enactments to try and make the trading community more prudent," he wrote in 1866. "I should be sorry to see any interference to prevent persons overtrading or speculating. Let everyone invest his money as he pleases; let everyone trade on what capital he pleases—borrow money at what rate and on what security he pleases; but the trading community must be taught at some time or other that no such establishment as the Bank of England can provide ready money beyond a certain clearly established limit, and that limit is the money left in their hands by their depositors."

The thoroughgoing defeat of Hankey's ideas is incorporated in statute books, regulatory precedent, and political philosophy in all four corners of the earth. (An English schoolmistress who lost her savings in a London bank defalcation in 1892 wrote a supplicating

letter that, by itself, might have canceled Hankey: "I can only sob
out in the night [the only time I can allow myself the luxury of cry-
ing], 'Oh God, I have worked so hard, and looked forward to my
little home, with my books, so longingly, save me, oh save me from
the workhouse. . . .' ") One by one, prudence, overtrading, speculation, capital, and credit became the government's business. Also
contra Hankey, ready money is today what central banks are prepared to deliver by the carload. The Federal Reserve is not only the
lender of last resort but also the liquidity provider of first resort. It
seeks to prevent financial crises just as it tries to forestall recession,
joblessness, and inflation. However, Hankey in defeat has had his
moments, not least in the early 1990s. The debris of the banking
and credit dilemma is in large part a consequence of the intellectual victory that Bagehot won in the 1860s.

THE HANKEY DOCTRINE, long defunct in 1946, was in that year given
a posthumous knock when the Bank of England was nationalized;
what the bank owed to the public and the British banking system
was thereby clarified. It owed everything.* Two years later, the central banks of the Netherlands, and West Germany were nationalized, and the word *macroeconomic* entered the English language. Now
a legal structure and a term of art were made available to support
policies already long established. What was, in effect, a forced draft
of interest rates for the duration of two world wars became a
makeshift of the cold war as well. At this writing, the federal funds
rate is almost as much an article of government property as the
USS *Nimitz*.

---

* "If the Bill is administered in the spirit in which it was drafted," said the then-
governor of the bank, T. S. Catto, at a dinner on the eve of the change of control, "we
need have few fears for the future. That future I cannot predict but I can say this, that
there is nothing in the structure of the new charter which would prevent the continued confidence, prosperity and prestige of the Bank." The pound sterling was another
matter, as Catto did not get around to observing: for it, the ways were greased.
    As for the stockholders, the importance of their removal was symbolic, but the
symbol was potent. "Their rights, in excess of their conventional dividend, have already sunk to the neighborhood of zero," John Maynard Keynes had contended in
1924. "But the same thing is partly true of many other big institutions. They are, as
time goes on, socializing themselves"—with an assist from the intellectuals, of course.

The principal financial end product of the exertions of the 24,000 employees of the Federal Reserve Board is, in fact, this one interest rate. Little or nothing in the education or experience of a silk-hatted practitioner of central banking under the gold standard would have prepared him to anticipate that the federal-funds targeting technique would be the fruit of 100 years of monetary progress. Neither could he have guessed that in a day and age of paperless securities trading, computer-generated checks, $1.5 trillion per day international payments systems, and electronic data processing, the central bank of the world's leading financial power would require a staff 21 times larger than the Bank of England (not then possessing computers) did when Great Britain was at the zenith of its financial power. Then again, the future is no longer allowed to go unanticipated: it must be forecast to be improved on.

If the old theorists did not foresee that the Federal Reserve would set an interest rate as the now-defunct Interstate Commerce Commission set freight rates, neither did they envision the era of perpetual payments deficits. Still less did they anticipate a world in which a reserve country's payments deficit would continuously and prosperously be recycled through the deficit country's money and capital markets.*

They could not have anticipated these developments without a preview of the principles of central economic planning, including the idea that the future can be accurately divined by a committee of public servants. Although this notion, qua notion, has sold at a sharp discount since the collapse of the Berlin Wall, it continues to thrive on Wall Street. "We're going to get a soft landing," a man from Kemper Financial Services told *USA Today* in March

---

* The American payments deficit persisted, in part, because it served two sets of interests. The participating central banks intervened not only to support the dollar but also to suppress the unwanted appreciation of their own currencies against the dollar and other major currencies. In this, they sought to protect and promote their United States–bound exports. The weaker the U.S. dollar against the Thai baht or the Japanese yen, for example, the higher the prices of those countries' products in dollar terms. The higher their prices, the lower the volume likely to be sold in American stores. If, as it sometimes seemed, the Third World's nouveaux riches central banks were propping up a drunk Uncle Sam, they were helping not just any drunk but an old and valued customer.

1995. "God bless the Fed." (A year later, the Fed's stock was not one-eighth of a point lower. "The people who run the Fed today are near geniuses," remarked David Braver in conversation. "Thank God for Alan Greenspan," wrote Tob Norton in *Fortune* magazine; Norton's piece was headed, IN GREENSPAN WE TRUST.) Enjoying the levitation of assets denominated in dollars, investors understandably conceived a higher opinion of the dollars themselves. Not only are managed currencies viable, the market has come to believe, but also the doctrine of managed currencies is coherent.

It was coherent enough to generate stable (if very low) rates of economic growth, very low rates of inflation, and some of the most luxuriant years ever seen on Wall Street. To gold-minded critics, each of the feats of contemporary central banking seemed the public policy equivalent of a lucky catch: the fans had no right to expect another one.

Admiration of the earlier system was not great-great-great-grandfather worship; nor, for the most part, did the critics believe that the old philosophy, rules, and institutions could be easily grafted onto the Clinton era. What undergirded the gold standard was not merely a commitment to conservative finance but also, and more fundamentally, a belief in conservative politics.* Laissez-faire was the shared political consensus. There was a perceived moral dimension to the financial arrangements of the day as well. "We are all destined in the world to earn our bread by the sweat of our brow," declared Hankey in 1873, "and I know of no trade or calling in which high religious and moral qualities can be more sensibly appreciated and brought to bear for practical utility in our journey through life than in that of Banking."

Bears and antiquarians were stuck: the more they studied the old arrangements, the less they believed in the new ones. They were under no delusion that the City of London of a century ago was paradise. The senior staff of the Bank of England, which had gone three decades without a raise in the middle nineteenth century, must not have been alone in yearning for a taste of what a subsequent generation would learn to call "creeping inflation." Janet

---

* "Liberal," in nineteenth-century nomenclature.

Courtney had a cog's view of the bank's efficiency: ". . . the great bars of gold and silver in the fortress-like bullion vaults, brought in from Lothbury under guard through an archway which looked as if it ought to have a portcullis; the almost human gold-weighing machines, which spat out sovereigns sideways and let the rest fall in a steady stream into copper vessels like coal pans—all the significant evidence of Britain's wealth and British solidarity, so picturesque, so historic, so reassuring, and, in the long run, so unbearably tedious. I used to wish a bomb would explode and wreck the Bank as the only way to get out of it. . . ."

Just in time for its 1894 bicentennial, the bank was shamed by its own chief cashier, Frank May, the stiff-necked veteran of 42 years, who, among other acts of misconduct and misappropriation, made an illicit loan to the financial editor of *The Times*. In the midst of the scandal, the bank came in for some sharp criticism by setting itself above the people who nominally owned it. "There is no outside audit of its books," one critic wrote; "its stockholders have no control whatever over the management. Under the charter shareholders are supposed to meet and elect directors and governors at stated periods, but this list has dwindled into mere routine and pantomime. The 'House List,' as it is called, is always elected as a matter of course, so that the board is really co-operative. It is thus, in great measure, 'a family party.' " Seen in this light a century later, the Bank of England bears a certain retrospective resemblance to one of the New York mutual savings banks that was driven into the ground by self-perpetuating managements. Then, too, sometimes, the Old Lady stooped to feud with other commercial banks in London. In a very real sense, they were its competitors. "When it came to the health of the British banking system," Gallarotti writes, "it was not always clear that the Directors of the Bank of England wished to prevent shocks, especially if that meant knocking off some erstwhile competitors." Anticipating the dubious practices of central banks to this day, the bank did not immediately report sensitive or embarrassing transactions. Thus, the mortification of a loan from the representative of a foreign power, the Bank of France, in 1836 was first disclosed in 1840. Decades later, in the financial tumult that led up to World War I, a single sentence in a memo from the British Treasury captured the bank's ambiguous (and, in the context of contemporary American financial life, unimaginable) public character: "The Bank of England cannot be expected to endanger its modest dividends by heroic measures." It is recorded that "all the good monetary economists of the late 19th century thought that something better than the gold standard could be achieved, and that the defenders of the gold standard were a lesser breed. . . ."

No doubt, the gold standard was calculated to annoy the intellectuals, who could perfectly well see its faults, and who could just as perfectly imagine themselves at the head of an alternative monetary arrangement, one that did not function through inadvertence. Yet a kind of serendipity was the system's principal genius and beauty. The outcome most directly sought by each central bank was not a melioration of the business cycle, a rise in stock prices, or a fall in bond yields but its own continued institutional prosperity. Price stability and low unemployment were, in effect, by-products of the pursuit of dividends for the proprietors of the bank. Over the span of three-and-a-half decades in the so-called core countries of the gold system—the United States, Great Britain, France, and Germany—wages, capital formation, and national output each grew by rates high enough to panic a 1996 bondholder. (Not the least of the drawbacks of the pure paper standard is the bond markets' morbid fear of growth; having no good reason to trust a fiat currency for any span of time resembling the maturity of a long-dated security, creditors have come to treat inflationary growth and noninflationary growth as one and the same menace.) One great achievement of the gold-standard years is that high growth and low inflation were achieved without headlong pursuit of macroeconomic targets. "The confidence in the stability of exchange rates was visible in the structure of foreign-exchange dealings," Gallarotti writes; "transactions in currencies on a firm gold basis were usually not hedged against exchange risk because of the expectations that rates would stay within the gold points."

As for bond yields, there was a shortage of drama. The turn of the century brought a gradual rise in long rates (forecast by almost nobody, as we have seen), but in none of the 35 years of the international gold standard did a central government security in America or Great Britain yield more than an annual average of 3.63 percent. Such interest-rate excitement as there was occurred in the money market. As bond yields were stable, bill yields were volatile; it was through money rates that the market adjusted to the ebbs and flows of domestic and international liquidity. The lower a country's gold reserves, the more volatile its money rates. In both Great Britain and the United States, short-dated interest rates were considerably more prone to lurch up and down between 1870 and 1914 than they were even in the tumultuous decades following the eclipse of Bretton Woods. The reason is easily explained: in the City of London, money rates were customarily set by the market; the Bank of England customarily followed. To the extent that no incorrect rate was imposed from the bank, to just that extent could buyers and sellers make their own mistakes. They could, and did err, both to the downside and the upside, as in the frenzied rise and fall of South African gold mines in the 1890s. ("Speculation has seized the public mind to an unprecedented degree, and the Stock Exchange had become the center of the national life," an observer recollected some time after the event.) The cardinal Austrian monetary sin of setting a subsidized or a punitive rate was therefore one that the Bank of England was usually innocent of.

What was different about speculation in the gold-standard era was not so much the upside as the downside. On rare occasions, the bank would lead a salvage operation of a threatened financial institution, as it did in the Baring failure in 1890. For the most part, however, the financial markets were their own keepers. The importance of reputation, and the evanescence of credit, were concepts more tangible in a day when it was the duty of no governmental authority to dress a small speculative wound with an interest-rate balm. ("We must be as careful of our credit now as if we were still creating it," cautioned a partner of an East India merchant in 1891, the year after the Baring disaster.)

The prevailing structure of interest rates constituted another sobering influence on speculative markets. In London from 1880 to 1914, money-market rates were usually higher than long-term government bond yields. The significance of such an alignment was that nothing could be gained by borrowing short and lending long—that is, by taking a calculated risk of the kind that caused the

U.S. savings and loan industry to come to grief in the early 1980s or the hedge-fund industry to nearly inherit the earth in 1991–93 or that precipitated the bond market convulsion of 1994. It was not that the citizens of gold-standard finance lacked the speculative urge. The great impediments to prolonged, lusty, and wild-haired booms were the obstacles to borrowing money. There was less money to be had, for one thing, and a banker had more to fear by overlending, for another. Also, owing to the structure of interest rates and the modus operandi of the Bank of England, there could be no certainty that a low money-market interest rate would stay low. What the bank did not do (as the Fed did, in 1993) was to sit on the money market for the express purpose of effecting a domestic financial result. As for the financial forbears of George Soros, they speculated mainly on the stability of the principal gold-standard currencies (if one should happen to fall to the lower end of its trading range), not on their devaluation. Belief in the convertibility of the money of gold-standard nations was a bedrock article of faith. "The system has become so much a matter of course to the vast majority of those engaged in commerce here as to appear a law of nature." So Colonel Robert Williams, president of the Gold Standard Defense Association, declared in 1897, a time when some agitation for a bimetallic standard—silver and gold together—did cast the shadow of a doubt (soon erased).

A CENTURY LATER, the nongold system also seemed, to many, a law of nature. To the faithful, Alan Greenspan had saved the banking system, foreshortened the recession, and sustained a stock market boom. They beheld a work of genius. No doubt, skeptics mused, there was much to be said for the feats (whether or not they had been knowingly brought to pass by monetary policy). The greater issue was whether they entailed any adverse consequences to the financial markets, the economy, to either, or both. How could they not?

Central bankers could not know what they pretended to know, what the financial markets hoped they could know, or what the law (at least in the United States) required them to know. They could not know exactly where the United States economy had been; an accurate navigational sighting awaited the receipt of revisions to the national income accounts, which were always late in coming. Still less could they be sure where it was at the moment or (even less) where it might be going. Their ability to forecast interest rates or real growth was in no way improved by the fact that their motives were disinterested and public-spirited. Even supposing that the Fed saw the future clearly, before it jelled, there was one thing, only, it could do about it. To believe in the efficacy of the Federal Reserve System's chosen operating system, it was necessary to believe that the manipulation of a single interest rate could guide the largest economy on earth. It was literally fantastic.*

Observing the unfolding prosperity of the mid-1990s, the gold-minded critic was sometimes put in the untenable position of a Stalinist-era member of the American Communist Party. Plainly, the financial markets were going up, and a boom was in progress; disaster (in the form of a full-blown credit contraction) had been skirted. Just as plainly, however, according to orthodox writ, such an outcome was not strictly possible. The upside was authorized, certainly: there would be booms. But the absence of a downside was admitted in no classical text. Sooner or later, the Fed would settle on the wrong federal funds rate; if too low, as in 1993, an inflation would ensue, either of prices or credit; if too high, as it seemed late in 1995, the timing of the inevitable bust would be moved up. However, there was no telling just when that might be. Meanwhile, the

---

* The Federal Reserve didn't doubt, however. In a speech to the Mortgage Bankers Association early in 1996, William J. McDonough, president of the Federal Reserve Bank of New York, explained the low inflation rate in terms of monetary anticipation. "The pre-emptive approach was highlighted early in 1994," said McDonough, "when the Fed began firming monetary conditions because of our concerns over inflation re-emerging. While there was no apparent acceleration in actual price inflation at that time, the buildup of underlying inflationary pressures was evident in various forward looking indicators and forecasts of the economy.

"The main reason we need a pre-emptive approach is that monetary policy works with uncertain and long time lags. Estimates of these lags vary widely, but most of the effect of monetary policy on economic activity seems to take place within one or two years and its impact on inflation usually takes longer. Thus, I think the appropriate horizon for Federal Reserve policymakers is one to three years."

McDonough described the clairvoyance system of monetary management without actually naming it.

world seemed to veer ever closer to perfection. The bears listened sullenly to radio advertisements in which Betty Sinnock, one of the famous "Beardstown Ladies," authors of a best-selling folksy investment book, urged her listeners to "Invest in the greatest companies in the world—you'll find them at the New York Stock Exchange, and have fun!"

Having no fun, the bears steeled themselves with the fact that every monetary system in history has come to grief, and that one based on false premises could hardly prove the exception. The odds had been stacked against even the ones that were based on true premises. (Just as Janet Courtney had sometimes wished, the Bank of England and the international gold standard were done in by bomb blasts; what she didn't anticipate was that the damage would be war-induced.) Following the international gold standard, successive, ersatz gold standards—the post–World War I gold-exchange standard and the post–World War II Bretton Woods system—had each failed, the second one only after two and a half decades of creditable service. The post–Bretton Woods era was itself getting long in the tooth in 1996: it was finishing up its own quarter century. It was not unreasonable to begin to anticipate a change.

"Is there a role for gold in monetary policy?" inquired an essay in a journal of the Federal Reserve Bank of Chicago in 1994. Not so many decades ago, the question might have been framed: "Is there a role for monetary policy under a gold standard?"

The obsolescence of the old ideas is not so remarkable; as our story has taught us, financial ideas are cyclical. Derivatives, managed currencies, and the lucrative, risky practice of borrowing short and lending long represent not merely accepted contemporary institutions, but also proscribed historical ones. Each was once a heresy.

At this writing, no trace of heresy attaches to the industrialized world's paper money or to the central banks that manage it. Together, to the bulls, they hold out the possibility of life without cyclical limits. Thus, if the Federal Reserve can facilitate a capital investment boom by suppressing the federal funds rate, why can it not keep on suppressing it? If the one correct funds rate can prolong an upturn, why should there ever be a downturn? If the

United States can import as much as it likes, paying in the dollars that it can issue without restraint, why does it not import every single Mercedes Benz car and Yves Saint Laurent evening creation offered for sale? If the wages of sin (as financial sin was traditionally defined) is prosperity, why stint on the sin?

Nineteen ninety-three, with its 3 percent federal funds rate, seemed a year borrowed from the Austrian text: a quintessential credit inflation with all the short-term bullish consequences attending on the propagation of surplus credit. Yet for all that Wall Street worried about the possible bearish consequences of that kind of inflation, Röpke might as well never have lived. Nineteen ninety-five, with its building U.S. payments deficit and volatile dollar exchange rate, seemed a clear-cut case of the abuse of a reserve currency. Yet neither was Rueff's memory honored in the financial markets. Not only did the dollar not visibly lose as an international store of value, but also nobody seemed to expect that it should.

The consensus of opinion was that a new age had arrived. Bear markets, recessions, and product cycles (especially of computer products) had supposedly been conquered. Monetary policy in America had allegedly succeeded where central economic planning in the Old World failed. Booms connote inflation, but the coast-to-coast acquisition of computers and computer-related paraphernalia was held to be a bulwark against price inflation, then and for all time.

The low incidence of slumps, bear markets, and serial bank runs seemed an unalloyed benefit and the prelude to even greater uninterrupted prosperity. Certainly, human suffering at the ebbs of market cycles was much reduced. Whether the depressionless modern economy was a net provider to human progress over the course of complete economic and investment cycles, however, was still an open question. Is it permitted in market economies to promote the upside while suppressing the downside? Through which capitalist institutions can human error be rectified, if not through the money-losing ones?

THE SPECULATIVE lilt in American finance is to some extent built in. "The discovery, colonization and early development of America was a speculative enterprise," Walter Werner and Steven T. Smith wrote in their history of the early years of the New York financial markets, "and it is not surprising that the spirit of speculation ran high both before and after the Revolution." In the first administration of Andrew Jackson, an American commentator celebrated the institution of boom and bust in his young country. As will be instantly apparent, he wrote in the boom portion of the cycle. "In the midst of all this speculation," expostulated Michael Chevalier in 1835, "while some enrich and some ruin themselves, banks spring up and diffuse credit; railroads and canals extend themselves over the country; steamboats are launched into the rivers, the lakes and the sea; the career of speculators is ever enlarging, the field for railroads, canals, steamers and banks goes on expanding. Some individuals lose, but the country is a gainer; the country is peopled, cleared, cultivated; its resources are unfolded, its wealth increased. Go Ahead!"

The panic of 1837 presently followed, and with it a severe depression—it would have reduced Clement Juglar to tears of admiration—and a banking crisis, induced by Jackson's contractionary banking policies. The elegiac flight of Chevalier's prose was inspired, in part, by a 25-fold expansion in bank capital (as against a $1\frac{1}{2}$-fold increase in population) in the years 1830–37. The credit inflation was a thing of beauty for as long as it lasted; speculation flowered in land and securities. A measure of the public's disappointment with the unfolding bust was a bill submitted in the New York state legislature to outlaw equity trading. It failed, but so did most of the members of the New York Stock & Exchange Board.

When the speculative stars are aligned, new ventures have usually found capital in the American public markets. As long ago as the boom year of 1791, for example, the Society for the Establishment of Useful Manufactures raised funds in a nascent stock market. Shares were sold on the installment plan. (When the company turned out not to be the General Electric of the first Washington administration, payments on subscriptions stopped.)

Two centuries later, as we have already seen, latter-day Societies for the Establishment of Useful Manufactures still find willing backers. In America, as in few other countries, a new business can be financed in the capital markets and an unsuccessful business can be resuscitated in the bankruptcy courts. And in no other bond market in the world can a corporation return to borrow time and again after sticking its creditors in the eye with a "tactical" bankruptcy filing (as Texaco did in 1987) or a leveraged restructuring (e.g., Marriott in 1993).

Only in America, perhaps, could a visionary college professor raise money in the stock market to finance a not-yet profitable venture in superconductivity, or a bankruptcy-bound retailer line up a big loan to tide it over during reorganization. The particular American business genius lies in beginnings and endings as much as in great, moneymaking middles. But the aptitude for bankruptcy is not often seen in the public sector. In Washington, the standing policy toward failure is asphyxiation: recessions are cut short (or headed off at the pass), bank failures arrested, bear markets intercepted, and insolvent neighboring countries bailed out. All around, the American way of bankruptcy is unique. In most countries, a failed business is sold for the benefit of its creditors. A failed American business may be sold, but it may also be conserved. If it is saved, it is saved not so much for its creditors as for its employees, management, and stockholders. More and more, bankruptcy is a state of necessity, convenience, or transition. Less and less shame seems to attach to it. (In 1994, almost 10 percent of the individuals who obtained federal refuge from their creditors were, at the moment they filed, current on their credit-card debts; they apparently expected to become imminently uncurrent. Or perhaps life has been imitating art. GOING BROKE AND CUTTING LOOSE, a *New York Times* headline beckoned in early 1996. BANKRUPTCY HAS NEW APPEAL FOR MUSIC GROUPS CHAFING AT THEIR CONTRACTS.)

How could a conservative Swiss banker be made to understand the United States? In America a bankrupt retailer in everyday operation is designated by the courts to be a "debtor-in-possession." This might seem an error in translation: surely, the gnome wonders, "creditor-in-possession" is the intended usage? But no, it is "debtor." The debtor is the failed business, or more exactly, the stockholders and management of the failed business. What they possess is the business. Their possession overrides the claims of the senior creditors. Even more amazing: retaining possession, they can lawfully borrow money in bankruptcy.

Before the Chandler Act of 1938, there was no such thing as a debtor-in-possession, much less a debtor-in-possession loan. The 1938 reform permitted a DIP-finance forerunner, "trustee certificates of indebtedness." This innovation permitted a trustee to borrow more easily to support the rehabilitation of special corporate cases (e.g., a railroad deemed essential to the public interest or an office building just a few thousand dollars short of completion). Forty years later came a new bankruptcy act and a more general application of the post-petition-financing idea: favored, so-called superpriority, status for DIP creditors and the proposition that the management that got a company into bankruptcy should remain in position to try to lead it out again. It is a situation as far removed from debtors' prison as group therapy is from Sing Sing.

The modern perfection of DIP finance awaited the right circumstances and the right inventor (it would certainly not be Thomson Hankey). Darla Moore, of Chemical Banking Corp., beheld the rise of junk-bond finance in the 1980s and saw that it was bound to fall. Under her leadership, Chemical proceeded to lend to companies that had already borrowed themselves into bankruptcy.

Could anything be so reckless? The truth was that few kinds of lending were so riskless. The DIP lender is senior to every other unsecured lender; none can be paid at all until he or she (or it) is paid in full. Thanks to this "superpriority status," an intelligently structured loan to a bankrupt is tantamount to an investment-grade credit. According to Moore, the incidence of loss in DIP-related lending has been just about zero. "That was what was so glorious about it," she said wistfully. There were (and indeed *are*) other glorious features, including the fact that so few DIP borrowers actually use the money. They pay the fees to borrow it but, usually, find that the mere promise of the loan is enough to restore their financial credibility. Vendors ship merchandise or raw materials, confident that they will ultimately be paid. "The irony was that if we put it up they never used it," said Moore. "If we didn't put it up, they would have been in a tailspin. That would have liquidated them, probably."

· · ·

BUT SEGMENTS OF the American economy seemed to cry out for liquidation. For example, in the fashion-forward, slow-pay segment of the department-store industry, Barneys did. The 14-store retail chain made a fundamental business error by overexpanding on the brink of the dress-down era, but it found a money partner to keep it going: Isetan of Japan. When, even then, it could not keep going, it filed for protection under the Federal Bankruptcy Code. This was in January 1996. Tellingly, Barneys contended that it was not actually impaired, even though its debt was 18 times larger than its equity. Striking this attitude, management furthered the suspicion of some observers that the bankruptcy system had come to serve as a tool for business improvement. High up on the list of available improvements was lease-breaking, the answer to the prayers of the company that could make a profit except for the inconvenience of paying rent at the rate it had contracted.

More and more of the garment industry—manufacturers, wholesalers, and retailers—fit this description. Too many stores, too much consumer debt, and the wearing of too few suits and neckties on weekdays combined to cripple it. Seventh Avenue dressed in widow's weeds, and *Women's Wear Daily* conveyed a sense of coast-to-coast depression. (When, in 1893, a member of the London Stock Exchange showed up for work one sweltering summer day in a straw hat instead of in the customary tall "chimney pot," he stirred a financial comment: "In view of this revolutionary development, Consols [i.e., perpetual British government bonds] should be sold." Nobody seemed to draw a comparable inference from the popularity of "dress-down Fridays" in 1995.)

No depression was under way, but the bankruptcy courts were full. Only one source of this heavy patronage was the sorry state of the retailing business; another was the consequence of humanely intended reform. As the government has sought to stamp out recessions, so it has tried to improve the process of going broke. However, the banking system (periodically aided and abetted by the tax code) has continued to set the kind of interest rates that ignite cyclical booms. Low interest rates stimulate building, as we have noted before, and very low interest rates stimulate overbuilding, in office towers, department stores, chemical plants, semiconductor fabricating plants, or coffee bars, according to taste and technology. The redundant portion of the capital goods stock thrown up in the boom is what helps to cause the distortions that precipitate the recessions that inspire the periodic liberalization of the bankruptcy laws. It is the business of the bankruptcy code to deal with (in part) the consequences of interest rates like 3 percent.

As so often happens with reform, however, actual results have veered away from legislative intent. The rash of retail bankruptcies in 1995, some of them undertaken for business-improvement reasons, spread fear and distress among manufacturers and landlords. The risk the manufacturers faced was not only the straightforward possibility of the failure of a company on the brink (a failure that would tie up a manufacturer's unpaid invoices for months or years on end). It was, in addition, that a retailer a few steps short of the brink would take the future into its own hands and seek the hospitality of the bankruptcy courts without the traditional prerequisite of actual insolvency. Manufacturers lived in dread of such prophylactic filings. So thin were profit margins that the loss of even one large order in nine meant disaster.

The famine of the garmentos was owing in large part to the softness of prices in the stores. The weakness in pricing was owing, in turn, to the surplus of stores; in the 10 years ended in 1995, according to the International Council of Shopping Centers, the number of retail square feet per American citizen had risen to 19 or so from about 15. ("There's too many competitor stores," said Leslie H. Wexner, chairman of The Limited Inc., speaking for retailers the world over. "Not too many of ours.") The excess was partly a consequence of the bankruptcy laws, partly of the tax laws, and partly of interest rates and the accessibility of credit. The reason a bankrupt retailer could lower its prices was that (with the court's dispensation) it could stop paying its bills. Thus, it tended to nudge its competitors toward the courtroom doors. At this writing, the Caldor chain (bankrupt as of September 18, 1995) is working to spread the blessings of rock-bottom retail prices throughout its network of 166 discount stores in 10 East Coast states. Its competition is as distressed by this turn of events as the public must be pleased.

By forestalling Caldor's liquidation—indeed, by facilitating its continued expansion—the Federal Bankruptcy Code helped to perpetuate the industrywide conditions that had pushed the company into Chapter 11 proceedings in the first place. The plethora of stores brought to mind the surplus of banks as well as the redundancy of commercial aircraft. In the varied cases of apparel, airline seats, and syndicated bank loans, profit margins were shrinking under the press of competition. Plainly, there were too many competitors. What prevented the less successful from leaving the field? Who or what was gumming up the works of failure? Filippe Goossens, a senior analyst at Moody's with experience in retailing and airlines, reflected on the problem shortly after Caldor became a Chapter 11 case. "Under a capitalist system," said Goossens, "the capital is supposed to flow out when profits decrease, but here, by giving debtors a second chance and allowing debtor-in-possession financing, capital flows in." Prior to 1938, the most common outcome of a bankruptcy proceeding was liquidation: of fixed investment, hopes, and employees, along with error (either of the capitalists or the government). "I'm not saying that there shouldn't be second chances or debtor-in-possession financing," Goossens added, "but it is being abused, I think."

In any case, Caldor, the country's fourth-largest discount retailer, was actually profitable in the last calendar quarter before it filed. It had had a poor August—same-store sales fell by 10.4 percent—and this news was disseminated to the far-flung TV audience of Dan Dorfman. As trade creditors abandoned ship, Caldor's management sought the safe harbor of Chapter 11. Then, in a turn of events rarely seen on the high seas, the captain said that his ship was seaworthy after all. "Our business today is fundamentally sound," declared the chairman, Don Clarke, shortly after the filing, "and we will continue to implement our strategy. This is not a company that is deteriorating."

Oddly enough, from a narrow financial point of view, it presently became sounder. A debtor-in-possession, Caldor received the standard bankrupt's relief: it no longer was bound to pay its existing, or "pre-petition," lenders. Because Caldor could raise new, post-petition funds in the DIP market, and because it received the court's permission to dig into the funds it had formerly laid aside as collateral against its pre-petition debts, bankruptcy was instantly restorative. It was, indeed, to this limited extent, a boon, and Clarke told *Women's Wear* that life would go on for the company much as before. No mass closing of stores was anticipated, he said, because most of its stores were profitable.

For Caldor, to listen to Clarke, the state of bankruptcy was almost as desirable as the state of solvency. However, it was plainly not as desirable for the creditors and stockholders of his corporation, nor for its vendors and competitors. As we have seen, what distinguished the American experience in the worldwide real estate slump of the 1990s was its ready admission of error and the writing down of (or writing off) buildings that proved unsalable at the hoped-for inflated price. Similarly, it was the incapacity of the Japanese to confront their own real estate errors that contributed so signally to four years (and counting) of stagnation.* Comparing the two experiences, it is impossible not to appreciate the wisdom of the trader's maxim that the "first loss is the best loss," and to wonder if Clement Juglar, philosopher king of the slump, might not have understood something about the uses of adversity.

IN THE AGE OF cyberwonder, it has been implied that the old cyclical theories have been superseded by the new technology. There is a modicum of truth in this suggestion. Thus, a kind of computer software known as "electronic data interchange" has introduced a new level of efficiency to inventory management, production planning, and delivery schedules. All of these activities may now be carried out computer-to-computer, i.e., on-line. "We're moving more and more to a built-to-ship economy, all electronically linked," an automotive-

---

* A footnote to the Barneys bankruptcy is that Isetan Inc., the Japanese company with which it unluckily teamed up in 1989, was financially crippled by fending off the unwanted advances of Shuwa, a Japanese real estate developer. In the end, Shuwa failed, and Isetan had to be rescued by Mitsubishi Bank. It is a cinch, however, that neither Japanese company could have plausibly discussed the step that Barneys talked about after *it* filed for bankruptcy. What Barneys told *The New York Times* was that it might go public after it exited from Chapter 11. In the eyes of Barneys' management, evidently, the stock market, like one of Walter Bagehots' central banks, was a lender of last resort.

supply executive marveled to Thomas Petzinger Jr. of *The Wall Street Journal* in the spring of 1996.

However, as the old masters were able to show in a previous age of wonder, it is the theory that is so helpful in explaining the technology. "The history of crises and cycles teaches us further," wrote Röpke in 1932, "that the jumpy increases in investment characterizing every boom are usually connected with some technical advance. In fact, the beginnings of almost every modern technical achievement—the railway, the iron and steel industry, the electrical industry, the chemical industry and most recently the automobile industry—can be traced back to a boom. It seems as if our economic system reacts to the stimulus of some technical advance with the prompt and complete mobilization of all its inner forces in order to carry it out everywhere in the shortest possible time. But this acceleration and concentration has evidently to be bought at the expense of a disturbance of equilibrium which is slowly overcome in time of depression."

The words "in time of depression" connote a fatalistic acceptance of a cyclical event that was outlawed in the United States by the Employment Act of 1946. Even if someone actually campaigned for the presidency on a pro-depression platform, he or she, if elected, could not lawfully seek to induce a depression. (Depressions may be lawfully fostered only through accident, not design.) To this extent, Röpke is out of date.

However, no act of Congress can repeal the tendency of the marginal rate of profit to decline in industries overcrowded with fixed investment. In markets, as has been repeatedly demonstrated, too much is frequently followed by too little. Röpke and others, taking this truism further, taught that busts are the products of booms. The upside actually causes the downside, since the structure of production is distended during the credit inflation. Foundry is layered on warehouse, or semiconductor fab on motherboard plant. In turn-of-the-century Vienna, it was believed that a capital-goods boom had to be taken out of the hides of the consumers who involuntarily financed it. In premillennial America, with its credit cards and home equity loans, it is harder to contend that the bulge in capital investment (and simultaneous liftoff in stock prices) is depriving the consumer of anything; or, rather, of anything in the short run. Over the long run, it is problematic. Insofar as consumer incomes fail to keep up with the pace implied by the gait of consumer borrowing, people will have to retrench. As it is, the extra dollar of consumer expenditure is requiring a larger and larger unit of consumer borrowing.

The deterministic view of cycles clashes with the modern view. It is widely believed in 1996 that recessions are the products of policy error. To the Viennese mind, they are the products of investment error, and investment error is the product of credit inflation. Credit inflation, as we have seen, is the product of subsidized interest rates. Knowing something about late-twentieth-century America that Röpke could not know, we may take the analysis a step further. Subsidized interest rates promote not only bank lending but also securities issuance (more than would be forthcoming under nonsubsidized interest rates) and stock market levitation. When the yield curve is positively sloped, as it was in 1993, a low federal funds rate promotes bond speculation. The definition of a too-low rate, to repeat, is one set below the expected rate of return on capital investment. It follows, if one lines up with Röpke, that downturns serve the useful purpose of clearing away boom-time debris. The Dallas skyline is enough to illustrate the point that overinvestment sometimes goes to "pathological" lengths (to use Röpke's word).

To see the glass as half empty, every great boom is the agent of the redundant railroad, steamer, canal, or bank (or its modern-day equivalent); to see it as half full, every great boom is the means to the end of an acceleration in the pace of material progress. "[T]oo many who examine the boom and bust, or the boom-bust syndrome in general, see only the bust and ignore the boom," Werner and Smith write. "Typically, following a cyclical upswing and crash, securities markets are left in a stronger position than before the upswing. They take two steps forward and one step back." Or, to quote Röpke himself, trying to put the best face on the last year of the Hoover term, "In this light, the crisis and depression appear as growing pains of the economic system from which we cannot escape so long as economic development proceeds by jumps instead of moving in a smooth even rise."

In the 1995 bull market, technology was easily the jumpiest department of the national economy. High-tech capital spending outstripped low-tech capital spending for the first time in 15 years, at least. At the heart of the boom was the computer, and at the heart of the computer was the semiconductor, the memory unit engineered to exacting, millionth-of-an-inch tolerances. Microprocessors—devices made of semiconductors—can, at this moment, compute in a minute what it would take the average person 120 years to do, assuming that the average person could stick to it. The semiconductor, to quote an interested corporate party, "is the archetype postmodern machine: a device made of inexpensive raw materials—like sand, air and other natural elements, such as aluminum and tungsten—to which the value of human creativity is added. That value creates enormous wealth."

The computer enriched the world, from the consumer-electronics manufacturers of Japan and South Korea to the software colony of Seattle to the semiconductor-making enclave of Boise, Idaho. Boise was the home of Micron Technology, expert maker of computer chips, especially the standard, four-meg models. "We're rolling out the chips," boomed J. R. Simplot, Micron's largest stockholder, a billionaire octogenarian and an archetype American optimist, who made one fortune in the potato and another in the semiconductor. MR. SPUD was the legend on his Idaho license plates (one-half of McDonald's french fries are supplied by the Simplot Co.), but it might as well have said MR. CHIP, MR. BULL, or, space permitting, MR. BUYDONTSELL. In only 24 months, 1994–95, the value of Simplot's interest in Micron vaulted by more than $2.5 billion, to $3.4 billion. Simplot himself owned no computer— "Hell, boy," he told Andrew E. Serwer, of *Fortune* magazine, "I came before the goddamn typewriter"—but he heard the music of the computer revolution as clearly as any cyberchild. "Son," he told Serwer, also paternalistically, "these computers are big, but they're going to get bigger. Bigger than the goddamned wheel!"

Simplot had lived through commodity cycles before, but he seemed to think that the semiconductor was not a commodity. (It is easy to understand this misconception; no mere potato is created in a clean room in which the air is refreshed about five times a minute.) In so many words, he predicted unbroken technological prosperity. Certainly, the success of his own career had been more or less unbroken, even though the markets in which he operated had had their ups and downs.*

In the mid-1980s, Micron had found itself on the wrong side of a falling semiconductor market. Japanese producers, basking under a weak yen, flooded the United States with imports. Micron struggled to survive. In this it succeeded, but it struggled anew in the recession and slowdown of the late 1980s and early 1990s. As recently as 1992, earnings totaled all of $6.6 million on sales of $506 million. It was one in a line of years of uninspiring annual results. On a decade-long chart, the price of its stock is recumbent in the neighborhood of $5 a share. Then came deliverance. In the 12 months ended June 1, 1995, Simplot's company earned no less than $705 million on sales of $2.4 billion. By late summer, a share of Micron had surged into the low $90s.

One cause of this aurora borealis was the coming of age of the personal computer. Another, closely related to the first, was a persistent shortage of computer memory chips. For years the prices of semiconductors had mainly gone down (as had the prices of most electronic marvels); now they went sideways or up. A third cause of prosperity was the boom-inspiring American monetary climate. Low interest rates, and the consequences of low rates, were partly responsible for the shortage of chips as well as for the spending that was intended to end the shortage. Japan, then as now a major chip maker, entered its slowdown-cum-debt contraction in 1990. It was in no position to spend as it had on new semiconductor fabricating capacity. Each "fab," as the adepts call them, costs as much as $1 billion to build and equip, and each

---

* Notoriously, in 1976, the potato market, of which Simplot happened to be short, went up. When the time came to settle accounts, he did not send cash, as the market expected him to, but potatoes. He did not send the Maine variety, however, as the futures contract stipulated, but the Idaho kind, which he grew. The indignant longs sued, and eight years of prosperity for the opposing attorneys unfolded. At the end of the day, Simplot paid a $50,000 federal fine and a $1.4 million judgment in a civil suit. He was exiled from futures trading for six years. Thus driven into the speculative wilderness, he began to make his second fortune in Micron. It was not the kind of poetic justice that the potato longs wished on him.

finished semiconductor chip is the product of as many as 200 production steps. Before very long, however, the case for gearing up
production became irresistible, and all hands—South Korea, Taiwan, Japan, the United States—turned to. By late 1995, announcements of new fabs were spilling out of fax machines at the
rate of approximately one a week.

Though a marvel, the semiconductor is also a commodity: dynamic random-access memory wafers are peas in a pod. (Technical
competition in the semiconductor field takes the form of innovation in chip design and manufacturing processes, but one maker's
end product is much the same as another's.) As with premodern
commodities, the price of the semiconductor has tended to fall
along with the cost of its production. The demand for semiconductors has only tended to rise, however, and in this respect the computer chip is a uniquely favored commodity. But in another respect
it is uniquely disfavored. The capacity to produce computer chips,
unlike (for example) the capacity to mine precious metals, is rising
by leaps and bounds. When the price of silver shot up in 1993–94 to
about $5.80 an ounce from less than $4 an ounce, not one new primary silver mine was dug (in the United States, environmental regulations stand in the way of any such project; it takes as many as
five years to get a new mine in production.) It may be said, on the
bearish side of silver, that some industrial invention might one day
render it obsolete, thereby collapsing its price. However, the same
objection holds with equal force for the semiconductor—or perhaps with greater force because of all the capital and brainpower
devoted to advancing the cause of obsolescence. Almost certainly,
wheat is a more permanent fixture of human existence than the
memory chip. The tactical question in the early autumn of 1995
was whether the supply of semiconductors would soon overtake the
demand. The strategic question was whether the business cycle, as
described and diagnosed by the Austrian theorists, was a thing of
the past, or whether it was unfolding before the gimlet eyes of the
technologists.

The makers of computers and computer memory devices did
not hold the answers. The topic being the future, the discussion
meandered inconclusively. The bulls contended that the semicon-

ductor cycle was a thing of the past. In view of what had come before, the bulls spoke ex cathedra. The predictive authority of people who had owned Micron Technology from $5 or $10 all the way up to $80 or $90 a share was impossible to exaggerate. What they predicted next was that the demand for semiconductors would be insatiable. One day in September, following simultaneous announcements of new semiconductor fabs by Motorola, Hitachi, and Mitsubishi Semiconductor America, one of the leading optimists favored the press with a statement: "The industry collectively is deciding they are going to have to invest more to meet the rising demand. . . . The shortages are worsening." The shortages of chips would be compounded by shortages in the equipment that was used to make the chips: Wall Street had spoken.

It was about this time that *Fortune* was in Boise observing two of Micron's fabulously rich original backers, Tom Nicholson and Ron Yanke, in their native Idaho habitat. (A *Fortune* photographer subsequently found them in another special habitat, the waters in Jackpot, Nevada; the two were bathing naked, their benevolent faces shaded under cowboy hats: they were the spits of bull-market serenity.) The observation began with a predawn breakfast at Burns Brothers truck stop. After breakfast, Serwer reported, the pair climbed into Yanke's truck to drive to the airport to take a ride in Yanke's personal aircraft. While still en route, the two received word that Micron had fallen two points on New York Stock Exchange trading. It was the beginning of what would prove to be a landslide, but the signs still seemed propitious. "Yanke flips on his Motorola cellphone and calls his broker," *Fortune* chronicled. " 'Get me 10,000 shares of Micron.' Done deal. A $750,000 stock trade out of a 1.5-ton Dodge Ram."

For a time in the summer of 1995, it seemed that high-tech common stocks were themselves in acute shortage. In July 1995 alone, an index of the stocks of 36 semiconductor equipment makers—Applied Materials was the leader—rose by 16 percent; through the first seven months of the year, the group climbed by 100 percent. The chief aerodynamic property of the companies was the imagination of the buyers; equipment sales, for the second year in a row, were growing faster than semiconductor sales. Plainly, or so it seemed to the remnant of doubters, such a thing could not go on indefinitely.

Experts predicted that sales of memory chips would grow by 20 percent a year into the year 1999. The ubiquitousness of semiconductors prompted the chairman of NEC Corp., Tadahiro Sekimoto, to call them "rice for industry." Thus, a 20 percent rate of growth did not begin to hint at the romance of the situation. Windows 95, a new computer operating system created by Microsoft Corp., would propel the world into a higher, more intense state of computer consciousness, it was universally understood. The existing Microsoft operating system, Windows 3.1, already ran 80 percent of the world's personal computers; Windows 95, retailing for $89, while supplies lasted, was bound to succeed it. Thirty million copies would be sold in the first year, enthusiasts projected. An enraptured public would be unable to help itself. Beholding the power and magic of the new Windows (15 million lines of computer code had gone into it), it would not only buy the operating system but also the software and hardware to match. "The same thing is going to happen with Windows 95 as happens when you buy a house," explained Russ Stockdale, Microsoft's product manager for Windows 95. "You're going to get new furniture for that house. You go out and buy appliances and hook up utilities and with Windows you'll want to get optimized software and upgrade to a multimedia machine and get all kinds of other stuff."

"I love that program," said Simplot, speaking for semiconductor manufacturers on every continent. "It uses all kinds of memory." A new riot for computer memory would thus be superimposed on the permanent riot.

The tub thumping recalled the rollout of New Coke in 1985, but Windows could be neither tasted nor poured. It was real enough to computer devotees, however, and the name given by Microsoft insiders to the August 24 Windows' launch festivities was "Geekfest 95." "The coming era of information at your fingertips whenever you want it, for whatever you want, will make life just plain better and much different than it is today," said the Microsoft chairman, Bill Gates, many months before the Empire State Building was lit up to mark the actual appearance of the puffy-white-clouds-set-in-a-blue-sky box on the shelves of the world's retail stores. Icons world-wide were hired for the long-awaited unveiling. The Rolling Stones sang what became the unofficial Windows theme song, "Start Me Up," and the entire 1.5-million-copy press run of the August 24 edition of *The Times* of London was distributed, free, courtesy of Microsoft: indeed, more than free, as readers also received a 24-page supplement extolling the qualities of Windows.

"Regardless of its merits, we'll all be using Windows 95," the editor of an influential industry newsletter was quoted as saying on Geekfest eve, underscoring the impression that Windows, more than software, was destiny. On Wall Street, Windows was treated as the greatest product introduction in the history of the stock market. There would not be one Christmas in 1995, the bulls anticipated, but two, the first to begin on August 24: not at 9 A.M., either —who could wait?—but at the stroke of midnight. A Gates speech was broadcast live by satellite worldwide, and Incredible Universe stores hosted Windows premier parties, complete with contests for the Best-Dressed Nerd. (Actually, the first copy of Windows was sold in the computer-literate country where the dawn of August 24 shone first: New Zealand. Naturally, this epochal retail transaction was broadcast on the Cable News Network. Slightly to the west, in Sydney, a four-story-high box emblazoned with Windows 95 logos was towed into Sydney Harbor on a barge; in the Philippines, the first copy of Windows was hand-delivered to President Fidel Ramos himself.)

Enthusiasts claimed that shortages of semiconductors, and of semiconductor fabrication manufacturing capacity, would last for years. "The kind of demand projections we have would require the industry to spend over the next five years about three times the amount of money spent in the last five years for fab construction," an economist from Texas Instruments told *Grant's Interest Rate Observer*. "This means we will require three to four new wafer fabs coming on stream each month. So the moment you stop reading in the newspapers that at least one new wafer fab is coming on stream each week, then we will need to be worried about capacity shortages."

Perhaps nothing, not even Windows, could vindicate the hopes and dreams of Geekfest. The New Hampshire–based technology analyst Fred Hickey all along insisted that Windows would flop, as indeed it did, at least in comparison to its advance billing (17 million copies were sold by the end of 1995, approximately half of original expectations), but the recognition of this uncomfortable fact was months in coming. Pending clarification, technology-stock investors operated under the assumption that the semiconductor had cast off its commodity clothing and donned the uniform of permanent indispensability. The government-subsidized semiconductor fab was the new badge of economic development, observed a New York investor, William M. McGarr, superseding the state steel mill and the state airline and tying with the government-owned central bank. Within a week of each other in early November, Singapore and Malaysia each trumpeted new fab investment projects, Singapore announcing the relocation of hundreds of companies to make way for the unhindered construction of not one single fab but a great fab park. "A global search for chip-making capacity is accelerating to a near-frenzy," *The Wall Street Journal* reported at about the same time. "To meet demand that could surge through the decade, semiconductor companies are junking time-tested business plans, forging unusual alliances, and building factories at an unprecedented pace. They're shrugging off some experts' concerns that the industry will repeat its mid-1980s dive caused by excess capacity. Caught up in the scrambles are both industry giants, such as No. 1 Intel Corp., and smaller companies that make chips for an array of gadgets in addition to personal computers."

If excesses-in-the-making were not always mistaken by the mass of observers as the manifestation of progress, there would be no excesses. Thus, in 1994 and 1995, the semiconductor, as distinct from the drilling rig, chemical plant, or office tower, was widely regarded as the instrument of human progress. When, also in the fall of 1995, Treasury Secretary Robert Rubin uttered the platitude that the inflation rate was low, he spoke for the overwhelming majority of financially literate Americans for whom the inflation rate began and ended with the consumer price index. "The important point," Röpke had observed, entering an advance demurrer, "is not that the general price level rises but simply the circumstance that additional quantities of money and credit are supplied to the economic system, calling forth dangerous disturbances in the structure of production."

In the fall of 1995, however, the disturbances seemed purely wholesome. The combination of enlightened central banking and revolutionary high tech had restored the financial world of the 1950s, with next to no inflation and rising productivity besides, the bulls contended. Central-bank mastery of the business cycle had taken some of the suspense out of reading the newspapers, but (as it was strongly believed) there was ample compensation for this omission in the stock tables, in which prices predictably went up. The remaining element of suspense was by how much they would rally.

The dogma of the mutual-fund era was reducible to a few basic articles. The market believed in central banking, the information content of the consumer price index, and in high technology: both the economic contributions of computers and the securities that the computer companies issued. The general class of investment asset in which it believed was stocks.

If the mutual-fund enthusiasts were right, high-tech stocks would not blow up in the faces of their admirers as they had done in the down portions of previous cycles. There would be no overheating in the mid-1990s, just as there had been no true underheating (only a brief recession) in the early 1990s. It was said (in so many words) that central banks were on the threshold of achieving permanent financial room temperature.

Such was the attitude of the mass of investors in the autumn of 1995. It was a state of complacency in no way disturbed by the frenzied pace of fab construction in Taiwan or by the alarming explanation, proffered by Frank C. Huang, president of UMAX, a Taiwan-based maker of computer parts, that most Taiwanese didn't know what else to do with their money except to build fabs. Certainly, money was no problem, except in the sense of there being too much of it. The fruit of a long-running payments surplus with the United States was a rising stockpile of dollars. Taiwan's savings rate was high, and its lenders were forthcoming; all in all, the country was awash with bank credit. When Power Chip Semiconductor Co. of Taiwan needed the equivalent of NT$13.5 billion (U.S.$500 million) with which to put up its own plant, a 24-bank syndicate duly supplied it; nobody seemed to object that Power Chip was brand new. Among the other new entrants in the Taiwan semiconductor industry was Chia-shi, which, before it discovered the most important technology of our time, raised livestock.

IN 1992 (a poor year for lending), Eagle Federal Savings Bank of Bristol, Connecticut, purchased seven unwanted branch banks in Danbury. The price: the equivalent of 1 percent of the money on deposit. The seller: the financial salvage agencies of the U.S. government.

In 1995 (a better year for lending), Eagle signed a letter of intent to sell the same seven branches to another Danbury institution, Union Savings Bank. The price: the equivalent of 9 percent of the money on deposit.

What changed so drastically in such a short span of years was, first of all, the credit contraction of the early 1990s. It ended. Then, promptly, a new boom began, touched off by low interest rates. Also, the New England economy recovered. And finally, the humble bank deposit went from surplus to scarcity. At low ebb in 1990 and 1991, the banking system gave every appearance of having too little capital; at the mid-decade high-water mark, it seemed to have too much. One could plot the growth in the capital of American national banks at four-year intervals all the way back to the turn of the century and not find a more prosperous interval than the one that ended in 1995: equity capital grew (propelled by the banks' earnings) by 10.5 percent per annum. A stock market that had not so many years before despaired of the banks' solvency now worried about their prosperity. An embarrassment of riches afflicted even the banks' regulators. The insurance fund of the Federal Deposit Insurance Corp., apparently insolvent in 1991, now was filled to overflowing, and history was made on November 14, 1995, when the FDIC's board voted to suspend the premium payments it had always demanded of the healthy banks it insured; their money was now deemed redundant.

Tackling the unfamiliar problem of too much of a good thing, bankers implemented prosperity-attenuation plans. They repurchased their own stock, merged with other banks (or were merged into them), or stepped up their dividends. However, if the end in view was the neutralization of capital, it was to no avail. In 1989, the beginning of the end of the credit expansion of the 1980s, 4,165 national banks possessed $114 billion in equity capital: at year-end 1995, there were just 2,861 national banks in commission, but they controlled $190 billion in equity capital. What was significant was not the shrinkage in the number of banks but the growth in the capital of the banks that remained. Without capital, a bank can't lend. Plainly, the national banking system could lend as never before.

Analysts at Montgomery Securities, San Francisco, writing in the fall of 1995, forecast that the nation's 50 largest banks would alone propagate another $100 billion of equity capital in the next three years, "an amount," said the firm, "which we believe will be impossible to deploy at comparable risk-adjusted returns to those currently being earned. We anticipate that roughly $35 billion of the total equity generated will be paid in dividends, leaving a $65 billion 'problem.' "

But whose "problem"? Not the borrowers': the price of a bank loan was cheap and becoming cheaper. Nor, immediately, the stockholders': it was their capital, and they had every reason to hope that it would compound even faster (for one thing, a fattened equity account provided padding against the losses that inevitably surface in the down portion of the cycle). Nor still, on first blush, the nation's: low-priced credit facilitated the extra transaction, and it was the marginal unit of activity that sped the process of growth. Then whose problem, exactly? Everyone's, eventually, if the excessive capital were deployed in the usual way. Too much lending would give gave rise to the kind of distortions in the architecture of the economy that caused the booms that preceded the busts.

The caboose of the train of the 1980s rolled by in the summer of 1994, when the Dallas Bank Fraud Task Force was disbanded following seven years of investigation into Texas boom-time banking practices. Even as the agents were packing their cardboard boxes, however, the mortgage market was reverting to the manic competitive pitch of 1987–88, the period without which the Dallas Bank Fraud Task Force would not have been able to have obtained its 239

convictions. Thus, certain California savings and loans were offering teaser rates of less than 4 percent on adjustable-rate mortgages
when the going rate in the secondary mortgage market was 6 percent or more. In general, lenders were settling for less documenta-
tion, lower down payments, and lower incomes. "So what's the
mortgage banker to do?" asked one practitioner rhetorically in The
American Banker. "It takes courage, but the answer is: 'Just say no!'
Don't chase volume by stretching credit. It just takes too much interest to make up for unpaid principal."

Sage advice, but unheeded. Dreamworks SKG, the multimedia
entertainment brainchild of Jeffrey Katzenberg, Steven Spielberg,
and David Geffen, was scarcely formed in March 1995 when it
lined up a $1 billion loan at a nominal rate of interest (just one-half
of one percentage point over the banks' wholesale cost of funds).
The maturity of the promised credit was no less than 10 years, by
conventional bankers' lights the equivalent of eternity (Thomson
Hankey insisted on 90 days). Were these terms not overly favorable
to the entrepreneurs, as talented as they were? A banker who hoped
to join the lending syndicate explained why they were not: "For
banks interested in lending to the media," he said, "this deal is almost a must."

In place of the words "lending to the media," weathered hands,
orienting themselves to the new credit cycle, could mentally sub-
stitute the phrases, "lending to Latin America," "lending to the
energy industry" or "lending to Donald Trump." As in previous expansions, the glory of the transaction seemed to count for as much
to the bankers as the hoped-for profit.

A regulatory rebuke shortly followed, directed not against any
one transaction but the new credit zeitgeist. Addressing the Bankers
Roundtable on April 8, the chief of the Office of the Comptroller
of the Currency, Eugene A. Ludwig, disclosed the creation of a National Credit Committee to monitor the sobriety and diligence of
the principal credit offenders of the previous cycle, the nation's
larger banks. "Almost without exception," Ludwig told his bankers'
audience, "the OCC's credit quality tracking studies have shown a
slippage in credit standards, first a slippage in pricing of the AA
credits, then a softening in pricing in the BB credits and a further

slippage of underwriting terms." He noted, for instance, that the standard minimum payment on a credit-card balance had declined to 2 percent from 5 percent and that "Some issuers are targeting consumers with less-than-stellar credit reports, because they know these customers are likely to carry larger balances." Furthermore, lending to the lower strata of automobile buyer was becoming commonplace, as was advancing loans against the equivalent of 100 percent of a borrower's home equity. Ludwig, sounding more saddened than angered by this slippage, exhorted, "We must all work very hard together to make sure that standards do not slip further."

Readers of the Sunday *New York Times* awoke the next day to find a report on this slightly arcane subject occupying column six of page 1—the place given over to the most newsworthy development in the world in the preceding 24 hours. Besides quoting Ludwig, the *Times* added (among other facts and opinions) the testimony of the chief economist of the National Association of Home Builders, David F. Seiders: "Banks that wouldn't talk to us a year ago are calling us." The gravity of Ludwig's warning was either vitiated or amplified, depending on the interest of the individual reader, by the advertisement that filled most of the page onto which the front-page story spilled. "Low rates," teased the advertising copy. "No points. No application fees. No closing costs. Chase Manhattan offers Smart Borrowing Made Easy with our new, tax deductible Home Equity Line of Credit."

The cycle did not stop there, of course. By the autumn, a loan to a presentable, or even a not-quite-presentable, wholesale borrower was as cheap as it had been during even the late 1980s. Now that financial knowledge was more widely distributed than ever before, the value of a bank's credit judgment, such as it was, was lower than it had been in the days when banks possessed unique knowledge; lower also, in consequence, was the typical bank's lending margin. Thus, late in 1995, the Kingdom of Spain, striving to reduce its public deficit from the equivalent of 5.9 percent of GDP (the European Union's requirement for membership was a deficit equivalent to no more than 3 percent of GDP), was able to secure a five-year bank loan at exactly four basis points, or four-hundredths of one percentage point, over the bankers' own cost of funds. It was the very next thing to free money. In the corporate loan market, also in the fall of 1995, Crown Paper borrowed $350 million at $2\frac{3}{4}$ percentage points over the lenders' cost of funds. The credit wrinkle in this transaction was that, at the latest reporting date, Crown's cash flow did not suffice to cover its interest expense. Hoping that it would, bankers strenuously lent.

They lent with particular gusto to the American consumer. In 1991, credit-card purveyors mailed 975 million solicitations; in 1995, they mailed almost three billion, the great bulk of them attempts to persuade credit-card borrowers to switch brands. Not only were commercial banks and credit-card-issuing finance companies competing, but so, too, was a new kind of finance company dedicated to serving speculative-grade people. The new, so-called subprime, lender aimed to charge an interest rate high enough to earn a profit even after a certain and (as it was hoped) predictable credit loss. The business plan was to exploit the well-known tendency toward unnecessary worry about consumer borrowing. The new entrepreneurs justifiably believed that conventional underwriting standards in the past had been overly cautious. Ever since its invention as a legitimate, law-abiding institution, consumer credit had elicited the unfounded concern that people would borrow the country into a depression. They never did. The traditional cause of banking difficulties was that too many big loans were extended to too few borrowers. Consumer loans, by contrast, are small (on average, no more than $1,500), and diversified. Furthermore, as any American consumer could attest, a credit-card balance did not bear the kind of rock-bottom interest rate attached to billion-dollar lines of credit to start-up media companies. One paid 18 percent and up.

Or one had. Throughout the 1990s, terms were relaxed and costs reduced. More and more loans carried a floating rate of interest, and interest rates mainly fell; and more and more lenders offered blue-light specials, for instance, no application fee or no annual service charge. At great length, competition also forced down borrowing rates. For the first six months, a new card-carrying debtor might pay no more than 6 or 8 percent, after which he or she could pay off that debt by taking advantage of a new, fabulous, never-to-be-repeated teaser-rate offer from a competing borrower.

True to historical experience, no calamity struck the consumer debt market, but the omens turned unfavorable. In the spring of 1996 George Salem, bank analyst with the firm of Gerard Klauer Mattison & Co., listed the distinguishing features of the credit-card lending business in the mid-1990s: a record number of cardholders; a sharp rise in the number of cards per borrower; a sharp decline in the stigma of filing for individual bankruptcy protection; intense competition among the 7,000 or so card purveyors (competition that found partial expression in the increased frequency of mailings to high school and college students); brilliant profits in 1994 and 1995; and—a credit-cycle concomitant—signs of rising losses in 1996 and beyond.

Partly, the growth in credit cards was evolutionary and irreversible. Shoppers who paid by credit card earned miles toward a free airplane ride; no comparable enticement was offered by the Treasury for paying with cash. However, the facts could not be blinked that the percentage of the average consumer's disposable income devoted to servicing installment debt continued to set new highs or that—an ominous sign of the times—casino gambling debts had begun to crop up in personal bankruptcy petitions. ("Though the evidence is still sketchy," reported Sandra Ward in *Barron's* in June 1996, "there's no question that the gambling craze is leading to fierce financial pressures.")

Where had all the puritans gone?

CHAPTER SEVEN

REVERSION TO THE MEAN

C YCLES IN MARKETS are inevitable, irrepressible, and indispensable. Even if some all-knowing central bank could create a
state of economic perfection—measuring out growth in ideal, noninflationary doses, neither too much nor too little—human beings
would respond by overpaying for stocks and bonds. In this way they
would restore imperfection.

Bidding up the prices of financial assets, people would not stop
until they had overvalued them. In consequence, the marginal
business would find the means to finance the extra, gratuitous capital project (and the marginal consumer to pay for the items thereby
produced). Redundant products and services would tumble into the
world's marketplace. Before very long, the marginal rate of return
on invested capital would fall short of even the low expectations of
the average bull-market investor. The extra, uncommitted dollar
would seek safe harbor in a bank account instead of a mutual fund.
At this moment, if not before, the boom would fall down in a heap.
The function of bear markets and cyclical downturns, as we have
seen, is to cut short the train of error.

In fact, something very much like this process (without, to date,
the culminating bear market) has been under way in recent years. In
the 1980s throughout the industrialized world, asset prices rose
on the wings of debt. What followed in America in the first half of
the 1990s was Wall Street's conception of heaven on earth. The rate
of borrowing declined, but no mass destruction of asset values en-

sued. White elephants were selectively culled, but (as the Bank for
International Settlements has demonstrated in a remarkable study
in its 1995–96 annual report) the value of the overall American herd
increased: "Real aggregate asset prices," a composite measure of
stock prices, residential real estate prices, and commercial real estate
prices, continued to push higher, higher, even, by mid-decade, than
the peaks registered in the leveraged-buyout phase of the previous
expansion. Nothing like this revival was seen in Japan, France, or the
United Kingdom, to name three other debt-encumbered nations; in
none of them has the aggregate level of asset prices thus far managed to stage a recovery to the old boom-time highs.

On the face of things, no outcome could have been more desirable. Beneath the surface, however, which is where our narrative
has taken us, there are ample reasons to doubt. The remarkable
state of American financial prosperity has had many side effects,
not least a thoroughgoing change in perception about risk and cycles. What the average investor had come to understand was that
there is no risk to speak of, that there is one cycle (the upward one),
and that any setback to prices should be seized on as a buying opportunity. "Too bad about yesterday's rally," grumbled a personal-
finance columnist in *The Wall Street Journal* in March 1996,
expressing regret about a lost opportunity for bargain-hunting.
". . . [F]or investors who hang on long enough to enjoy the recovery, a full-blown market crash would be mighty rewarding." It is exactly the kind of argument that most of H. J. Nelson's readers
found unconvincing when, more than a half century ago, the stock
market consisted of almost nothing except bargains.

The lack of volatility in business activity and stock prices has
been one of the hallmarks of the 1990s. Indeed, stability itself has apparently taken its place as a goal of national economic policy. Not
only have the financial authorities attempted to stamp out crises, as in
Mexico following the 1994 peso devaluation, but also they have intervened to try to level out unwanted fluctuations in commodity prices.
Thus, in short order in April 1996, the U.S. government rhetorically
intervened in the oil and cattle markets, seeking a downward and upward adjustment in prices, respectively; and when the copper market
was devastated by scandal two months later, *The Financial Times* re-

ported that a pair of central banks—the Bank of Japan and the Bank of England—had, with help of regulatory authorities in the United Kingdom and the United States, launched a "coordinated effort" to put things right. Evidently, no speculative sparrow could fall to earth without governmental approval. As for the Fed, in 1994 it raised the federal funds rate to choke off an inflation that, except in the prices of financial assets, had not yet occurred. Although there was no inflation to be seen, the policymakers indicated, it was theirs to be visualized. It was a case of monetary management through anticipation. Thomson Hankey, the nineteenth-century governor of the Bank of England who so stoutly resisted intervention, could have scarcely imagined it.

The Fed's success in implementing this, the clairvoyance method, has (by Wall Street's lights) been complete. To the theoretical objection that nobody can know what the Fed pretends to know, or, indeed, must know, to run the kind of monetary policy in which every calamity is prevented, a practical speculator may reply that somebody seems to know enough to perpetuate a wonderful bull market. Wall Street is, to this extent, a believer. And believing in what Hankey doubted, it has willingly shouldered greater and greater risk. Anyway, stock prices have been going up long enough to condition an entire generation of investors to doubt the Robert Lovett thesis that there is no security in securities; what they have seen with their own eyes is the validity of the Edgar Smith thesis that stocks excel in the long run (and, indeed, in the short and medium runs).*

The feats of macroeconomic management so widely attributed to the Fed have only deepened faith in the certainty of steady returns through patient investing. The money that poured into equity mutual funds in 1996 was put to work at once, not held in reserve against the rainy day that—so two decades of experience suggested—would never come. There was, indeed, little need for pru-

---

* One of the fine, clarifying headlines of the manic phase of the bull market was published in *The Wall Street Journal* of May 20, 1996: SUMMER STOCK RALLIES DON'T EXCITE SOME: ONE EXPERT SAYS SPRING, FALL AND WINTER ARE BETTER. Apparently, financial correction was reserved for the lesser seasons, for instance, in the New England states, mud season.

dence, as prudence had been defined in a dangerous and accident-prone world. Inasmuch as the downside of the financial or credit cycle had been dampened down or even managed out of existence, an investor was liberated from the old, cautionary rules. In effect, a dual speed limit was established in the American economy: 40 miles an hour or so in commerce, manufacturing, agriculture, and the other nonspeculative occupations; 120 miles an hour on Wall Street. Professional equity investors who tried to proceed at a slower speed, by hoarding cash, for example, or by buying bonds, put their careers at risk. (A well-publicized, premature move by Magellan Fund, flagship of Fidelity Investments, into bonds early in 1996 caused general disappointment, with investors withdrawing and Magellan chief Jeffrey Vinik resigning. It was a dull portfolio manager who did not get the message that the greatest risk in a bull market is the risk of not being fully invested.)

However, the growing faith in stability has become a powerful force for instability. As fear has receded, so has speculation increased. "Despite being laid off a few weeks ago, even Jake Rahiman is helping push stocks higher," *The Wall Street Journal* reported in February. "The 29-year-old professional recruiter in New York plunged his $30,000 severance pay into stocks. 'I figure I'll get a better return on my money in the short term as well as the long term if I put in the market, especially since the market is doing so well.'" The market had been doing so well because so many people have been acting as their forbears would never have dreamt of acting at the bottom of the cycle in 1942.

The direction of things can be plainly seen out of the windows of *Grant's* Wall Street offices. By day, tourists file into the New York Stock Exchange visitor's gallery or take pictures of each other with the exchange looming behind them, like Chartres. From time to time, a newly listed company celebrates the admission of its stock for trading by staging some appropriate street theater: the designer Donna Karan waving from a stock exchange balcony to photographers on the sun-drenched street below (causing a *Women's Wear Daily* reporter to liken her, at that instant, to Eva Perón), for example, or the Boston Beer Co. (as *The New York Times* reported) "reenact[ing] the Boston Tea Party, sort of, on Broad Street." By night, sedans idle in lines stretching west along Wall Street from the head-quarters of J. P. Morgan & Co. to await the day's, or early morning's, discharge of tired bankers (such was the crush of underwriting busi-ness that the Morgan employees routinely worked into the wee hours). All day long, starting in the early summer of 1996, demoli-tion crews tore out the interiors of a pair of aging, formerly obsolete Wall Street skyscrapers, Nos. 40 and 45. Thanks to new tax rules, as well as to bull-market optimism, the buildings—indeed, the entire neighborhood of lower Manhattan—was getting a new lease on life. Just as *The Journal of Commerce* prophcsicd in 1952, Wall Street was becoming more and more a residential neighborhood, like Soho.

In general, the view from *Grant's* conformed to the picture of the up-phase of Röpke's capital cycle. Moreover, the national data cor-roborated the local sights. Throughout the economy, capital spend-ing was on the upswing. As noted by Van Hoisington, a Texas bond investor, the growth in producers' durable equipment accounted for an average of nearly 30 percent of the growth of the American GDP in 1993, 1994, and 1995. The great bulk of this expenditure was computer-related, as might have been expected. However, as might not have been expected, the computer business expanded it-self into a state of oversupply and demoralization (semiconductors being a particular soft spot), the existence of automated, up-to-the-minute information about computers notwithstanding.

Then again, in speculative gales, emotion often overrides infor-mation. Even if a certain course of action does not seem reasonable, it may sometimes be irresistible. Thus, in March 1996, John Larkin, a transportation analyst at Alex. Brown & Sons, warned trucking industry executives not to buy more rigs just to beautify their balance sheets in expectation of some future initial public offering (or, more familiarly, IPO). "Adding equipment simply for growth does not cre-ate value," Larkin observed. "Indeed, if the existing public carriers are all growing to satisfy equity investors rather than growing to haul freight because it's available, then overcapacity is inevitable."

In 1996, the urge to sell new shares was almost as intense as the urge to buy them, and IPO issuance approached the volume of the record-holding year of 1993. Representatives of the class of 1996 included Yahoo!, an Internet company, Planet Hollywood, a celebrity-restaurant-concept company, Lucent Technologies, an AT&T-spinoff technology company, Saks Holdings, a leveraged department store chain, and Gumtech International, a high-concept chewing-gum maker ("Love Gum," "Buzz Gum," and "Repose," for instance).*

There had never been a gaudier market. It took the cake in terms of trading volume, in the value of a New York Stock Exchange seat, and in the number of investment clubs dedicated to buying low and selling high. ("Investment clubs . . . are going online," *The New York Times* reported in July. "In the process they are transforming themselves from the traditional kaffeeklatsch of friends sitting around the kitchen table trading tips from their brothers-in-law and dentists into far-flung networks of cyberspace browsers who pounce on breaking news, sometimes even before it reaches Wall Street professionals.") The 1996 market set new records in margin debt, expressed as a percentage of personal income, and in stock market capitalization, expressed as a percentage of GDP (more than 90 percent in March 1996, noted the analyst James A. Bianco, compared to 81 percent in August 1929, just before the deluge that so inspired Röpke). "But in what might be a first for Wall Street—and a test of just how hungry investors are for information about the Internet—the Wall Street securities firm Morgan Stanley Group Inc. is republishing one of its research reports as a commercial book," *The Wall Street Journal* disclosed in March. One newspaper story topped another.

In May, at what may or may not prove to be the ultimate peak of the speculative frenzy, Presstek, a New Hampshire–based devel-

---

* Concerning Gumtech, *Grant's Interest Rate Observer* noted in March that the offering constituted a kind of speculative litmus. "Working against the success of this transaction," we wrote, quoting from the prospectus, "is the company itself ('limited operating history'), its products ('no scientific proof of efficacy'), its underwriter ('lack of underwriting experience'), its cash flow (numbers surrounded by brackets), its potential regulatory difficulties . . . and the number of pages in its new prospectus devoted to a listing of selling shareholders (six).

"Working in favor of the offering, on the other hand, is the fun-filled spirit of the marketplace. Taking one thing with another, we would rule out nothing."

The registered shares—about $7 million worth—were duly sold in April. In the spring of 1996, just as we suggested, the most prudent policy was to expect anything.

oper and licenser of digital-imaging technology, was valued at 670 times earnings. Essentially everything that Presstek sold, it sold to Heidelberger Druckmaschinen AG, a subsidiary of a Mannheim, Germany, conglomerate. This entire conglomerate—Rheinelektra AG—had a stock market capitalization equivalent to $2 billion. Presstek, one supplier to one Rheinelektra subsidiary, had a stock market capitalization in the sum of $3.2 billion. In the preceding 12 months, Presstek had revenues of a mere $33.5 million.

"Risk has ceased to have any negative implications," said a man who was betting against Presstek and stocks like it—unsuccessfully, at that moment. "That's what is happening within the market. Investors are gravitating to the stocks with all the risk they can find."

The 1968 market was just as wackily speculative as the 1996 market, but the technology was not then available to accommodate all potential comers; the Mates Fund, one of the hottest of the late-1960s era, was overwhelmed by cash inflows of $1.5 million a day. Nowadays, the Clearing House Interbank Payments System, a computer network connecting 100 or so banks worldwide, easily accommodates currency-trading volumes on the order of $1.3 trillion a day. Late in the 1960s, 15 million shares a day almost incapacitated the Big Board; in the spring of 1996, a single stock, Comparator Systems Corp., priced in pennies and traded over-the-counter, generated volume of 150 million shares a day. Now, no technological barrier stands between American investors and an epochal stomachache. Wall Street has lost its gag reflex.

Predictably, the risks to savings are the greatest just when they appear to be the smallest. By suppressing crises, the modern financial welfare state has inadvertently promoted speculation. Never before has a boom ended except in crisis. In anticipation of just such an outcome, a skeptical Seattle investor, William A. Fleckenstein, founded a hedge fund in 1995 to buy cheap stocks and to sell dear ones. He named it The RTM Fund, the initials signifying "reversion to the mean." They may be the financial watchwords for the millennium.

Notes on Sources

In general, sources are alluded to, if not actually cited, in the text. Additional notes follow.

CHAPTER I: HEIRS TO 1958

1. Joseph R. Slevin's nine-part series on the Eisenhower-era Treasury-bond liquidation was published in the *New York Herald Tribune* beginning September 1, 1958. A definitive critique of the same events was published jointly by the Treasury and Federal Reserve System in July 1959. The *Monthly Economic Letter* of the National City Bank weighed in with a Treasury-market study in June 1960.

2. *The Life and Times of The Equitable* by John Rousmaniere (self-published by The Equitable Life Assurance Society in 1995) illuminates the life and career of the inflation-hating Thomas I. Parkinson. The chairman was in peak rhetorical form before the Chicago Bond Club on November 1, 1945 (text obtained from the Equitable).

3. "Investments in Common Stocks by Life Insurance Companies," by Shelby Cullom Davis, in *The Analysts Journal*, July 1945, provides a window on the investment mind of the late, great New York moneymaker. For a personal reminiscence of Davis, see David Shiff's interview with Davis's grandson, Christopher Davis, in the June 1994 edition of *Emerson, Reid's Insurance Observer* (published privately in New York).

4. The literature of the "creeping inflation" debate of the late 1950s is fascinating and suggestive (although inflation was then creeping upward instead of sideways). A sample includes Roy L. Reierson, "Business Fluctuations and Inflation: Is Inflation Avoidable?," in the *American Economic*

317

Review, May 1957; Malcolm Bryan, "The Idea of Creeping Inflation," *The Commercial & Financial Chronicle,* November 21, 1957; Sumner H. Schlichter, "Thinking Ahead," *Harvard Business Review,* September–October 1957; and Allan Sproul, "The Sickness of Inflation," *Fortune,* July 1959. A collection of Sproul's writings (*Selected Papers of Allan Sproul,* 1980) was published by the Federal Reserve Bank of New York, of which Sproul served as the president from 1941 to 1956.

5. As for Malcolm Bryan, one of the most plainspoken central bankers of all time, some biographical information is contained in Richard H. Hamble, *A History of the Federal Reserve Bank of Atlanta, 1914–1989,* self-published by the Atlanta Fed in 1989.

6. Notes of the research meetings conducted by Lehman Brothers at the time of the organization of One William Street Fund were kindly made available by Lehman. As for Ernest Havemann's wonderful article, it was published in the September 15, 1958, issue of *Life.* A very different kind of bullish stock market document appeared in 1968: *Managing Educational Endowments: Report to the Ford Foundation,* by the Advisory Committee on Endowment Management.

7. Roy Harrod's essay, "Why the Dollar Price of Gold Must Rise," was published in the *Economic Journal,* September 1958. The annual reports of the Bank for International Settlements are always must reading. Also worthwhile are Allan Sproul's "Gold Convertibility Is No Assurance of Monetary Stability," *The Commercial & Financial Chronicle,* November 10, 1949; "The Price of Gold," in the National City Bank's *Monthly Economic Letter,* June 1958; and "United States Gold Losses," Kansas City Federal Reserve Bank *Monthly Review,* September 1958. The position of the orthodox monetary school of the early postwar period was distilled in one sentence in the October 27, 1949, edition of *The Commercial & Financial Chronicle:* "Devaluation of a currency is like the amputation of one's arm or leg; it is a great misfortune," wrote Professor Walter E. Spahn of New York University.

8. Among the more-or-less recent books that address the topics of the dollar, gold, or both are Milton Gilbert, *Quest for World Monetary Order: The Gold-Dollar System and Its Aftermath* (1980); Robert Solomon, *The International Monetary System: 1945–1981* (1982); Donald F. Kettl, *Leadership at the Fed* (Yale University Press, New Haven, Conn., 1986); and Steven Solomon, *The Confidence Game: How Unelected Central Banks Are Governing the Changed World Economy* (Simon & Schuster, New York, 1995). Marriner S. Eccles, *Beckoning Frontiers* (1951), is the autobiography of the long-sitting Fed chairman who collided with Harry S Truman. Joseph Nocera, *A Piece of the Action: How the Middle Class Joined the Money Class* (Simon & Schuster, New York,

1994), approaches the revolutionary year of 1958 from the point of view of the American consumer.

CHAPTER 2: TALLEST BUILDING ON EARTH

1. The triumvirate of Robert A. M. Stern, Gregory Gilmartin, and Thomas Mellins has captured Wall Street, and many other neighborhoods besides, in their *New York 1930: Architecture and Urbanism Between the Two World Wars* (Rizzoli International Publications, New York, 1987); an encore volume, *New York 1960: Architecture and Urbanism Between the Second World War and the Bicentennial*, was written by Stern and Mellins, this time teaming up with David Fishman (The Monacelli Press, New York, 1995). Another new work in the high-rise genre is *Form Follows Finance: Skyscrapers and Skylines in New York and Chicago* (Princeton Architectural Press, New York, 1995). A practitioner's viewpoint on lower Manhattan real estate is available in *Zeckendorf: The Autobiography of William Zeckendorf,* with Edward McCreary, 1970.

2. Newspaper sources on the developer Louis Adler include an ironically headlined story in the May 9, 1930, *New York Telegram:* BUYER OF WALL STREET BLOCK GOT THE DEAL BY NOT "FIDDLING."

3. *Fortune* gave the tower at 40 Wall Street a top-to-bottom appraisal in 40 WALL STREET: X-RAY OF A SKYSCRAPER, July 1939. The firm of Starrett Brothers was profiled in the *Barron's* dated May 19, 1930, and the failure of J. A. Sisto & Co. was reported in the October 4, 1930, *Commercial & Financial Chronicle.* The underpopulated New York skyscraper was the subject of an essay by Elmer Davis in the June 1, 1932, issue of *The New Republic.*

4. For details on the finances of the Forty Wall Street Corp., see the annual editions of *Moody's Manual of Investments (Industrial Securities).*

5. Robert A. Lovett's "Gilt-Edged Insecurity," a brilliant, bearish, period piece, appeared in the April 3, 1937, *Saturday Evening Post.* In June 1937, *Fortune* published "Wall Street, Itself," a description of the somewhat shrunken financial district (the 1937 bear market was to reduce it even further).

6. Donald G. Simonson and George H. Hempel, in "Banking Lessons from the Past: The 1938 Regulatory Agreement Interpreted" (*Journal of Financial Services Research*, 1993), look back from the perspective of the early 1990s on the debt predicament of the mid-1930s.

7. The source of the fact that just 15 percent of Wall Street was occupied by stock and bond brokers in 1941 is the September 24, 1942, *Commercial & Financial Chronicle.* The archives of the New York Stock Exchange contain a wide variety of information about the securities firms that did not give

up the ghost in that dispirited time. Periodicals include the annual *Fact Book* and a monthly magazine, *The Exchange,* as well as the annual financial reports of the stock exchange itself. H. J. Nelson, better known by his pen name, "The Trader," wrote perceptively on the stock market every week in *Barron's.* Nelson was steadfastly bullish; for a bearish view of stocks in 1941, see Frederick H. Ecker, quoted in Shelby Cullom Davis's essay in *The Analysts Journal,* July 1945.

8. Alvin H. Hansen's "Economic Progress and Declining Population Growth," was published in the March 1939 *American Economic Review.* The story of Emil Schram's stunted raise was reported in the January 1946 edition of *Fortune.* John Templeton appeared in *Barron's,* November 17, 1952. The doleful report in *The Journal of Commerce* spanned two days, August 5 and 6, 1952.

9. The now-defunct Seamen's Bank for Savings published a history of 30 Wall Street on the occasion of the opening of its new office there in 1955. Joshua Lippincott's postmortem of an earlier institution that occupied the same address is quoted in Walter B. Smith, *Economic Aspects of the Second Bank of the United States* (1969).

10. John Brooks's peerless *Once in Golconda* (1969) describes the bomb blast of 1920. *Business Week,* in the issue of July 16, 1955, described the unfolding prosperity at ground zero some 35 years later. The declining fortunes of Seamen's are documented in its own annual reports, 10-Q reports, and other SEC filings. As for the recent history of 40 Wall Street, published sources include, among many others, *Crain's New York Business* (e.g., the issue of February 7, 1994: "Lenders Unloading Downtown Properties"). New York City's 1993 *Plan for Lower Manhattan* is a handy reference of amazing facts, including the number of square feet of office space put up in the financial district during the 1980s: 25 million.

CHAPTER 3: THE THING WITHOUT A NAME

1. Owing to revisions in the national income accounts, the precise magnitude of the 1990–91 recession is, at this writing, in flux. However, the basic judgment rendered by a number of research economists (including that of Stephen McNees in the January–February 1992 edition of the *New England Economic Review* of the Boston Fed) is intact: the slump was mild.

2. Clement Juglar is quoted in Theodore Burton, *Financial Crises and Periods of Industrial and Commercial Depression* (1907); Juglar's own *Des Crises Commerciales et de leur Retour Périodique en France, en Angleterre et aux Etats Unis* was published in Paris in 1889.

3. Dramatic new research on the growth of government spending around the world is contained in a December 1995 working paper of the International Monetary Fund: "The Growth of Government and the Reform of the State in Industrial Countries," by Vito Tanzi and Ludger Schuknecht.

4. G. L. S. Shackle is quoted in A. W. Mullineaux, *Business Cycles and Financial Crises* (University of Michigan Press, Ann Arbor, Mich., 1990).

5. An antidote to the "downsizing of America theme" was produced long before downsizing became a seven-part series in *The New York Times* (which was, for the bibliographic record, March 3–9, 1996). "A Report on American Living Standards: These Are the Good Old Days," comprised most of the 1993 annual report of the Federal Reserve Bank of Dallas.

6. Further proof of how little is new under the sun is available in David Cahan's wonderful 1917 novel, *The Rise of David Levinsky*, which traces the life and business career of a thrusting cloakmaker in turn-of-the-century New York.

7. Lionel Robbins's *The Great Depression* was published in London in 1934; Wilhelm Röpke's *Crises and Cycles* (translated from the German and revised by Vera C. Smith) came along in 1936; and Gottfried von Haberler's *Prosperity and Depression: A Theoretical Analysis of Cyclical Movements* appeared in 1937. All can be read with pleasure today, the subject matter notwithstanding. The late Murray Rothbard, one of the great figures in the American wing of the Austrian school, published his revisionist history of the Hoover years, *America's Great Depression*, in 1963. Victor Zarnowitz's exhaustive survey of the business-cycle literature filled 57 pages of the June 1985 issue of the *Journal of Economic Literature*.

8. For the 1920–21 depression, see Benjamin M. Anderson, *Economics and the Public Welfare: A Financial and Economic History of the United States, 1914–46* (initially published in 1949 but reissued in 1979 by Liberty Press, Indianapolis). Anderson was an economist at what, when he started, was still the Chase National Bank; Alexander Dana Noyes, author of *The War Period of American Finance: 1908–1925* (1926), was the financial editor of *The New York Times*. Each man took an active part in the world's business. For Truman's foreshortened business career, see Robert H. Ferrell, *Harry S. Truman: A Life* (University of Missouri Press, Columbia, Mo., 1994). There is an excellent chapter-length account of the 1920–21 depression in *Prosperity Decade: From War to Depression, 1917–1929*, by George Soule, published in 1947 as the eighth volume in a nine-volume economic history of the United States.

9. The omniscient *New Republic* essayist wrote ("Production vs. Prices") in the June 2, 1920, issue; the estimable Garet Garrett did a better job on the same subject in the November 3, 1920 issue.

10. As for the Japan of the 1920s, see Hugh T. Patrick's "The Economic Muddle of the 1920s," in *Dilemmas of Growth in Prewar Japan,* edited by James William Morley (1971). David Asher is the author of "Convergence and Its Costs: The International Politics and Geo-Political Ramifications of Japanese Economic Liberalization, 1918–1932," an unpublished essay he wrote while at Cornell University in 1990–91. Junnosuke Inouye's *Problems of the Japanese Exchange Rate* was published in 1931, the year before its author's exchange-rate-related assassination. See also Norio Tamaki, *Japanese Banking: A History, 1859–1995* (Canberra University Press, 1995). The *Economist*'s report on Japanese finances was published in the June 12, 1920, issue (in that pre–e-mail era, it bore a May 3 Tokyo dateline).

11. David Asher's *Whatever Happened to the Miracle?,* by which the author ironically means the Japanese bubble, appeared in the spring 1996 issue of *Orbis.* A brawl of correspondence, pro and con, was published in the summer issue. See, too, Eugene Dattel's *The Sun That Never Rose: The Inside Story of Japan's Failed Attempt at Global Financial Dominance* (Chicago, Probus Publishing, 1994), which explains the hopelessness of the Japanese financial setup. The anonymous Bank of Japan functionary is quoted in *Japan's Banks and the "Bubble Economy" of the late 1980s,* by Tomohiko Taniguchi, a 1993 monograph of the Center of International Studies, Program on U.S.-Japan Relations, Princeton University. Also on point is Yukio Noguchi, "The 'Bubble' and Economic Policies of the 1980s," which appeared in the summer 1994 *Journal of Japanese Studies.*

12. Andrew Smithers, eponymous head of Smithers & Co., London-based economic consultants, is the author of "Japanese Equities: Will the Rigging Have to Stop?" (November 1, 1994) and "Japan: Growing Problems for the PKO" (February 15, 1995).

CHAPTER 4: MIRACLE CURE

1. Source of the comparison of money-center banks, then and now, is Moody's Investors Service for the 1932 numbers and standard quarterly financial reports for the current ones.

2. Jay Chiat was quoted in *The Wall Street Journal* of April 17, 1995.

3. Alan Blinder reflected on the near perfection of Federal Reserve monetary management in *The Financial Times* of May 18, 1995.

4. For an account of the evolution of bankers' attitudes toward real estate collateral, see the author's *Money of the Mind: Borrowing and Lending in America from the Civil War to Michael Milken* (Farrar, Straus & Giroux, New York, 1992).

5. What the leading American banks did to themselves in the 1980s boom is the subject of John H. Boyd's and Mark Gertler's essay, "The Role of Large

Banks in the Recent U.S. Banking Crisis," in the winter 1994 issue of the *Quarterly Review of the Federal Reserve Bank of Minneapolis*. See also Sangkyun Park, "Explanations for the Increased Riskiness of Banks in the 1980s," in the July/August issue of the *Review of the Federal Reserve Bank of St. Louis*.

6. *Junk Collapse Renews Focus on LBO Credit Quality*, by Christopher T. Mahoney, was published by Moody's Investors Service on March 17, 1990.

7. The extensive 1990s Citicorp bibliography is a journalistic mirror to the cycles of finance. "The Collapse of Citibank's Credit Culture," by Ida Picker and John W. Milligan, the cover story of the December 1991 issue of *Institutional Investor*, appeared at the bottom of the bank's fortunes; "The Wizard of Citi," by Matthew Schifrin, a resoundingly positive piece on the chairman of Citicorp, John Reed, appeared in the March 13, 1995, issue of *Forbes*, less than four years later. It has not yet been shown to be the top. *Wriston: Walter Wriston, Citibank, and the Rise and Fall of American Financial Supremacy*, by Philip Zweig (Crown Publishers, New York, 1996) is an ultra-thorough account of the life and times of Reed's predecessor.

8. Details on the volatile credit markets of 1990–91 are drawn from *Grant's Interest Rate Observer* and The *American Banker*, among other sources; the Equitable was analyzed in the September 1992 edition of *Emerson, Reid's Insurance Observer*. Kevin Donovan and Andrew Bary, writing in *The Wall Street Journal* on May 31, 1991, were among the first in the financial press to identify the significance of the speculation in short-dated Treasuries.

9. Martin Mayer's *Nightmare on Wall Street: Salomon Brothers and the Corruption of the Marketplace* (Simon & Schuster, New York, 1993) deals extensively with the 1991 Treasury-note corner.

10. Gordon Ringoen spoke on the "carry trade" at a conference sponsored by *Grant's Interest Rate Observer*, on October 27, 1992. The banks' note-buying binge of the early 1990s was described in the second quarter 1994 edition of the *Federal Reserve Bank of Kansas City's Economic Review*, "Causes of the Recent Increase in Bank Security Holdings," by William R. Keeton.

11. Alan Greenspan floated his claims for the Federal Reserve's foresight in testimony before the Senate Banking Committee, on May 27, 1994.

12. "Does the Fed Influence Interest Rates?" was the question posed by Daniel L. Thornton in the January 1995 edition of *Monetary Trends*, a publication of the Federal Reserve Bank of St. Louis. Volcker's skeptical remarks on central banking were contained in his foreword to *The Central Banks*, by Marjorie Deane and Robert Pringle (Hamish Hamilton, London, 1994).

13. The 1991–92 credit chronology is drawn from the pages of The *American Banker*.

14. Rueff's warning (slightly premature) of impending disaster was published in the July 1961 issue of *Fortune* magazine: "The West Is Facing a Credit Collapse." His book, *The Monetary Sin of the West*, was published in 1972.

15. Alan Greenspan's mid-1980s consulting arrangement with Charles Keating was disclosed in *The Wall Street Journal* on November 20, 1989.

CHAPTER 5: THE CANFIELD MARKET

1. *Luck: The Brilliant Randomness of Everyday Life,* by Nicholas Rescher (Farrar, Straus & Giroux, New York, 1995), addresses some of the philosophical issues of gambling, while *Sucker's Progress: An Informal History of Gambling in America from the Colonies to Canfield,* by Herbert Asbury (1938), is a chronicle of the action.
2. *Canfield: The True Story of the Greatest Gambler,* by Alexander Gardiner (1930), is an account of the life of one of the Edwardian-era practitioners; *I Want to Quit Winners,* by Harold S. Smith with John Noble (1961), is the autobiography of one of the mid–twentieth century ones. *Gambling without Guilt: the Legitimization of an American Pastime* by John Rosecrance (Brooks/Cole Publishing Co., Pacific Grove, Calif., 1988) and *Sagebrush Casinos: The Story of Legalized Gambling in Nevada* (1953) are histories of the highly cyclical business of taking bets. "What Del Webb Is Up To in Nevada," by Tom Alexander, in the May 1965 *Fortune,* describes a financial environment in which the public capital markets still recoiled from gambling.
3. The story of the five-year-old gambling boom in Tunica County, Miss., is told in fine weekly installments in *The Tunica Times.*
4. *Grant's Interest Rate Observer* is the primary source for the description of the new-issue boom of the early 1990s.
5. "Inefficiency in the Market for Initial Public Offerings," by Jonathan A. Shayne and Larry D. Sonderquist, an essay published in the May 1995 issue of the *Vanderbilt Law Review,* is the source of the claim that initial public offerings are typically overvalued.
6. Andrew Dickson White's essay *Fiat Money Inflation in France* (reprinted by The Bank of New York, New York, in 1980) discourses on the institution of paper money: White was against it.
7. *Modern Investment Management and the Prudent Man Rule,* by Bevis Longstreth (Oxford University Press, New York, 1986), is an understandable treatment of the evolution of what a fiduciary may and may not do with other people's money. Just how much the law has evolved is clear from reading Justice Samuel Putnam's decision in *Harvard v. Amory* (Octavius Oickering, *Reports of Cases Argued and Determined in the Supreme Judicial Court of Massachusetts,* vol. IX, second edition; Boston, 1855). For a contemporary discussion of the use and abuse of conservatism in fiduciary investment, see Shelby White, "The Price of Prudence," *Forbes,* September 25, 1995.

8. William "Beau" Duncan's comments on optimism were immortalized in *Investor's Business Daily*, October 27, 1995.

CHAPTER 6: CONSEQUENCES OF 3 PERCENT

1. *Grant's Interest Rate Observer* was perhaps the first to discuss the monetary-cum-gambling significance of the construction of the Stratosphere tower in Las Vegas (December 22, 1995).
2. Two excellent monographs were prepared for the occasion of the 300th anniversary of the Bank of England in 1994: *The Development of Central Banking*, by Forrest Capie, Charles Goodhart, and Norbert Schnadt, each a British academic; and *Modern Central Banking*, by Stanley Fischer of the Massachusetts Institute of Technology.
3. *The Central Banks*, by Marjorie Deane and Robert Pringle, cited previously, canvasses the contemporary monetary scene. Thomson Hankey, *The Principles of Banking, Its Utility and Economy; with Remarks on the Working and Management of the Bank of England*, 4th ed. (London, 1887) surveys the Victorian one. Vera C. Smith, *The Rationale of Central Banking* (1936, but republished by Liberty Press, Indianapolis, in 1990) fills the chronological breach; on the institution of central banking, Smith is a convincing skeptic.
4. Giulio M. Gallarotti's *The Anatomy of an International Monetary Regime: The Classical Gold Standard, 1880–1914* (Oxford University Press, New York, 1995) looks back at the period in which Hankey lived. It is just as engrossing as a monetary history—or, more exactly, comparative analysis of monetary systems—can be. David Kynaston, in his second volume of *The City of London: Golden Years, 1890–1914* (Chatto & Windus, London, 1995) vividly describes the everyday workings of the financial world that dealt in gold money.
5. *Wall Street*, by Walter Werner and Steven T. Smith (Columbia University Press, New York, 1991), is a history of the formative years of American markets. The material on bankruptcy is drawn from the September 29, 1995, issue of *Grant's Interest Rate Observer*.
6. The bullish *Fortune* article on Micron Technology was dated November 27, 1995. Taking the bearish side of the argument on semiconductors was (and continues to be, at this writing) *The High-Tech Strategist*, a newsletter edited and published by Fred Hickey, of Nashua, N.H. The August 20, 1995, *Wall Street Journal* discussed Microsoft's rental of *The Times* of London (GATES SEES IT AS ADVERTISING; PRESS CRITICS SEE A WINDOW CLOSING ON PAPER'S ETHICS). The May 1, 1995, *Electronic Business Buyer* was the source of the arresting claim that many Taiwanese didn't know what else to do with their money *except* to build a semiconductor fabrication plant.

7. There is a vast Wall Street literature (most of it highly perishable, for better or worse) on banks and the economics of lending. One fine specimen, *A Blatant Disregard for Economic Returns,* published in July 1995 by Lawrence R. Vitale and Mark E. Raisbeck of Bear, Stearns & Co., contends that banks have resumed lending at too narrow a profit. The theoretical issue that underlies the practical investment issue—are there too many banks, or not enough bank failures?—was addressed in 1993 in a collection of papers by the Federal Reserve Bank of New York: "Studies on Excess Capacity in the Financial Sector" (1993). George M. Salem's excellent study of personal indebtedness—*Bank Credit Cards: Loan Loss Risks Are Growing*—was distributed by Gerard Klauer Mattison and dated June 11, 1996.

Index

Page numbers enclosed in square brackets indicate textual references to notes on sources

Norris, Frank, and psychological components of speculation as depicted in *The Pit*, 27–28

O'Connor, J. F. T., Roosevelt administration comptroller, under whom banking regulation subordinated to New Deal economic agenda, 75–76
Office of Price Administration (OPA), 15
  and rent control, 11
Office of the Comptroller of the Currency (OCC), 76–77, 302
Once in Golconda (Brooks), [320n. 10]
One William Street Fund, as landmark investment event of 1958, 38–39, [318n. 6]
Onoue, Nui ("Bubble Lady"), charges of fraud against, 154
"Operation Twist," 52
optimism
  as general attitude of American investors, 263
  source of 1990s financial revival, 163–65, 193–94
Organization of Petroleum Exporting Countries (OPEC), reduction in power of, with advent of free oil markets, 122
outsourcing, of standard corporate functions, 121

Parkinson, Thomas I., 16–21, [317n. 2]
  criticism of, against "fictitious money" practices of Federal Reserve, 19
  intense opposition of, to inflationary fiscal policies of Roosevelt and Truman, 16
  leadership of, toward higher-yielding investments, 16–18
  Rousmaniere's account of life/ career of, [317n. 2]
Patman, Representative Wright (Texas), anti–Wall Street stance of, 33

Patrick, Hugh T., on 1920s Japan, [322n. 10]
Perot, Ross, 179, 193, 197
Persian Gulf War, effect of, on U.S. economy, 203–204
Planet Hollywood, 314–15
President's Council of Economic Advisers, establishment of, 13
Presstek, speculative frenzy in valuation of, 314–15
price controls
  during 1940s and early 1950s, 10–12
  shortages as a result of, 10–11
principal-only strip, and derivative securities risk, 105
Prudential Insurance Company, 226
"prudent man" rule (Prudent Investor rule), and responsibility of fiduciary, 259–62, [324n. 7]
Putnam, Samuel, *Harvard v. Amory* decision of, and the "prudent man" rule, 259–62, [324n. 7]

Rasminsky, Louis, on Bretton Woods agreements and control of international monetary system, 53
real aggregate asset prices, and mid-1990s recovery in United States, 310
real estate
  breakdown of 1980s, 170–72
  commercial banks' loan growth (mid-1980s to early 1990s) provided by, 172
  depression, 132
  manic effects of overvaluation on, 63–64
  speculation in, boomlike phenomenon of, 131
  worldwide slump (1990s) in, Japanese vs. American response to, 289
Real Estate Auctioneers Association, 40 Wall Street as largest ever foreclosure-auction bid (1940) in 80-year history of, 74

speculation (*continued*)
as downward influence on money
interest rates, 127
emotion often overrides information in, 313
Federal Reserve's countercyclical
objectives as fuel for, 33–34
in government securities, outcry
against, 33–34
inadvertent promotion of, by politi-
cal/financial policy of suppressing crises, 315
increase of, and concomitant loss of
fear/growing faith in stability,
312
investors' predilection toward, 7–8
and junk bonds, 83
nature of, in gold-standard era,
278–79
Presstek as example of frenzy in,
314–15
psychological component of, as
depicted in Frank Norris's
novel *The Pit,* 27–28
spirit of, endemic to American
psyche, 282–83
surge of, in 1990s, 5–6
and "Texas hedge," 105
speculator
in business of risk dispersal, 221
distinguished from gambler, 222
distinguished from investor, 220–21
Spielberg, Steven, creator (with David
Geffen and Jeffrey Katzenberg)
of Dreamworks SKG, 302
Sproul, Allan
on gold convertibility and monetary
stability, [318n. 7]
on perils of price inflation, 52
Standard Oil Company of New Jersey,
235
Steinhart, Michael, charges against,
in scheming to corner 1991
Treasury-note issue, 188–89
Standard & Poor's 500 Index, 7, 22,
268
Standard & Poor's new-issue index, 247

Starrett Brothers, [319n. 3]
collapse of American price structure unanticipated by, 63–64
record construction of 40 Wall
Street by, 63
stock market
current belief in indefinite rise of, 7
rise of, as instrumental in cure of
banking system and flowering of
entrepreneurial capitalism, 217
rising prices contain the "germ" of
falling prices in, 250–51
stocks, rise in price of, as macroeconomic stimulus, 243–44
Stratosphere
capitalization of, 267–68
construction of, analogous to construction of 40 Wall Street, 267
Sucker's Progress (Asbury), a history of
gambling in America, 224
swords-to-plowshares movement, beneficiaries of, 123n.
Sylla, Richard, 21

Templeton, John M. [320n. 8]
on capital gains tax rate, 91
Terkel, Studs, 119
"Texas hedge," as failed defensive
speculation strategy, 105
Theory of Public Finance, The
(Musgrave), 44n.
"Thing Without a Name," 166
30 Wall Street
formerly the world's largest storehouse of gold, 108
headquarters for *Grant's Interest Rate
Observer*
one-time headquarters for defunct
Seaman's Bank for Savings, 58,
[320n. 9]
site of former U.S. Assay Office, 58,
93
Thornton, Daniel L., on Federal
Reserve's doubtful influence
on money-market interest rates
(1983 to 1994), 197–98,
[323n. 12]

About the Author

James Grant founded *Grant's Interest Rate Observer* in 1983. He is the author of several books, including *Money of the Mind: Borrowing and Lending in America from the Civil War to Michael Milken*, which *The Financial Times* named the best financial book of 1992. A regular commentator on CNN and a panelist on *Wall Street Week* with Louis Rukeyser, he lives with his family in Brooklyn, New York.